An Introduction to Government and Politics

A Conceptual Approach

Second Edition

An Introduction to Government and Politics

A Conceptual Approach

Second Edition

Mark O. Dickerson
Thomas Flanagan

NELSON CANADA

©Nelson Canada,
A Division of International Thomson Limited, 1988
Published in 1988 by
Nelson Canada,
A Division of International Thomson Limited
1120 Birchmount Road
Scarborough, Ontario M1K 5G4

Originally published by Methuen Publications in
1986.

Canadian Cataloguing in Publication Data
Dickerson, M.O., 1934-
    An introduction to government and politics

2nd ed.
Bibliography: p.
Includes index.
ISBN 0-17-603450-1

1. Political science. I. Flanagan, Thomas, 1944-
II. Title.

JC131.D52   1988   320   C88-094002-6

DESIGN: William Fox/Associates

Printed and bound in Canada
4 5 86 90 89 88

Contents

Acknowledgments

We would like to recognize the many people who have helped make this book possible. Special thanks are owed to numerous students at the University of Calgary, Mount Royal College, and Medicine Hat College who used the text in draft form. Peter Milroy of Methuen Publications suggested that publication would be worthwhile and thereafter saw the book through press. The previous head of our department, Anthony Parel, always encouraged our efforts, and our colleagues Frank MacKinnon, David Thomas, James Keeley, Rainer Knopff, Neil Nevitte, and Les Pal made helpful comments on portions of the manuscript. Also, we are grateful for the useful comments made by instructors using the first edition in their classes.

We would like to thank professors Sidney Pobihushchy and Richard Noble, University of New Brunswick, for their valuable comments on an earlier draft of Chapter 30, which has been added to this edition. The Constitution Act, 1982 is reprinted from Peter W. Hogg, *Constitutional Law of Canada*, 2nd ed. (Toronto: Carswell, 1985). Cecile Calverley and Judi Powell brought us into the modern age in 1985 by keying the second edition into the University of Calgary's word processing system, and Ann Griffiths provided much help in getting it ready for printing. We must take responsibility if any errors remain after all this assistance.

Introduction

This book is a text for a first-year course in political science. Although designed for use in Canadian universities and community colleges, it does not focus solely on Canadian government. We use Canadian examples of general principles together with examples from the British and American political systems, which have historically been of great importance to Canada.

In teaching introductory courses in political science for more than a decade, we have encountered thousands of students. This experience has taught us something about the virtues and vices of the present approach to social studies in the Canadian schools. On the positive side, many students come to university with an active curiosity about politics and a healthy scepticism about orthodox opinions. They are eager to learn more about a field whose importance they recognize. But students are handicapped by certain deficiencies in the social studies curriculum:

- They have neither historical information nor a historical perspective on events. History has perhaps suffered more than any other discipline from integration into social studies.
- They have little specific information about the institutions of Canadian government. Most students entering university would not be able to say how a judge is appointed or what an order-in-council is. Their acquaintance with government has been more in the realm of current affairs, with heavy emphasis on "issues" as portrayed in the mass media.
- They are accustomed to discussing politics but not to using rigorously defined concepts. They are used to a looser mode of reasoning than that which must prevail in an academic discipline.

We have tried to prepare a text that does something about each of these problems. About a lack of historical background we can do relatively little because we are dealing with a course in political science that cannot replace the systematic study of history. However, we do attempt to put important topics in a historical or developmental perspective, and we supply some information about watershed events such as the French or Russian revolutions. We also refer whenever possible to authors, from Plato to Keynes, whose reputations are established and who are important historical figures in their own right. Furthermore, there is only a limited amount we can do to give the student detailed facts about Canadian political institutions, for that requires a course in Canadian government.

We believe we have been more successful in dealing with the conceptual problem. The material in this book is arranged in a careful sequence. Concepts are introduced

1

one at a time, elaborated, then used as the basis for explaining further ideas. Important terms are italicized where they first occur or where they are thoroughly explained, and they are listed at the end of each part of the book for easy reference. These listed terms are used consistently throughout the text. The result, we believe, is to equip the student with a comprehensive, interrelated, and logically consistent vocabulary for the study of politics. In Part Four of the book, we offer a way to conceptualize the process of politics and organize or arrange the many ideas and concepts introduced in the first three parts. Being able to conceptualize politics as a coherent process is an essential first step to becoming a student of politics, evaluating politics, and becoming a critic of one's own political system.

We are keenly aware that this effort at consistency means contracting the scope of meaning attached to some important terms. Political scientists are often not in agreement about the way they use many of the significant terms in the discipline: politics, nation-state, and democracy are only a few examples that have caused well-known disagreement. Our experience has been that students at the introductory level cannot absorb all these debates about the meaning of terms that they are encountering for the first time. Thus we have narrowed the meaning of many terms without, we hope, departing from the mainstream of current usage. Readers will undoubtedly criticize our handling of this or that concept, but we hope that the pedagogical benefit of a consistent, interrelated vocabulary will compensate for any misunderstanding in meaning. It is a considerable advantage to be able to explain, for example, liberalism in terms of previously established concepts, such as society, state, and coercion, that the student has already assimilated.

The book is divided into four parts that constitute what we believe is a logical point of departure for the study of government and politics. Part One is a definition of terms, ideas, and concepts basic to political science. Knowledge of words such as state and society, authority and legitimacy, and law and sovereignty is essential when starting a systematic study of politics. Part Two discusses the ideological bases on which modern political systems are founded. Liberalism and socialism, the fundamental ideological systems in the modern world, are considered in the context of the political spectrum from communism to fascism. Forms of government are the subject of Part Three. Here we classify different sets of characteristics that exemplify basic political systems—liberal-democratic, authoritarian, totalitarian, parliamentary and presidential, federal and unitary. In Part Four, government as a process is examined. A complex interaction of individuals and political institutions produces law and public policies for a society, and this interaction is viewed as a systematic process. While the model of politics is hypothetical, examples are drawn principally from Canada, the United Kingdom, and the United States to demonstrate how the process works in reality.

This conceptual approach makes it advisable to cover the material in the same order in which it is presented in the book. It is particularly important to read Part One before Part Two, and Parts One and Two before Parts Three and Four. However, it would be allowable to reverse the order of Parts Three and Four because the logical interrelation is not as structured in the latter part of the book, which is more institutional in focus, compared to the former part, which is more theoretical.

Our work is meant to be objective and dispassionate, but that does not mean that it is "value free" or without commitment. We consistently try to point out the value of the leading ideas of the Western world's political tradition. We pay particular attention to two different and sometimes opposing clusters of ideas, both of which are of great importance. One is a group of concepts centred around constitutionalism and including notions such as the rule of law and individual freedom. The other set of ideas involves democracy and allied concepts, such as majority rule and popular sovereignty. For the last two centuries, the Western world has tried to combine both these directions into the system of government known as constitutional or liberal democracy, in which majorities rule within a legal context and which prevents the oppression of minorities. This form of government has not always been stable and successful even in its countries of origin in Western Europe and North America, and it has been adopted only sporadically in other regions of the world. Living in Canada where liberal democracy seems securely established, we are apt to take it for granted; but it is far from being an obvious or universal form of government.

The origins of political science lie in the classical period of Greek philosophy, whose greatest writers were Plato and Aristotle. The Greek philosophers did not cultivate political science as a specialized discipline in the modern sense, but they thought and wrote systematically about government. They were concerned above all with the place of politics in contributing to a life of excellence and virtue. Greek philosophy, and with it the habit of systematic reflection upon government, became part of the cultural tradition of the Western world. Political science continued to exist as a branch of moral philosophy, and important contributions were made by authors who also wrote in other areas of philosophy: Thomas Aquinas, Thomas Hobbes, John Locke, Benedict Spinoza. Such writings, extending over more than two millennia, constitute a rich body of wisdom that is still the foundation of political science.

In the eighteenth century, political science started to differentiate itself from moral philosophy—not yet as an independent study, but as part of the new science of political economy. Writers like Adam Smith, by training a moral philosopher, began to study and write accounts of the workings of the market. This did not take place in a vacuum; it corresponded to the reality of a society in which market processes were becoming emancipated from traditional restraints or governmental control. The study of government was a junior partner in the new science of political economy, whose emphasis was on the market. Government appeared as an auxiliary to accomplish certain functions not well performed by free trade. In any case, chairs of political economy were established at Western universities in the late eighteenth and nineteenth centuries. During this period much work—which today we would call political science—was also done in faculties of history and law, especially under the guise of comparative and constitutional law.

Economics and political science began to split apart in the second half of the nineteenth century as scholars increasingly began to specialize. The discovery of the principle of marginal utility in the 1870s made it possible for economics to become mathematical, hence more specialized and remote from the everyday concerns of government and politics. Universities in the United States took the lead in establishing autonomous departments of political science, which united the work of professors who might previously have been found in political economy, history, and law. Political science in its modern academic form thus stems from developments in the United States in the late nineteenth century. The first department of political science was created at Columbia University, New York City, in 1880; by the outbreak of World War I in 1914, there were forty such departments.[1]

Why in the United States? For one reason, this rapidly expanding country was opening scores of new universities that were not bound by old traditions about academic specialities. More profoundly, the United States as a nation generated by an act of revolution has always been fascinated with government. University political science was a logical extension of the civics education that was so important in the public schools. Also, these early political scientists tended to be moralistic crusaders for governmental reform (for example, Woodrow Wilson, the only political science professor ever to become an American president).

In the first half of the twentieth century, political science as an academic discipline remained largely an American phenomenon. A few chairs were established in universities in other countries, but political science was usually found under the wing of law or economics. However, after World War II, political science was adopted around the world along with so many other cultural exports. Perhaps a deeper reason than mere imitation of the American behemoth was the tremendous expansion of the scope of government in the second half of the twentieth century. Whereas the small state of the laissez-faire era could be understood fairly easily within the study of political economy, the large and interventionist state of the present seemed to demand its own specialized discipline.

Political science in Canada must be seen in this historical context. In 1950 there were only about thirty political scientists in Canada, generally employed in university departments of political economy.[2] Their main periodical was the *Canadian Journal of Economics and Political Science*. In the 1960s these departments began to split into economics and political science as enrolments increased and more staff were

---

[1]David M. Ricci, *The Tragedy of Political Science: Politics, Scholarship, and Democracy* (New Haven, Conn.: Yale University Press, 1984), pp. 60–61.

[2]Alan C. Cairns, "Political Science in Canada and the Americanization Issue," *Canadian Journal of Political Science* 8 (1975), p. 196.

hired to cope with an unprecedented expansion of universities. In 1967 the former *CJEPS* was split into the *Canadian Journal of Political Science* and another review for economists. The academic emancipation of political science in Canada is now complete. Two major universities, Saskatchewan and Toronto, maintained joint departments of economics and political science as late as the early 1980s, but even these two departments have now been divided along disciplinary lines. The term political economy, instead of covering the entire territory of economics and politics, as it once did, now refers to the study of certain narrower subjects, such as economic intervention by government, that require information and insights from both disciplines in order to be understood.

Intellectually, political science has undergone some major changes in this century. When it achieved academic autonomy, its practitioners were equipped with the methods of their forebears in philosophy, political economy, law, and history. These methods were chiefly the narrative, chronological, and descriptive study of political institutions, coupled with philosophical reflection on matters of good and evil as applied to government. Undoubtedly the biggest development in the twentieth century has been the impact of quantitative methods pioneered in the other social sciences. From social psychology has come the methodology of the opinion survey, which is now used in political science to study elections and public opinion. Economics has contributed its econometric and statistical techniques, which can be used to construct formal models of many kinds of political behaviour. Generally speaking, the new methods have been tied to a realignment of interest away from formal constitutional structures to other phenomena, such as political parties, pressure groups, elections, and collective behaviour.

The discipline was intensely divided in the 1950s and 1960s between adherents and opponents of the new methods, with many extreme claims being made on both sides; but that furor has largely disappeared. Political scientists who use quantitative methods now co-exist peacefully with colleagues who rely on the old techniques of description and reflection. It now seems to be accepted that political science is an inherently pluralistic discipline united not by possession of a single method, but by concern with a common subject. Because aspects of politics and government may require different approaches, political scientists may in their research methods resemble philosophers, sociologists, historians, lawyers, economists, or anthropologists; yet all feel that they are united in a joint enterprise to understand the many facets of government and politics.

PART ONE

Basic Concepts

1 Society, Government, and Politics

We are all social beings who need the support of others not only to live well but even to survive. There is no record of a time when human beings lived as isolated individuals, coming together only to mate. As far as we know, people have always lived in groups at least as large as the family or band. The usual term for such groups, large or small, is *society*.

No one has created or designed society. It results from an infinite number of human transactions, from which stable and predictable patterns emerge. Society is not a person or organization with a will of its own, but a setting in which we carry out our lives. We often speak metaphorically of society "doing" or "wanting" something, but this must not be taken literally. Only individual men and women have wills, which they combine using deliberate techniques of organization. This cannot be true of society as a whole because it is not a conscious formation. Society as such cannot act or decide anything.

Sociologists usually define society as a human group whose members live by common rules of conduct and that has a plausible claim to self-sufficiency. Both of these points need clarification. By rules of conduct we mean not just enforceable commands, but regularities or predictabilities of behaviour. All human activities, whether marriage, work, or recreation, are carried on within a framework of such rules. Society exists when people share so many rules of conduct that they are able to understand, predict, and react to one another's behaviour. According to Western rules of conduct, a smile represents happiness or pleasure; however, a Japanese, unacquainted with the system, might interpret a smile as a sign of anger. It does not particularly matter whether a smile means pleasure or anger so long as it is understood in the same way by everyone concerned. Understanding and living by these rules that govern interpersonal relations is the essence of social order.

Human beings, of course, are not the only social animals. There are social insects—bees, termites, and ants—as well as mammals—hyenas, wolves, chimpanzees, baboons, and many others. The study of animal societies has in recent decades been one of the most dynamic scientific fields and has yielded many insights that, with appropriate caution, can sometimes be transferred to the study of human society.[1] The common denominator in both animal and human societies is rules of conduct—predictable, regular patterns of behaviour that integrate individuals into a social whole. The major difference between animal and human societies is that the vastly greater intelligence of human beings allows them not only to understand social rules of conduct but also to change them by conscious decision.

Self-sufficiency is a more problematic concept. Few, if any, societies have ever been self-sufficient in the literal sense of requiring nothing at all from other societies—no husbands or wives, no trade goods, no new ideas or techniques. Perhaps a more reasonable test of self-sufficiency is whether a society could survive if its ties with other societies were broken, but even this test does not give very clear results. Western society could undoubtedly survive if deprived of oil from the Persian Gulf, but it would have to undergo profound changes to do so.

Consideration of both rules of conduct and self-sufficiency shows that it is hard to draw clear lines between societies in the modern world. The volume of international movement of people, commodities, and ideas is so enormous that self-sufficiency has almost vanished. Rules of conduct have also become widely diffused. The ascendancy of Western society since the fifteenth century has spread many Western cultural practices around the earth: education and literacy, modes of dress, table manners, forms of economic activity, and much more. To a certain degree, the world has become one society with regional differences merging into one another. One can travel and even work in the major cities of all continents without the feeling of crossing profound lines of social demarcation.

This vagueness of the term society means that we use it in different ways to express different realities. We may speak very broadly of an entity such as Western society to refer to the peoples of Europe and the new societies they founded overseas as an extension of their mother countries. In this broad sense, Western society is more or less a synonym for Western civilization. At other times, we may speak of societies as if their boundaries were the same as the legal and territorial boundaries established by governments. Thus it is common to refer to Canadian society or American society, even to Alberta or Toronto society. Even while speaking in this way, it is essential to recognize that society and government are different things. Society is a general matrix of activity formed by similarity of conduct and frequent interaction; *government* is a specialized activity of making and enforcing public decisions that are binding on the whole community.

All effective governments carry out at least the following functions: they protect society from external attack, enforce rules of conduct within society, and settle disputes between members of society. The common denominator of these functions is order, both internal and external. Government requires the selective use of force to attain a stable and durable social order. Beyond this minimum function, government may also be used as a service agency for members of society. This is particularly true of modern governments, which deliver mail, pave highways, operate health insurance schemes, and provide old age pensions. But these service functions are optional; the essence of government is the maintenance of peace within the social order.

We may conjecture that the earliest concern of government was to ensure the very survival of the group. To defend against attack or to choose where to hunt or forage were potential matters of life and death, so that co-operation could not be left purely to individual whim. Lack of agreement about fighting or hunting might endanger the entire group, so the need for universality necessitated at least a degree of coercion. Survival depends not only on self-defence and finding food but also on preserving peace within the group, which in turn demands conduct according to accepted rules—for example, pertaining to property and marriage. Violation of these can endanger survival and thus requires coercive action to punish violators.

But why should rules of conduct need enforcement? Why do human beings not always obey them spontaneously? The problem of obedience is vastly more complicated in human beings than in other animals because of our greater intelligence. Humans are able not only to follow rules but also to understand and formulate them, reflect upon them, and try to manipulate them for their own ends. This means there may be differences of opinion about what rules of conduct apply to particular situations. Honest, principled conflict of opinion about right and wrong is a recurrent dilemma of human existence. But even if we could always agree in the abstract about which rule of conduct to follow, there would still be a problem of enforcement, as shown by the following argument.

Suppose a society has the customary rule that all able-bodied men will fight to defend the tribe. Such a rule is in the common interest because it facilitates the survival of the group. But one man may say to himself: "If I don't fight, while everyone else does, the group will probably still survive, and I can eliminate the risk to myself. Thus I will hide." If this hypothetical person knew that his refusal to fight would precipitate a similar refusal on the part of many others, he would probably not refuse because he could see that his society would be destroyed. But he has an incentive to break the rule as long as he can count on others to continue to obey it.

The same reasoning applies to acts of thievery. Thieves do not want to abolish the rules of conduct that guarantee private property; they merely want a special advantage for themselves. They want their own property and a share of others' as well.

Thus there is an interesting paradox at the centre of human existence. People need society to survive, and social life depends on following common rules. Yet the existence of rules inexorably sets up an incentive for some to try to gain special advantages over others by breaking the rules while others abide by them. It is in the rule breaker's long-range interest to observe the rules so that society may exist, but it is in his or her short-range interest to break the rules as long as others keep them.

Moral training is one answer to this dilemma; government is another. It is an attempt to increase compliance with rules by using coercion against those who would break them. The intelligence that enables a person to understand social rules and tempts one to break them has also encouraged the evolution of government to punish violations.

There is yet another paradox. If governments were too successful in enforcing rules, progress would be impossible. One aspect of social change is the replacement of one rule of conduct by another; this is possible only if pioneers are able to experiment with new ways of doing things. If society is to progress, either government must be less than totally efficient or else some areas of social life must be held outside the sphere where rules are coercively enforced. The latter is the Western solution of limited government, reserving a sphere of privacy to individuals within which they can establish or vary their own rules of conduct as long as they do not destroy the right of others to do the same.

Up to this point we have described government as a process, a set of activities extending over time. It is now time to broach the question of the structure of government—that is, who performs the activities, and how are the performers organized for collective action? Studying the structure of government is a major part of political science because, although the process of government is universal to all societies, the structure of government is infinitely variable.

In the so-called primitive government of tribal societies, there is little or no specialized structure. Necessary activities are performed by all qualified members of the tribe, usually males who have passed the age of maturity. As required, they hear and settle disputes, decide when to travel or rest, punish lawbreakers, and fight to defend the tribe. Good examples are the tribes of native peoples, such as the Sioux and Blackfoot, that once roamed the great plains of North America. There were tribal chiefs, but they did not wield the coercive power we today associate with government. They could persuade others but not enforce their will upon them. Indeed, during much of the year the tribe was split into small, wandering bands that were little more than extended families. A specialized structure of government existed only when the families assembled for collective action, such as the buffalo hunt. Then the authority of the chief was enforced by men from the military societies who became a temporary and voluntary police force. They settled quarrels and enforced rules necessary to the hunt, such as not prematurely attacking the buffalo herd. During this period of close co-operation, men from the military societies could seize and destroy property, flog offenders, and even inflict the death penalty; but when the hunt was over, this primitive apparatus of government disappeared. The Cree and Ojibwa, whose lives in the northern forest did not include the large-scale co-operation of the buffalo hunt, had even less government. The traders of the Hudson's Bay Company, uncertain who the leaders of these tribes were, virtually created chiefs by singling men out for special attention.[2]

There is a broad, evolutionary correlation between the increasing complexity and sophistication of social life and the increasing specialization and permanence of governmental institutions. The native peoples of the northern forest did not need any organized authority to co-ordinate their solitary hunting, whereas those of the plains needed at least an intermittent structure of authority to maintain order during buffalo hunts. An agricultural existence, where land is subdivided and property rights created, usually leads to a permanent structure of government, at least when this existence goes beyond simple slash-and-burn agriculture, in which the tribe is still very mobile. The growth of cities and large-scale enterprises such as irrigation again occurs along with an increase in the size, complexity, and permanence of government institutions, creating monarchs, armies, judges, tax collectors, and so on.

From now on, when we speak of government we mean this sort of enduring, specialized structure that is found in all complex societies. Another word meaning much the same thing is state, but we will not use it until after Chapter 4 because it has certain other connotations to be explored later. There is no such thing as a society without government, at least without the process of government, but it is quite proper to speak of a *stateless society*. Indeed, that is a common way of describing societies such as those of the Sioux or Blackfoot, which had little or no specialized structure of government. Again, we see why it is so important not to confuse society with government or the state.

A concept often associated with government is *politics*. The word comes from the Greek *polis*, usually translated as "city-state." The *polis* was the typical Greek form of political community at the time of Socrates, Plato, and Aristotle, who were the founders of political science. The *polis* consisted of a city, such as Athens or Sparta, plus some surrounding hinterland, including smaller towns and villages. It has given us a number of related words having to do with the idea of the common good, such as "politics," "police," "polite," and "policy."

Curiously, politics is one of the most disputed terms in the vocabulary of political science. Almost everyone uses it as an occasional synonym for government, but beyond that it has received a wide variety of meanings, some of which are discussed in this chapter. The various definitions tend to emphasize different aspects of politics. We believe that each contains an element of truth and that a satisfactory understanding of politics must be comprehensive and multifaceted.

One definition comes from Bertrand de Jouvenel, an eminent French political scientist. According to Jouvenel, "we should regard as 'political' every systematic effort, performed at any place in the social field, to move other men in pursuit of some design cherished by the mover."[3] Politics was for him the activity of gathering and maintaining support for human projects.

This is a very broad definition of politics, one that cuts across all areas of human life. Politics can be found in business, sport, religion—wherever people are mustered for collective effort. However, in the rest of the book we will be less concerned with politics in the private sector of existence than with politics in the public sector, where politics is related to government. As an example, consider the Greenpeace Foundation, which has given itself the mission of influencing government to preserve certain forms of wildlife. Greenpeace has its own internal politics, necessary to keep the organization functioning, and it also engages in politics in the larger public sphere as it tries to affect the actions of government. By staging highly publicized disruptions of seal hunting, it helped to bring about the virtual abolition of that activity as a commercial venture. Its activity was political in the sense that it mobilized popular opinion around an issue and brought pressure to bear on government to achieve its objective.

Whereas Jouvenel's conception of politics emphasized support, another common approach is to equate politics with conflict. J. D. B. Miller writes that politics "is about disagreement or conflict."[4] Alan Ball carries this even further; for him, politics

> involves disagreements and the reconciliation of those disagreements, and therefore can occur at any level. The children in a nursery with one toy which they both want at the same time present a political situation.[5]

Ball's definition is not too far from Jouvenel's, for in real life mobilizing supporters for some project almost always involves overcoming conflicts of opinion or desire. But there are also conflicting situations that do not seem political in any usual sense. There is certainly conflict if a mugger tries to take someone's wallet, but it is not a political action because no collective project is envisioned. To be political, a crime has to be linked to some vision of reordering society. It is thus a political act, as well as a crime, for a revolutionary group to kidnap a politician in the hope of inciting the people to rise against the government.

A distributive conception of politics is expressed in the title of Harold Lasswell's book *Politics: Who Gets What, When, How.*[6] In Lasswell's view politics is the distribution of the good things of earthly life: wealth, comfort, safety, prestige, recognition, and so on. David Easton means the same thing when he says that politics is the authoritative allocation of values, values meaning not moral ideals, but those things in life that people desire.[7] There is certainly much merit in this approach; it draws attention to the fact that the winners in conflict, those who succeed in mobilizing support for their projects, also usually allocate to themselves and their followers a generous share of material and social benefits. But the distributive approach runs the risk of merging politics with other activities. Wealth, for example, can be distributed by impersonal economic transactions of buying and selling, which are not necessarily political acts. They can become political by promoting a cause—as in the case of campaigns to buy products manufactured within the country—but they are not intrinsically political.

The approach in this book is based on the premise that politics and government are a part, but not the whole, of social activity. Distributive politics is a concept that threatens to engulf all of society and make it political. Our position is that society is in danger of being overpoliticized and that government should be kept within certain limits, where it has an essential but still limited role to play.

Politics, then, is a distributive process of conflict resolution in which support is mobilized and maintained for collective projects. Government—decision making and rule enforcement—is thus laden with politics at every level. For one thing, government cannot carry out its various functions unless it is based on some popular support. It will probably lose that support if it proves unable to maintain internal and external peace and to provide services desired by the population. Government in a democracy must have an especially high level of popular support, and elections are an important way of indicating this. Hence in popular usage, the term politics has come to be associated with elections and related things, such as political parties. Going into politics usually means running for elective office. This popular usage is valid as far as it goes but is only one aspect of politics in the broader sense.

The political rationality of maximum support sometimes yields different results than the economic rationality of maximum efficiency. For example, most economists, regardless of ideological commitments, agree that rent controls, as an isolated intervention in an otherwise open market economy, tend to create a shortage of rental housing.[8] They encourage demand while simultaneously discouraging supply. Yet all Canadian provinces except Alberta and British Columbia have some form of rent control. The policy is economically irrational but politically attractive to those who must get elected to office by courting popularity with different groups of voters. Candidates recognize that the ballots of tenants far outnumber the ballots of landlords. (On the other hand, landlords on the average probably have more money than tenants, and this may be a resource they can use to political advantage.)

To an extent, politics has acquired a bad name because its rationality differs from that of other activities. Generally, there is little praise for someone who has advanced her career through politics; we likely refer to her as a flatterer or apple polisher who manages to win the support of influential people even if her work is mediocre. In the larger arena of public affairs, to say that an issue has become a "political football" is to imply that those in government are emphasizing political questions of conflict and support while neglecting the economic or administrative aspects of the issue. This may seem like an unscrupulous abandonment of principle. Yet if a politician ignores the need for popular support, he may find himself out of office and unable to implement his principles at all.

Politics has been called "the art of the possible" and "the art of compromise" because it must resolve disagreements among people with different opinions and desires. Compromise is usually needed if violence and coercion are to be avoided, although there are times when coercion is necessary to deal with those who have broken rules and harmed others. Political problems rarely have a satisfying "solution"; usually the best that can be obtained is a "settlement," that is, an arrangement that makes no one perfectly happy but with which everyone can live.[9] The English political scientist Bernard Crick calls politics "the activity by which different interests within a given unit of rules are conciliated by giving them a share in power in proportion to their importance to the welfare and the survival of the whole community."[10] Citing Aristotle, Crick argues that politics is not unity but harmony, the peaceful and co-operative co-existence of different groups, not their reduction to a single imposed pattern.

To recapitulate: Government and politics are universal aspects of human existence. *Government is the process that makes and enforces rules and decisions for society; politics is the activity of reconciling conflicts and gathering support that makes government possible.* Government and politics both arise from the necessity for people to live in societies, which means abiding by common rules and settling conflicts in such a way that the community is not endangered. Government and politics involve coercion, but not for its own sake. One reason why rulers resort to force is to lessen the use of force by private individuals against each other. Government and politics, therefore, are more and more indispensable as civilization advances. As our way of life becomes more complicated, we can less afford to have our plans upset by random, forcible intrusions of others on our person, property, or expectations. Government can be the great guarantor of the stability of expectations, making it possible for other human endeavours, such as religion, art, science, and business, to flourish. Where government is working well, the political process is continually and unobtrusively providing settlements to conflicts that might otherwise tear society apart. In fact, politics may work so well that the ordinary person may take it for granted and have very little need to be concerned with it.

Even if government is an essential aspect of the human condition, we are not always reconciled to it. There is in Western history a persistent belief that we may someday attain a perfectly harmonious, conflict-free form of society in which government would be unnecessary. One form of this belief is the Judaeo-Christian idea of the Kingdom of God on earth or the Kingdom of the Saints.[11] Human conflict would cease with the definitive triumph of goodness, when there would be no ruler but the Messiah himself. Secular versions of the same hopes also exist. The early French socialist Henri Saint-Simon (1760–1825) wrote that eventually the "government of men" would be replaced by the "administration of things," a formula later echoed by Lenin.[12] They both hoped that in a future world where everyone was comfortable and gross inequalities had vanished, people would become so peaceable that governmental coercion would be unnecessary. The same expectation is embodied in the Marxist doctrine of the "withering away of the state," which teaches that government will eventually become obsolete after a communist revolution.[13] But none of these visions of the future has ever come to pass, and we must still rely on politics and government.

2   Power

Power in the broadest sense is the capacity to achieve what one wants. The word is derived from the French verb *pouvoir*, meaning "to be able." Power can be the physical, muscular ability to perform a task such as lifting or running, or it can be the intellectual capacity to solve a problem.

In our field of study, power means the ability to induce others to do what one desires. In this sense and according to our conception of politics as acquiring and retaining support for human projects, power is inherently political. Power is to politics as money is to economics: it is the medium of exchange, the universal common denominator. Political power, however, is not a simple thing. We may distinguish three major forms of it: influence, coercion, and authority.

INFLUENCE

Influence is the ability to persuade some to do the will of another, to convince others to desire the same objective. Rational arguments about self-interest or the public interest may be used, or an emotional appeal to love, friendship, or loyalty may be made. The important point is that the targets of persuasion act voluntarily; they are not conscious of restraints upon their will because they have freely chosen to agree. Of course, they may agree either because they have come to think that the action is right and justified in itself or because they think they will reap personal benefit from it. We regard it as influence to induce people to act by offering rewards or bribes as well as by appealing to their reason or emotions.

Influence is always at work in the realm of government. Candidates for office in a democratic system obtain their goal by persuading their fellow citizens to vote for them. Once in office, they are besieged in turn by requests from individuals and groups who would like government to do something on their behalf. They seek, for example, to convince government that a road should be built along one route rather than another or that taxes on one group should be lowered and the revenue recouped by increased impositions on another group. Government also seeks to influence the behaviour of those over whom it rules. For example, in recent years, the government of Canada has undertaken extensive advertising campaigns to exhort Canadians to exercise more, drink less alcohol, conserve energy, and support Canadian unity.

COERCION

Coercion is the deliberate subjection of one will to another through fear of harm or threats of harm. Compliance is not voluntary but results from fear of unpleasant consequences.

Coercion can take many forms. *Violence* is physical harm, such as beating, torture, or murder. Imprisonment is not directly violent but is enforced by violence if a prisoner tries to escape. Other forms of coercion are monetary penalties imposed by government or strikes and lockouts, during which people deliberately combine to threaten others with losses in the marketplace. There is an infinite number of ways to harm or threaten people, and most rely ultimately on violence. We must pay a fine for a traffic violation to avoid imprisonment. Employers must submit to the economic setback of a legal strike. If they repudiated their agreements to bargain collectively with the unions, discharged their workers, and tried to hire a new work force, they would break the law and could be fined or even imprisoned.

An example that falls between coercion and persuasion is manipulating someone by providing false or misleading information. Motivating someone to act on false information is probably closer to coercion in essence, even though it takes the form of persuasion. The one who is "persuaded" would not have acted voluntarily had the truth been made accessible; in that respect the result is similar to coercion because it secures involuntary compliance.

Note that coercion is only one among many constraints on our behaviour. We are all faced with natural circumstances that limit our possibilities. One person would like to be a professional basketball player but does not have the height, strength, or agility. Some people would like to work all night but feel the need to sleep. These are real constraints, but it makes no sense to call them coercive.

Modern governments try to control most forms of coercion and, especially, violence. Ordinary persons are prohibited from violently assaulting each other or seizing property. They are supposed to refrain from violence except in self-defence or in disciplining their children, and limits are enforced even in these situations. Government uses its near-monopoly on violence to protect society from external attack, enforce rules of conduct, and punish those who violate them. To these ends, it develops a complex apparatus of armed forces, police forces, prisons, and courts.

One partial exception to the governmental control of coercion is in the field of industrial relations. In the twentieth century, governments have set up collective bargaining as an arena in which employees and employers resort to economic coercion to achieve their objectives. Yet the exception is perhaps not as great as it seems. Collective bargaining was introduced to civilize labour relations, which were previously marked by a high degree of overt violence. Government now tries, more or less successfully, to legalize a degree of economic coercion and thus keep both sides from resorting to violence.

Government forbids its subjects to use violence against it. Whatever their other differences, all governments are identical in their resistance to acts of political violence because they undermine the very existence of the state. Using force and threatening to use force against government are defined as political crimes.[14] A government that cannot resist such threats will not long survive.

Coercion is a powerful tool, yet no government can depend solely on it. Society has so many members, engaging in so many different activities, that everything cannot be coercively directed. Even if it were possible, it would be too expensive; coercion is very labour-intensive. But in any case, it is logically impossible for everything to depend on coercion. Coercion demands firm organization on the part of the coercers. What holds them together? More coercion? If so, who provides it? At some point, we must go beyond coercion to a principle that holds followers together for joint action, something that makes it possible for them to coerce others—in a word, authority.

AUTHORITY

Authority is a form of power in which people obey commands not because they have been rationally or emotionally persuaded or because they fear the consequences of disobedience, but simply because they respect the source of the command. The one who issues the command is thought to have a right to do so, and others are thought to have an obligation to obey. The relationship between parents and children is a model of authority. Sometimes parents must persuade their children to do something, and occasionally they may have to resort to coercion; but normally they can command with the expectation of being obeyed.

All governments possess at least some authority and strive to have as much as possible, for obvious reasons. Something more than influence is necessary to guarantee predictable results. Coercion produces compliance, yet it is very expensive and furthermore is possible only if a substantial number of people are held together by authority. Thus authority is an inescapable necessity of government.

It is safe to say that most people most of the time are acting in deference to authority when they do what government wishes. They stop at red lights, file tax returns, and pay medicare premiums because they realize that such actions have been commanded. (Of course, there may be other motives as well.) Their consciences may bother them if they disobey what they know to be right. How else can we explain the fact of obedience even under conditions where punishment is highly unlikely? Most drivers obey traffic lights even at 3:00 A.M. on a deserted street not solely because they fear a hidden police officer but also because they might feel a little uncomfortable about violating an authoritative rule. Nevertheless, not everyone is always deferential to authority, so coercion is extremely useful in motivating by fear those who are not susceptible to feelings of obligation. Coercion is present as a background threat, as with a soldier who may be prompted to obey out of fear of a court-martial. But this coercion, though important, is only an adjunct to authority. Coercion by itself could not produce the united action necessary to hold a court-martial.

Authority is sometimes held to be the opposite of freedom, but that is a misunderstanding. We are all surrounded by a multitude of authorities: family, school, church, state, and so forth. Freedom cannot mean escape from authority, for that is impossible so long as we remain social beings. More clearly, freedom means an uncoerced, voluntary choice among authorities. One mark of freedom is not doing as one pleases but voluntarily assuming obligations through obedience to a chosen authority. "A man is free when and to the extent that he is his own judge of his obligations, when none but himself compels him to fulfil them."[15] In fact, authority is not only compatible with freedom, it is essential to it. Voluntary submission to commands produces the kind of stable society that makes it possible for individuals to plan their own lives. Widespread loss of respect for authority entails a rise in coercion as leaders strive to re-establish order. It may seem paradoxical, but it is true that authority is nowhere more indispensable than in a free society.

Finally, we must distinguish between *natural* and *public authority*. The former exists whenever one person spontaneously defers to the judgment of another. Little children tagging after big children, students seeking out teachers in the early days of the medieval university, the disciples of Jesus recognizing him as one who "spoke with authority"—all these are examples of natural authority. Each of us is always surrounded by numerous natural authorities—friends, relatives, colleagues— and each acts as an authority to others on occasion. Natural authority is simply another term for the human tendencies to follow and imitate, as well as lead and initiate, that are the bonds holding society together.

Public authority, in contrast, is deliberately created by human agreement. The English language recognizes the difference between natural and public authority in an interesting way. We say that an expert on baseball statistics "is an authority" in his chosen field but not that he is "in authority" in that field. But when we describe, for example, a policewoman, we do not say she "is an authority" by virtue of any personal quality but rather that she is "in authority" by virtue of power entrusted to her by government. Her uniform is a visible sign of the public or artificial authority that she wields. To be a natural authority, one must have special personal qualities. To hold public authority, one has only to be in a position or office that carries with it rights of command.

Political science, at least with respect to modern government, is largely the study of public authority. However, natural authority still plays a significant role. Particularly in revolutionary or unstable situations, people are drawn to unusual leaders who seem to exude a personal magnetism. Individuals such as Louis Riel and Adolf Hitler had followings that transcended any office. Thus they were charismatic in the proper sense of that much-abused word, which will be discussed in the next chapter.

3   Legitimacy and Authority

Although we often speak of "having" or "possessing" authority, that usage is misleading because it makes authority seem to be a quality of a person, such as red hair or a deep voice. But in fact, authority is a social relationship. No one has authority as such; one has it only if others respect and obey it. *Authority* is one pole of a relationship, of which the other pole is *legitimacy*. When we emphasize the right to command, we speak of authority; when we emphasize the response to command, we speak of legitimacy. Authority is focussed in the one who commands; legitimacy is the feeling of respect for authority that exists in those who obey and makes authority possible. It is the same type of relationship that exists between leadership and "followership." Neither makes sense without the other.

Both authority and legitimacy are moral or ethical concepts; that is, they involve perceptions of right and wrong. We feel that one in authority has a right to command. Similarly, we feel that it is right to obey, that we have a duty or obligation to do so. Governmental power without legitimacy is only coercion or force; with legitimacy, power becomes authority.

Obligation is the link between authority and legitimacy, as illustrated in the following diagram:

Authority ——————— Obligation ————————→ Legitimacy
(right of command)   (sense of duty)   (belief in rightness of government)

We experience a feeling of obligation in response to commands when we are convinced that those who exercise authority are justified in doing so.

Public authority survives only as long as it has substantial legitimacy in society. It is not necessary that literally everyone, or even a numerical majority, accept the legitimacy of a particular government; but there must be at least a loyal minority, strong and united, to withstand potential opposition. Maintaining legitimacy is the supreme task of politics. If legitimacy collapses, so will public authority, to be replaced by another claimant to power.

Because authority and legitimacy are such central facts of political life, they are an important focus of study in political science. One of the major contributions to understanding them was made by the German sociologist Max Weber (1864–1920), who devised a well-known classification of three kinds of authority/legitimacy: traditional, legal, and charismatic.[16] These "ideal types," as Weber called them, are always found mixed together in political systems. They are intellectual models that never exist in pure form in reality yet help observers to understand what they see.

TRADITIONAL AUTHORITY

Traditional authority is domination based on inherited position. Hereditary monarchs provide a good example of traditional authority. They hold the right of command not because of extraordinary personal qualities or because they have been chosen by others, but because they have inherited a position from a parent or other relative. The arrangement is regarded as legitimate because it has the sanction and prestige of tradition; things have been done that way from time immemorial.

The feudal system of medieval Europe was chiefly one of traditional authority. At the apex of authority were the monarchs, who inherited the position. They appointed judges, administrators, and military commanders who owed them personal allegiance; their authority was only an extension of the monarchs'. Many governmental functions were performed by members of the caste of nobles, who also inherited social positions by right of birth. The system rested on the common people, who were born into a social position out of which it was extremely difficult to rise. Throughout the system, command and obedience were associated with inherited social rank, sanctified by tradition. A similar arrangement characterized much of the rest of the world until very recently and still prevails in Saudi Arabia, for example, where authority is vested in the royal family and a number of related clans.

LEGAL AUTHORITY

The central concept of *legal authority* is that general rules are binding on all participants in the system. Authority is exercised only when it is called for by these rules. It is associated not with persons who inherit their status, but with legally created offices that can be filled by many different incumbents. It is a "rule of law, not of men" (see Chapter 7 for a further discussion of this phrase).

In Canada and Great Britain authority is primarily legal, although the external symbolism is still traditional. A hereditary monarch reigns but does not rule, while actual power is wielded by politicians who are elected to office under a strictly defined system of laws. A prime minister is in authority as long as he or she is in office but has no personal status after dismissal. Those who work for government are no longer merely the monarch's personal servants, and their allegiance to the Crown means loyalty to the government as a whole, not just to a particular person within it. There is no longer anything like a hereditary caste of nobles to exercise governmental functions. The House of Lords, which still survives in Britain, is but a symbolic reminder of the vanished age of traditional authority. The basis of legitimacy on which the system rests is no longer acceptance of status and loyalty to personal authority, but loyalty to the constitution, which is a legal system above persons.

However, traditional elements still remain within contemporary legal authority. Law itself is hallowed by tradition. As rule-following animals, we quickly build up habits of compliance to those in power. Over time it begins to seem right to obey, simply because that is the way things have been done in the past. It is undoubtedly true that habit is a powerful source of governmental legitimacy. We obey because we are accustomed to, because we have always done so. Reflective thought is not necessarily involved. This is probably a good thing, for if we had to continually reconsider the legitimacy of government, we would have time for little else.

The great trend in modern political history is for traditional authority to be replaced by legal authority. This long, slow, and painful process began in Great Britain and its American colonies in the seventeenth century, continued in Europe in the eighteenth and nineteenth centuries, and has engulfed the entire world in the twentieth century. It is the political aspect of the wider social process known as *modernization.* Social changes gradually and cumulatively alter the perception of political legitimacy, so that the process is punctuated at certain points with the dramatic collapse of a traditional regime and its replacement by a new system of legal authority. The great popular revolutions of modern history must be seen in this context:

1688	Glorious Revolution	Stuarts overthrown by English Parliament
1776	American Revolution	American colonies declare independence from British Crown
1789	French Revolution	Bourbon dynasty replaced by a republic
1911	Chinese Revolution	Manchu dynasty replaced by a republic
1917	Russian Revolution	Romanov dynasty overthrown; Russian empire becomes Soviet Union

These are only a few of the many revolutions that in three centuries have transformed the political face of the globe. Together they make up what is often called the "world revolution." The essence of this world revolution was memorably stated by the French writer Alexis de Tocqueville, who made an extended tour in 1831–1832 of the United States and Canada. Describing the great social inequality of the traditional order, he wrote:

On the one side were wealth, strength, and leisure, accompanied by the refinements of luxury, the elegance of taste, the pleasures of wit, and the cultivation of the arts; on the other, were labor, clownishness, and ignorance. But in the midst of this coarse and ignorant multitude it was not uncommon to meet with energetic passions, generous sentiments, profound religious convictions, and wild virtues.

The social state thus organized might boast of its stability, its power, and, above all, its glory.

But the scene is now changed. Gradually the distinctions of rank are done away; the barriers which once severed mankind are falling down; property is divided, power is shared by many, the light of intelligence spreads and the capacities of all classes are equally cultivated.[17]

This social equalization described by Tocqueville is inseparably tied to legal authority, in which individuals are governed by universal rules applicable to all. It cannot co-exist for long with the hereditary classes and ranks of traditional authority. The worldwide transition from traditional to legal authority is the single most important political event of our times, furnishing the context in which everything else takes place.

CHARISMATIC AUTHORITY

Charismatic authority differs from both of the other forms because it is based not on inherited status or on legal office, but on the perception of extraordinary personal qualities. Weber defined charisma as

> a certain quality of an individual personality by virtue of which he is set apart from ordinary men and treated as endowed with supernatural, superhuman, or at least specifically exceptional powers or qualities.[18]

Charisma was originally a theological term derived from the Greek word for "grace" or "spiritual favour." Jesus was an example of charismatic authority in this original sense. People listened to him because of the extraordinary qualities they perceived in him, such as the ability to work miracles. The charismatic authority of Jesus was seen as a threat by the existing authorities of the Roman state and the Jewish religion, who collaborated in putting him to death.

Generally speaking, charismatic leaders are prophets, saints, holy people, shamans, or similar figures. Their legitimacy does not depend on tradition or law, but on their followers' belief that they speak to them directly from God. Their transcendental claim to authority often places them in conflict with mere traditional or legal authorities. Some of our most striking and well-known historical figures were charismatic in this sense: the Biblical prophets who brought God's message to the Hebrews, as well as Joan of Arc, whose heavenly visions inspired her to help drive the English from France.

Louis Riel is Canada's best example of a charismatic figure. On December 8, 1875, he underwent an experience of mystical illumination that convinced him that he was the "prophet of the New World." He believed himself endowed by God with a personal mission to create a new religion in North America. His own people, the Métis, would be a chosen people like the Hebrews. They would revive many Jewish practices, such as polygamy and circumcision, and merge them into a revised version of Roman Catholicism. Riel preached this novel doctrine to the Métis at Batoche during the North-West Rebellion of 1885. The rebels formed a sort of provisional government, but Riel did not hold office in it, wishing rather to be recognized as a prophet. Each morning he assembled the Métis forces to tell them of the divine revelations he had received during the night. He promised his followers that God would work a miracle to defeat the expeditionary force sent by Canada. When the miracle did not happen and the uprising was crushed, Riel was convicted of high treason. He went to the scaffold believing that he, like Christ, would rise from the dead on the third day after his execution.[19]

The term charisma is also applied to political leaders who base their claims to rule on an alleged historical mission. Adolf Hitler, for example, believed that he had a special mission to restore Germany's greatness. He came to this conviction as he lay in hospital in 1918, having been blinded by a British gas attack on the Western front. His blindness coincided with Germany's surrender, and when he recovered his sight, he became convinced that he might be the means of Germany's restoration to greatness. The title Hitler always preferred was *Führer*, which means "leader"; it emphasized that his authority radiated from his personality, not from an office that he happened to occupy.

Charisma may also be collectively shared, as in the political thought of the Ayatollah Khomeini, the symbol and leader of the revolution that swept the Shah of Iran from power in 1979. Khomeini is one of the jurists who specialize in the study of the Shari'a, the Islamic law. "The jurists," according to Khomeini, "have been appointed by God to rule."[20] The state must also have secular legislative and executive authorities, but the jurists have overriding, divinely given power and responsibility to ensure that all government is carried on within the principles of the Shari'a. Thus the jurists as a group are endowed with special authority directly by God; Khomeini sees himself less as a special individual than as the most prominent representative of a charismatic class.

In popular or journalistic usage today, charisma has been debased to mean little more than popularity. It is attributed to democratic politicians, such as President John Kennedy in the United States or Pierre Trudeau in Canada, who were momentarily popular but who did not make claims like those of Riel or Hitler. Neither Kennedy nor Trudeau claimed to be anything more than officeholders in a structure of legal authority; they certainly did not claim to rule on the basis of divine inspiration or a world-historical mission. To call popular politicians charismatic confuses the nature of their support and at the same time deprives the vocabulary of social science of an indispensable word.

Charisma, like authority in general, is not a thing that a leader "has"; it is a social relationship based on the followers' perception of the legitimacy of the leader's claims. The most important question is not how Joan of Arc, Louis Riel, or Adolf Hitler could utter such extraordinary claims about themselves, but how they could find such a receptive audience. The short answer is that charismatic leaders are accorded legitimacy in times of crisis or grave unrest when other forms of authority appear to have failed. Joan of Arc came to the rescue of France during the Hundred Years War at a time when England had the upper hand and it seemed that France might be conquered. The traditional authority of the French monarch seemed incapable of meeting the challenge. Riel preached his radical gospel to the Métis when the disappearance of the buffalo and the replacement of their ox trains by railway and steamboat threatened to destroy their way of life. It was a challenge that the traditional Métis authorities, the patriarchs of the clans, were helpless to meet. Hitler came to power at a peculiar point in German history. The traditional authority of the kaiser had been destroyed by Germany's defeat in World War I. The legal authority of the Weimar Republic, never deeply rooted, was gravely shaken by the runaway inflation of the early 1920s and the international depression of the early 1930s. Driven to desperation, the German people, particularly the middle class, turned to Hitler's promise of salvation.

If charisma is a response to crisis, it is difficult to see how it could be very long-lasting. As stability is restored, we would expect a return to traditional or legal authority. Weber was well aware of this tendency, which he called the "routinization of charisma."[21] The more successful prophets or leaders are in creating a following, the more either they or their followers find it necessary to create an enduring structure of authority that can exist over generations. The legacy of Jesus is the Christian Church. If Riel had been successful in the North-West Rebellion, he would eventually have had to take on some role other than prophet. Once the Shah was overthrown, Khomeini approved a new Iranian constitution that institutionalized and regularized the authority of the Islamic jurists, who will carry on after his death. From a long-range point of view, political history seems to alternate short, intense upheavals of charismatic authority with longer periods of normalcy.

4   Sovereignty and the State

The term *sovereign*, derived from the Latin *super*, meaning "above," literally denotes one who is superior. It was first used in its modern sense by the French author Jean Bodin toward the end of the sixteenth century. Writing in the midst of fearful wars between Catholics and Protestants, Bodin sought to obtain civil peace by establishing the monarch as the supreme authority whose will could decide such disputes. Bodin's idea was that in any community, there ought to be a single highest authority not subject to other human authority. He wrote in *Six Livres de la république* (1583):

> Sovereignty is the absolute and perpetual power of a commonwealth. . . . The sovereign Prince is only accountable to God. . . . Sovereignty is not limited with respect to power, scope, or duration. . . . The Prince is the image of God.[22]

The Romans had a conception somewhat like sovereignty that they called *imperium*, the concentrated, undivided power of government. Bodin, who was a student of Roman law, tried to revive the idea of centralized power in an age in which it either did not exist or existed in only an imperfect way. To understand why this should be so, we must recall some facts about the feudal society of medieval Europe. Each person was subject to a feudal overlord, but there was in reality no effective pyramid of authority culminating in the monarch. The nobles were often autonomous for all practical purposes. So were many city-states in Italy and along the Rhine. Overall, the pope exercised a claim to rule in religious matters through his bishops. The Church not only maintained its own system of ecclesiastical courts but also had a power of taxation by which money flowed to Rome. It would have been impossible to find a single sovereign—a "highest" authority—and indeed, except for the authority of God, the concept did not exist. This helps to explain why the religious wars of the Protestant Reformation were so protracted. Various nobles gave their support to one side or the other, and there was no effective central power to keep them all in check.

Bodin's idea of the sovereign took hold in the revulsion against this warfare and became well established in the seventeenth and eighteenth centuries. This was the age of "absolute monarchs"—so called not because they could do whatever they pleased, but because there was no human authority superior to theirs.

However, it is less the person than the power that is of interest here. *Sovereignty* can be conceived as the authority to override all other authorities. Family, employer, church—all social authorities—must yield to the sovereign's power when it is turned in their direction. Concretely, sovereignty is a bundle of powers associated with the highest authority of government. One is the power to enforce rules of conduct, which means establishing tribunals, compensating victims, and punishing offenders, and includes the power of life and death. Another is the power to make law, which encompasses creating new law, amending existing law, and repealing old law. Sovereignty also includes the control of all the normal executive functions of government: raising revenue, maintaining armed forces, minting currency, and providing other services to society. Moreover, in the British tradition, sovereignty implies an underlying ownership of all land. Private ownership of land "in fee simple" is in law a kind of delegation from the sovereign, who can reclaim any parcel of land through expropriation. Compensation to the private owner is customary but not necessary. Finally, sovereignty always means the power to deal with the sovereigns of other communities as well as the right to exercise domestic rule free from interference by other sovereigns.

Sovereignty was exercised by individual sovereigns in the Age of Absolutism, but it can also be placed in the hands of a small group or an entire people. In England the pretensions of the Stuarts to absolute monarchy were decisively defeated by Parliament in the Glorious Revolution of 1688. This victory ultimately led to the theory of *parliamentary sovereignty*, articulated by William Blackstone in his *Commentaries on the Laws of England* (1765–1769). Blackstone held that the supreme authority in England was Parliament, defined as the Commons, Lords, and Crown acting together under certain procedures.

Parliamentary sovereignty is still the main principle of the British constitution. It means that Parliament may make or repeal whatever laws it chooses; one Parliament cannot bind its successors in any way. Parliament is still the highest court in the land and cannot be overruled by the judiciary. The executive authority of government symbolized by the Crown can be exercised only by ministers who are responsible to Parliament. A hundred years ago A. V. Dicey, one of the greatest British constitutional experts, claimed facetiously that "Parliament can do anything except make a man into a woman." The progress of medical science has now removed even that limitation.

While Blackstone was developing the theory of parliamentary sovereignty, Jean-Jacques Rousseau's *Social Contract* (1762) set forth the great alternative of *popular sovereignty*. Rousseau taught that supreme authority resided in the people themselves and should not be delegated. Laws should be made by the people meeting in direct-democratic fashion, not by electing representatives to legislate for them. "The people of England," wrote Rousseau,

> deceive themselves when they fancy they are free; they are so, in fact, only during the election of members of Parliament: for, as soon as a new one is elected, they are again in chains, and are nothing.[23]

Rousseau's ideal of direct democracy is so difficult to attain in a commonwealth of any size that other writers have retained the notion of popular sovereignty by redefining it in a less ambitious way. For example, the American Declaration of Independence (1776) stated that governments derive "their just powers from the consent of the governed." This moderate formulation of popular sovereignty, stressing consent rather than actual rule, underlies modern representative democracy.

In fact, the three alternatives of personal, parliamentary, and popular sovereignty are not mutually exclusive. All three have to be employed to explain the present reality of, for example, British government. Queen Elizabeth is still sovereign in the symbolic sense that she represents the power of the state; she "reigns but does not rule," as the saying goes. Parliament is legally sovereign in its control over legislation and all aspects of government, but Parliament does not exist in a political vacuum. The most important part of Parliament is the House of Commons, whose members are elected by the people. Interpreters of the British system argue that popular sovereignty exists in the political sense that Parliament depends on public support. If Parliament uses its legal sovereignty contrary to public opinion, the people will eventually be able to elect new members of the House of Commons. In the long run, popular sovereignty is as much a fact of British politics as is parliamentary sovereignty.

If the British situation is complex, the Canadian is even more so. With a heritage of representative democracy based on the British model, Canadians share the same balance of personal, parliamentary, and popular sovereignty. The Queen is the sovereign of Canada as she is of Great Britain and some other members of the Commonwealth; and Canada also has a legally sovereign Parliament whose political composition is determined by a voting population. But Canada's federal system also divides power between levels of government. The federal Parliament and the provincial legislatures each have a share of sovereign law-making power. The provinces, for example, have control of education but cannot coin money or raise an army. The federal government controls interprovincial trade and commerce, but not property or civil rights, which are provincial matters.

The inevitable disputes between levels of government about the precise distribution of powers are settled in the courts, which have a power not needed or possessed by the British courts: judicial review. *Judicial review* is the ability of the courts to declare that actions taken by other branches of government violate the constitution. This includes the power to nullify legislation passed by one level of government if it invades the jurisdiction of the other. The Canadian system may be described as a variant of British parliamentary sovereignty in which sovereignty is shared by a number of parliaments or legislatures and tempered by the ability of the courts to declare legislation unconstitutional. The result is that, in comparison to the British model, Canadian sovereignty is divided, not concentrated. This arrangement is some distance from Bodin's original conception of sovereignty as a single, undivided centre of power.

The same is true of the United States, where a federal system divides sovereign power among levels of government. A further complexity of the American constitution is that the president, the chief executive officer, is neither a symbolic figure like the British monarch nor an actual ruling sovereign like a seventeenth-century king. Sovereignty is divided between the president and Congress, so that both must agree in order to make law, wage war, and perform other governmental acts.

Sovereignty may also be delegated in effect to administrative agencies or even private bodies. Marketing boards, professional associations, and trade unions recognized under collective bargaining legislation all exercise a small, delegated share of the state's sovereignty. Much of modern politics consists of a competitive struggle among organized groups to persuade the government to delegate a share of sovereign power to them so that they may use it to benefit their members.

These examples show that Bodin's original desire to locate sovereignty entirely in one place has not been fully realized. The bundle of sovereign powers that exists conceptually may be divided among different hands. Some fragmentation of power helps ensure that sovereignty is exercised within the rules established by the constitution. It is perhaps better for a free society that power is divided in this way because concentrated, unopposed power is a standing temptation to abuse by the one who wields it.

However, even if sovereignty is internally divided and delegated within the state, it still makes sense to inquire whether a government is able to control a certain population on a given territory, free from interference by other governments. This is actually the most frequent use of the term today, to denote autonomy from outside control in international affairs. Sovereignty in this sense is claimed by all governments and endorsed by international law, but it is as much myth as reality. Governments always interfere with each other to a degree, and only the biggest powers possess unhindered control over their own affairs. Yet sovereignty remains the central concept in all thinking about relations between states.

This discussion of sovereignty makes it possible to develop the concept of *state*, which was mentioned previously but not fully explained. A state is defined by the united presence of three factors: population, territory, and sovereignty. A state exists when a sovereign power rules over a population residing within the boundaries of a fixed territory. Canada is a state, as are Great Britain and France. Quebec, on the other hand, is not a state; it has people and territory, but not a sovereign government (except to the limited extent in which a province in a federal system has a share of sovereignty). Some members of the Parti Québécois wish to turn Quebec into a state by attaining full sovereignty. The Palestinians, in further contrast, are a people who have neither territory nor sovereignty of their own. They live scattered among Israel, Jordan, Lebanon, and several other states of the Middle East. In order to create a Palestinian state, which is a dream of the Palestine Liberation Organization, it will be necessary to obtain both territory and sovereignty.

The state is the universal form of political organization in the modern world. The earth's entire land mass, with the exception of Antarctica, is divided into territories under the control of the approximately 160 ostensible sovereign states.[24] Thus we tend to take the state for granted as the only conceivable form of political organization. But in fact, the combination of people, territory, and sovereignty that we call the state is, historically speaking, a fairly recent invention. The word itself was not widely used before Machiavelli, the author of *The Prince* (1513).

Governmental processes in tribal societies are carried on without the state form of organization. Before the coming of the Europeans, the Sioux and Cree did not have fixed territories with stable boundaries. They had traditional lands on which they hunted and gathered food, but the limits of these lands always overlapped with those of neighbouring tribes. The peoples themselves were in constant movement. The Cree and Ojibwa, for example, moved off the Canadian Shield onto the Prairies only after their contact with the fur trade provided them with firearms. Using their new weapons, they compelled other tribes to make room for them. If there were no stable borders, there was also no rigid definition of a people. Tribes could split apart, such as the Sioux and Assiniboine, or become close allies in spite of linguistic differences, such as the Cree and Ojibwa. There was also no specialized structure of government culminating in sovereign authority. In tribal government there is no army or police; these roles are filled by the men of the tribe as the occasion warrants. The men may also act as a sort of legislative assembly, reaching decisions by discussion and consensus. They may act as a court for settling disputes, or that job may fall to the chief. There is almost surely a chief or headman, but he is *primus inter pares* ("first among equals") and does not possess anything resembling sovereignty. Thus laws are enforced, decisions are made, and government exists; but these are stateless societies because there is no sovereignty, division of labour, or specialization in government.

Like hunting societies, the earliest agricultural societies were also stateless. Farming took place in autonomous villages that could handle their collective affairs without a specialized machinery of government. How, then, did the state arise? The answer almost certainly lies in warfare. Armed clashes between hunting tribes do not lead to the formation of a state because the losers migrate to new hunting grounds; roughly the same is true of primitive agriculturalists, as long as arable land is available. But where new land is not readily accessible, warfare produces a social hierarchy of victors and vanquished enforced by coercion. A specialized state machinery of armies, courts, tax gatherers, and other officials evolves as the conquerors enrich themselves at the expense of the conquered.[25] The consolidation of conquered territory under a strong monarch leads to the state form of organization.

Once created, the state is a powerful, expansive force. It easily prevails over neighbouring agricultural communities if these have not formed their own states. It may find tougher opposition in warlike nomads, who may even overrun the territorial state, as has happened so often in the history of Europe and Asia. Over thousands of years, tribe after tribe of warlike barbarians from the steppes of Eurasia descended upon the empires of China, India, the Middle East, and Europe.

Often the conquerors do not destroy the state; they take it over and install themselves as rulers and are sometimes able to extend the state's territories to new dimensions. At other times, the conquest may be such a shock that the state machinery deteriorates and requires a long period to be rebuilt.

Modern European states stem from such an interregnum. Invasions of German and other barbarians destroyed the highly developed state of the Roman Empire. The invaders installed themselves as rulers in medieval Europe but did not initially create a full-fledged state system. There were rudimentary specialized structures of government, but territorial boundaries between authorities were not clear. For hundreds of years, the king of England was nominally a vassal of the king of France, while England had important territorial holdings in France. The Catholic church in all parts of Europe carried on activities, such as raising revenue or conducting court trials, that would be considered governmental today. The political history of modern times is the emergence of separate, sovereign states out of the overlapping, interlocking jurisdictions of medieval Europe.

This development of the state runs like a thread through the familiar epochs into which Western history is customarily divided. Although the subject is far too big for a complete discussion here, we can at least mention some of the main stages.

During the Renaissance (fifteenth and sixteenth centuries), there was a great revival of interest in classical antiquity. Knowledge of Latin and Greek became more widespread, and many forgotten works of art, literature, and science were recovered. Revival of these interests culminated in what is often referred to as humanism, one of the great contributions of the Renaissance. One consequence of this was a heightened knowledge of Roman law, whose concept of *imperium* helped pave the way for sovereignty. Legal advisers trained in Roman law guided monarchs toward assertion of centralized control over their territories.

The Reformation (sixteenth and seventeenth centuries) broke the political power of the Catholic church. In England and parts of Germany, new Protestant churches were created that were firmly subordinated to the state (Queen Elizabeth II is still head of the Church of England, for example). In countries such as France and Spain, which remained Catholic, church administration was shorn of independent political power, and the pope lost his ability to intervene in internal political disputes. Another aspect of the Reformation, the increased use of vernacular languages rather than Latin, also strengthened the developing states of Europe by fostering the notion of a different official language for each state. The dialect of Paris became the language of France, the King's English became the standard speech of Britain, and so on.

The Enlightenment (eighteenth century) saw a relaxation of religious tension. Exhausted by more than a century of religious warfare, people turned their energies in a secular direction. Science and philosophy flourished under the patronage of monarchs who founded institutions such as the Royal Society of London to promote the advancement of learning. Scepticism, science, and the individual's control of his or her own destiny contributed to the development of the name by which the Enlightenment is best known, the Age of Reason. Hope and optimism became the qualities of a society that regarded itself as peaceful and reasonable. Interestingly, the Enlightenment in its political aspect is often known as the Age of Absolutism. The European continent was now more or less clearly divided into territorial states ruled by strong monarchs. They established standing armies, court systems, and police forces and in other ways developed a virtual monopoly of law enforcement and armed coercion. Further, they founded a professional bureaucracy capable of raising money through taxes and offering services to the population, such as the construction of harbours and highways and the promotion of agriculture. It was in this century that the state first took on a shape we would recognize if we could return to that era.

There was an important contradiction between the political thought of the Enlightenment, which was generally individualistic, and the political practice of the age, which was absolutist and monarchical. "L'Etat, c'est moi" ("I am the State"), said Louis XIV, emphasizing his personal sovereignty. In England this contradiction had been partially resolved by the establishment of parliamentary sovereignty in 1688. In Europe a revolution was delayed by more than a century and was correspondingly more violent when it came. The year 1789 saw a popular uprising against the French monarchy that proved to be the beginning of the end of personal sovereignty and traditional authority. Since then all the great royal dynasties have been overthrown or made purely symbolic, as in Britain. Yet the age of popular revolutions has not abolished the states created by the absolute monarchs; on the contrary, the state has been extended and perfected. Modern government enjoys armies, police, and bureaucracies that Louis XIV could never have imagined.

The crucial difference is that in the nineteenth and twentieth centuries, the state has become participatory. The absolute monarchs ruled over *subjects*, whereas the reality of the modern state is *citizenship*. This was dramatically demonstrated during the French Revolution, when for a time men addressed each other not as "Monsieur" but as "Citoyen."[26] Today each person is potentially a citizen, a member of an association in which all participate. Citizenship brings a variety of rights: personal rights, such as freedom of speech; political rights, such as the vote; economic rights, such as public education and pensions. The personal sovereign is now chiefly a symbol of the governmental powers exercised by a parliament in response to the wishes of the citizens. In Weber's terms, the modern state is the triumph of legal authority over traditional authority. Ideally, the modern state is not just a power over society imposed on it by force; it is a specialized instrument of society for the achievement of common goals. In its pursuit of these ends, it can become an association of all citizens, who share popular sovereignty and may be chosen to help wield parliamentary sovereignty.

A final comparison with tribal society may help to show how far political organization has evolved. The term citizen does not exist, and would have no meaning, in a tribal context. One could not become a Sioux or Cree citizen because to be Cree or Sioux was not a legal category. It was achieved by being born into the tribe or being adopted by a family. A stateless society, having no special governmental structure, could not have a legal status like citizenship separate from overall participation in the life of the tribe. But today all human beings in the world, with the exception of some refugees who may be stateless, are citizens of one state or another. Even resident aliens usually retain their prior citizenship unless and until they are admitted to citizenship in their new homeland. Sovereignty, state, and citizenship are so much a part of our lives that it is hard to imagine that they are not facts of nature, but the result of centuries of political evolution.

The participatory aspects of the modern state must not blind us to its origins in warfare and conquest. Any state is fundamentally an enormous engine of coercion, even if that coercive power is somewhat restrained by the legal form of authority. States are still predatory in their relations with one another; in spite of pious pronouncements about sovereignty, weak states are bound to be wholly or partially controlled by more powerful ones. Internally, the state machinery is also a temptation to the ambition and greed of social groups. Such concentrated coercive power can easily be used by one group within the state to elevate itself at the expense of another. To protect itself from taxation while loading taxes on others, to win official sponsorship of its language or religion, to make public services flow to it rather than to others—these strategies of using the state for special interest are as old as the state itself. Their existence should scarcely be surprising, because the original purpose of the state was precisely to protect the spoils of conquest. The modern legal and participatory state is a delicate and sometimes fragile modification of a brutal enterprise.

As a summary, let us link together four key concepts that have been discussed thus far: society, state, politics, and government. Society is the voluntary, spontaneously emerging order of relationships in which we co-exist with others and serve each others' needs, thus making possible human survival and even comfort. The state is the specialized structure of coercion that has evolved to protect the social order from internal disruption and external attack and to provide certain public

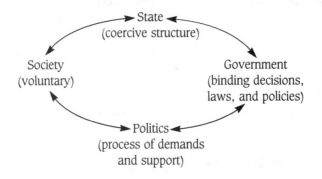

services to the community. Politics is the ongoing process that gives direction to decisions made by the state. Social factions compete to put pressure on public authorities to influence them to decide in certain ways, and support is tendered when the desired decisions are made. The state structure and the political process are both aspects of government, of making and enforcing decisions for society.

Interestingly, the ancient origin of words provides some up-to-date insights into these relationships. The word govern is derived from the Latin word *gubernare*, meaning "to steer a ship." The related Greek word *kybernein* is the source of the modern term cybernetics, the science of information. Government is a sort of cybernetic system for society—processing information, making decisions, and providing guidance. We will return to this topic in much greater detail in Part Four, where, with the aid of concepts derived from modern cybernetic theory, government will be discussed as a self-regulating system.

5   The Nation

What we described in the previous chapter as the modern, legal, participatory state, many authors prefer to call the *nation-state*. The word nation is added to state to emphasize that the state is participatory—that it is an association of citizens, not just a power coercively imposed on subjects. For reasons that will be discussed later in this chapter, the term nation-state raises all sorts of problems in Canada, and we prefer to use it sparingly. However, the term is widely used in political science, and the student will undoubtedly encounter it many times. Why does the word nation have these connotations of voluntary consent and active participation when it is added to state?

First of all, *nation* is sometimes almost a synonym for state. The United Nations is an organization to which only states can belong, so that groups like the Palestinians have only observer status. Could the United Nations just as well have been called the United States if that name had not already been taken by our southern neighbour? Probably not, for state suggests an association of the peoples of the world. They may communicate with each other through their governments, but if the term means anything, they are also involved as peoples.

This brings us to the nub of the issue. There are social realities called nations, which are conceptually distinct from states. Typical nations are the Americans, the French, the Germans. Who exactly are the Germans? They are not simply those who speak the German language, for German is also spoken in Austria and part of Switzerland. Germans cannot be identified with reference to a single state, for there are two German states: the German Democratic Republic (East Germany) and the Federal Republic of Germany (West Germany). Religion is also not the explanation, for the Germans are about equally divided between Protestant and Catholic. Clearly, to be German is to be aware of a certain identity, a certain definition of oneself.

The French writer Ernest Renan explored this topic in a well-known essay, "Qu'est-ce qu'une Nation?" (1882). He wrote:

> A nation is a soul, a spiritual principle. . . . A nation is a great solidarity, created by the sentiment of the sacrifices which have been made and of those which one is disposed to make in the future. It presupposes a past; but it resumes itself in the present by a tangible fact: the consent, the clearly expressed desire to continue life in common. The existence of a nation is a plebiscite of every day, as the existence of the individual is a perpetual affirmation of life.[27]

In contemporary language, we would say that the nation is an identity shared by a large number of people based upon, but not reducible to, objective factors such as common race, language, religion, customs, and government.

The nation, like the participatory state, is a product of modern European history. The peculiar identity we call the nation did not exist in medieval Europe. People thought of themselves in both broader and narrower terms: on the one hand as Christians or subjects of the Holy Roman Empire; on the other in terms of limited local identities. The first discernible nations to emerge were the English, French, and Spanish, and in each instance, the pattern was approximately the same. A strong monarchy established a stable territorial state within which local identities were merged over centuries into a wider national identity. The language of the court was extended over the realm, while local dialects were suppressed. The monarch's religion was made a state religion, and non-conforming groups were stripped of power or even expelled (Huguenots from France, Jews and Moors from Spain). Social disparities between the nobility and common people were gradually reduced as the monarchy, employing many commoners in its official service, stripped away the privileges of the aristocracy. The different estates of medieval society—nobility, clergy, freemen, serfs—were levelled into the universal category of citizens. Out of this often brutal exercise of state power emerged nations conscious of a common identity and destiny. An example of this is what happened in France after the revolution of 1789. With the king overthrown and the traditional enemies of France (Austria and Prussia) threatening war, the French rose to defend *la nation*. Huge armies of citizen-soldiers overran Europe, defeating the professional and mercenary armies of other states.

More than anything else, it was the French Revolution that awakened the spirit of nationality in Europe. Other peoples began to think of themselves as nations, even though they were not associated with a single strong state like the French or English. The Italians and Germans, for example, had lived for centuries divided among many states, large and small. Now movements of unification began that eventually resulted in the formation of the Kingdom of Italy (1861) and the German Empire (1871). Other peoples, such as the Irish and Greeks, who had long been ruled by foreign masters, began to assert their nationhood in frequent popular uprisings. One of the great themes of European history since 1789 has been the emergence of nations with a demand to create their own political entity—a nation-state. The process is now largely complete, though a few small groups, such as the Basques, Scots, and Bretons, still remain submerged minorities. One of the most striking political phenomena of recent years has been the "mini-nationalism" of such small groups: their attempts to assert themselves as full-fledged nations, even to the point of demanding political independence.[28]

In a different way, new nations were created elsewhere in the world by colonization. European immigrants flocked to the United States and Canada, Australia and New Zealand, Argentina and Chile. In different ways and at different times, each nation gained independence from its mother country, and political autonomy became the focus of new national identities. These are open, synthetic nations composed of immigrants of varied origins, whereas the traditional European nations are more closed, having grown up over a long period of common history. Both types of national identity seem equally viable.

A major development of the twentieth century is the spread of nationalism out of the European context to the rest of the world. The world revolution of modernization has made the nation the chief source of political legitimacy by weakening traditional social institutions such as the family, tribe, and village. It has also meant the destruction of ancient empires (for example, the Ottoman Empire) and the emergence of new nations from the wreckage (Turks, Syrians, Palestinians, and so forth). Another aspect is the attempt to fuse tribal identities into nationalities. Most of Africa was divided by the European powers along more or less arbitrary lines that bore little relation to patterns of tribal habitation. Now the Europeans are gone, but their colonial boundaries remain as the borders between sovereign African states. In most of these states, tribal identities are far more important than the sense of being Kenyan, Zambian, or whatever; but something similar could have been said of England or France five hundred years ago. Over time, at least some of these new states may create viable national identities. In the meantime, many are subject to chronic civil war among tribes, and the continent of Africa is troubled with millions of refugees, driven from their homes by political violence.

This brief historical survey confirms that nationality is not tied to any single objective factor. National identity is usually based on some combination of language, race, religion, and government, but none of these is either necessary or sufficient. The Swiss as a nation are religiously divided between Protestant and Catholic and linguistically divided among speakers of German, French, Italian, and Romansh; the focus of identity is government. Americans constitute a multiracial nation of Caucasian, Negro, Oriental, and Amerindian elements; there are also more than twenty million Americans whose first language is not English, but Spanish. In contrast to Switzerland and the United States, the small country of Lebanon, where all are of the same race and all speak Arabic, might seem well endowed to develop a coherent nationality; yet that unhappy country is torn by perpetual civil war among Christians and several sects of Moslems. One must look at each case separately to see what factors contribute to or make impossible the growth of national identity. The only safe generalization is that there is no universal formula.

As a form of identity, the nation is a subjective or psychological reality that transcends objective factors. That is what Renan meant when he called it "a plebiscite of every day." It depends upon human will. Ultimately, identity is a matter of what you wish to call yourself and what you can get others to accept. The nation as a psychological entity is a particular kind of social group, which must be distinguishable from other kinds of groups. Some of the main groups that overlap with the nation are racially, tribally, or ethnically based.

A *race* is a biologically defined group whose members share a gene pool, giving them physical characteristics in common, such as skin, eye, and hair colour. A race is the same as a subspecies; members of a race are physically identifiable and distinctive, but they can interbreed with members of other races and produce fertile offspring (as well as new races). Race differs from nation because it is only biological and not in itself a psychological identity. Members of the same race, such as American Negroes and African Negroes, may have absolutely nothing in common apart from genetic endowment. In Canada it was once customary to speak of the French and English as different races, and that usage is still sometimes encountered; but it is avoided by most people today, for it implies a biological difference that does not really exist.

A *tribe* has both biological and psychological dimensions. It is a group of people who are tied together by a myth of common ancestry and who think of themselves as blood relations. It is a sort of expanded family whose identity is often reinforced by distinctive language and customs. It differs from the nation in that members of the nation do not think of themselves as related by ties of consanguinity. Tribes and nations are not unlike each other in the way they furnish identity to their members, but they are different social structures that have arisen at different stages of social evolution.

The *ethnic group* is the hardest of these groups to define. Again, it is a mixture of psychological and biological elements. In North America ethnic groups usually share a common descent from some European or Asiatic nation. They may now feel Canadian or American but wish to preserve a slightly distinctive identity while still belonging to the larger nations. Thus we see many compound names: Japanese Canadian, Ukrainian Canadian, etc. The nation is an independent identity that stands on its own, while the ethnic group can be understood only as a part of a nation.[29]

Given that the nation is an inherently subjective reality, the distinction between it and a race, tribe, or ethnic group is often far from clear. Furthermore, the nation has a certain prestige lacking in the other types of groups. Consequently, it is a typical situation for a group to assert itself vis-à-vis other groups by insisting that it is a nation, while others try to cut it down to size by countering that it is really a race, tribe, or ethnic group. Several North American examples readily come to mind.

In the United States the religious movement popularly known as the Black Muslims (their most famous adherent is the boxer Muhammad Ali) maintains that Negro Americans are a nation—to be precise, the "Lost Found Nation of Islam."[30] This assertion is tied to the demand that as a nation with a full-fledged identity, black Americans should have their own sovereign state. Critics of the Black Muslims counter that Negroes as a distinct race are a special group within, but still part of, the American nation. In Canada the Dene people of the Northwest Territories elevated themselves from tribe to nation in the Dene Declaration of 1975: "We the Dene of the Northwest Territories insist on the right to be regarded by ourselves and the world as a nation."[31] In this they follow the Métis, who have insisted for a century and a half that they too are a nation, "The New Nation." Indians in general in Canada now refer to themselves as "the first nations."[32] Sceptics might counter that Indians are tribes and the Métis a racially mixed ethnic group. A similar issue arises in the case of French Canadians, who are often regarded by English Canadians as an ethnic group but who generally regard themselves as a nation. The difference is vitally important. If Indians, the Métis, and French Canadians are ethnic groups, they are only some among many within the Canadian nation. If they are nations, they are partners in a binational or multinational state. Furthermore, the status of being regarded as a nation implies at least the potential exercise of sovereignty. Even if the demand for statehood is not explicit at the present moment, it is implicit that the nation could be viable as a nation-state.[33]

Objectively, there is no right answer to the question of who constitutes a nation. It is not a scientific question of truth or falsity, but a strategic question of whether one social group is able to assert itself against others. The Dene will be a nation if they can convince others that they are a nation. If they do not succeed, they will have to be content with being regarded as a tribe, with the lower political status it entails.

Let us now return to the relationship between nation and state, in which there are several typical situations. Nation-states exist where the limits of common identity coincide with the boundaries of sovereign authority. The United States is a good example. There is a clearly defined frontier, within which lives a multitude of people who recognize the legitimacy of the state and share a common identity of being "American." Other contemporary examples are Sweden or Poland, where the state contains an almost homogeneous population. Perhaps more numerous are nation-states where one nation is clearly preponderant but minorities cannot be ignored. England has its Celtic fringe and its non-white immigrants; France has its Basques and Bretons; Israel has its Palestinians. If these minorities accept the legitimacy of the state, they can be regarded as ethnic groups within the nation. But in many cases the minorities, not content to be ethnic groups, struggle vigorously for national status or even a nation-state of their own, such as some Basques in France and Spain and most Palestinians in Israel.

A second situation is that of the *binational* or *multinational state*, where two or more nations co-exist under a single government. From one point of view, Canada is a binational state, a partnership of English Canadians and French Canadians, enriched by various ethnic groups and racial and tribal minorities. Belgium is a binational state, a partnership of Flemings and Walloons. India and the Soviet Union are vast multinational states, as was the Austro-Hungarian Empire.

If there are multinational states, there are also "multistate nations." Prime examples are: the German people, presently divided into East and West Germany; the Koreans, split into North and South Korea; the Poles at the end of the eighteenth century, when the state was parcelled out among Russia, Austria, and Prussia; and the Basques, who straddle the border between France and Spain. Nations can live submerged for hundreds of years with no state of their own and then reappear on the political stage, as the Poles did after World War I when the Polish state was re-created.

Applying these concepts to Canada is a challenging exercise. There is no single "correct" view, but a variety of views reflecting differing political positions. What may be called the official view of the Canadian government is that Canada is a bilingual, multicultural nation-state. There are two great linguistic groups, English and French, and many cultural groups (races, tribes, ethnic groups) that may adopt one or the other of the official languages; but there is only one overarching Canadian identity. There is only one Canadian nation, even though it is internally pluralistic. This view can be traced back to the Confederation debates, when it was strongly enunciated by the leading spokesman of French Canada, Sir George-Etienne Cartier. Cartier called the new state of Canada a "political nationality,"[34] by which he meant that the existence of a common government would create a national identity transcending linguistic and regional differences. These differences would continue to exist and would be reflected in provincial governments, but they would not be great enough to destroy Canada as one nation. Canadians, like the Swiss, would constitute a single people, even if they spoke more than one language.

Cartier's view appeals today to English-speaking Canadians, who are a large majority within this "political nationality," but it is less palatable to minorities. Most French Canadians believe, with considerable justification, that they are a nation separate from *les Anglais*. They can point not only to language but also to a heritage of religion, laws, and customs that makes them unique in North America. This consciousness of national identity does not necessarily imply a separatist political claim for a French Canadian state, although that is the aspiration of one wing of the Parti Québécois. It does imply a different attitude toward Confederation, perceiving French Canadians as partners in a binational state, not just as one group among many within the Canadian political nationality. Smaller groups, such as the Indians, Dene, and Métis, are now practising the same strategy by also claiming to be nations. If their claims are to be taken seriously, Canada becomes a multinational state of many partners.

The practical consequences of the different views are obviously considerable. Whether Canada is a nation-state, a binational state, or a multinational state will greatly influence the constitutional distribution of powers among the levels of government as well as the legal protection of the rights of social groups. Analysing the terms around which the debate is conducted does not resolve the argument, but it helps clarify the implications of all the positions.

6   Law

Law in the broadest sense means a rule or regularity of behaviour of any element in the universe. The motion of falling bodies on the earth or of the planets in the heavens is described by the laws of gravitation. Certain changes in living species are described by the laws of evolution. Human behaviour in dealing with scarce resources is described in the laws of supply and demand. Laws or regularities such as these make the universe intelligible. Without law there would be only the unpredictability of random motion and thus no order, life, or intelligence. Law is also the foundation of society, which is essentially a group of people living together under the same laws.

Although law is all-embracing, it is not monolithic. There is a subtle change in the character of law as one ascends the scale of creation from inanimate objects through plant and animal life to human beings. The higher levels have a greater element of self-guidance or freedom in the way they follow laws. Planets stay in their orbits exactly. Crops grow under certain conditions, but only the average yield can be predicted, not the growth of a particular plant. Animals mate at a certain time of year, but not with clockwork regularity. People usually try to buy cheap and sell dear in the marketplace, but any individual may depart from this model for personal reasons.

The variability of human behaviour raises the problem of enforcement (which does not exist for inanimate objects and lower life forms but may have parallels among the higher social animals). From now on, when we use the term *law*, we shall mean a rule of human conduct that is enforced by the community with coercion or violence if necessary.

Law is only one of several kinds of rules that we follow. Our behaviour is guided by *instincts*, of which we may not even be aware. Innate desires for nourishment, sleep, and shelter surely contribute to regularities of human behaviour. However, these basic impulses are always mediated by higher forms of rules. A purely personal rule of conduct is usually called a *habit*. We must all drink, but some of us habitually drink coffee, while others take tea at certain times of the day. Habit gradually merges into *custom* as the aspect of social determination becomes greater. The fact that most adults in the Western world drink either coffee or tea results from their seeing others drink the same beverages. In some other spheres, the social element is even more predominant. Such things as politeness and appropriate clothing and table manners are elaborate codes of conduct, customary in a particular society, that we learn through imitation and parental instruction.

Habits and customs all create regularities of human behaviour without coercive enforcement because deviation from the norm carries its own penalty. Someone

42

who cultivates a habit such as daily jogging will probably feel a certain self-induced distress by departing from that practice. In a different way, one will also feel distress by flouting normal customs of politeness because others avoid the company of those who create unpleasantness. In neither of these instances is there true enforcement, only a spontaneous reaction that helps keep our conduct in accustomed channels.

Some things are so socially important, however, that they cannot be left to spontaneous self-correction. Ordered society demands that, at the very least, we know which family we belong to and which material things are within our control. Thus all societies have rules about the family and property that are coercively enforced. Other areas of life, too, are subject to law in this sense of enforcement. Typically, enforcement is required when the rules are of primary importance to peaceful co-operation and when the rewards of breaking the rules, relative to the costs, are particularly attractive. Violating table manners makes one incur heavy social penalties for little apparent gain, so that enforcement is unnecessary; but stealing someone's property is such an attractive proposition that sanctions against such behaviour are needed.

The enforcement of law performs a number of functions for society, conveniently remembered as the four Rs: retribution, restitution, rehabilitation, and restraint. Retribution is the punishment of those who violate the norms of society. Restitution is the provision of compensation to those who have been damaged by rule breakers. Rehabilitation is a change in conduct that will prevent lawbreaking in the future. And restraint is the deterrence that is imposed by fear upon those who cannot be swayed by other means.

Two general points about rules are worth noting. First, we do not need to "know what" a rule is in order to follow it, we only need to "know how" to act. Language, for example, is a complex system of rules recorded in grammar books. We all learn to speak by imitation before we have any ability to say what the rules are. Similarly, children learn what kind of behaviour is just and fair long before they develop an abstract notion of the rules of justice. A child of three or four, who does not even know the word justice, can honour a rule of not grabbing other children's toys. Second, rules may be, but are not necessarily, designed by conscious intelligence. They may also develop over time in an evolutionary process of trial and error, as is true of habits, customs, and a great many laws.

These observations help to explain the two main kinds of law. The older kind of law found in all societies is evolutionary or *customary law*, which arises gradually without ever being "made" at an identifiable moment in time. The newer kind of law, *legislation*, is consciously formulated and deliberately constructed. Both kinds of rules are equally capable of being enforced, hence both are equally valid as law. Let us first consider customary law.

All human communities, no matter how primitive, have enforceable rules of conduct. They may not be written down, and no one may be able to articulate them, but they exist and are enforced nonetheless. Such laws embody the experience gained by a community in its struggle to survive. Rules of conduct that contribute to survival and comfort tend to be adopted over time. The requirements of internal order and external peace and strength promote enforcement of these rules.

Laws of this type are reason—tacit reason—and not command because no one has ever issued them. Typically, the community attributes divine origin to them, as the Jews regarded the Mosaic law as a product of divine revelation. Belief in divine origin is a way of saying that no one has created the laws and simultaneously emphasizing their importance for the life of the community.

Society took a step toward assuming conscious control of law when laws began to be written down instead of merely being honoured in practice and trusted to folk memory. Such deliberate recording of laws, however, should not be confused with true legislation. Early legal systems, such as the laws of Hammurabi in Babylon and the Twelve Tables in Rome, were regarded not as a new creation by the sovereign, but as a recording of ancient laws that had existed from time immemorial.[35] They had always been valid laws, but they were now being written down to avoid misunderstanding.

A rather similar attitude underlies the *common law* of the English-speaking peoples. Prior to the Norman Conquest (A.D. 1066), there were several bodies of law in the different regions of England. The Norman kings set up a unified system of courts throughout the realm that for a time competed with older local courts. The traditional courts gradually fell into disuse as the English found the king's justice to be fairer and more predictable. The king's courts, however, continued to interpret the old customary laws, of which many were generally acceptable and became common to all the courts of the realm. Thus there was never a radical break with the past.

Common law is essentially the sum of a vast number of cases decided by English courts since the Middle Ages. Most of these cases were decided not by reference to a written law, but by a process of reasoning based on the needs of ordered liberty. Certain principles, such as security of possession of private property and the enforcement of contracts, can be applied to a multitude of disputes. Application yields results, which then serve as models or *precedents* for subsequent cases. The courts generally observe the rule of *stare decisis*, which means "to stand by what is decided," that is, to follow precedent. Adhering to the example of past decisions allows the law to grow in an orderly or predictable way. By studying prior cases, one can have a fair idea of how future disputes will be decided. In this way, an enforceable body of law can grow up over centuries without ever being issued as general commands. It is "judge-made" law, although "made" is perhaps not the best word. It might be better to speak of "finding" the common law, as was done in the Middle Ages. The law, or abstract rule, is gradually discovered through experience with a number of concrete cases.

The great advantage of common law is its flexibility, because it can forever be applied to new situations. It need never become obsolete so long as judges have a reasonable freedom to follow precedents. For example, when radio waves were first commercially used early in this century, the law was faced with a novel situation. Questions arose, such as whether one could broadcast on a frequency already being used by another transmitter. Judges immediately began to cope with these problems, reasoning by analogy with other forms of property.

Common law, having grown up in England, was transported to all the British colonies. It is still very much alive in Canada, the United States, Australia, and New Zealand, guiding a great deal of our lives in areas such as personal property, contracts, and family matters.

But valuable as it is, common law has certain inherent limitations. At any given time, it is liable to contain conflicting precedents on unsettled points of law, and conflict means uncertainty. It may also become very complex as precedents multiply over the centuries, and complexity is another source of uncertainty. Finally, there is no guarantee that the common law process produces desirable results. Judges may box themselves in by making a series of undesirable decisions, creating an impasse that may take decades or centuries to resolve.

One solution to these problems is to codify an existing body of common law to reveal its principles with greater clarity. An example of this is Justinian's Code, produced in the sixth century A.D. by order of Justinian, emperor of the surviving eastern half of the Roman Empire. The code systematized the results of a thousand years of Roman customary law. In the early years of the nineteenth century, Justinian's Code served as a model for the French lawyers whom Napoleon commanded to codify the complex body of French customary law. The Napoleonic Code is an all-encompassing system that forms the basis of law in France as well as in other European countries, such as Italy and Spain.[36]

Codification in the common law countries, although important, has not gone as far. In Canada the private law of the province of Quebec, governing such things as property and contracts, was systematized in the *code civil* of 1866;[37] private law in the other nine provinces remains an uncodified extension of the common law. There are thus two legal systems of private law in Canada, so that three judges of the Supreme Court of Canada must be from Quebec in order to deal with appeals from that province. The criminal law, in contrast, is unified in a single Criminal Code, which by Act of Parliament in 1892 replaced the common law in those matters.

The production of legal codes is a final step toward deliberate control of law. This conscious creation of law is legislation. It may result in a *statute*, which is a particular piece of legislation, or a *code*, which is a comprehensive set of inter-related rules. In general, the realm of legislation is known as *positive law* because it is "posited" or put in place by society, in contrast to laws that have spontaneously evolved and are "found," not "made."

The concept of legislation has been understood since antiquity, but until the last two centuries it played only a restricted role in governmental affairs. Statutes in Britain were most often passed in the domain of *public law*, the law that creates agencies of the state and controls the relations between state and subjects. Statutes defined political crimes such as treason, created state machinery such as police forces, navies, and government departments, and provided for raising revenue through taxation. There was relatively little legislation in the field of *private law*, which controls the relations of individuals to one another. Matters such as contracts and family were largely left to the evolution of common law. Here the state's role was to enforce the rules that gradually emerged from judicial precedents, but not directly to create rules by legislation. Exceptions occurred but were relatively infrequent.

All this has changed in the last hundred years. The modern state now legislates freely in private as well as public law. The general rule is that common law retains its validity only until the state supersedes it by passing statutory law. In Canada large areas of what used to be common law have been replaced by legislative statutes or codes. One good example is labour relations. In the nineteenth century, relations between employer and employee were regulated by the common law of contracts, employment being considered the contractual exchange of money for work. But all the provinces, as well as the federal government, now have comprehensive labour relations statutes that have replaced the common law. They have established the framework of collective bargaining—certification of bargaining agents, negotiations, strikes, arbitration, and so forth—which is far different from what existed under the common law.

The expansion of legislation has certain advantages. Legislators can foresee situations and try to prevent conflicts, whereas common law adjudication must wait for conflicts to arise. Legislation can be created or changed in a relatively short time, whereas it may take decades for solutions to evolve in common law. As well, legislation seems to offer greater certainty because the law is not inferred from precedent but is laid down in express terms.

This certainty, however, is partly illusory. No matter how perfectly designed statutes may be, ambiguous language can never be wholly avoided. Also, statutes are soon overtaken by the course of events and need to be adapted to new situations. Continual legislative amendment is not practical; the statutes must be interpreted in particular disputes as they are brought before the courts. A sequence of cases will arise in which the courts will usually follow precedent according to the rule of *stare decisis*. In this way, legislation becomes subject to the same sort of evolutionary forces that guide the development of common law.

The flowering of legislation in this century has been based upon prior developments in the field of *jurisprudence*, or the philosophy of law. The early theorists of sovereignty tended to define law as simply the command of the sovereign. Thomas Hobbes wrote in the *Leviathan* (1651) that law

> is to every subject, those rules, which the commonwealth hath commanded him, by word, writing, or other sufficient sign of the will, to make use of, for the distinction of right and wrong. . . .[38]

To make matters perfectly clear, Hobbes added that "the sovereign is the sole legislator."[39] His view was later developed into the doctrine of *legal positivism* by the English writers Jeremy Bentham and John Austin.

Legal positivism holds that all law is the command of the sovereign. In its pure form, it does not entertain questions about the substantive reasonableness of law. It is concerned only with procedural issues, such as whether the sovereign's will has been clearly articulated and properly made known. It is assumed that the sovereign—monarch, parliament, or the people themselves—may create any law whatsoever, as long as the prescribed procedure is followed.

Obviously, from the positivist perspective, common law is not really law, or is at best a highly imperfect form of law, because it has never been formally commanded. Positivists have tried to rationalize common law by arguing that its legal status arises from the announced determination of the sovereign to enforce what the courts find the law to be. But this is only a logical expedient that does not do justice to the great difference between common and statutory law. Hence it is not surprising that common law has been in retreat during the last century and that legislation has been expanding to fill its place.

We see an important danger in the philosophy of legal positivism to the extent that it anchors law in the will of the sovereign rather than in the behavioural norms of society. Our view is that all law stems ultimately from society rather than from the state. This happens in different ways for common law and legislation, as illustrated by Figure 6.1.

FIGURE 6.1

The Social Origins of Law

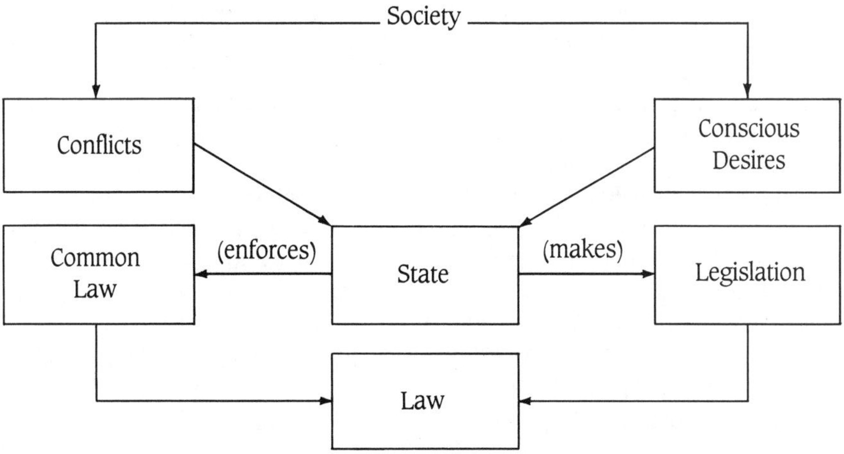

Common law and legislation are two different expressions of social ideas about right conduct. The former emerges from conflicts of action, and the latter is created according to deliberate plan; but both rest upon the people's conception of what is just. Legal positivism, in contrast, threatens to put the state above society, to treat it not as a special agency within society, but as a power ruling over it. If that is done, laws become rules imposed upon society by force, not an expression of social morality. This corresponds in real life to the situation of conquest, where a state imposes itself upon unwilling subjects and maintains its rule by coercion. The absence of legitimate authority has to be compensated by sheer force. But conquest is not the normal condition of politics, and law is not normally maintained by brute force. Yet legal positivism, as Hobbes understood perfectly well, puts the sovereign above the law by claiming to be the source of law, not just the means by which law is enforced or proclaimed. This position is a threat to the accumulated wisdom of the Western political tradition that all should be subject to the same laws— rulers and ruled alike. This is the ideal of constitutionalism, which is discussed in the next chapter.

The preceding discussion sheds some light on the much-debated question of whether law leads or follows social change. Any answer must take account of the distinction between judge-made law and legislation. Normally, judges are a conservative force in society, both in developing common law and interpreting legislation. The rule of *stare decisis* tends to make them look to the past for guidance. Their tenure in office, which deliberately (and rightly) insulates them from political pressure and public opinion, may also leave them somewhat removed from social change. For example, the common law served as a restraint on organized labour long after the labour movement had become so powerful that it needed more adequate legal recognition. The solution of collective bargaining finally came through legislation rather than the evolution of common law. In this instance, social change clearly ran ahead of the law until remedial legislation was introduced. But judges are not necessarily a conserving force in all circumstances. Since the 1950s, the American judiciary has played an activist or intervening role in areas such as race relations. Judicial orders have required measures, such as the bussing of schoolchildren to achieve racial balance, which are probably opposed by a majority of the American public.

If judges can be either behind or ahead of public opinion, so can legislators. In Canada the Lord's Day Act remained on the books until 1985, when the Supreme Court held that it conflicted with the Canadian Charter of Rights and Freedoms.[40] For a number of years before 1985, it was apparent that this law had become so anachronistic that it was scarcely enforceable and was routinely flouted by numerous otherwise law-abiding citizens. But legislators refused to act, preferring to leave this emotional issue to the courts. On the other hand, legislators sometimes race ahead of public opinion, as in the abolition of capital punishment in Canada. There has been a long-term trend toward less physical forms of punishment, and

Canadians may eventually turn decisively against the death penalty, as they have against torture and flogging. But in the meantime, if opinion polls can be believed, a large majority of the population, about 70 per cent, wish that capital punishment had not been abolished.[41]

Experience suggests that law may be a little behind or a little ahead of popular feeling without causing much trouble; but if the discrepancy becomes great, signs of distress will appear. The law will be widely disobeyed, and escalating levels of coercion will be needed for enforcement—phenomena that show that law does indeed come from society and is not just the command of the sovereign. Neither legislation nor judge-made law is immune to the danger; but in a sense, each is a partial corrective of the other. Legislation can replace outmoded common law, while judicial interpretation can help adjust legislation to social change.

7   Constitutionalism

A *constitution* is a set of fundamental rules that generally:

1. Establishes the powers and responsibilities of the legislative, executive, and judicial branches of government.
2. Allocates powers to different levels of government, such as federal, provincial, and local.
3. Enumerates the rights of citizens against each other and against the government, as in a bill of rights.
4. Stipulates a procedure for amendment of the constitution.

The words fundamental rules are used advisedly because a constitution comprises both laws that are enforceable in the courts and customs, or *conventions*, that are enforceable only in the sense that a government may lose political support by violating them. A convention is a practice or usage that is consistently followed by those in government, even though it is not legally required. According to a leading authority on the British constitution, a convention is not just any custom that happens to be observed. To be considered a convention, a practice must exist for a good reason, and those who follow it must be consciously aware that they are following a rational rule.[42]

Although useful, the distinction between law and convention is not as solid as it appears because courts have no power to enforce anything unless they are obeyed by those who control the coercive apparatus of the state. This obedience is at bottom no more than a convention, based upon politicans' belief that public opinion wishes the courts to be obeyed. In the last analysis, law and convention are two related manifestations of the same spirit of constitutionalism and the rule of law.

The older type of constitution, which used to be very common but now survives in only a few countries such as Great Britain and New Zealand, is usually called *unwritten*. The name is not quite exact, for the British constitution is written down, at least in large part. But it is not written down in a single place; rather, it must be pieced together from studying many different sources. Unwritten in this context really means "uncodified." Also, there exist as part of the British constitution many conventions that are not written down at all.

Much of the British constitution consists of statutes of the King-in-Parliament. The oldest such text is the *Magna Carta* (Great Charter), which King John was forced to sign in 1215, before Parliament even existed. Later adopted by Parliament in statutory form, it established the principle that the monarch had to rule within the law of the land. Further restrictions on royal power were contained in the Bill of Rights (1689), which, for example, prevented the monarch from levying taxes without the consent of Parliament. The Act of Settlement (1701), as well as fixing the succession to the throne, protected the independence of judges by making it impossible for the monarch to dismiss them without cause. The Parliament Act (1911) imposed several restrictions on the powers of the House of Lords as compared to those of the House of Commons.

These and many other statutes passed over hundreds of years make up the legal framework of the British constitution, but more than statutory law is involved. Because statutes almost always raise problems of interpretation when they are applied, the body of case law that has developed around the statutes must be considered part of the constitution. Also, the very existence of Parliament does not rest on statute, but on the common law or prerogative powers of the monarchs who first established the practice of calling Parliaments for consultation. In an important sense, the statutory structure of the British constitution has been raised on a common law foundation.

Many of the most important institutions of British government rest not upon law at all, but only on convention. The Cabinet and prime minister are mentioned briefly in some statutes, but the offices have never been deliberately created by legislation. Similarly, it is conventional that the monarch not refuse assent to a bill properly passed by Parliament, that she or he invite the leader of the majority party to form a Cabinet, and so on.

This short sketch of the British constitution shows one important characteristic— its flexibility. The written part, that is, the constitutional law, is no different from any other type of law; all law, constitutional or otherwise, may be changed by an Act of Parliament. An Act of Parliament cannot be unconstitutional as long as specified procedures are adhered to, and Parliament could even free itself from existing procedures if it chose. The conventions are particularly flexible because they are essentially usages that are in constant evolution. This peculiar flexibility of the unwritten British constitution has led some observers to say that it is not a constitution at all; and indeed it may be thought of as a synonym for the ensemble of governmental institutions at any moment.

All of this is in striking contrast with the American constitution, the world's oldest surviving written constitution. It is a systematic, deliberately designed document, drawn up at the constitutional convention at Philadelphia in 1787. In a few pages this text arranges the legislative, executive, and judicial powers of the state, divides government into federal and state levels, and deals with some other necessary matters. Rights of the individual are enumerated in the Bill of Rights, the first ten amendments to the constitution, approved almost immediately after adoption. The amending process was made intentionally arduous so that the constitution could not be lightly changed by the transitory desire of whoever happened to be in power. Amendments must be approved by a two-thirds majority in both houses of

Congress and subsequently ratified by three-quarters of the states. Not surprisingly, this very difficult procedure has been used successfully only twenty-six times as of 1986.

The difficulty of the process is revealed by the curious history of the proposed Equal Rights Amendment (ERA): "Equality of rights under the law shall not be denied or abridged by the United States or by any State on account of sex." Congress approved the ERA in 1972, setting a period of seven years for ratification by three-quarters of the states. When only thirty-five states of fifty had ratified by 1978, Congress extended the deadline until 1982;[43] but even with the extension, the approval of the requisite thirty-eight state legislatures was never obtained, and the ERA is now dead.

This rather rigid amending process has not hampered constitutional evolution in the United States as much as might be expected because the courts have taken on the function of declaring the meaning of the constitution in specific applications. A large body of case law has grown up that is indispensable to understanding the constitution; this case law is flexible in much the same way as common law. For example, the Supreme Court held in 1896 in *Plessy v. Ferguson* that it did not violate the constitution for states to require racially segregated coaches on railway trains.[44] If the facilities were "separate but equal," the situation did not violate the "equal protection" clause of the Fourteenth Amendment. But in 1954 the Supreme Court departed from this precedent in the famous case of *Brown v. Board of Education*, holding that segregated schools were necessarily injurious to the minority race and thus contrary to the principle of equal protection of the law.[45] The point for our purpose is that the American constitution is, to a large extent, what the courts say it is. Judicial interpretation of the constitution has probably gone further in the United States than in any other country in the world.

Although the word convention is not used as a technical term in American constitutional law, there is inevitably an element of custom in the American constitution. The power of the courts to declare legislation unconstitutional is not mentioned in the text of 1787. Chief Justice John Marshall first claimed this right in the seminal case of *Marbury v. Madison* (1803); it ultimately rests upon the acquiesence of Congress.[46] Another example of constitutional custom was the practice established by the first president, George Washington, of serving no more than two terms of office. This precedent was followed until World War II, when Franklin Roosevelt, because of the dangerous international situation, chose to run for a third and then a fourth term. This violation of the custom touched off such a reaction that the Twenty-Second Amendment, ratified in 1951, officially wrote the two-term principle into the constitution. Custom, having proved insufficient, was translated into constitutional law.

The British and American constitutions make an instructive contrast. The former is unwritten and flexible, the latter written and rigid. The former can be amended by simple statute, the latter only by an elaborate amending process. Judicial decisions play a role in both instances, but a far larger role in the American model, where they supply the flexibility that is missing in the constitutional text.

The Canadian constitution may be seen as a blend of the two types. Although there is no central, systematic document of the American type, there is a substantial written core to the Canadian constitution. As in the British model, this core consists of a series of statutes; but contrary to the British constitution, these statutes can no longer be amended or repealed by a simple Act of Parliament.

The starting point of the written constitution is now the Constitution Act, 1982, whose first thirty-four sections are known as the Canadian Charter of Rights and Freedoms. The Charter sets forth limitations on the powers exercised by both the federal and provincial legislatures and governments. The rest of the Constitution Act, 1982, covers aboriginal and treaty rights of native peoples, future constitutional conferences, ownership and control of natural resources, and – most important for this discussion – the process to be followed in amending the constitution.

Schedule I to the Act lists a further thirty statutes and orders-in-council, some Canadian and some British in origin, that are now assured of constitutional status and can therefore be amended only by the approved procedure mentioned above. The most important of these thirty items is the British North America Act, 1867, now renamed the Constitution Act, 1867. The British Statute created the Dominion of Canada in 1867 and set up the federal system as well as the legislative, executive, and judicial institutions of government – all of which exist to this day. A large number of the thirty items are amendments to the British North America Act made between 1867 and 1982 by the British Parliament at Canada's request. The amendments have all been restyled ''Constitution Act, 1871,'' or ''1940,'' or whatever year is appropriate. Another large fraction of the scheduled items consists of statutes and orders-in-council by which Canada was enlarged to its present boundaries – for example, the Manitoba Act, 1870, the British Columbia Terms of Union, the Alberta Act, etc. These have all retained their original names. Finally, there is the Statute of Westminster, 1931, a piece of British legislation by which Britain renounced the right to legislate for Canada except to amend the Canadian constitution, a duty retained until nine provinces and the federal government finally reached agreement in 1982 on an amending formula.

Prior to 1982, those parts of the written constitution that were British statutes (the most important parts) could be amended only by the British Parliament. The normal procedure was for a joint address of the Canadian Senate and House of Commons to request the king or queen to have the British Cabinet introduce the needed amendment into Parliament, a request that was never refused. Although the mechanics of the procedure were under federal control, it became conventional to seek provincial agreement to amendments affecting the provinces – this usually, but not always, meant unanimous consent of the provincial governments. The Constitution Act, 1982, has now removed constitutional amendment from the realm of convention to that of law. For certain fundamental matters such as the existence of the monarchy and the composition of the Supreme Court, the agreement of all provincial legislative assemblies must be added to that of the Senate and the House of Commons. Other questions require only resolutions of the legislatures of at least two-thirds of the provinces, containing among themselves 50 per cent of Canada's population, plus consent of the federal Senate and House. In either case, the Senate actually has only a suspensory veto. If the Senate does not agree to the resolution within 180 days of passage by the House of Commons, and if the House then repasses the resolution, the governor general will proclaim the amendment, assuming the requisite degree of provincial consent. There are a few more niceties that need not concern us here; the main point is that the amending procedure is relatively rigid and will not be used frequently. Some observers predicted that it was so inflexible it would never be used, but it has in fact already been used successfully to add some amendments to s. 35 of the Constitution Act, 1982, which deals with aboriginal and treaty rights.

Because the statutes that comprise our written constitution are far from crystal-clear, judicial interpretation is an essential part of Canadian constitutional law. This has been true since 1867 with respect to the allocation of powers between the federal and provincial governments as set forth in ss. 91 and 92 of the Constitution Act, 1867. It is only by virtue of court decisions that we know, for example, that the federal government has the power to legislate a national system of wage and price controls under conditions of economic emergency, including a high rate of inflation.[47] None of this, not even words such as price control or inflation, exists in any explicit fashion in the Act itself. Since 1982, the interpretive function of the courts in constitutional matters has become much wider because the Canadian Charter of Rights and Freedoms, which is a constitutional text, covers so much territory. The courts not only have the function of "power allocation," of saying whether the federal or provincial governments have the right to legislate on a particular matter; they also have the function of "power denial," of saying that no government, federal or provincial, may do such things as abridging freedom of the press or taking away the right to vote.[48] Canada is now very close to the United States, and far from Great Britain, in the extraordinary importance assumed by the courts in saying what the constitution means.

In another way, however, we remain very close to Great Britain. The Preamble to the Constitution Act, 1867 states that Canada desires to have "a Constitution similar in Principle to that of the United Kingdom." These words have imported into Canada a large body of British constitutional convention covering such matters as the use of the royal prerogative, the appointment of a prime minister and cabinet, the need to maintain support in the House of Commons, and so on. The working machinery of parliamentary government in Canada is largely based on convention. The Constitution Act, 1867 does not even mention the prime minister or cabinet; an uninformed reader of the Act would assume that the governor general and the Queen's Privy Council for Canada were the chief executive authorities in Canada. Even in 1867 that was far from true, and it is not at all true today. But the outmoded language of the written constitution is meaningful because it is supported by many conventions, such as the existence of Cabinet as the working committee of the Privy Council and the reliance of the governor general upon the advice of cabinet ministers.

All constitutions, whether of the British unwritten, the American written, or the Canadian hybrid type, are ultimately a manifestation of an underlying attitude or spirit of *constitutionalism*. This is the belief that government is not the master of society, but an instrument within it. It exercises the powers of authority and coercion for the general welfare by doing things that other agencies cannot do; but it is still part of society, not elevated above it. It is, to use another common term, a *limited state*. The constitution is the expression of that limitation because it stipulates which powers will be exercised by which person. Perhaps more important, it also states which powers are not to be exercised by anyone in government but are to be left to the people, such as the power to decide how God will be worshipped. A constitution possessed by an unlimited state would be mere camouflage; if government could do whatever it chose, its actions would not be restricted by rules, and its discretion would be complete.

RULE OF LAW

Closely related to constitutionalism and the limited state is the concept of the *rule of law*. This phrase is more readily understood if it is considered as a shortened form of the expression "the rule of law, not of men." It means that to the greatest extent possible, people should not be subject to the unhindered discretion of others, but that everyone—rulers and ruled alike—should obey known, predictable, and impartial rules of conduct. We can distinguish several layers of meaning in the idea of rule of law:

Maintenance of Law and Order. At the most elementary level, the government must maintain law and order so that people are, as much as possible, prevented from attacking each other. The enforcement of law in this sense allows us to count on security of person and property. Yet it is not enough for sovereigns to restrain us from despoiling each other if they themselves are not so restrained. Simple law and order must be complemented by restrictions upon government itself. The ideal of the rule of law leads logically to constitutionalism and the limited state.

No Punishment without Law. The subject should be liable to punishment by government only for violation of law. "No punishment without law" (*nulla poena sine lege*) is an old maxim of English common law. It prevents rulers from using their coercive power arbitrarily against persons who are the object of their dislike. People cannot be punished just for who they are; they must commit concrete acts that violate known laws. This aspect of the rule of law is an important safeguard of individual freedom because it means that people are free to do anything not explicitly forbidden by law. A 1935 law of the German Nazi regime provides an example of the opposite situation:

> Any person who commits an act which the law declares to be punishable or which is deserving of penalty according to the fundamental conceptions of a penal law and sound popular feeling, shall be punished. If there is no penal law directly covering such an act it shall be punished under the law of which the fundamental conception applies most nearly to the said act.[49]

Under such a broadly defined "law," one could be punished for any action disliked by someone in authority. The meaning of the rule of law is entirely extinguished, even if the form of legislation is preserved.

Discretion. Not all government activity can be reduced to impartial enforcement of rules. There is also a large and important element of *discretion*. This appears in law enforcement when the judge assigns a sentence to a convicted offender, and it is even more prominent in the service activities of the state. If government is to defend the country from external enemies, it must have discretion to locate military bases in suitable spots, choose effective models of weapons, and promote capable officers. If government is to build roads, it must plan their location, acquire land, and contract for grading and construction; and none of these things can be achieved without discretion.

But discretion need not be complete; it can and must be hedged with limiting rules. Government, for example, must have the discretion to acquire land; but there can be rules ensuring that owners will be compensated at fair market value and that they may appeal to the courts if they are dissatisfied with the state's offer. Similarly, government's discretion in letting contracts can be controlled by requiring that bids be submitted by contractors in an open competition. The rule of law requires that where governmental discretion is necessary, it should be exercised within a framework of rules that discourages arbitrary decisions and offers recourse if arbitrariness does occur.

Government Subject to Laws. Government and its employees must be as subject to law as are those who are ruled. This is the great principle that was established in the English-speaking world by the Magna Carta. It means today that the powers of government must be founded on either common law or legislation. For example, it may be necessary in the interests of national security to open the mail of persons suspected of treasonous or seditious activities. This is a power that common law gives to neither government nor private citizens. If it is to be exercised at all, the rule of law requires that it be explicitly approved by legislation setting forth the appropriate conditions. If postal surveillance is carried on without legislative authorization, government employees are in effect acting outside the law, and this is contrary to the rule of law.

This aspect of the rule of law was reaffirmed in Canada in the celebrated case of *Roncarelli v. Duplessis*.[50] In 1946, when Maurice Duplessis was premier and attorney general of the province of Quebec, he ordered the Quebec Liquor Commission to revoke the liquor licence of Roncarelli, who owned a small restaurant in Montreal. The only reason given was that Roncarelli was an active Jehovah's Witness and had furnished bail money for his colleagues who had run afoul of Quebec's laws prohibiting the distribution of religious literature. The Supreme Court of Canada ultimately concluded that Premier Duplessis had acted without any legal authority whatsoever because Roncarelli's religious activities were unconnected with the statute under which his liquor licence had been granted. Duplessis was required to pay financial compensation to Roncarelli for the damage caused to his business. His position as premier did not confer on him any immunity for actions taken outside the law.

Recognized Procedures. Law itself should be made by known and accepted procedures and is binding only if these procedures are followed. In the common law system, if a judge violated accepted rules in hearing a case—for example, by not allowing one side to speak—the resulting decision would be reversed on appeal and would not become a precedent contributing to the law. Similarly, legislation can be created only if Parliament follows all its rules of procedure. An attempt by the Canadian House of Commons to legislate without the assent of the Senate and the governor general would be contrary to the rule of law. Of course, these legislative procedures are not immutable; they are contained in the constitution, which can be amended. But amendment itself requires fixed procedures for its accomplishment, as shown by the Parliament Act in Great Britain (1911).

This statute, which reduced the power of the House of Lords to approve legislation to a suspensory veto, was a fundamental amendment to the British constitution. The House of Commons initiated the change, but it did not become effective until it had been approved by the House of Lords itself. If the Lords had not acquiesced, King George V, on the advice of the Cabinet, would have appointed enough new members to that House who were committed to the change in order to tilt the balance in favour of the Act. And he would have been acting legally because the power of appointment is part of the British monarch's prerogative or common law powers. Thus a constitution may be changed in virtually any direction, but the rule of law requires that the amendment take place according to recognized procedures.

The rule of law, in the five dimensions described above, is significantly connected to the individual freedom so highly prized in the Western world. A society of free people is possible only if the rule of law is more or less adhered to. Although it may seem paradoxical, freedom is the consequence of law, not its opposite. "We are all slaves of the law," said Cicero, "that we may be free."[51] Rules of conduct make possible a stable, ordered society in which we can plan our lives with reasonable expectations about how others will respond to our initiatives. For example, freedom to drive a car depends on a complex set of rules of the road, control of property depends on rules of ownership, and so on.

Normally we think of law in a negative way, as a restraint on our behaviour. But law also has its positive side. While restricting the behaviour of some to violate social rules, it lets the remainder maximize their freedom of action. If lawbreakers were not restrained, they would use fear and intimidation to limit the freedom of others. A society that lives under the rule of law uses coercion selectively in order to prevent people from coercing each other. The result is enhanced freedom for all who abide by the laws. But the protection of liberty under law is not complete until the protecting power, the sovereign, is itself bound by constitutional restraints. As James Madison, the drafter of the American constitution, wrote: "In framing a government which is to be administered by men over men, the great difficulty lies in this: you must first enable the government to control the governed; and in the next place oblige it to control itself."[52] Hence maintaining a free society depends ultimately on deferring to the constitution and refusing to amend it except by a procedure that is itself part of that same constitution.

Of course, no society manages to live up to the ideal of the rule of law at all times. Perpetrators of crimes sometimes go unpunished, or even worse, innocent persons may be punished for actions they did not commit. The wealthy or the well-placed may succeed in skirting the law through personal influence. Those in government may use their position to obtain special privileges for themselves. But an ideal is nonetheless important even if it is not fully adhered to; things, after all, would be much worse if no one even tried to live up to the ideal. It still retains its validity as a standard by which to judge the performance of government.

8 International Politics and International Law

Relations between states stand in sharp contrast to relations among citizens within the state. Whereas the rule of law characterizes domestic politics, at least under favourable conditions, it exists to a much lesser degree in international politics. The explanation of this situation has to do chiefly with the nature of sovereignty and the state.

The world has always been divided among different human communities. Humans, for most of our existence, probably existed in small nomadic bands that lived by hunting and gathering. Around 8000 B.C., agriculture began to make settled life possible, and around 4000 B.C., specialized governmental structures began to control fixed territories. States in the full sense of the term arose in the valleys of the Nile and the Tigris and Euphrates rivers. History since that time has seen the gradual expansion of the *state system* across the globe. In recent times, the European powers finally succeeded in bringing the entire world into the state system, dividing up the less developed areas among themselves. Since World War II, these colonies have emerged as states in their own right, generally retaining the sometimes artificial territorial boundaries created by the colonial powers.

The world political system now consists of about 160 nominally sovereign states. Colonies and dependencies have almost entirely disappeared, except for a few special cases, such as Hong Kong and Namibia (South-West Africa). Hong Kong will revert to Chinese sovereignty in 1997; in the meantime, as a British colony, it furnishes China with a convenient means of commercial access to the world of international trade. Namibia is a former German colony that was given to South Africa to administer after World War I. South Africa now retains it as a buffer against hostile African states to the north. The few other colonies still existing in the world are the result of special circumstances. Because colonies are dependencies of sovereign states, it is correct to say that the world's entire habitable land mass has now been parcelled out among these states. The relatively few nomadic peoples that still exist, such as the cattle herders of sub-Saharan Africa, are all at least nominal subjects of one or another state.

In theory, each of these 160 or so states is sovereign and master of the people and territory within its boundaries, but in reality things are not quite so simple. Sovereignty often exists *de jure* (in law) but not *de facto* (in fact). In many states, sovereignty is so weak that large areas are virtually out of control of the central government. The government of Lebanon, for example, before it was invaded by Israel in 1982, had lost almost entire control of the Palestinian refugee camps as well as other districts dominated by militias of the country's various factions. The central government's control of many areas is still exceedingly weak after Israel's withdrawal in 1985. Sovereignty in many African states is also very tenuous, as in Angola and Mozambique, where large areas are dominated by rebel movements hostile to the governments.

There are many states whose sovereignty vis-à-vis external powers is more fictitious than real. The government of Campuchea (Cambodia) has been little more than an extension of the government of Vietnam ever since 1978, when Vietnam invaded Cambodia, deposed the regime of Pol Pot, and made Heng Samrin prime minister. South Africa is gradually converting the Bantu homelands into units that have many of the trappings of statehood, but which clearly are satellites of itself. In both these situations, other states have shown their suspicion by withholding *diplomatic recognition*. They realize that there are entities called Cambodia and the Transkei, but they do not enter into official relations with them because they doubt their sovereignty. (Of course, many other reasons may cause states to withhold diplomatic recognition.)

Beyond such evident examples lies a whole range of cases in which one state controls another to a greater or lesser degree. The nations of the Warsaw Pact, such as Czechoslovakia and the German Democratic Republic (East Germany), are very closely allied to the Soviet Union. Soviet troops stationed on their soil (except Romania's) severely limit governmental freedom of action. Not surprisingly, no Warsaw Pact state, except occasionally Romania, ever opposes the Soviet Union in the United Nations or other international bodies. At a considerably different level, the states of the North Atlantic Treaty Organization (NATO) are all ultimately dependent upon the nuclear arsenal of the United States for their strategic security. Although the United States may be able to influence their decisions, these states often demonstrate the vitality of their sovereignty by opposing the United States on matters of foreign policy. France and Greece have, at different times and for different reasons, unilaterally loosened their ties with NATO without coercive retaliation by the United States.

Obviously, the conception of a world system of equally sovereign states does not fully accord with reality, but it is the dominant intellectual model of our era.[53] Those who conduct international relations generally speak as if the model were valid, even if their actions sometimes belie their words. The whole structure of international law in its modern form is premised on sovereignty.

The most obvious fact about the state system is that while there is international politics, there is no sovereign international government. States try to win one another's support for projects of mutual benefit, but there is no sovereign power over them all. Sovereignty is divided among states, not concentrated above them.

This has important consequences for *international law*. Laws, it will be remembered, are enforceable rules of conduct. Within a state, enforcement is performed by those who wield sovereign power. Within the international sphere, who will enforce the laws that regulate the intercourse among sovereign states? If voluntary compliance fails, self-enforcement is one possible alternative. One state may try to punish another by breaking diplomatic relations, forbidding its nationals to trade with or visit the offender, or at the most extreme, undertaking military action. Such measures can take the form of an individual state acting on its own behalf or a group of states agreeing to act collectively. But even a widespread agreement is still dependent on the good faith of the parties and is consequently a weaker instrument than sovereign power.

The international society of states is in much the same position as human societies without the invention of government. Rules of conduct exist, but enforcing them is problematic because no specialized agency exists that has an authoritative monopoly on coercion. Of course, individual, spontaneous enforcement is possible. A person can avenge an injustice done to a relative, or a group can band together to form an association of vigilantes. Such enforcement techniques are not unknown even where sovereign authority exists, but they have obvious drawbacks. One is that they are voluntary, which can encourage shirking. Why should one avenge another if one's brother will do it? Another is lack of impartiality. No man should be judge in his own case, says an old proverb. These difficulties are just as much in evidence in the international sphere as in the domestic.

The situation, however, is not quite as hopeless as it may seem. In stateless societies where rule enforcement is uncertain, spontaneous avoidance plays a great role in the regulation of conduct. Those who break the sacred laws of the tribe may be so thoroughly shunned by their fellows that they are in effect cast out of society. Similar processes operate in international society. A state that frequently or flagrantly violates international law, unless it is so powerful that it can prevail by pure force, will find it hard to maintain commercial, cultural, military, and diplomatic contacts with other states. Self-interest may thus exert some pressure toward conformity with norms of international behaviour.

The difficulty of enforcement sometimes makes it appear that international law does not really exist, and indeed, a thoroughgoing legal positivist would have to deny the validity of so-called international law because it is not a sovereign command. However, it is more generally held that international law is real enough but that the absence of a sovereign-enforcing power creates special problems.[54]

From where does international law come? Like domestic law, it can either be deliberately made or emerge spontaneously, so it shows parallels to both legislation and common law. International law is deliberately made in the form of an agreement or *treaty* between two or more states. A treaty is essentially a contract that the signatories agree to observe. It is a particularly solemn form of agreement, in which the contracting parties bind themselves according to internationally recognized methods of negotiation and ratification. Once ratified, treaties create binding obligations on states in somewhat the same way as legislation binds individual conduct. The analogy is only partial because legislation is binding on subjects even if they do not agree with it, whereas treaties are binding on states only after they voluntarily accept their obligations. Similarly, an individual may not repudiate legislative acts of the sovereign, but a state may *abrogate* a treaty, that is, unilaterally declare it to be no longer valid. Thus Iraq in 1980 abrogated its border treaty with Iran before invading that country. The absence of sovereign-enforcing power creates these crucial differences between legislation and treaties.

Treaties may be signed between two states (*bilateral*) or more than two states (*multilateral*). The latter form has become highly developed in this century with the assistance of international organizations such as the League of Nations, the United Nations, and the European Economic Community (Common Market). Elaborate codes of conduct have developed, in areas such as labour relations, human rights, and treatment of prisoners of war, that are in fact multilateral treaties adhered to by many states.

International law is also deliberately made by the formal resolutions of bodies that, like the United Nations, have been set up by treaty. That body was established by the Charter of the United Nations, now adopted by 158 member states. One of the important principles embodied in this charter is the recognition of national sovereignty. Respect for the sovereignty of individual member states significantly influences the operations of the UN. For example, the UN General Assembly may adopt resolutions on issues of international importance, but they are not enforceable if they are disregarded by member states.

The UN also sometimes engages in military actions, such as when it sent peacekeeping forces to Cyprus in 1964. This action was directed at resolving the controversy between Greece and Turkey when they chose to support Greek and Turkish Cypriots, respectively. But the UN force was deployed only after the government of Cyprus agreed to allow UN troops on its soil. Because the UN is not a sovereign body, it is not empowered to act without the consent of the nations involved in a dispute. If the UN's decisions are to carry any force in international politics, they must be accompanied by voluntary compliance by individual states.

International law has also developed spontaneously in much the same way as customary law in domestic jurisdictions. As states have had dealings with one another, certain practices have emerged as standard. Generally, their utility is not difficult to discern. For instance, diplomatic immunity provides a means whereby states can communicate with one another through ambassadors. The evolution of custom is strengthened by consciously reflecting upon broad ethical principles that transcend international politics. Keeping promises is, as a general rule, regarded as a virtue in all societies. Society can survive some exceptions, but no society could possibly exist if this rule were systematically flouted. Thus it is not surprising that keeping agreements figures prominently in international law.

Such customary international law was already well understood in ancient times. It was known to the Romans as the *jus gentium*, "the law of nations." It was understood to be not the enactment of a sovereign power, but the general practice of the civilized portion of humanity. Certain authors of the seventeenth and eighteenth centuries performed a special service to the development of the *jus gentium* by systematizing the existing law of nations in the light of general principles. Hugo Grotius's book *On the Law of War and Peace* (1625) was a particular landmark. Grotius and similar figures, such as Samuel Pufendorf and Emer de Vattel, have long been cited as authorities in international law, like Blackstone and Coke in British law. Their writings have become as much a part of tradition as the customs and usages themselves.

Finally, there is an International Court of Justice at The Hague that hears disputes between states arising under international law. Other disputes are sometimes submitted to voluntary arbitration. Decisions in these cases become evidence for future interpretation of the law. But it must be borne in mind that these courts and arbitrators do not command an apparatus of enforcement, so complying with decisions remains voluntary. In 1984, for example, the United States refused to recognize the International Court of Justice jurisdiction in a decision condemning its mining of Nicaraguan territorial waters. The mining, however, had already ceased because of political opposition, both domestic and foreign.

Almost all the factors discussed above were exemplified in the affair of the American hostages in Iran. In November 1979, the American embassy in Iran was stormed by a large number of so-called student militants who took as hostages about fifty American diplomatic personnel. A nation's embassy is, according to international law, exempt from the jurisdiction of the receiving state. Furthermore, diplomatic personnel are supposed to be immune from detention by the host country. This is an ancient part of the *jus gentium*, as well as an explicit provision of a multilateral convention adhered to by both Iran and the United States. Diplomatic personnel suspected of espionage, as Iran alleged of the Americans, can be expelled on short notice by the host country, but not detained or otherwise harmed.

The student militants did not seem to act at the outset under instructions from the government of Iran, but it could not help but become involved. In fact, it became an accessory to the hostage-taking when it refused to take measures to restore the embassy to the Americans. The Iranian government also supported the demands of the hostage-takers, such as the return of the Shah and his family fortune to Iran. Thus a private initiative quickly became a confrontation between states.

The United States proceeded to use all the normal "enforcement" machinery of international law. It obtained from the Security Council of the United Nations a resolution calling on Iran to release the hostages. When Iran refused, the United States brought a case before the International Court of Justice at The Hague and obtained a favourable judgment that Iran ignored. The United States also asked the Security Council to impose economic sanctions against Iran, that is, to call on member states to refrain from trading with Iran; this measure was blocked by a Soviet veto.

Along with this legal strategy, the Americans from the beginning resorted to self-enforcement. President Carter signed an executive order freezing all Iranian assets in American financial institutions. Subsequently, the United States and its NATO allies announced a partial economic embargo against Iran. The United States also deployed a carrier task force in the Indian Ocean as a scarcely veiled military threat.

In reality, the American military options were not attractive. Iran could be severely punished, but that might result in the death of the hostages. Also, military action might destabilize the entire region, on which the world depends for a good part of its oil supply. To complicate matters even more, the Soviet Union proceeded to occupy Afghanistan, enhancing its strategic position along Iran's eastern border. American action from the south could have triggered a Soviet thrust from the north. In desperation, President Carter finally authorized a clandestine rescue mission that failed in the Iranian desert when equipment malfunctioned.

Given that legal institutions such as the United Nations and the International Court of Justice failed to get Iran's consent and that there were no feasible opportunities for military self-enforcement, why were the hostages finally returned in 1981, even though the United States did not meet the original Iranian demands? One factor was spontaneous avoidance. By openly flouting international law, Iran made many nations reluctant to deal with it. It became difficult for Iran to obtain loans, conclude trade agreements, and purchase military supplies. Iran's isolated position became even more untenable after it was invaded by Iraq,which occupied part of its territory. Iran's war effort was severely hampered by shortages of military equipment that could only be obtained abroad. In the long run, international public opinion helped accomplish what legal resolutions, economic sanctions, and military threats had failed to achieve.

This example demonstrates two things:

1. International law is a real influence on the conduct of nations, a set of norms to which nations tend to return in the long run because all other alternatives are unsatisfactory.
2. In the short run, international law is often impossible to enforce at a reasonable cost.

The result of this uncertainty is that states cannot let themselves be guided solely by international law. All states reserve the right to act in their *national interest*; that is, in matters of vital concern to their continued existence and prosperity, states will take, and feel themselves morally justified in taking, whatever steps are necessary to defend their interests. Because the rule of law in international affairs is so uncertain, states must be prepared in the last analysis to take things into their own hands.

Certain examples of national interest are well known. In 1823 President James Monroe of the United States proclaimed the Monroe Doctrine: the United States would not tolerate any military adventures by European powers in the Western Hemisphere and would react with force if necessary to prevent them. The doctrine was subsequently used to justify American interventions in Central American republics to support regimes sympathetic to American interests. In 1968 the Soviet Union justified its intervention in Czechoslovakia with the Brezhnev Doctrine: no socialist country would be allowed to revert to capitalism. In 1980, at the time of the Iranian hostage incident and the Soviet intervention in Afghanistan, the United States proclaimed the Carter Doctrine: the United States considered the Persian Gulf an area vital to its national security and would use all necessary means, including military force, to prevent domination by hostile powers. None of these three doctrines rests upon international law; each is a unilateral assertion of national interest, as interpreted by the state itself. Others violate it at risk of reprisal up to, and including, war.

Self-interest, of course, is a vital principle of all human society; but where government is effective, self-interest is constrained by the rule of law. We are not free to pursue whatever goals we choose regardless of law; the sovereign will punish actions where there is adequate public power. National interest in international society is on a different level from the self-interest to which we are accustomed because the absence of sovereignty virtually compels each state to think first of its self-preservation.

The concept of national interest, however, creates interesting problems. Who determines what is really in the interests of the nation? We often look at international politics as if states were simple entities in which those who control the government could define and pursue the national interest. Yet the national interest is never self-evident. Even with such a basic matter as territorial integrity, there are often groups within a state who would favour dismembering it or allowing portions of its territory to be annexed to other states. On less fundamental issues, opinion is even more divided. Is it, for example, in the national interest to try to encourage local industry by establishing protective tariffs? Manufacturers and organized labour are likely to say yes; consumers are likely to say no. One side will emphasize creating or maintaining jobs in the protected industry, the other will complain about the increased cost to the consumer of that industry's products. How the national interest is defined on such an issue will depend largely on the constellation of domestic political forces.

International politics, then, is linked to domestic politics in two ways—by the internal struggle to define the national interest as well as by the impact of international policies upon subjects of the state. In spite of these important links, we will not pursue the study of international politics further in this text. The absence of a central sovereignty makes international politics so distinctive that it is customary to study it separately, so that its special terminology, problems, and issues can be treated at length. Although in the rest of this book we treat the international context as a sort of fixed backdrop to domestic politics, the student should remember that political science is not complete until the international system is subjected to analysis and its links with domestic politics are explored.

Notes

1. The seminal work is Edward O. Wilson, *Sociobiology: The New Synthesis* (Cambridge: Belknap Press of Harvard University Press, 1975). Later literature is reviewed in Charles J. Lumsden and Edward O. Wilson, *Promethean Fire: Reflections on the Origin of Mind* (Cambridge: Harvard University Press, 1983), pp. 189–191.

2. Marcel Giraud, *Le Métis canadien* (Paris: Institut d'Ethnologie, 1945), pp. 57–61.

3. Bertrand de Jouvenel, *The Pure Theory of Politics* (New Haven, Conn.: Yale University Press, 1963), p. 30.

4. J. B. D. Miller, *The Nature of Politics* (Harmondsworth: Penguin, 1965), p. 14.

5. Alan P. Ball, *Modern Politics and Government* (London: Macmillan, 1971), p. 20.

6. Harold D. Lasswell, *Politics: Who Gets What, When, How* (New York: Peter Smith, 1950). First published 1936.

7. David Easton, *A Systems Analysis of Political Life* (New York: John Wiley & Sons, 1965), p. 21.

8. F. A. Hayek et al., *Rent Control: A Popular Paradox* (Vancouver: Fraser Institute, 1975), p. xvi.

9. Jouvenel, *The Pure Theory of Politics*, pp. 204–212.

10. Bernard Crick, *In Defence of Politics*, rev. ed. (Chicago: University of Chicago Press, 1972), p. 22.

11. Norman Cohn, *The Pursuit of the Millennium*, rev. ed. (New York: Oxford University Press, 1970).

12. V. I. Lenin, "The State and Revolution," in *Selected Works* (Moscow: Progress Publishers, 1967), vol. II, p. 345.

13. Marx himself did not use the phrase "withering away of the state." It was popularized by his collaborator, Friedrich Engels. See his "Socialism: Utopian and Scientific," ch. 3, in Karl Marx and Friedrich Engels, *Selected Works* (Moscow: Progress Publishers, 1968), pp. 417–436.

14. Liberal democracies define political crimes narrowly as the use of force, or the advocacy of such use, against the state. Totalitarian and authoritarian regimes extend the definition to include peaceful opposition to or criticism of the state. The definition of a political crime is an almost infallible test of the genuineness of liberal democracy.

15. Bertrand de Jouvenel, *Sovereignty: An Inquiry into the Political Good*, trans. J. F. Huntington (Chicago: University of Chicago Press, 1957), p. 262.

16. H. H. Gerth and C. W. Mills, eds. and trans., *From Max Weber* (New York: Oxford University Press, 1950), Part II.

17. Alexis de Tocqueville, *Democracy in America*, ed. Andrew Hacker (New York: Washington Square Press, 1964), pp. 9–10.

18. Cited in Reinhard Bendix, *Max Weber: An Intellectual Portrait* (Garden City, N.Y.: Doubleday, 1960), p. 88, note 15.

19. Thomas Flanagan, *Louis "David" Riel: "Prophet of the New World"* (Toronto: University of Toronto Press, 1979).

20. Cited in J. G. Ismael and T. Y. Ismael, "Social Change in Islamic Society: The Political Thought of Ayatollah Khomeini," *Social Problems* 27 (1980), p. 614.

21. Gerth and Mills, *From Max Weber*, p. 297.

22. Cited in Jacques Maritain, "The Concept of Sovereignty," in W. J. Stankiewicz, ed., *In Defense of Sovereignty* (New York: Oxford University Press, 1969), pp. 44–46.

23. Jean-Jacques Rousseau, *The Social Contract* (New York: Hafner, 1947), p. 85.

24. It is difficult to say precisely how many states there are because of certain anomalous cases. Some "mini-states," such as Monaco, Andorra, and San Marino, do not carry on a full range of relationships with other states; their foreign policy is conducted by larger neighbours. Other difficult cases include governments in exile, states that lack universal recognition (Taiwan), and puppet or buffer states (Namibia). Various states claim portions of Antarctica, but the claims conflict and have never been resolved.

25. Robert L. Carneiro, "A Theory of the Origin of the State," *Science* 169 (21 August 1970), pp. 733–738.

26. It is unlikely that this usage extended to women. While women were involved in the uprisings against the monarchy, they were generally not active participants in politics. Throughout this text, man and men are used when discussing the thoughts and writings of certain political thinkers to reflect the historical context of the writings.

27. Cited in Hans Kohn, ed., *Nationalism: Its Meaning and History*, 2nd ed. (Princeton, N.J.: D. Van Nostrand, 1965), p. 139.

28. Louis L. Snyder, *Global Mini-Nationalism: Autonomy or Independence* (Westport, Conn.: Greenwood Press, 1982).

29. This approach to ethnicity corresponds to current popular usage in North America, but the social science literature sometimes uses ethnicity as a very wide term to embrace all sorts of communal identities: racial, tribal, national, religious, etc.

30. Theodore Draper, *The Rediscovery of Black Nationalism* (New York: Viking Press, 1969), ch. 5.

31. Mel Watkins, ed., *Dene Nation: The Colony Within* (Toronto: University of Toronto Press, 1977), p. 3.

32. Menno Boldt and J. Anthony Long, "Tribal Traditions and European-Western Political Ideologies: The Dilemma of Canada's Native Indians," *Canadian Journal of Political Science* 17 (1984), pp. 537–553; Thomas Flanagan, "Indian Sovereignty and Nationhood: A Comment on Boldt and Long," ibid. 18 (1985), pp. 367–374.

33. Michael Asch, *Home and Native Land* (Toronto: Methuen, 1984), p. 34.

34. P. B. Waite, *The Confederation Debates in the Province of Canada/1865* (Toronto: McClelland and Stewart, 1963), p. 50.

35. Friedrich A. Hayek, *Law, Legislation and Liberty*, 3 vols. (Chicago: University of Chicago Press, 1973–1979), vol. I, p. 81.

36. John Henry Merryman, *The Civil Law Tradition: An Introduction to the Legal Systems of Western Europe and Latin America* (Palo Alto, Calif.: Stanford University Press, 1969).

37. John E. C. Brierly, "Quebec's Civil Law Codification Viewed and Reviewed," *McGill Law Journal* 14 (1968), pp. 521–589.

38. Thomas Hobbes, *Leviathan* (New York: E. P. Dutton, 1950), p. 226.

39. Ibid.

40. *Queen v. Big M Drug Mart*, April 24, 1985, [1985] S.C.C.D. 5905–01.

41. The Gallup Report, February 13, 1982.

42. W. Ivor Jennings, *The Law of the Constitution*, 5th ed. (London: University of London Press, 1959), p. 136.

43. J. N. Peltason, *Corwin & Peltason's Understanding the Constitution*, 8th ed. (New York: Holt, Rinehart and Winston, 1979), p. 236.

44. *Plessy v. Ferguson*, 163 U.S. 537 (1896).

45. *Brown v. Board of Education*, 347 U.S. 483 (1954).

46. *Marbury v. Madison*, 1 Cranch 137 (1803).

47. Peter Russell, "The Anti-Inflation Case: The Anatomy of a Constitutional Decision," *Canadian Public Administration* 20 (1977), pp. 635–665.

48. F. L. Morton, ed., *Law, Politics and the Judicial Process in Canada* (Calgary: University of Calgary Press, 1984), pp. 262–267.

49. Jennings, *The Law of the Constitution*, p. 52.

50. [1959] S.C.R. 121.

51. Cited in Friedrich A. Hayek, *The Constitution of Liberty* (Chicago: Henry Regnery, 1968), p. 462.

52. Alexander Hamilton, John Jay, and James Madison, *The Federalist* (New York: Modern Library, n.d.), p. 337.

53. Robert A. Klein, *Sovereign Equality Among States: the history of an idea* (Toronto: University of Toronto Press, 1974).

54. See the discussion in J. L. Brierly, *The Law of Nations*, 6th ed. (Oxford: Clarendon Press, 1962), pp. 68–78.

Vocabulary

society
government
stateless society
politics
polis
power
influence
coercion
violence
authority
natural authority
public authority
legitimacy
traditional authority
legal authority
modernization
charismatic authority
sovereign
imperium
sovereignty
parliamentary sovereignty
popular sovereignty
judicial review
state
subjects
citizenship
nation-state
nation
race
tribe
ethnic group
binational state
multinational state
law
instinct

habit
custom
customary law
legislation
common law
precedent
stare decisis
code civil
statute
code
positive law
public law
private law
jurisprudence
legal positivism
constitution
convention
unwritten
Magna Carta
constitutionalism
limited state
rule of law
discretion
state system
de jure
de facto
diplomatic recognition
international law
treaty
abrogation
bilateral treaty
multilateral treaty
jus gentium
national interest

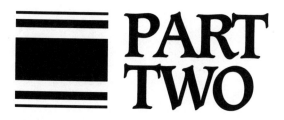

PART TWO

Ideology

9   Ideology

It was discussed in Part One that governmental authority and legitimacy rest upon a network of beliefs about people, society, and the purpose of government. Speculation about these matters, which is known as political philosophy or political theory, was the first aspect of political science to develop, having been already well cultivated by the Greek thinkers of classical antiquity. What is said of philosophy in general—that "all philosophy is a footnote to Plato"—is equally true of the special field of political philosophy. All the great issues were already addressed in the writings of Plato and his pupil Aristotle.

Plato (ca. 429–347 B.C.) made a distinction that is still crucial to the study of political beliefs. He distinguished between *episteme*, which we might translate as "true, well-founded knowledge," and *doxa*, or "opinion." *Episteme* is knowledge that can be demonstrated by logical argument from first principles, whereas *doxa* is an opinion that may be at least partly true, but that believers cannot fully expound. They accept it because they have confidence in its source. To take a non-political example, consider the proposition that the earth revolves around the sun. We all "know" this is true, but few of us can justify our belief except by referring to the authority who has taught us. Only a scientifically instructed minority can develop the proposition from the first principles of physics; the rest of us accept it as a matter of *doxa*. The field of political philosophy deals with both *episteme* and *doxa*. It tries to achieve *episteme* through discovery of valid first principles and deduction of results from them. It also studies the *doxai* found in society to see whether they are logically coherent and whether they reflect a more disciplined form of knowledge. The studies of *episteme* and of *doxa* are not wholly separate and generally reinforce each other, for analysing the opinions that philosophers encounter is the first step in their pursuit of higher levels of understanding.

The usual contemporary word for political *doxa* is *ideology*, described in a well-known textbook in these terms:

> An ideology is a value or belief system that is accepted as fact or truth by some group. It is composed of sets of attitudes towards the various institutions and processes of society. It provides the believer with a picture of the world both as it is and it should be, and, in so doing, it organizes the tremendous complexity of the world into something fairly simple and understandable. . . .
> An ideology must be a more or less connected set of beliefs that provide the believer with a fairly thorough picture of the world.[1]

Remember that we have defined politics as the activity of gathering and maintaining support for collective projects. Support might be obtained by offering bribes or making threats, but in the long run it has to rest on persuasion. Ideology furnishes a basis for political persuasion by providing certain assumptions and values to be held in common. More specifically:

1. Ideology is not a mere personal opinion, but a social belief, that is, accepted by large numbers of people and passed on by the normal channels of cultural transmission. If we feel surrounded by enemies at home and at work who wish to ruin us, that is personal paranoia; but if as a leader of the Soviet Union we feel that our country is encircled by hostile capitalist powers who wish to destroy it, that is a tenet of communist ideology.

2. Ideology always involves a mixture of factual and moral beliefs. Because governmental legitimacy is an inherently ethical problem, ideology always contains beliefs about how people should act and what they should consider right or wrong.

3. Ideology, as a mass belief, is somewhat simplified. The infinite complexity of the world is reduced to simpler ideas that can be understood by large numbers of people who, after all, must devote most of their time to concerns other than the study of politics.

4. An ideology is not a random collection of opinions, but a more or less organized system of beliefs that fit together logically. It is important to say "more or less," for the integration is never perfect. All of us have some surprising contradictions in our opinions. However, there is a big difference between an orderly, interrelated set of ideas and an assortment of unrelated opinions.

In this sense, ideologies are espoused by intellectuals in politics: lawyers, teachers, journalists, and politicians who carry on public debate in ideological terms. But it is doubtful whether many ordinary people, even among a well-educated populace, can be said to have ideologies.[2] They are more likely to believe in an assortment of rather conflicting ideological fragments: to be liberal on some points, socialist on others, and so forth. They are not bothered much by inconsistency in their views because they probably do not think very often about social and political questions. Examples of contradictory thinking frequently turn up in public opinion polls. It is routine, for example, for respondents to say that taxes are too high while simultaneously demanding higher levels of public spending on roads, schools, and old age pensions.

One interesting aspect of the term ideology is the negative connotations it carries. It is often used as a weapon to degrade ideas with which one disagrees. Dismissing them as "mere ideology" is a common tactic in argument. The reasons why this is possible are worth knowing.

The word ideology was coined in 1796 by the French philosopher Antoine Destutt de Tracy, who gave it a meaning quite different from the one it bears today. For Destutt de Tracy, ideology was to be the name of a new science, the study of human consciousness in all its aspects. When Destutt de Tracy, who had once been a supporter of Napoleon, began to criticize the emperor, the latter responded by ridiculing Destutt de Tracy's new science of ideology as an obscure doctrine and those who espoused it as "ideologues." The concept of ideology probably would have died out except that Marx and Engels picked it up and redefined it to express one of the most noteworthy ideas in their system. They used it as part of their theory that all human thought rests upon an economic basis, that art, science, literature, law, and political thought reflect the underlying economic conditions of their creators. Marx wrote that one should always distinguish the "economic conditions of production," which are the essence of class conflict, from the "legal, political, religious, aesthetic, or philosophic—in short, ideological—forms in which men become conscious of this conflict and fight it out." Economic relations are the "foundation, on which rise legal and political superstructures and to which correspond definite forms of social consciousness."[3]

Marx's view was bound to put derogatory connotations on the term ideology, for he regarded his own theory not as ideology, but as science—scientific socialism. The beliefs of others were ideology, whereas his were science. Marx had a profound, although debatable, reason for thinking this, but it is easy to see how the word could become a mere polemical weapon in the hands of others. Moreover, there is much that is obviously true in Marx's insight. The intellectual world clearly does have some relation to the economic milieu that surrounds it. Marx's insight is so significant that the term he used to express it was bound to become popular.

However, as always happens, the word has become detached from the particular theory that gave it currency. Today, when a belief system is labelled an ideology in a derogatory way, detractors might mean any of several things. They might imply that the beliefs are not really thought through and would not stand comparison to a well-developed philosophy (like their own). Or they may mean that the beliefs are a not very subtle expression of self-interest on the part of some group that is trying to assert itself. Or, following the sociologist Karl Mannheim, they might mean that the beliefs are a rationalization of the status quo, inherently conservative in function.[4]

Our use of the term is not intended to have any of these special implications. We use ideology simply as a convenient, contemporary word for political ideas in action—ideas not as they are found in the philosopher's study, but as they motivate large numbers of people. However, students should be aware of the many other connotations of the term because they will certainly encounter them elsewhere.

Part Two will discuss four of the main ideologies in the contemporary world: liberalism, conservatism, socialism, and nationalism. Up to a point, it is useful to analyze them as systems of ideas or beliefs. But remember that all ideologies are abstractions. They do not really exist; what exists are real people with their individual thoughts, and organizations that adopt statements or programs. It is unlikely that the beliefs of any person or organization fit perfectly the description given here of particular ideologies. Yet there are tendencies and common concerns that unite diverse thinkers, even if they do not agree on every point. Think of ideologies as broad tendencies of thought existing over long periods of time. No two people identified as liberal or socialist think identically, but there are certainly recognizable patterns in their ideas. Above all, do not think of ideologies as fixed creeds, from which a thinker who varies on any point is excommunicated. It is a waste of time to argue whether someone "is" or "is not" a liberal, conservative, or socialist. With this proviso in mind, the concept of a structured ideology can be a helpful device for showing how ideas are interrelated.

Although it is perhaps not readily apparent, these four ideologies are members of an interrelated family. All are peculiarly modern systems of thought. Although they have earlier roots, they have taken on distinctive form only in the last two hundred years. None of the terms liberalism, conservatism, socialism, or nationalism was used to denote a system of thought before the early decades of the nineteenth century. The isms furnish the terms of discourse about politics in the modern world, but they are not a universal or permanent vocabulary of humanity.

Another similarity is that all four are secular in orientation. Belief in God can be and has been combined with each of them, but it is not essential. All four ideologies are humanistic, not in the sentimental sense of kindness or generosity, but in the philosophical sense of being human-centred. All four have human happiness on earth as an unquestioned goal. Each has a different way of getting there, but the goal remains the same. Jeremy Bentham (1748–1832), an early liberal, expressed this when he said, "The business of government is to promote the happiness of the society, by punishing and rewarding,"[5] not to fulfill the will of God or prepare us for the next life. These may be important things, but they are not the business of government. Marx's humanism was even more aggressive, picturing belief in God as a barrier to people creating happiness for themselves. "Religion," wrote Marx, "is only the illusory sun about which man revolves so long as he does not revolve about himself."[6] The humanism of the four modern ideologies is not always as forceful as it is in Marx's teachings, but it is a common trait. This means that the arguments among them are instrumental ones about the best means for achieving their ultimate goal of human happiness on earth.

Also, the ideologies we study presuppose a widespread belief that society is something that human beings can change, reform, or mould according to their desires. Liberalism, socialism, and nationalism all have programs or agendas of social change to be undertaken by government; conservatism differs by believing that society is too complex to be easily improved by conscious human designs. However, it would not exist as a self-conscious ideology except for the challenges posed by the other ideologies. If it had not occurred to anyone that humanity could take charge of and deliberately improve society, there would have been no occasion for the development of a conservative ideology that argues against such possibilities. Thus the modern confidence in social improvement is the backdrop to all contemporary ideologies.

Finally, all four ideologies stem from the same historical situation, symbolized by the French Revolution: the transition from traditional to legal authority and legitimacy. Broadly speaking, liberalism celebrates this transition as human emancipation from bondage. Conservatism is suspicious of it, fearing that the accumulated wisdom of the past will be lost if the transition is too abrupt. Socialism is ambiguous about it, welcoming the demise of traditional authority but also fearing that the freedom created by legal authority will produce a new aristocracy of wealth even more exploitative than the old aristocracy of inherited privilege. Nationalism also welcomes the transition to legal authority, but it seeks to formulate a new form of political identity to replace traditional ones. Thus it is no accident that the great ideologies of our age appeared almost simultaneously on the political scene at the end of the eighteenth century. The French Revolution and the Napoleonic Wars were the visible signs of underlying social change. These events in Europe proved to be a rehearsal for similar changes throughout the world. This is the unifying theme of our era, often called the age of ideology.

10   Liberalism

The word liberal comes from the Latin *liber*, meaning "free." Before it became a political word, it had well-established usages, such as a "liberal" (generous) giver or the "liberal arts," referring to the studies suitable for a freeman. It was first used as a political term in Spain during the Napoleonic Wars, becoming common later in the nineteenth century with the establishment of the Liberal party in Britain. The ideas of liberalism, however, are older than the name. Broadly speaking, liberalism is a product of the constitutional tradition of the West. More specifically, it is an outgrowth of the English Whig tradition of liberty under law. Prominent Whig thinkers were John Locke (1637–1704) and Edmund Burke (1729–1797) in England, Adam Smith (1723–1790) and David Hume (1711–1774) in Scotland, and Thomas Jefferson (1743–1826) and James Madison (1751–1836) in America. These men never called themselves liberals, but they elaborated the principles later known as liberalism. They were followed by writers such as John Stuart Mill (1806–1873) and his French contemporary Alexis de Tocqueville (1805–1859), who consciously thought of themselves as liberals.

The history of liberalism reveals four interrelated principles involved in the broad concept of freedom: personal freedom, limited government, equality of right, and consent of the governed. These concepts, which have all appeared earlier in our discussion of constitutionalism, can be briefly recalled here:

1. *Personal freedom*, as understood by liberals, refers to the absence of coercion in the various realms of life. It includes free speech, religious liberty, private property, and the right of political opposition.

2. *Limited government* means that the state is understood as an instrument serving a particular function in society rather than being in general charge of all society.

3. *Equality of right* implies that all must abide by the same laws, enforced impartially by the state.

4. *Consent of the governed* means that government emanates from the people, is responsible to them, and may be changed by them; it is a moderate and practical way of implementing the doctrine of popular sovereignty.

These four principles mark the entire liberal tradition from Locke, who did not yet call himself a liberal, to the twentieth century. Indeed, these principles are so widely accepted today that almost everyone in the Western world pays at least lip service to them. However, there is also a deep division within liberalism that must be carefully examined. From this point on we will distinguish the older *classical liberalism* from the newer *reform liberalism*.

Classical liberalism was the dominant ideology in the nineteenth century in North America, Britain, and much of Western Europe. It accepted these four principles in a straightforward and literal way. In particular, it identified personal freedom with a free market or *laissez-faire* economy. Reform liberalism, which began as a reform movement within the British Liberal party at the end of the nineteenth century, has become dominant in the twentieth century. It is an attempt to graft certain features of socialism onto the liberal tradition, in particular to use the state to modify the market system without abolishing it altogether. The differences between classical liberalism and reform liberalism may be summarized in terms of the four principles.

PERSONAL FREEDOM

For classical liberals, freedom is simply the absence of coercion. Without totally rejecting this definition, reform liberals try to add another dimension. They usually think of freedom in terms of capacity, arguing that freedom from coercion means little unless means of attaining it are provided. Canadian journalist Pierre Berton expressed this position in his book *The Smug Minority*:

> A poor man is not free and a destitute man is as much a prisoner as a convict; indeed a convict generally eats better. A man who can't afford a streetcar ticket, let alone real travel, who can exercise no real choice in matters of food, clothing, and shelter, who cannot follow the siren song of the TV commercials, who can scarcely afford bus fare to the library let alone a proper education for himself or his children—is such a man free in an affluent nation?[7]

Berton is saying that the poor man is not really free, even though he is not being actively coerced. Absence of financial means limits his opportunities in life as effectively as if he were kept down by force.

This difference in understanding freedom is not a trivial matter; it is at the heart of the difference between the old and the new liberalism. The classical liberal emphasizes the absence of coercion, freedom in the sense of being left alone to do as one wishes, as long as it does not infringe on the freedom of others to do likewise. Reform liberals, on the other hand, may wish to use governmental power, even coercion if need be, to reduce the freedom of some in order to provide economic opportunities for others. They justify this in terms of freedom, arguing that they are increasing the sum of "real" liberty in society by furnishing people the means to achieve their goals. The two kinds of liberals talk in the same words but do not speak the same language. Their different conceptions of freedom lead to different ideas about the role of the state in economic life. In particular, economic freedom and the market system are no longer accorded the same primacy in reform liberalism as in classical liberalism.

However, even if reform liberalism now differs significantly from classical liberalism, the former can be seen as a logical outgrowth of the latter. Understanding freedom as absence of coercion implies the primacy of individual will—doing what you want. Reform liberalism purports to be a more effective way of enabling more individuals to obtain the objects of their desire, using the power of the limited state, if necessary. Both versions of liberalism agree (and differ from other ideologies) in celebrating the fulfilment of individual desire as the highest good.[8] This individualistic outlook and understanding of freedom is absent from conservatism, socialism, and nationalism.

LIMITED GOVERNMENT

Classical liberals see the state in negative terms. Its role is primarily to prevent people from harming each other through force or fraud. To this end, it uses force to protect the community from external attack and punish people who commit acts of aggression or deception against each other. Beyond this the state does relatively little, leaving people to work out their own destiny in society. The classical liberal idea of government has been caricatured as the "night-watchman state," as only the caretaker of society. Reform liberals accept these caretaking functions, but they wish to add to them a positive or interventionist state role of promoting freedom in the additional sense of capacity. They want the state to be a positive force, ensuring social "welfare" in the broad sense—leisure, knowledge, security—for those who might otherwise not achieve these goals. These two different views of freedom lead to two different conceptions of the duties of the state.

EQUALITY OF RIGHT

For classical liberals, equality of right means only that all abide by the same rules. It definitely does not imply *equality of condition* (equality of outcome or result). Classical liberals accept that there will always be inequality of wealth, status, and power. One might even say that for them, equality of right is the right to become unequal.[9] Reform liberals, while not committed to a wholesale equalization of conditions, wish to reduce economic and social differences. They have often adopted what was originally a socialist formula, *equality of opportunity*.

It is easy to see that equality of right and equality of condition are two different things: one corresponds to a negative, the other to a positive, use of the state. But equality of opportunity is an elusive concept; it seems at first glance only to call on the state to ensure that none of us are prevented by others from having a chance to make a success of ourselves. If that were all that was meant, it would be little different from equality of right. However, equality of opportunity in today's vocabulary usually implies a claim for positive state action to equalize people's starting points in life. Opportunities, by themselves, are never equal. One child is born to wealthy parents, another to poor. One child is born to industrious, thrifty parents who save for education and encourage progress through school, while another is born to parents who care nothing about learning. One child is born with an attractive face; another is not so endowed. Obviously, the state can do little about many of these inequalities; but if equality of opportunity is to have any meaning, the state must take positive steps to overcome handicaps that cannot reasonably be blamed on the child. Thus government may provide public schools, trying to ensure that all children start with the same sort of education, or at another level it may offer low-interest loans to help young people obtain jobs or professional training that their parents might not be able to afford. Such measures go much further than the classical liberal conception of equality of right.

CONSENT OF THE GOVERNED

Consent of the governed, to classical liberals, did not necessarily mean democracy in the sense of universal suffrage. It was enough if government was accountable to a sizable section of the population. Thus some classical liberals in the nineteenth century often favoured a *property franchise*—a requirement to own a stipulated amount of property before receiving the right to vote. Visualizing government as being largely the protection of property, they felt it was reasonable to entrust government to those who possessed substantial amounts of property and who paid most of the taxes to support the state. Reform liberals, in contrast, are strongly democratic. Because they put so much emphasis on using the state positively to provide for the common welfare, they naturally feel it is important that everyone have a share of political power. Classical liberals, having a much more restricted view of state action, do not see democracy as such an urgent necessity, though they need not oppose it in principle.

Reform liberalism has much in common with democratic socialism. It differs from socialism in that it has adopted the liberal rhetoric of freedom rather than the socialist rhetoric of planning, but the specific ideas about the role of the state in society are similar in the two ideologies. For historical reasons, the term socialist has been unpopular in North America, whereas it is more respected in Europe. Many who are known as liberals in contemporary North America might well be social democrats if they lived in Europe.

One final note of special relevance to Canadians: this text discusses the two types of liberalism as ideologies, that is, small-l liberalism. The ideologies are only loosely connected with the capital-L Liberal party of modern Canada. The Liberal and Progressive Conservative parties both contain members whose ideologies are, in our terms, classical liberal as well as reform liberal. The Liberals lean a bit to the reform liberal (left) side of the political spectrum, the Conservatives to the classical liberal (right); but the difference is not profound. An idea of the magnitude of the difference is given by the results of a recent survey of opinions among university students. On a scale of neoconservatism (which in this context means about the same as classical liberalism) ranging from a low of 4 to a high of 20, those who identified themselves as federal Progressive Conservatives had a mean score of 14.5; Liberals, 11.7; and New Democrats, 10.3.[10]

CLASSICAL LIBERALISM

The ideology of classical liberalism calls for a policy of freedom, defined as the absence of coercion, in all areas of human life—social and economic as well as political. This notion of extending freedom consistently to all aspects of life was gradually worked out by a series of important English, Scottish, and American thinkers from John Locke to John Stuart Mill. A brief sketch of this development is useful to emphasize that ideologies are not static, timeless systems of ideas. They are more like a conversation carried on across generations in which ideas are created, amplified, modified, and sometimes discarded. An overriding concern with freedom gives classical liberalism coherence, but no two thinkers within the tradition have had precisely the same opinions.

Politically, liberalism grew out of the struggle of the English Parliament with the Stuart monarchs during the seventeenth century. At the level of power, the revolution of 1688 established the supremacy of Parliament over the monarchy. At the level of ideas, the revolution established that governmental authority is not derived directly from God, as the Stuarts had tried to maintain, but resides ultimately in the people themselves, who delegate it to the sovereign. Rule is a trust that can be removed if it is abused. The sovereign must rule within the law of the land, as made by Parliament and interpreted by the courts. Arbitrary government is unconstitutional and cause for opposition. The people have a moral right to rise up in arms to overthrow an arbitrary government and re-establish the rule of law. In Weberian terms, this is the triumph of legal over traditional authority.

The ideas animating the Glorious Revolution were given classic expression in John Locke's *Second Treatise of Government* (1690). Locke argued that men deliberately create government by agreement among themselves in order to achieve a reliable, impartial enforcement of law. The purpose of government was fundamentally to protect men in their "life, health, liberty, or possessions."[11] Government was not authorized "to destroy, enslave, or designedly to impoverish the subject."[12] Arbitrary rule in the manner of the Stuarts had just this result, so that the English were right to resist and depose them:

> Wherever law ends, tyranny begins if the law be transgressed to another's harm. And whosoever in authority exceeds the power given him by the law, and makes use of the force he has under his command to compass that upon the subject which the law allows not, ceases in that to be a magistrate and, acting without authority, may be opposed as any other man who by force invades the right of another.[13]

Locke's arguments were repeated in the American Declaration of Independence of 1776. Drafted by Thomas Jefferson, this text is the most concise and memorable statement of the political theory of classical liberalism:

> We hold these truths to be self-evident, that all men are created equal, that they are endowed by their creator with certain unalienable rights; that among

these are life, liberty, and the pursuit of happiness; that to secure these rights governments are instituted among men, deriving their just powers from the consent of the governed; that whenever any form of government becomes destructive of these ends, it is the right of the people to alter or to abolish it, and to institute new government.[14]

Similar ideals animated the early days of the French Revolution. In August 1789, the National Assembly adopted the Declaration of the Rights of Man and of the Citizen, which declared:

> The end of all political associations is the preservation of the natural and imprescriptible rights of man; and these rights are liberty, property, security, and resistance of oppression.
>
> The nation is essentially the source of all sovereignty; nor can any individual, or any body of men, be entitled to any authority which is not expressly derived from it.[15]

These quotations portray the ideals of the rule of law and the consent of the governed, but they are not democratic in the strict sense of saying that all men should have an equal vote in choosing their rulers. The political theory of classical liberalism called for equality before the law and equality of right in respect to person and property, but not equality of political participation. Although writers like Locke and Jefferson wrote of man and men in the generic sense, they and their contemporaries generally applied their ideas only to property-owning adult males, a numerical minority of society. The incorporation of democracy into liberalism occurred at a later stage and will be discussed as part of reform liberalism.

The demand that government be bound by law was part of a larger concern for freedom of the individual. People ought to be surrounded by a private sphere in which government would not intrude. This was worked out first in the area of religion, disputes about which were an important part of the quarrel between Parliament and the Stuarts. Locke's *Letter Concerning Toleration* (1689) held religion to be a private matter:

> The care of souls cannot belong to the civil magistrate because his power consists only in outward force; but true and saving religion consists in the inward persuasions of the mind, without which nothing can be acceptable to God.[16]

His conclusion was that all religions should be tolerated by the state as long as they did not disturb civil peace by meddling in politics.

Regarding religion as a private matter was congenial to the increasingly secular outlook of the Enlightenment. It also coincided with a growing feeling that communication ought to be as free as possible. The First Amendment to the American constitution (1791) established a wide freedom of speech and press:

Congress shall make no law respecting an establishment of religion, or prohibiting the free exercise thereof; or abridging the freedom of speech or of the press; or the right of the people peaceably to assemble, and to petition the government for a redress of grievances.[17]

At about the same time, the Declaration of the Rights of Man and of the Citizen enunciated an even broader principle—that not only thought and speech, but also conduct should be left alone by the state as long as they did not coercively invade the rights of others:

Political liberty consists in the power of doing whatever does not injure another. The exercise of the natural rights of every man, has no other limits than those which are necessary to secure to every *other* man the free exercise of the same rights; and these limits are determinable only by law.[18]

John Stuart Mill brought all these themes together in his book *On Liberty* (1859), which is perhaps the best-known statement of the value of freedom in the English language. *On Liberty* asserted "one very simple principle":

The only purpose for which power [coercion, in our terms] can be rightfully exercised over any member of a civilized community, against his will, is to prevent harm to others. His own good, either physical or moral, is not a sufficient warrant.[19]

The book tried to prove that in the long run, we would all be better off if the state was restrained from prohibiting "experiments in living," provided they were not coercive of others. Freedom to experiment with new ideas and new ways of doing things would encourage progress through discovery of better alternatives to present practices.

In the economic sphere, classical liberalism is identified with the free market. Locke did not have a fully developed theory of the market, but he helped lay the foundations by stressing that a major purpose of government was the protection of private property. The principles of the market were brought to light in the eighteenth century by numerous writers, of whom the most famous is Adam Smith. His *Wealth of Nations* (1776) used the metaphorical term invisible hand to describe the results of the individual seeking to promote his own self-interest:

He intends only his own security; and by directing that industry in such a manner as its produce may be of the greatest value, he intends only his own gain, and he is in this, as in many other cases, led by an invisible hand to promote an end which was no part of his intention. Nor is it always the worse for the society that it was no part of it. By pursuing his own interest he frequently promotes that of the society more effectually than when he really intends to promote it.[20]

Smith articulated in this passage a central belief of classical liberalism: that the common good can be served by individual initiative without state direction in the economic sphere. Much the same thing was meant by a French contemporary of Smith, who coined the term laissez faire (let alone). The terms invisible hand and laissez faire both imply that human needs are best served by free competition in the economic marketplace. Government has to enforce the rules of property and agreements that make competition possible, but it need not otherwise direct the process. These thinkers of the Enlightenment did not develop their ideas in a vacuum, of course. They were trying to encourage governments to end many restrictive practices that hampered market competition. Governments commonly set high tariffs to discourage imports of certain goods, conceded monopolies to favoured interests, attempted to fix prices, and in other ways meddled in the market.

In time, Smith's advice was taken, at least in North America and Western Europe, and governments largely disengaged themselves from the cruder forms of direct intervention in the market. The doctrine of free trade and open competition was further adopted in John Stuart Mill's *Principles of Political Economy* (1848), which became the single most widely read textbook of economics in the second half of the nineteenth century. Through Smith and Mill, public opinion became imbued with the virtues of the market system.

Let us turn to a more systematic exposition of classical liberalism and its leading idea, freedom as the absence of coercion. Locke and Jefferson derived their view of freedom from certain ideas about "natural rights," but we will not follow their line of thought here because it rests upon certain metaphysical and theological premises that are no longer universally shared. Rather, we will follow the thinking of those who defend freedom in terms of its utility for attaining the other goals of human society. This instrumental approach, which Mill took, is espoused today by two of the most distinguished advocates of classical liberalism, the economists Milton Friedman and Friedrich Hayek,[21] Nobel Prize winners in 1974 and 1976, respectively. Their argument for freedom reads approximately as follows:

People must live in communities in order to survive and live well. The efforts of each contribute to the welfare of all. How can all these individual efforts best be co-ordinated for the common good? One obvious answer is to set up a central source of direction, but liberals believe that people make better use of their talents if they are left to solve their own problems in their own way. Society is so complex that no central power can direct it as efficiently as individuals can, acting in a decentralized way. Freedom may seem inefficient, but it is in the long run the most effective principle of social life; for there is no intelligence that can look after people's affairs better than they themselves can. This is more evident the more advanced and complicated society becomes. A single mind might succeed in directing a small clan or tribe with few and primitive wants, but it could hardly cope with the demands of our complex civilization.

Individual initiative does not preclude co-operation. As David Hume pointed out in a famous example, two men would quickly discover how to row a boat across a river. Trial and error would show them how to work the oars together.[22] Society is a great self-regulating order whose parts are continually adjusting to each other through the processes of communication and exchange. Co-operation exists, but it is decentralized co-operation achieved through mutual consent, not directed from above. Order emerges as each person, pursuing individual good in an individual way, responds to the initiatives of others. Following Hayek, we will call this emergent, decentralized, voluntary order *spontaneous order* to distinguish it from a deliberately imposed pattern, which we will call *organization*.[23]

Classical liberalism holds that spontaneous order is more effective than organization in dealing with situations that involve vast amounts of information. An organization, as a structure under deliberate control, is limited by the wisdom of those who run it, whereas spontaneous order, as a decentralized network of mutual co-ordination, does not limit the information that can be used by the participants. Concrete examples will help make this argument clear.

The economic marketplace is a spontaneous order, not under the control of any one person or committee. Freely moving prices are the signals by which participants communicate to each other the relative abundance or scarcity of commodities. The discipline of economics is centred around the almost miraculous ability of the market to clear itself, that is, to bring supply and demand into equilibrium. Using the information conveyed by prices, producers and consumers are able to adjust their expectations so that the quantity produced equals the quantity desired. Classical liberals believe that no organized authority, such as a central planning agency, can perform this feat of matching as well as the self-ordering market process. As factual verification, they point to the shortages and surpluses of essential commodities that are chronic features of life in the state-managed economies of Eastern Europe.

This view of markets is based on several factual presuppositions. At a minimum, it assumes that (1) there are many buyers and sellers (2) who trade freely without coercion and (3) who know what they want and what goods and services are available. It further assumes that (4) entry to the market is relatively open, so that new participants can always undermine any collusion that may arise among present participants. It also assumes that there is a legal framework that (5) protects property and (6) enforces contracts, thereby making commerce possible. Under these conditions, it is argued, all exchanges are mutually beneficial; because participants have a variety of choices, they do not consummate certain transactions unless they find them superior to others. As we will see later, those who criticize the spontaneous market order often do so not because they oppose its intrinsic logic but because they believe that one or more of these six presuppositions does not actually exist.

Note that the market order requires behaviour limited by rules of conduct to prevent mutual coercion. Such rules include, at a minimum, respect for individuals and their property and keeping agreements or contracts. These rules are necessary for the general welfare; but it will always be in the interest of specific individuals to violate them, as long as others abide by them, because they will thereby gain a special advantage over their fellows. Those who violate rules while expecting others to abide by them are known in the jargon of contemporary economics as *free riders*. Tax evasion, for example, is usually free riding because it is not a protest against government as such, but merely an attempt to enjoy the benefits of government without paying for them. Hence government is necessary for spontaneous order as the means of enforcing those rules without which order breaks down.

Coercion is necessary to discourage and punish free riding. Society can live with a few persons of this type, but others may soon imitate their example. If that happens, rules of conduct collapse and with them the possibility of a co-operative spontaneous order. It is the essential role of government to make spontaneous order possible by enforcing general rules of conduct necessary to it. Beyond that, according to classical liberalism, government should allow individuals to pursue their own interests as they understand them.

This is not a rose-coloured view of society. There is no guarantee that individuals properly understand their own best interests or how to attain them. But the liberal believes that it is unlikely that the state knows better than individuals themselves. Hence reliance on the individual is the most effective general policy, even though it may fail in individual cases. Freedom means failed experiments and frustrated expectations, but failure and frustration are the means of learning and improvement.

Adam Smith's description of the duties of government has never been surpassed as a statement of classical liberalism:

> According to the system of natural liberty, the sovereign has only three duties to attend to; three duties of great importance, indeed, but plain and intelligible to common understandings: first, the duty of protecting the society from the violence and invasion of other independent societies; secondly, the duty of protecting, as far as possible, every member of the society from the injustice or oppression of every other member of it, or the duty of establishing an exact administration of justice; and, thirdly, the duty of erecting and maintaining certain public works and certain public institutions, which it can never be for the interest of any individual, or small number of individuals, to erect and maintain; because the profit could never repay the expense to any individual or small group of individuals, though it may frequently do much more than repay it to a great society.[24]

The first two points should be clear, but the third requires some comment. Smith was thinking of certain activities that are not profitable in a free market because it is difficult to charge for them. For example, it would not pay an entrepreneur to beautify a city because it is difficult, if not impossible, to devise a way to charge people for looking; or it seldom pays an entrepreneur to subsidize basic scientific research because profitable application is so uncertain.

In contemporary economics, such activities are known as *collective goods*. They are defined as goods and services that are not divisible among individuals but are consumed in common. A traffic light, for example, shines for all who are near the intersection. The fact that one person sees the light does not make it less available for others, in contrast to food or clothing, which cannot be used simultaneously with others. Collective goods have an inherent free-rider problem. It is obvious that if people are going to feed and clothe themselves, they have to pay for what they consume (assuming the state is doing its job of prohibiting theft); but it is tempting for them to hold back their share of the cost of a collective good, hoping that others will pay for it and they will be able to enjoy the benefits free of charge. How many streetlights would there be if they were supported by voluntary contributions?[25] The state is used to help provide collective goods by ensuring that we all pay our fair share. The state's monopoly on coercion can be used to collect taxes to pay for harbours, roads, scientific research, urban beautification, and many other desirable things. The liberal justification of this procedure is that government is being used to help people attain what they actually want, not to impose goals upon them despite their own desires.

Classical liberals have always recognized the category of collective goods, but they have usually not been eager to see too many services offered by the state. Adam Smith, certainly, had only a few things in mind when he wrote the *Wealth of Nations*. The problem is that collective goods must be financed by taxation. Revenue drained from individuals to government leaves that much less available for private decisions in the market. Classical liberals have generally been confident that private ingenuity will find a way to offer in the market goods or services that substitute for governmental provision of collective goods. For example, a movie is a sort of collective good because many people consume it at once; but it can be marketed by simply selling the right to a seat.

One crucial point is that beyond the three functions of government mentioned by Smith, the state has no mandate to "correct" the results of the marketplace by transferring wealth from rich to poor. Inequality is seen as an inevitable result of free competition. In the long run, it will even benefit the poor, as capital is reinvested to create new opportunities of employment and production. The classical liberal believes that economic advances may initially benefit only a restricted few, but over time their advantages become more widely disseminated. Innovations such as television or computers, which at first are expensive luxuries, eventually become articles of mass consumption.

At one level, classical liberals object to coercive state *redistribution* of wealth and income because they believe it is economically inefficient. To work properly, the market requires free bargains made knowing data about supply and demand that are furnished by prices. One who gains wealth by responding to these price signals is regarded as contributing to the welfare of others, not as taking away from them wealth that must be repossessed by the state. The prospect of gaining wealth is an important incentive for leading self-interested people to contribute to the common good by providing what is profitable in the marketplace.

At another level, classical liberals also object to coercive redistribution because they believe it clashes with equality of right, a concept they strongly uphold. Equality of right means, among other things, that the property of each is equally protected, regardless of how much there is. Now, the essence of redistribution is to take from the rich because they are rich and give to the poor because they are poor; such a policy means that the two classes are not treated equally before the law.

Classical liberalism was certainly not egalitarian in the sense of equality of condition. However, it was an important force for attaining equality before the law. Typically, liberals have agitated for abolition of special privileges enjoyed by some groups and disadvantages imposed on others by the power of the state. Liberals have fought against slavery and privileges of the nobility, against discrimination imposed on ethnic or religious minorities, against monopolies and tariffs that favoured special interest groups, against government patronage in employment and public works. Many of these goals have been largely achieved in the Western democracies, so that classical liberalism today seems "conservative," in favour of preserving the status quo; and indeed, classical liberals in this century are often called, and call themselves, conservatives (more on this later). But in the early nineteenth century, liberalism was a reforming force, very much in favour of great changes in the status quo.

The economic, social, and political perspectives of classical liberalism are closely related to one another. They all amount to saying that in the various spheres of life, people should be free to lead their own lives within universal laws that apply equally to all for the sole purpose of preventing coercion of others. Society is a game played fairly according to accepted rules. As in any game, there are winners and losers, but that does not justify a sudden change of rules at half-time to handicap the winners and help the losers. In any case, society is not really one game, but many games being played simultaneously, so losers may seek out games at which they are more adept. The function of government is to make sure that all players abide by the rules of the various games. Government is not a coach, but an umpire or referee—limited in task, but nonetheless indispensable.

Although classical liberalism is logically consistent in its views on government, it seems to many observers to lack concern for those who are not favoured by ability or good fortune. It is all very well, say its critics, to draw comparisons with athletic events, but losing a football game does not have the same pervasive effects on one's life as a low economic position. The confidence of the classical liberal that in the long run, free enterprise and the market system will raise the living standards of all does not do much now for those who are less well-off. Even those who concede the wealth-creating potential of classical liberalism may dislike the unequal distribution of wealth that seems to accompany it. And even if the economic inequality generated by the market system is no greater than in other systems, many critics object to the classical liberal's willingness to accept this inequality as an inescapable fact. It should be possible, they say, to do better—to have the admittedly useful aspects of the market while using government to ensure that all citizens have a decent standard of living, adequate medical care, education for their children, and financial security in times of accident, sickness, unemployment, and old age. Sentiments like these have encouraged reform-minded liberals to develop a more positive conception of government's role in society.

REFORM LIBERALISM

Curiously, John Stuart Mill, who was perhaps the best-known exponent of classical liberalism, also appears in retrospect as one of the pioneers of reform liberalism. One aspect of his thought that pointed toward the future was an emphasis on democracy. His father, James Mill, had been the first prominent thinker in England to openly espouse representative democracy as the only acceptable form of government. J. S. Mill was somewhat less enthusiastic about democracy than his father, but he still advocated the extension of voting rights to all adults, men and women alike. Fearful that this new mass of uninstructed voters might use the franchise for selfish purposes such as confiscating property, he proposed that the educated receive multiple votes; however, in historical perspective, his support of democracy seems more politically significant than his reservations about it.

Since Mill, liberalism has become securely attached to democracy, going far beyond the right to vote. Today liberals take for granted the right to vote and insist on other forms of public participation in government, such as public hearings, consultation before the passage of legislation, and publication of government documents. This emphasis on mass participation is considerably different from the earlier classical liberal idea of government as the affair of the propertied class.

Mill was also a key transitional figure in the development of economic interventionism among liberals. Though he remained committed to the free market system, he was deeply pained by economic inequalities. He wrote in the *Principles of Political Economy*:

> If the institution of private property necessarily carried with it as a consequence, that the produce of labour should be apportioned as we now see it, almost in an inverse ratio to the labour—the largest portions to those who have never worked at all, the next largest to those whose work is almost nominal, and so in a descending scale, the remuneration dwindling as the work grows harder and more disagreeable, until the most fatiguing and exhausting bodily labour cannot count with certainty on being able to earn even the necessaries of life; if this or Communism were the alternative, all the difficulties, great or small, of Communism would be but as dust in the balance.[26]

Mill flirted with socialism as a way of redressing these inequalities but ultimately rejected it on the grounds that property could be made more equal within the market system. He thought that taxes on large inheritances plus encouragement of enterprise ownership by workers could produce the best of both worlds: a reformed system of competition that would preserve the market's ability to solve complex problems of allocation while not generating such great inequalities. Though he remained a classical liberal in outlook, Mill helped popularize the idea that present inequalities of condition within the market system were intolerably large.

The decisive step toward reform liberalism was taken by T. H. Green (1836–1882), professor of philosophy at Oxford University. It was Green who redefined the concept of freedom to include not only the absence of coercion but also the presence of means or capacity:

> When we speak of freedom, we should consider carefully what we mean by it. We do not mean merely freedom from restraint or compulsion . . . we mean a positive power or capacity of doing or enjoying something worth doing or enjoying and that, too, something that we do or enjoy in common with others.[27]

The context of this new definition of positive freedom was Green's argument that the state would have to abridge liberty of contract in order to secure a higher standard of living for the less fortunate. Green achieved lasting influence by formulating the quest for equality of condition in terms of the attainment of freedom. In this way, he made it possible for liberalism to incorporate within itself equality of condition, which had previously been seen as a socialist issue. Green is the true father of reform liberalism as a unique combination of liberal and socialist concerns.

Although Green was an academic philosopher, his ideas had considerable practical effect. He and like-minded professors at English universities educated a generation of students who rose to prominence in the Liberal party. Imbued with the spirit of reform in Green's egalitarian sense, they laid the foundations of the welfare state when they came to power in the first decade of the twentieth century. They adopted the income tax as a means of redistribution; involved the state in social insurance programs such as unemployment insurance and old age pensions; and fostered through permissive legislation the power of organized labour. In Canada William Lyon Mackenzie King was nourished on the same ideas. The complexities of Canadian federalism required him to move slowly, but by the time he retired as prime minister in 1948, he had launched the welfare state. This reformist trend has been continued by other Liberal prime ministers, notably Lester Pearson and Pierre Trudeau. Their governments expanded unemployment insurance and welfare payments and launched a national medical insurance scheme. The thrust of all these reforms is to guarantee, through state action, the financial security of all residents of Canada. The welfare state is often described as a safety net, a minimum standard of living below which no one needs to fall, assuring a minimum financial capacity to all to pursue their goals in the marketplace.

Another landmark in the development of reform liberalism was the work of the economist John Maynard Keynes. His *General Theory of Employment, Interest and Money* (1936) argued that the spontaneous order of the market had a fatal flaw when it came to money. The economy could fall into a permanent depression characterized by high unemployment of labour and underuse of other resources. Government could counteract this by appropriate fiscal and monetary measures. Keynes's theory, which is much too complex to explain here in full, put government in a curious position vis-à-vis the economy. It was not the central planner demanded by socialism, but it was much more than the rule enforcer of classical liberalism. It was now responsible for maintaining prosperity and full employment, duties that were explicitly accepted by the governments of Britain, Canada, and the United States at the close of World War II.

A striking feature of reform liberalism is that, while it has departed significantly from the economic freedom of classical liberalism, it has preserved and even intensified the commitment to freedom in other spheres of life. Contemporary liberals tend to be strongly in favour of freedom of expression, even of legalizing blasphemous and pornographic material that earlier liberals might have rejected on grounds of public decency. Similarly, reform liberals today often advocate loosening many restrictions on behaviour, for example, legalizing marijuana or all sexual relations between consenting adults. Pierre Trudeau's famous remark that "the state has no place in the bedrooms of the nation" is a fair statement of the attitude of reform liberals in these matters.

The apparent paradox of reform liberalism's restriction on freedom in economic life coupled with permissiveness in other areas can perhaps be explained by the individualistic and hedonistic character of all liberal thought, classical or reform. All liberals see society as essentially a means of enabling individuals to do what they want without preventing others from doing likewise. Reform liberals believe that their economic interventions will help individuals toward the satisfaction of their desires. Their general outlook remains individualistic and libertarian, even when they advocate increased state supervision of the economy.

In summary, reform liberalism is more democratic than classical liberalism, though the difference is more of degree than kind. Reform liberalism preserves and even enhances the general commitment to freedom of classical liberalism, except in the realm of economics, where a definite break has occurred. There reform liberals call for an expanded, "positive" state role to reduce inequalities of condition and guarantee a minimum standard of living for all. This is expressed in the rhetoric of positive freedom, but it can also be understood as a moderate form of the socialist vision of equality of condition. At bottom, reform liberalism is a sort of hybrid between classical liberalism and democratic socialism.

Ideologies do not undergo such profound changes without cause. The rise of reform liberalism was chiefly motivated by concern about the new working class created by the Industrial Revolution. The rural poor flocked to cities such as

Birmingham, Manchester, and London to work in factories. It is a much-debated question whether their standard of living as industrial workers was lower or higher than it had been as agricultural labourers, but the objective fact is perhaps not as important as the subjective perception.[28] The new working class, concentrated as it was in industrial towns and cities, was far more visible than the rural poor. Extensive urban slums created a widespread belief that poverty and wretched living conditions were caused by the market system. The new developments in liberalism were an attempt to share the wealth more widely and, in the minds of some, stave off the socialist revolution that would occur if the condition of the working class did not improve. ·

The industrial working class has been at least partially integrated into Western society, so that the distinction between working class and middle class has lost much of its force; but reform liberals have gone on to champion the cause of other groups perceived as downtrodden: racial minorities, women, and the entire Third World. One student of liberalism has termed this the "suffering situation."[29] The spontaneous order of society and the market in particular are indicted for not according equitable treatment to workers (blacks, native peoples, women, homosexuals, the physically and mentally disabled, and so on). The "oppressed" group is not seen as responsible for its own fate; the state is summoned to use its power on behalf of these groups, who are thought to be not fully able to advance themselves.

Another development encouraging the ascendancy of reform liberalism has been the growth of large corporations and the reduction of the number of competitors in key markets. Many industries—automobile, steel, and petrochemical, for example—are dominated by a few giant firms. Reform liberals argue that this situation of oligopoly substantially releases these firms from the constraints of market discipline by weakening competition. Many of them take the position that the factual presuppositions of effective competition no longer exist and therefore government must play a regulatory role to protect society from exploitation by corporate giants.[30] Classical liberals would dispute this analysis, arguing that, for example, while there may be only a few automobile makers in North America, foreign firms are able to offer stiff competition now that improved transportation has unified the world market. Also, a dynamic and advanced economy offers many alternative products. There may be only a few steel companies, but competition still exists because steel is challenged for many purposes by wood, glass, cement, aluminum, plastics, and other structural materials.[31] This classical liberal rejoinder has its supporters, but the reform liberal attitude toward large corporations has been extremely influential in shaping regulatory legislation.

Reform liberalism has been the dominant ideology of the Western world in the twentieth century, with adherents in parties of all labels. However, there were signs in the late 1970s and early 1980s of a breakdown in the reform liberal consensus that had prevailed since World War II. Keynesianism has been largely discredited in practice because politicians have used it to legitimize recurrent deficit spending, with inflationary effects. There has been something of a revival of classical liberalism in both the United Kingdom and the United States under the governments of Margaret Thatcher and Ronald Reagan. Thatcher and her advisers have been particularly influenced by the writings of Friedrich Hayek, Reagan and his advisers by the works of Milton Friedman. Both administrations speak of reducing the size of government and deregulating the economy, privatizing government-owned enterprises, inaugurating a new era of free market growth, and lessening our preoccupation with equality of condition and social security.

About two months after the Conservatives won the Canadian general election of 1984, Finance Minister Michael Wilson tabled an agenda paper, entitled *A New Direction for Canada*, which seemed to point in this same direction. It identified the "intricate web of regulations, subsidies, and other forms of intervention" as a major hindrance to the economy.[32] It spoke of deregulating industries and reviewing the benefit level of social programs, especially unemployment insurance. But it is not yet clear whether the Mulroney government will pursue this agenda with the same energy as have those of Mrs. Thatcher and Mr. Reagan.

The main issue raised by reform liberalism is the conflict between freedom in the classical liberal sense and state coercion, which the reform liberal must use in the provision of collective goods and the pursuit of positive freedom. This conflict frequently recurs in the various domains of government policy.

We have already seen how classical liberals recognized governmental responsibility to provide collective goods but were rather cautious about the scope of such operations. Reform liberals have been much more eager to supply collective goods through the state. "Private affluence, public squalor" was the slogan coined in the 1950s by John Kenneth Galbraith, a leading North American liberal.[33] By it he meant that the public sector was starved in comparison to the private. Much more should be spent on collective goods, such as urban beautification, scientific research and education, the fine arts, and protection of the environment. Providing such collective goods increases our standard of living in some respects, but because they are supported by coercively collected taxes, they reduce the freedom to decide how to spend one's own money.

A similar dilemma occurs in the social insurance programs of the *welfare state*, which protect against the contingencies of life—unemployment, poor health, injury, and old age—that render people incapable of fully looking after themselves. Governments in this century have established massive quasi-insurance programs to which all are obliged to pay contributions and from which all derive benefits in time of need—for example, unemployment insurance and the Canada Pension Plan. These are unlike private insurance plans because membership is compulsory, premiums are not proportional to risk, and they are almost always actuarially unsound (expenses exceed contributions). This latter feature requires that they must be subsidized from general tax revenues. Why is membership always compulsory in these plans? Chiefly in order to subsidize high-risk individuals at the expense of low-risk persons, who might not voluntarily enroll in the plan. For example, despite the growing incidence of layoffs in education, a public school teacher with several years of experience still has something close to guaranteed lifetime employment. Making an uncoerced choice, she might well decide not to purchase unemployment insurance if it were for sale on the market. In comparison, an unskilled labourer subject to periodic layoffs might badly desire unemployment insurance but would find himself faced with prohibitive premiums because of his level of risk.

Compulsory membership in a universal scheme, as a way to pool risks, is the solution generally adopted by the architects of the welfare state. The coercion employed seems a small loss to the reform liberal, who is convinced that no one is really free without economic security and medical care. However, the classical liberal regrets the coercive aspects of the plan and asks whether a coercive solution imposed today might not prevent the appearance in the market of unsuspected alternatives. A compulsory state scheme of pensions, for instance, might discourage private insurance companies from trying to create policies to do a comparable job.

Forcing low-risk people to join a plan in order to subsidize high-risk people is fundamentally an act of redistribution. This opens up a topic of lively debate between classical and reform liberals: the pursuit of social justice. To the classical liberal, *justice* is not a problematic concept. It is simply the virtue of protecting individuals in the possession of everything they have accumulated within the ac-knowledged rules of conduct. The most famous definition of justice comes from Justinian's Code: "Justice is a firm and unceasing determination to render to every man his due."[34] As an old proverb has it, "to each his own." Justice does not say anything about the relative size of holdings; it simply says that holdings must be respected, regardless of their size. Equal justice under law means that small holdings are as much protected as large holdings, not that holdings will be equalized. But reform or welfare-state liberals typically talk about *social justice*, which is not the protection of property as such, but the partial equalization of property to reach some conception of a desirable range of holdings. The fundamental idea is that the outcome of free action in a spontaneous order should not be allowed to reach too great a degree of inequality. Extremes of wealth and poverty are criticized as violations of social justice, even if they have arisen without violation of law.[35]

The demand for the state to enforce social justice implies redistribution, that is, taking property from those who have more in order to give it to those who have less. This by definition must clash with the classical liberal's conception of justice, which would not permit the state to take such action. From the viewpoint of the classical liberal, governmental redistribution to achieve social justice is simply theft. It is a violation of the freedom of some in order to increase the wealth of others. This differs in principle from the state provision of collective goods, which is intended to be a restriction of the freedom of all for the benefit of all.[36]

Apart from compulsory participation in social insurance schemes, the main vehicle of redistribution is the progressive income tax. A *progressive tax* is one whose rate rises as the amount to be taxed increases. It is not just a matter of "the more you earn, the more you pay"; for that would also be true if everyone paid, for example, a flat 10 per cent of income as tax. Someone who earned $10,000 would pay a tax of $1,000, $20,000 of earnings would mean a tax of $2,000, and so on. A progressive tax means "the more you earn, the higher percentage you pay." Whereas the reform liberal praises this as implementing social justice and approaching equality of condition, the classical liberal decries it as a coercive violation of the equality of right. The preferred alternative of the classical liberal is the flat-rate tax. Its supporters in the United States maintain that a uniform rate of less than 20 per cent, combined with abolishing the many tax deductions that have grown up along with the progressive income tax, would raise more revenue than the present system.[37]

Numerous other policies espoused by reform liberals have redistributive intentions and sometimes redistributive results, although these results are not always what was intended. Price-fixing is one of the most common strategies. Sometimes this takes the form of a legally established floor, as in minimum wage legislation. The theory here is that any employed person ought to earn enough to achieve some minimum standard of living. Sometimes price-fixing means setting a ceiling, as in rent controls or the pricing regime for oil and natural gas that was followed in Canada before the National Energy Program was discontinued in 1985. The justification offered for such maxima is that those who sell essential commodities should not be able to make unduly large profits.

All of these policies, which are quite numerous today, have a common theme: it is believed that the free market yields results that are not compatible with social justice. It is alleged that tenants pay too much rent, employers do not pay high enough wages, or prices for farmers' crops are too low. It is up to the state to redress the imbalance.

One difficulty with such programs is determining how much is enough. Classical liberals can point to the impersonal workings of the marketplace, and socialists can appeal to strict equality of condition as a goal. Few welfare-state liberals would feel comfortable with either ideal, but they do not have a precise one of their own. Thus there is a peculiar quality of dissatisfaction in the present welfare state. No matter how much has been done, there is always a cry for more reform, more progress, more humanitarianism, more state action.

Fundamentally, such policies face the dilemma of all interventions. An *intervention* is an isolated attempt to impose a particular result upon a spontaneous order. Rent controls, for example, are an intervention in a market economy because they impose a price for a single commodity, while other prices are determined by supply and demand. All price-fixing is an act of intervention, as is setting quantities—for example, allowing dairy farmers to produce only a stipulated volume of milk each year. Every intervention is a coercive imposition on the market.

Interventions are attractive to the reform liberal because they seem to offer a path to social justice. Legislation can provide everyone with decent housing at an affordable price or require all employers to pay a living wage. But interventions suffer in a special way from the unintended consequences that plague all human action. An isolated governmental control on the market leaves economic actors free to seek an escape from losses. For example, on the supply side, landlords faced with rent controls shift their investment capital into another field. The result may be that they postpone new buildings, convert existing structures to condominiums, and decrease maintenance on existing units. On the demand side, tenants take advantage of a perceived bargain. As housing is more affordable, they feel less impelled to double up or otherwise reduce consumption of space. Demand is enhanced while supply is discouraged, resulting in a perceived shortage of rental accommodation. Some lucky consumers, those who happen to be in units they like, get a bargain, but many others, particularly those who need to move or young people seeking their first apartment, face a difficult situation. Landlords suffer a one-time loss but now move their capital to more remunerative investments. The long-term "redistribution" is from one class of tenants to another—hardly the social justice that the policy-makers had in mind.

From the point of view of classical liberalism, these results are predictable. Moving prices are the indispensable signals by which individuals co-ordinate their behaviour in the market. Fixing these prices by coercive state action means the signals can no longer work. Hence it is not surprising that unintended and undesirable consequences arise. The example of rent controls is not an exceptional instance. It is a paradigm of what happens, in one degree or another, with all interventions.

This problem helps us understand one of the most basic differences between classical and reform liberalism. Classical liberals are committed to a process: spontaneous order in general, the market in particular. The process depends on the government maintaining freedom, equality of right, and justice. The process may yield some objectionable results, such as economic inequality, but these must be accepted as unavoidable side effects of an otherwise beneficial system. Reform liberals are also committed to spontaneous order and the market, but they believe that government can be used to improve particular results of the process. The state can provide collective goods and economic security, redistribute income, and in other ways add social justice to the outcome of market competition. When classical liberals point to the unintended consequences of interventions, reform liberals may acknowledge their existence but may also feel it is worth the price if positive freedom has been promoted.

Fundamentally, the dilemma of reform liberalism is to preserve the market system while using government to achieve certain supplementary objectives, especially maintaining a decent standard of living for all. This requires a discriminating use of governmental power, for the seemingly shortest path to the goal does not always lead directly to it. Heavy-handed interventions such as rent controls often cause more harm than good. In the field of rental housing, government might be able to make accommodations more affordable by reviewing its own land-use and building regulations, thus streamlining the process of land development and construction. In general, there is much room for improvement of all the rules of agreement and exchange upon which the market rests. Improvement of general rules rather than selective interventions may allow reform liberals to accomplish their goal of helping the less well-off without impairing the market system.

11   Conservatism

To conserve is to save or preserve. Thus we would expect a conservative to be a person who wishes to keep society as it is and who is sceptical about change. *Conservatism* in this sense is a disposition "to prefer the familiar to the unknown . . . the tried to the untried, fact to mystery, the actual to the possible, the limited to the unbounded, the near to the distant, the sufficient to the superabundant, the convenient to the perfect, present laughter to utopian bliss," stated Michael Oakeshott, a contemporary British political theorist and a well-known conservative.[38]

This preference for the existing present over the conjectural future rests on a sober assessment of human nature. The Canadian historian W. L. Morton put it this way:

> To the theologian, this is the belief in original sin, the belief that man is by nature imperfect and may be made perfect only by redemption and grace. In philosophic terms, it is a denial of the fundamental liberal and Marxist belief that human nature is inherently perfectible, and that man may realize the perfection that is in him if only the right environment is created.[39]

According to conservative thinking, the limitations of human nature make it imprudent for society to embark on large-scale ventures of social transformation. Much that is good may be lost with little likelihood of reaching "utopian bliss."

This attitude can also be defended using arguments drawn from social science, particularly the idea of spontaneous order. The main point is that spontaneous order acts as a vast filter for selecting desirable and discarding undesirable innovations. Such an order consists of millions of intelligences freely co-operating under suitable rules. Any innovation, say a new idea in science, a new trend in art, or a new product in business, is subjected to the repeated, independent scrutiny of countless people who must decide whether to accept, imitate, or purchase. Any given individual may make a poor decision, but there is a strong presumption that in time, the right decision or course of action will emerge. This is especially true because the testing process continues over generations.

Thus there is some reason to assume that the present way of doing things is socially useful. If a better way existed, chances are it would have already been adopted. But this is only a probability, not a certainty. The fact that progress occurs shows that some innovations do have value, even if most do not. Thus the conservative tends to adopt a cautious attitude toward changes, wanting to see their usefulness demonstrated before adopting them. This is not hostility to change or improvement as such, but rather respect for wisdom inherited from the past and caution in the face of an unknown future.

Reformers, whose proposals seem so obviously beneficial in their own eyes, are naturally impatient with this conservative attitude. Conservatives would reply in their defence that existing institutions already have the tacit approval of millions of minds over generations. That is a strong counterweight to the reformers' confidence in their own ideas. They may in fact be correct, but they must bear the burden of proof.

An interesting consequence of conservatism is respect for habits and customs whose rationale may not be immediately apparent. Conservatives assume there is tacit wisdom in inherited patterns of behaviour. People may not understand all the reasons for what they do, but they may still be doing the right thing by following custom. Reformers, in contrast, are often quick to condemn what they do not understand, preferring conscious reason to inarticulate habit.

The conservative theory of change is closely associated with the Anglo-Irish parliamentaran Edmund Burke (1729–1797), who gave it an influential formulation. Burke was moved to reflect upon change by his observation of the French Revolution. In 1789 Louis XVI convened the Estates-General, a medieval type of consultative body that had not met since 1614. His goal was to raise new taxes, but events quickly escaped from his control. The Estates-General converted itself into a National Assembly and declared France a constitutional monarchy. Change followed change with dizzying rapidity. The Declaration of the Rights of Man was adopted and a parliamentary system created. The last remnants of feudalism were abolished, and the property of the Catholic church was nationalized. The old provinces were replaced by geometrically drawn *départements*. Even weights and measures were affected, as the National Assembly commissioned the preparation of what became the metric system. All this, as well as much more, was quickly done in an exalted spirit of reform: the rationalism of the Enlightenment, finally put into practice, would remodel society.

The results were not what had been expected. Within four years, France was under the dictatorship of Maximilien Robespierre, in what historians usually call "the Terror." France was also at war with the rest of Europe. Louis XVI and Marie Antoinette had been put to death on the guillotine, a novel form of execution. Thousands of other opponents of Robespierre also went to the guillotine, and he himself was finally removed from power in the same way. Political stability was restored only by Napoleon, who ruled at least as autocratically as, and far more effectively than, any of the Bourbon monarchs had done.[40]

Burke wrote *Reflections on the Revolution in France* (1791) before the worst excesses began, but he correctly predicted that turmoil and despotism would grow out of such a radical break with the past. People are not wise enough to remake society all at once; they must rely on the accumulated wisdom of the past, contained in customs, traditions, and practices:

We are afraid to put men to live and trade each on his own private stock of reason; because we suspect that this stock in each man is small, and that the individuals would do better to avail themselves of the general bank and capital of nations and ages. Many of our men of speculation, instead of exploding general prejudices, employ their sagacity to discover the latent wisdom which prevails in them. If they find what they seek, and they seldom fail, they think it more wise to continue the prejudice, with the reason involved, than to cast away the coat of prejudice, and to leave nothing but the naked reason; because prejudice, with its reason, has a motive to give action to that reason, and an affection which will give it permanence.[41]

The contemporary reader is struck by Burke's praise of prejudice, which is today a negative word implying unfair discrimination. For Burke, prejudice meant literally "prejudgment" that contained the "latent wisdom" of past experience. People are not able to think their way through each new situation, so they must fall back on rules of thumb that have served them well in the past. Take the modern example of a landlord who may refuse to rent to tenants under twenty-one years of age. In defence, several unhappy experiences can be cited with young tenants who gave noisy parties, were delinquent in their rent payments, and did not take care of the apartment. The landlord's "prejudice" against a category of people is, in a sense, unfair and irrational because not all members of the category behave the same way. Yet is it irrational for the landlord to rely on prejudice if there is no better way of predicting behaviour? Past experience, limited as it may be, is better than nothing as a guide to the future. The conservative view expressed by Burke is that prejudice is not just an irrational closing of the mind, but a necessary way of dealing with a world in which complete information is rarely available.

As the psychologist Gordon Allport has pointed out, "the human mind must think with the aid of categories. . . . Once formed, categories are the basis for normal prejudgment."[42] The prejudgments are necessary and useful; they "become prejudices [in the modern sense] only if they are not reversible when exposed to new knowledge."[43] The challenge for conservatism is to combine open-mindedness about new developments with attachments to traditional values.

Burke was not opposed to change as such (he had earlier spoken in defence of the American Revolution). But he wanted change to be gradual, so that the inherited wisdom of the past might not be lost:

We must all obey the great law of change. It is the most powerful law of nature, and the means perhaps of its conservation. All we can do, and that human wisdom can do, is to provide that the change shall proceed by insensible degrees. This has all the benefits which may be in change, without any of the inconvenience of mutation. This mode will, on the one hand, prevent the *unfixing old interests at once*: a thing which is apt to breed a black and sullen discontent in those who are at once dispossessed of all their influence and consideration. This gradual course, on the other hand, will prevent men, long under depression, from being intoxicated with a large draught of new power, which they always abuse with a licentious insolence.[44]

The conservative attitude toward change is perhaps best expressed in the old adage, "If it is not necessary to change, it is necessary not to change." In the absence of some compelling reason for innovation, it is desirable not to tamper with the status quo, which has at least shown some degree of viability. Alternatives that are superficially attractive may turn out to be much worse when they are tested in practice. In evaluating proposed reforms, the conservative is aware that one is comparing something that exists and whose faults are therefore apparent to an idea that does not yet exist and whose faults may be unsuspected.

Conservatism is a prejudice (in Burke's sense) against using the state's coercive power to sponsor large efforts of social change. The conservative will eventually give grudging approval to change that has taken place spontaneously through the accumulation of many individual decisions, testing the effects of innovation at each stage. To use the state as an agency of rapid reform shortcuts this process and may commit society to beautiful but unworkable visions.

Conservatism is conveniently described as an attachment to the present or status quo, but that is an oversimplification in one important respect. Conservatives are often highly critical of present trends, comparing them unfavourably with their image of the past. This is not incompatible with their view of gradual change, for the testing period of complex innovations may well extend over decades or generations. Conservatives often feel that we are headed in the wrong direction and should return to the example of the past before it is too late. Therefore they can find themselves in the position of making proposals that are themselves innovative vis-à-vis present arrangements. Burke, for example, wanted the revolutionary government of France overthrown and the monarchy restored. When we refer to the status quo, we mean the present not as an isolated moment in time, but as an extension of a long past. It is really the prolonged experience of the past that the conservative values, not the mere present existence of a custom, practice, or institution. Under normal conditions—when the state has not forcibly induced social changes—the conservative is satisfied with the present as an organic outgrowth of the past.

Burke expressed this unity of past, present, and future by speaking metaphorically of the state as a partnership across generations:

> It is a partnership in all science; a partnership in all art; a partnership in every virtue and in all perfection. As the ends of such a partnership cannot be obtained in many generations, it becomes a partnership not only between those who are living, but between those who are living, those who are dead, and those who are to be born.[45]

No one has better stated the conservative's sense of continuity. For Burke, this continuity was further buttressed by a belief in divine order as the foundation of social order. Other conservatives have reversed this relationship, seeing religion more as a useful support of society rather than as its basis. But whatever their differences of religious faith, conservatives all revere the social order as something larger and more important than the individual. Conservatives are always mistrustful of the rationalistic intellectual's confidence in individual judgment. Conservatives put more trust in the collective wisdom of society as expressed in customs, usages, and institutions.

As presented here, conservatism is an attitude, not a fullfledged ideology with a whole set of beliefs about people, society, and government. By the conservative's own admission, the status quo is always changing and is never the same from year to year. Conservatism's commitment to the status quo paradoxically entails gradually accepting new principles as the content of the present reality changes. In this way, conservatism differs markedly from liberalism or socialism, both of which are built around certain ideas regarded as universal truths. The classical liberal believes the market, and the socialist believes state planning, is the most effective means of meeting human wants. Each defends the preferred system where it exists and works for its introduction where it does not. The status quo is regarded as a secondary factor affecting the speed with which the desired goal may be achieved. The goal itself is derived intellectually as a matter of principle, and there is no commitment to what exists simply because it does exist.

All of this means that there is no single, unchanging body of doctrine that can be identified as conservative. Those who are so identified, or who identify themselves as conservative at certain times and in certain places, have had varying opinions about the major issues of government, depending on historical context. Not surprisingly, there are all sorts of conflicting pronouncements in the literature of political science about what conservatism "really" is. There has been more confusion about it than about any other ideology. But asking what conservatism "really" is, is a false question; ideologies have no existence apart from the beliefs of actual persons. The point is to understand the opinions of those who call themselves, and who are called by others, conservative.

Here we must confine our view largely to the Anglo-American tradition.[46] In continental Europe during the last two centuries, conservatism has often referred to the ideology of those who have not accepted the legal type of authority and legitimacy, who have wished to cling to the practices of Europe before the French Revolution: monarchy unchecked by representative government, a hereditary aristocracy, established religion, a traditional society of inherited status. Though Anglo-American conservatism also began with the reaction against the French Revolution, that reaction was not as total and violent because the status quo in England in 1789 was far removed from that in Europe. The revolution of 1688 had established parliamentary supremacy and religious toleration. Although an important aristocracy existed, it was closely tied to the business or mercantile class. In the newly independent American colonies, there was no nobility at all, the monarchy had been abolished, and religious freedom was nearly absolute. England and America in 1789 already were, to a great extent, what the early reformers of the French

Revolution wished to create. Anglo-American conservatism, epitomized by Burke, rejected their method of sudden, state-directed change but could not have rejected many of their aspirations without rejecting itself.

A glance at some of Burke's opinions shows the complexities of being a conservative in a society whose traditions were largely liberal. Burke's economic views were almost identical to those of Adam Smith. He praised the market in these terms: "Nobody, I believe, has observed with any reflexion what market is, without being astonished at the truth, the correctness, the celerity, the general equity, with which the balance of wants is settled."[47] Correspondingly, Burke was a strong advocate of private property and totally rejected the redistributive state. Politically Burke was a Whig, that is, a member of the party that, in broad terms, supported the rights of Parliament. He revered the memory of the Glorious Revolution, and he spoke in favour of the American colonies in their dispute with England because he thought they were being deprived of traditional English rights of self-government. All these positions sound very "liberal," seeming to imply freedom, constitutionalism, and the rule of law. On the other hand, Burke was a strong advocate of hereditary aristocracy, though he himself was not of that class. To ensure that the nobility together with merchants of great property retained control of English government, he opposed any extension of the right to vote, which in his day was quite narrowly restricted. His conception of equality before the law did not imply that literally the same laws would apply to all. He thought that society was necessarily divided into hierarchical levels and that this was something for government to protect because of its contribution to social stability.

Burke's "conservatism" (we use quotation marks because he did not think of himself as conservative) was a combination of economic liberalism and social conservatism. The precise elements of the combination are intelligible only in the light of the issues of his day. Since Burke, Anglo-American conservatives have held various ideas, depending on when and where they have lived; but they have generally followed his example in combining market economics with respect for the past and a hierarchical view of society. Two of the chief founders of Canada—Sir John A. Macdonald and Sir George-Etienne Cartier—fit this description exactly. Both were thoroughgoing advocates of the market system. Macdonald ultimately adopted a protective tariff, which violates the theory of free trade, only because he could not conclude a reciprocity agreement with the United States. Both were opposed to universal suffrage and regarded the United States as an instructive example of democracy run amok. Both were strong supporters of the British Empire and the Crown, seeing a constitutional monarchy as a valuable source of social stability. A recent study has said of these two statesmen:

It was not that the founders of the Canadian nation despised freedom; indeed, they revered it. But, for them, freedom arises from order, from restraint, not from unconstrained passions. The world they desired was the Burkean world, the world of order, restraint, sterner virtues and prudence.[48]

In the late twentieth century, the issues are, of course, somewhat different. Conservatives in the Anglo-American world have become reconciled to democracy, though they still fear that popular majorities may be mobilized politically against the rights of property. The major economic issue for conservatives today is protecting the market system from further state intervention or even reversal of the statist tendencies of reform liberalism and democratic socialism.

NEOCONSERVATISM

There has clearly been a conservative tide during the 1980s in many Western democracies. Over the past fifty years, it has become common to expect rapidly expanding state intervention in society. Following the Great Depression and World War II, the state was seen as a force for implementing a more just and equitable society. This belief in statism as a cure for the ills of libertarian societies may have run its course. Conservative electoral victories in Great Britain (1979 and 1983), the United States (1980 and 1984), West Germany (1983), and Canada (1984) all point to the fact that many voters are responding to politicians who advocate reducing some of the extensive activities of the state while encouraging individuals or social groups to find solutions for their own problems. It has become common to refer to this conservative revival as *neoconservatism*, a term first used in the 1970s by a circle of writers in the United States who had once identified themselves as liberals but had become disenchanted with recent developments in liberalism. We continue to use the traditional term conservatism because we see no fundamental change in ideology, even though popular support for conservative views has increased.

Many welfare liberal policies have much political appeal. At the same time, however, the record in Western societies shows that it is impossible for a centrally run bureaucracy to respond effectively to all claims made on it. Many policies, such as old age pensions and medicare, are still considered sacred, but there does seem to be a call for more selectivity in the scope of the welfare state. Politically powerful conservatives in the 1980s seem to be advocating neither absolute individualism nor absolute collectivism, but a balance between the two.

The economic credo of conservatives in Britain, Canada, and the United States has a number of common themes. First is the belief that the public sector has become too large and is crowding out the private sector. This leads to a demand for the "downsizing" of government activities. Conservative governments have tried to achieve this with wage freezes or rollbacks in the public service, across-the-board cuts in programs, and selective reductions in areas thought to be particularly overfunded. The main obstacle to reducing the size of government is that most of the budget of the modern state consists of services and transfer payments that are popular with large groups of electors: education, pensions, health care, unemployment insurance. Electors may agree in the abstract that government is too large and may vote for a conservative party that promises to do something about it; but they may become extremely irate when they see their favourite service cut back. The budget-cutting attempts of conservative governments, such as Premier Bennett's in British Columbia or President Reagan's in the United States, show that initial cuts build up a coalition of resistance to further cuts that is difficult to overcome.

A second typical conservative belief is that the private sector is hampered and restricted by government controls. The practical consequence of this line of thought is *deregulation*, that is, lifting governmental controls on market activity. In the United States the Reagan administration has deregulated the air travel industry, allowing airlines to change fares and routes as they wish. It has also decontrolled the price of oil and is moving in that direction for natural gas. Similar initiatives have been undertaken in other regulated industries, such as trucking. Overall, the Reagan administration has also tried to relax the burden of environmental and safety regulations on the private sector. The Conservative government of Brian Mulroney will certainly do at least some of the same things. Shortly after taking office, it effectively removed the power of the Foreign Investment Review Agency to block or otherwise regulate external takeovers of Canadian business. It subsequently returned oil to world prices and intends to allow more competition in the heavily regulated banking industry. In the summer of 1985 it announced further deregulation of air travel and trucking, including possibly the management of airports by local authorities.

A third watchword is *privatization*, the sale of publicly owned corporations and activities to the private sector. In the United States, where the federal government has not been a large owner of enterprises, at least in comparison to other countries, privatization has taken place mainly at the local level, involving services like garbage pickup and disposal, fire protection, and street paving. There is considerable empirical evidence that many services at this level can be provided more cheaply by the private sector than the public.[49] However, resistance from public sector unions, which tend to be stronger in Canada than the United States, has slowed the advance of local privatization in Canada. At the national level, the most spectacular steps have been taken by the Thatcher government in Great Britain, which has organized several sales of previously nationalized enterprises, the most notable being the sale of the entire telephone system through a public share offering. In Canada Joe Clark promised to privatize Petro Canada when he was prime minister in 1979, but that idea did not win popular support. It seems more likely that the Mulroney government will seek to sell off some less popular Crown corporations, such as the money-losing aircraft manufacturers acquired in the 1970s. Another possibility might be a limited public share offering in popular Crown corporations, such as Air Canada or Petro Canada, allowing a degree of private ownership in a mixed enterprise.

The main social issue for conservatives is protecting traditional institutions and practices in an era of rapid social change. They wish to defend the family in its traditional form, and this implies a number of political positions: making abortions difficult to obtain, discouraging youthful promiscuity, preventing "value free" sex education in public schools. In other ways, they want the state to help maintain traditional standards of conduct by inflicting harsher penalties for crime, including capital punishment, and enforcing stricter discipline in schools. Conservatives are generally against legalizing drugs, such as marijuana or cocaine, on the grounds that they promote a life devoted to pleasure rather than the fulfilment of duty toward others. Similar reasons account for opposition to pornography in films and publications. The common denominator in all these positions is a belief that a good society cannot be a mere collection of pleasure-seeking individuals. Social existence demands that human behaviour be restrained by institutions such as the family, church, school, and, if all else fails, the state.

Conservatives are particularly outraged by certain activities of the state that they interpret as weakening other institutions. For example, governmental sponsorship of homosexual rights is to them an attack upon the family, and government-mandated bussing of children to achieve racial balance is an attack upon the local school. Conservatism seems to have recently taken on new popularity in Britain and the United States, a phenomenon that political commentators call the "New Right." The American New Right tends to be closely allied with Protestant fundamentalism. Supported by television evangelism and sophisticated fundraising techniques, it has become highly aggressive in promoting the views of the "moral majority." There is no real equivalent in Canada to this peculiarly American variety of activist conservatism.

In international affairs, conservatives believe it is, above all, necessary to resist the expansion of communism and related forms of revolutionary socialism. Viewing the world in terms of the "East-West" split, they see communism as a threat to the social order of the Western world. Both the Thatcher and Reagan governments have emphasized military preparedness, and the latter in particular has spent vast sums on "rearming America." This desire for military strength can involve conservatives in a painful dilemma, for the armed forces, as part of the public sector, must be paid from tax revenues. Thus President Reagan's announced policies of reducing the size of government, balancing the federal budget, and increasing military spending have proved mutually incompatible. This complex of issues is, of course, much less important to Canadian conservatism. Mr. Mulroney's government will probably refrain from criticisms of American foreign and military policy and may lend rhetorical support from time to time, but it is unlikely to increase defence spending very much.

Apart from these broad similarities, there is at least one important line of division among contemporary conservatives. One group, the more orthodox and traditional-minded, believe that the highest priority of a conservative government should be to balance the budget and make people realize that, as Milton Friedman entitled one of his books, "There's no such thing as a free lunch." Once in power, conservatives of this type often raise taxes because they find themselves politically unable to cut expenditures enough to balance the budget. Another group of conservatives, often referred to as "supply siders," believe it is more important to reduce the burden of government on people by cutting taxes.[50] They would also like to downsize the scope of government; but they do not make a fetish of balancing the budget and can accept deficits with equanimity, believing that in the long run, a lower burden of government will encourage the private sector and result in sufficient tax revenues to achieve a balanced budget in the future.

Because contemporary conservative governments are likely to be composed of representatives of both camps, their pronouncements and policies are often a result of compromise. In the United States President Reagan has been more successful at cutting taxes than cutting expenditures and has consequently produced a series of large deficits accompanied, incidentally, by a spectacular economic recovery after a sluggish couple of years at the outset of his presidency. In Canada Finance Minister Michael Wilson's first budget seemed to tilt, at least rhetorically, toward the orthodox fiscal strategy of balancing the budget. But the proposed tax increases and expenditure reductions were modest, so that the deficit will probably not be reduced by much. In any case, it is clear that supply-side ideology is much weaker in Canada than in the United States.

This sketch of conservatism adds new difficulties to the problem of overlapping ideological labels. We have already noticed how classical and reform liberals are not black-and-white opposites but share considerable common ground. In different respects, conservatives and classical liberals also have much in common. Classical liberalism, exemplified in John Stuart Mill, espoused freedom in both economic and social matters. Reform liberals, while preserving a belief in freedom in social matters, wish to use the state to restrict economic behaviour. Conservatives have always been more favourable toward economic than social freedom. However, even where conservatism and classical liberalism converge, there is one decisive difference in outlook: conservative thought rejects the liberal postulate of individualism. Seeing people always in their social context, conservatives also reject the liberal notion of freedom as doing what one wants. They think of freedom rather in a moral sense, as the voluntary assumption of obligations to others. Like classical liberals, they reject the pretensions of the state to direct society; but they also reject the liberal vision of utility-maximizing individualism, preferring to emphasize the social institutions that structure individual existence.

In the everyday language of politics, at least in North America, the two terms liberal and conservative suffice. Liberal means what we have called reform liberal, and what other writers sometimes call "left-liberal" or "welfare-state liberal." Conservative means what has just been described in this chapter. Classical liberalism, as a consistent ideology of freedom in all realms of life, has relatively few adherents today, and the very term classical liberalism has little place in our contemporary vocabulary except to describe a past ideology.[51] For practical purposes, the ideological landscape in North America can be divided into (reform) liberal and conservative camps, corresponding roughly, but only very roughly, to the distinction between Liberal and Conservative or Democrat and Republican.

The situation in Europe is similar in substance but different in terminology because the name liberal is hardly used except in a historical sense. What is called liberalism in North America is usually called democratic socialism in Europe. The major reformist parties include either Labour or Socialist in their titles. Conservative, in contrast, means about the same thing as it does in North America and is often used as a rough description of the Conservative party in Britain, the Gaullists in France, and the Christian Democrats in Germany or Italy. All combine a favourable orientation to the market economy with a cautious attitude toward social change and some reverence for the past.

What we have called Anglo-American conservatism can be explained only in terms of the relative stability of North Atlantic society in the last two centuries. Cautious change and deference to the past can scarcely work in revolutionary circumstances, where change is so rapid that there is no continuity of tradition to guide present behaviour. One speculative explanation of the viability of Anglo-American conservatism is that England and its colonies are in fact the oldest modern societies, having undergone their modernizing revolution in the seventeenth century. A parallel transition from traditional to legal authority was delayed in France until 1789, in Russia until 1917, and is only now taking place in much of the Third World. Local forms of conservatism can hardly be very effective in the midst of such momentous transitions but may arise over time as legal authority develops a tradition of its own.

12   Socialism

Like liberalism and conservatism, *socialism* is not a single ideology. We use it as a global concept to include communism, social democracy, anarchism, syndicalism, and other ideologies that have a family resemblance because of certain common characteristics. Four of these are particularly important: planning, public ownership, equality of condition, and selflessness. We state them here in unqualified form, although it will become obvious that the several socialist schools accept them in varying degrees.

PLANNING
Socialists repudiate the market economy and wish to replace it with a planned economy, believing that society can emancipate itself from impersonal market processes and take conscious control of its economic affairs, deliberately planning them to maximize human happiness.

PUBLIC OWNERSHIP
Socialists dislike private ownership of productive property, such as land, factories, and stores, and means of transportation and communication. They believe such assets should be owned by the community, supposing that the benefits will then flow to all, not just to a restricted circle of private owners.

EQUALITY OF CONDITION
Socialists aspire to a high degree of equality of condition. While recognizing that people cannot be literally equal in all respects, they believe that much can be done to reduce major inequalities of wealth, income, social position, and political power. They see the planned economy and common ownership, though not desirable solely on grounds of equality, as important means to this end.

SELFLESSNESS
Socialists usually regard selfishness not as an innate human characteristic, but as a result of living in flawed social institutions. They are convinced that appropriate social change can produce new generations of people who are less selfish and more concerned about the welfare of others. This overall change in human behaviour will result from, and at the same time support, the first three objectives.

The biggest source of disagreement among socialists is the political question of obtaining and maintaining the power necessary to effect such changes in society. Almost every conceivable strategy has been canvassed: rational persuasion, teaching by the example of a working commune, winning democratic elections, a general strike of organized labour, insurrection of armed workers in major cities, and protracted guerrilla warfare among a rural population. We will explore these political questions during a historical sketch of the socialist family tree.

Common ownership of property is an ancient topic of philosophical speculation. Plato's *Republic* (ca. 380 B.C.) portrayed a *polis* in which the intellectual and military classes would share property and wives, although the ordinary people would continue to have private property and families. Thomas More's *Utopia* (1516) went further and extended common property to an entire society, but it was a satire on the England of More's day, not a serious proposal for implementation. Other philosophers toyed with socialism from time to time, but it was not viewed as a realistic project until the nineteenth century.

There is also a long religious history to socialism. The Acts of the Apostles report that in the first Christian community of Jerusalem, "the whole body of believers was united in heart and soul. Not a man of them claimed any of his possessions as his own, but everything was held in common."[52] Ananias and his wife Sapphira were struck dead by God for holding back on their contribution and lying to the community about it. Community of goods has repeatedly been reintroduced by Christian sects, particularly those who believe that the Second Coming of Christ to earth is imminent. The selfishness of private property does not seem to fit well with the Kingdom of the Saints. In Canada today, this kind of Christian socialism is practised by the Hutterites, who collectively own and operate large farms in the Western provinces. But our interest is in socialism as a secular, political ideology, not as part of religious doctrine.

Like so much else in modern politics, secular, political socialism made its debut during the French Revolution. A journalist named François Noël Babeuf organized an abortive communist uprising in 1796.[53] Its practical significance at the time was nil—the plot was broken up by the police, and Babeuf was sentenced to death. But the events, and particularly the speech Babeuf made at his trial, begin the story that leads to Marx, Lenin, and the socialist revolutions of our time.

Babeuf's goal was a short, successful insurrection in Paris on the model of several that had been attempted since 1789. Having seized the French state at the centre, he would institute a provisional government to crush the enemies of the people. Confiscating private property would lead to a "Grand National Economy." The market system of allocation would be replaced by a central storehouse where goods would be deposited, stored, and distributed to all as needed:

> It will be composed of all in complete equality—all rich, all poor, all free, all brothers. The first law will be a ban on private property. We will deposit the fruits of our toil in the public stores. This will be the wealth of the state and the property of all. Every year the heads of families will select stewards whose task will be the distribution of goods to each in accordance with his needs, the allotment of tasks to be performed by each, and the maintenance of public order.[54]

Babeuf did not desire or expect this system to create great wealth. He quoted with approval the words of Rousseau that "all luxury is superfluous—everything is superfluous above and beyond the sheerest of physical necessities."[55] To ensure that luxury did not creep into this Spartan society, money and foreign trade would be banned.

Babeuf's conspiratorial and insurrectionary approach survived his death, and it was complemented in the first decades of the nineteenth century by the *utopian socialism* of writers like Robert Owen (1771–1858) and Charles Fourier (1772–1837). They proposed not to seize the state by force but to teach by example, to found small-scale communities in which productive property would be jointly owned, all would share the necessary labour, and living standards would be more or less equalized. Unlike Babeuf, they did not seek to impose a regime of universal poverty; they believed that their communes would allow everyone to enjoy the luxuries previously reserved for the rich. Literally hundreds of these communes, based on various models, have been tried in practice, and some are quite famous, such as New Harmony, Indiana, run by Robert Owen, and Brook Farm, Massachusetts, modelled on the ideas of Fourier.[56] The utopian strategy of showing the world the merits of socialism on a small scale has not been fully successful, but neither has it been without effect. The Israeli kibbutz, for instance, is a lineal descendant of these early experiments.

The ideology of socialism was given classic formulation by Karl Marx (1818–1883) and Friedrich Engels (1820–1895). Their greatest innovation was transforming socialism into the doctrine of a single class—the industrial working class—which they renamed the *proletariat*. They mocked their predecessors as "utopian" for having aimed at the betterment of humanity by appealing to its reason. For Marx and Engels, socialism could be created only by the political victory of the working class. The proletariat was the "universal class" and embodied the future hopes of humanity; its political struggle would furnish the "material weapons" of socialist philosophy.[57]

Marx's emphasis on the working class gives an impression that for him the central issues were poverty, equality, and standard of living; but discovery of certain unpublished manuscripts of his youth has put the matter in a different light. "An enforced increase in wages," wrote Marx in 1843, "would be nothing more than a *better remuneration of slaves*, and would not restore, either to the worker or to the work, their human significance and worth."[58] The true issue was what Marx called *alienation*. A market system, he argued, reverses the right order of human priorities. Work, which ought to be people's highest activity, the expression of their creative powers, becomes merely a means of keeping themselves alive. Instead of valuing human activity for its own sake, people are driven to become acquisitive, storing up purchasing power. They lose control over what they produce as their products are bought and sold on the market. Property owners are equally dehumanized, even if they escape the impoverished condition of the proletariat.

The social alienation between owners ("*bourgeoisie*" in Marx's vocabulary) and workers was only one aspect of the larger alienation of all people from their human essence. Of course, that did not make class differentials less odious, and Marx depicted them with all his rhetorical power:

> Labour certainly produces marvels for the rich but it produces privation for the worker. It produces palaces, but hovels for the worker. It produces beauty, but deformity for the worker. It replaces labour by machinery, but it casts some of the workers back into a barbarous kind of work and turns the others into machines. It produces intelligence, but also stupidity and cretinism for the workers.[59]

Marx offered not only a moralistic critique of society but also an analysis of the course of history. He wanted to show not that capitalism ought to be destroyed but that it would destroy itself through its internal contradictions. Marx and Engels called their doctrine *scientific socialism* because they thought it was not just a morally attractive alternative, but a guide to what was bound to happen. Most of their writings do not deal with socialism at all; rather, they analyze the capitalist or market system to find the mechanism of its self-destruction. The class-divided market society would, by the victory of the proletariat in the class struggle, give way to a classless society. When property was collectively owned, there would no longer be a meaningful distinction between proletarians, who live by selling their labour, and bourgeois owners of industry, who become wealthy by employing labour.

Although the subject is much too complex for such a brief exposition, the main lines of the capitalist breakdown according to Marx can be briefly drawn.[60] One salient fact was the polarization of society. Capitalism would create a large working class who would be the "gravediggers" of the system. According to Marxian economics, the proletariat was doomed to impoverishment, maybe not in absolute terms, but at least in comparison with the rapidly increasing affluence of the bourgeoisie. The working class, led by socialist intellectuals such as Marx himself, would eventually seize the state and use it to abolish capitalism. Ironically, when the proletariat came to power, it would find that the system had already virtually abolished itself. The market process would have generated industrial monopolies, as only a few giant firms would have survived the rigours of competition. Without many competitors, the market would not work, even on its own terms. The new proletarian state would simply have to confiscate these monopolies from their bourgeois owners and set them to work under central planning.

Marx thought the uprising of the working class would probably come at the bottom of the business cycle, when unemployment, with all its attendant distress, was high among the proletariat. He had several reasons for thinking that these cycles could not be avoided. He drew from earlier economists speculations about the long-term tendency of the rate of profit to fall and added to it some rather inchoate ideas about overproduction. The full train of reasoning is too technical to pursue, but the conclusion is relevant: capitalism would destroy itself in a great crash.

Marx held that the ultimate victory of socialism was certain but not automatic; it required a deliberate political struggle. Marx proposed, and helped to bring about, the representation of the working class by organized political parties. He saw two means by which the workers' party could come to power: evolution or revolution. In constitutional states with a parliamentary system, the workers might struggle for the universal franchise. Once the vote was achieved for all, socialists could expect to be elected to power, for the proletariat would be a majority of society. Socialism would be a natural outgrowth of democracy. Simultaneously, Marx also proposed a revolutionary seizure of power, particularly where constitutionalism and the rule of law did not exist. In this he was influenced by the insurrectionary tradition stemming from Babeuf. Such a rising would produce a workers' government, the *dictatorship of the proletariat*. In a situation equivalent to civil war, the proletarian dictatorship would have to ignore the niceties of the rule of law, at least until its power was secure. This dual approach to gaining power was to prove fateful for the subsequent history of socialism. The two approaches, united in Marx, would ultimately split apart into separate and mutually antagonistic socialist movements.

Curiously, neither Marx nor Engels wrote much about socialism itself. What one mostly finds in their writings are theoretical passages such as the following:

> With the seizing of the means of production by society, production of commodities is done away with, and, simultaneously, the mastery of the product over the producer. Anarchy in social production is replaced by systematic, definite organisation. The struggle for individual existence disappears. Then for the first time man, in a certain sense, is finally marked off from the rest of the animal kingdom, and emerges from mere animal conditions of existence into really human ones. The whole sphere of the conditions of life which environ man, and which have hitherto ruled man, now comes under the dominion and control of man, who for the first time becomes the real, conscious lord of Nature, because he has now become master of his own social organisation. The laws of his own social action, hitherto standing face to face with man as laws of Nature foreign to, and dominating him, will then be used with full understanding, and so mastered by him. Man's own social organisation, hitherto confronting him as a necessity imposed by Nature and history, now becomes the result of his own free action. The extraneous objective forces that have hitherto governed history pass under the control of man himself. Only from that time will man himself, more and more consciously, make his own history—only from that time will the social causes set in movement by him have, in the main and in a constantly growing measure, the results intended by him. It is the ascent of man from the kingdom of necessity to the kingdom of freedom.[61]

From this we learn that man will attain true freedom by emancipating himself from natural and social constraints and taking over his own destiny, but we do not see the mundane details of a socialist state and society.

Some scattered passages from Marx and Engels give a rough idea of their views about what would happen after the workers came to power. Initially, there would have to be a transitional period in which the state gained control of property and put itself in a position to plan the whole economy. It is striking to read the list of transitional measures given in the *Communist Manifesto* (1848) and reflect that several of them have already been implemented, even by liberal or conservative governments:

1. Abolition of property in land and application of all rents of land to public purposes.
2. A heavy progressive or graduated income tax.
3. Abolition of all right of inheritance.
4. Confiscation of the property of all emigrants and rebels.
5. Centralization of credit in the hands of the State, by means of a national bank with State capital and an exclusive monopoly.
6. Centralization of the means of communication and transport in the hands of the State.
7. Extension of factories and instruments of production owned by the State; the bringing into cultivation of wastelands, and the improvement of the soil generally in accordance with a common plan.
8. Equal liability to all to labour. Establishment of industrial armies, especially for agriculture.
9. Combination of agriculture with manufacturing industries; gradual abolition of the distinction between town and country, by a more equable distribution of the population over the country.
10. Free education for all children in public schools. Abolition of children's factory labour in its present form. Combination of education with industrial production, &c., &c.[62]

Accomplishing these and other measures would supposedly make the state master of the economy, able to conduct central planning. But full equality of condition would take a long time to achieve. There would have to be an interim period when equality meant, in effect, "equal pay for equal work." All would be employed by the state, and ownership of property would no longer allow the wealthy to escape labour. But some would work more effectively and diligently than others, and they would be rewarded for doing so.

Beyond this stage, Marx's prognosis becomes visionary, almost mystical. The state, even though it would have to be large and powerful to conduct central planning, would lose its coercive character. This perhaps makes sense if we accept the premise that human quarrels are fundamentally caused by private property, so that the classless society would not need a state to maintain civil peace. At any rate, it was Marx's view that the state was always the tool by which one class dominated others, so by definition a classless society would be a stateless society. As Engels put it in a biological metaphor, the state would "wither away." Marx preferred to say that the state would be "transcended," that is, that people would learn to conduct their affairs without a centralized apparatus of coercion.

The transcendence of the state was linked to what Marx called the "higher phase of communist society," where "equal work for equal pay" would give way to a nobler form of equality:

> In a higher phase of communist society, after the enslaving subordination of the individual to the division of labor, and therewith also the antithesis between mental and physical labor, has vanished; after labor has become not only a means of life but life's prime want; after the productive forces have also increased with the all-round development of the individual, and all the springs of cooperative wealth flow more abundantly—only then can the narrow horizon of bourgeois right be crossed in its entirety and society inscribe on its banners: "From each according to his ability, to each according to his needs."[63]

At this advanced stage of development, the alienation of labour would finally be transcended. Work would become a freely creative activity performed for its own sake, not to be bought and sold. Men would express themselves in all directions, using their repertoire of human powers; there would be no economic necessity in the "kingdom of freedom" to force them to be narrow specialists. In an almost lyrical passage, Marx and Engels wrote:

> For as soon as the distribution of labour comes into being, each man has a particular, exclusive sphere of activity, which is forced upon him and from which he cannot escape. He is a hunter, a fisherman, a shepherd, or a critical critic, and must remain so if he does not want to lose his means of livelihood; while in communist society, where nobody has one exclusive sphere of activity but each can become accomplished in any branch he wishes, society regulates the general production and thus makes it possible for me to do one thing today and another tomorrow, to hunt in the morning, fish in the afternoon, rear cattle in the evening, criticise after dinner, just as I have a mind, without ever becoming hunter, fisherman, shepherd or critic.[64]

In addition to being theorists, Marx and Engels were political activists who contributed to the political struggle of the working class. Their first organization, the Communist League, is memorable only because the *Communist Manifesto* was written to be its program. More important was the International Workingmen's Association (1864–1872), commonly known as the *First International*, in which Marx and Engels were deeply involved. It was a loose association of socialist parties and labour unions in Western Europe, with headquarters in London. It split into hostile wings in 1872 when old factional differences became too strong to contain. The split was partly a clash of personalities between Marx and the Russian Michael Bakunin, but there was also an important ideological issue. Bakunin and his followers, who have subsequently become known as *anarchists*, thought that Marx was infatuated with the state. They believed the state could be destroyed fairly quickly in the aftermath of the workers' revolution, whereas Marx envisioned a period of state socialism leading up to the true classless society and the higher phase of communism. The anarchists feared, with considerable foresight, that the Marxian socialist state might turn out to be permanent rather than temporary.[65]

Although the First International collapsed, socialist parties continued to exist in various European states. They were reunited, excluding the anarchists, in the *Second International*, founded in Paris in 1889 to celebrate the centennial of the French Revolution.[66] Marx had died in 1883, but Engels was the elder statesman of the new organization, and Marxism was its ideology. With the Second International, socialism came of age in Europe. Socialist and labour parties thrived by following Marx's evolutionary strategy. None ever won a majority in an election, but they succeeded in electing substantial blocs of representatives in all countries where liberal and constitutional values kept politics open. Compromising their principles a bit, some socialist politicians even served as ministers in coalition governments. The Second International kept up a pretence of revolutionary rhetoric, but its political practice was overwhelmingly evolutionary and constitutional.[67]

In the Russian Empire, however, the absence of a parliament and constitution made the evolutionary strategy irrelevant. The Russian Social Democratic party was forced to be illegal, secretive, and conspiratorial. Vladimir Ilyich Lenin (1870–1924), leader of the wing of the party known as the Bolsheviks, was led by these conditions, so different from what Marx and Engels had known in Western Europe, to create a new style and a new theory of party leadership. Marx had expected the revolution to grow from the spontaneous class consciousness of the workers; the role of bourgeois intellectuals was not to create this revolutionary state of mind, but to lend it theoretical precision. Lenin, faced with a backward country and a small working class, tended to think of revolutionary consciousness as something transmitted by bourgeois intellectuals to the workers. This seemingly minor difference implied a new approach to the problems of party organization. The party had to be firmly controlled from the top because the workers' spontaneity could not be fully trusted. Lenin's theory of the disciplined party—*democratic centralism*—moulded it into an effective revolutionary weapon, especially suited to survival in the autocratic Russian setting.[68]

Lenin, incidentally, is associated with another major innovation in socialist ideology. Marx had always insisted that the socialist revolution would be a world revolution. But his view of the world was centred on Western Europe, and he apparently thought that the European nations would drag their empires with them into socialism. With his emphasis on Europe, Marx thought that the revolution would occur soon because capitalism, which was fated to put an end to itself, was well advanced there. Marx certainly expected a proletarian victory in his own lifetime. But when World War I broke out, he had been dead thirty years, and no socialists had come to power anywhere.

Lenin, who spent most of the war in Switzerland, used this period of leisure to write a pamphlet explaining the delay. *Imperialism: The Highest Stage of Capitalism* (1917) argued that the advanced nations had managed to postpone the revolution by amassing colonial empires. Overseas investments counteracted the tendency of the rate of profit to fall, while colonial markets temporarily solved the problem of overproduction. Merciless exploitation of the colonies could buy off the workers at home, creating a "labour aristocracy." But the imperialist solution could only be temporary because the world was finite and was now totally subdivided. World War I showed that the imperialists had begun to quarrel with each other. The socialist revolution would arise not from a business crash, as Marx had been inclined to believe, but out of the turmoil of war. Lenin's view left his revolutionary optimism intact by decisively broadening the scope of socialism from a European to a worldwide movement. "Capitalism," he wrote, "has grown into a world system of colonial oppression and of the financial strangulation of the overwhelming population of the world by a handful of 'advanced' countries."[69]

World War I tolled the death knell for the Second International. Although socialists had prided themselves on their internationalism, national loyalties prevailed in wartime. Most of the workers in the combatant states supported the war effort, effectively pitting the International against itself.

The *coup de grâce* was delivered by the successful socialist revolution in Russia. In February 1917, the Czar was toppled and a constitutional democracy created. In October of the same year, the Bolsheviks, led by Lenin, seized control of the state through insurrections of armed workers in Petrograd and Moscow. The Bolsheviks then created a dictatorship of the proletariat in which their party played the dominant role. Political opposition, even socialist opposition, was outlawed. These events were an agonizing test for the socialists of Western Europe, who had talked about revolution for generations. Now that they were confronted with one, they were appalled by its undemocratic aspects.

The result, after some years of indecision, was an irreparable split in the world socialist movement. Those who approved of Lenin and his methods formed *communist* parties in every country and gathered themselves in the *Third International* or *Comintern*. The official ideology of these parties was now Marxism as modified by Lenin, or Marxism-Leninism. In practice, the Comintern soon became an extension of the Soviet state, useful for foreign policy purposes. It was dissolved in 1943 by Stalin as a gesture of co-operation with the Allies during World War II. The individual communist parties continued and still continue today to be closely tied to Moscow, but the emphasis of organizations has shifted to the Soviet satellite states. In 1947 these were bound together into the *Cominform* (Communist Information Bureau), which in turn was replaced with the Warsaw Treaty Organization in 1956. Communist parties outside the satellite states are not as closely tied to the Soviet Union and occasionally disagree with Moscow over specific issues, such as Soviet military intervention in Hungary (1956), Czechoslovakia (1968), and Afghanistan (1979).

Those who opposed Lenin regrouped under the general name of *social democrats*. The parties still exist as the Labour party of Great Britain, Social Democratic party of Germany, and so on. Politically, they have kept to the course of constitutionalism and are well integrated into the political system. They form governments when they win elections and resign from office when they lose. Socialism, in the form of social democracy, is a familiar part of contemporary politics. The ideology has over decades become considerably diluted in comparison to the original Marxian version, so that social democrats today are hard to distinguish from reform liberals. Both espouse, to a limited degree, the typical socialist goals of central planning, common ownership, and equality of condition. Social democrats call for government to guide the economy through measures of spending, taxation, and regulation but not to replace the market by comprehensive planning. They wish some major enterprises to be publicly owned but do not advocate wholesale nationalization of all business. They approve of redistribution of income in the direction of social justice but not thoroughgoing, egalitarian levelling.

Several small socialist parties existed in Canada before the great split between communists and social democrats, but none was ever very significant. The first important party of the social democratic type was the Co-operative Commonwealth Federation (CCF), founded in Calgary in 1932. It drew together remnants of the old socialist parties, select trade unionists and farmer activists, and certain intellectuals who had been educated in Britain or influenced by British socialist thought. The party's first major program was the Regina Manifesto, adopted in 1933. It repudiated "change by violence" and promised to promote the socialist cause "solely by constitutional methods." Although the means would be peaceful, the end was declared to be far-reaching:

> We aim to replace the present capitalist system, with its inherent injustice and inhumanity, by a social order from which the domination and exploitation of one class by another will be eliminated, in which economic planning will supersede unregulated private enterprise and competition, and in which genuine democratic self-government, based upon economic equality will be possible. . . . We aim at a planned and socialized economy in which our natural resources and the principal means of production and distribution are owned, controlled and operated by the people.[70]

The CCF achieved some political successes, most notably the election of the first socialist government in North America in Saskatchewan in 1944, but its electoral support was badly eroded during the 1950s. In 1961 it converted itself into the New Democratic party with a much stronger tie to organized labour. Tellingly, the word socialism was not to be found in the New Party Declaration it adopted.[71] As in other countries, social democracy in Canada had relaxed its ideology considerably since the Depression. It presented itself no longer as a full alternative to the market system, but rather as a means of using the state as a reforming agency.

In certain ways, the history of socialism has turned out almost the opposite of the expectations of Marx, who saw socialism as the successor to capitalism. He had a grudging admiration for the market system as a means of accumulating wealth but regarded it as a temporary phase of human development. Socialism, he thought, would be able to make much more humane use of the productive powers unleashed by capitalism. But in fact, socialism has been least successful in just those countries that have been most capitalistic and, on Marx's grounds, most ready for socialism. In the industrialized countries, socialism has been effective chiefly in the attenuated form of social democracy, where it represents a reformist impulse within the system, not a polar alternative. The stronger form of communism came to power in the economically backward Russian Empire, and the Soviet Union has imposed it by force on the less advanced nations of Eastern Europe. Authentic communist revolutions, not the result of Soviet initiative, have also taken place in Yugoslavia, China, and Vietnam. The latter two are almost the opposite of what Marx had in mind: they are pre-industrial societies in which the capitalist system never got fairly started.

Very generally, we can see that socialism has become not the successor to liberalism, but an alternative to liberalism as a modernizing force. Socialism has found its greatest success in societies that began but did not make a complete transition from traditional to legal authority. Quite apart from the communist states, a large portion of the Third World claims to be socialist. Algeria, Syria, Iraq, Tanzania, India, Nicaragua: the list could be much longer. One source of social-ism's popularity in the Third World is that because it is anticapitalist, it can be used as an ideological weapon against the Western powers. Also, great disparities of wealth typical of many traditional societies seem to cry out for state-initiated redistribution. Common ownership and central planning have great appeal in societies where large portions of cultivable land are held by a few individuals and where great disparities of wealth exist between the landed and the masses who work the land. Most profoundly, there is a certain congruence between socialist collectivism and the communal institutions that still exist in much of the Third World. This view has been most clearly formulated by Julius Nyerere, president of Tanzania, who is a leading theorist of Third World socialism. Nyerere translates the word socialism into Swahili as *ujamaa*, which means literally "familyhood." He claims that in Tanzania, where society is still largely tribal, a socialist state can grow organically out of the family and tribe:

> Traditional Tanzanian society had many socialist characteristics. The people did not call themselves socialists, and they were not socialists by deliberate

design. But all people were workers, there was no living off the sweat of others. There was no very great difference in the amount of goods available to the different members of the society . . . traditional African society was in practice organized on a basis which was in accordance with socialist principles.[72]

Nyerere has enjoyed great prestige in the Western world, and Western governments have contributed remarkable amounts of aid to Tanzania to help this experiment in Third World socialism succeed. But in spite of foreign assistance, Tanzania has not achieved financial stability, and Nyerere is now talking about placing greater reliance on the market principle.

After this historical discussion, let us return to an analysis of the main ideas of socialism.

PLANNING

To varying degrees, socialists are generally hostile to the market, condemning it as anarchic, inefficient, and inequitable. They particularly condemn the pursuit of profit; in the words of the Regina Manifesto, the principle of a socialist society "will be the supplying of human needs and not the making of profits."[73] This formulation unfortunately obscures the problem. Profit in the market system is not antithetical to need; it is rather the means by which needs are met. The fact that people need food, clothing, shelter, and recreation and are willing to pay for them induces entrepreneurs to seek a profit by offering these goods for sale. The question is not need versus profit, but what is the most effective means of discovering and satisfying human needs. Is it the market system, with competition, floating prices, and the profit motive? Or is it a *planning* system, in which a central authority decides what to produce and allocates production to consumers?

Without claiming that the market is a perfect system, it can be said that it does demonstrably perform the job of matching production and consumption across a large number of commodities. Early socialists were quite naive about how difficult this task is. Babeuf's central storehouses could scarcely have coped with the problem; but he probably would not have cared because he wanted everyone to live in Spartan simplicity. Marx simply ignored the problem by refusing to speculate on the concrete features of a socialist society. After much painful trial and error, the Soviet Union and other socialist states have worked out a state planning machinery that is actually a hybrid between the planning principle and the market principle. The State Planning Committee, as it is called in the USSR, produces and continuously updates a national plan that specifies production quantities in the various industries: tons of coal and steel of various grades, kilowatt hours of electricity, barrels of oil, bushels of wheat, and so on. One industry supplies another as part of this plan rather than by market auction. The state uses the market to relate the industrial complex to the inhabitants of the country, who purchase the output at state-owned retail stores and sell their labour to the state as employer. Through this partial use of markets, the state refrains from trying to directly control the daily affairs of hundreds of millions of people.

These markets, however, are heavily controlled by the state. The labour market is restricted by lack of mobility: a worker on a collective farm, for example, is not legally free to leave the farm and seek work in a city. Also, prices for labour and consumer goods do not float according to supply and demand but are administered by the state. As might be expected, this leads to the shortages and surpluses of commodities that are frequent in the Soviet Union, as in all planned economies. When price is not used to ration scarce commodities, other forms of rationing must be used. One is direct assignment by authority, which distributes housing. The other is queuing. The ability to spend time waiting replaces the ability to spend money as a means of acquiring goods. Those with more money than time frequently resort to bribery and black markets.

State planners in Eastern Europe are very much aware of the difficulties of their system and would like to ameliorate them. Reform proposals that are suggested and sometimes adopted almost always amount to an extension of the market principle or at least decentralization of bureaucratic authority. Among Soviet satellites in Europe, Hungary has gone the furthest toward adopting market-inspired reforms.

Developments in the People's Republic of China after the death of Mao Zedong (1976) have also been significant. Once Deng Xiaoping gathered power securely into his hands, he launched a series of major economic changes. Foreign investment is now encouraged in certain "economic zones." Multinational companies are exploring for oil, while Western manufacturers are using the cheap labour of the People's Republic. State-owned enterprises have been given more latitude to decide what to produce, price the output, and hire and fire personnel. Rationing is being replaced by market sale as a way of distributing consumer goods. Perhaps most important in a country that is still overwhelmingly agricultural, the rural communes are being decentralized. Many decisions about what to grow are now made by teams or even individual households rather than the communal authorities.[74]

A much greater retreat from full-scale planning has taken place among social democrats in the Western world. In 1935 *Social Planning for Canada*, written by the leading intellectuals of the CCF, called for a National Planning Commission modelled on the Soviet example.[75] Today neither the NDP nor other social democratic parties advocate full-scale planning. Instead, they see the state as a means for guiding the market toward particular objectives, such as full employment, locating industry in depressed areas, advancing racial minorities, and energy self-sufficiency. To attain these goals, the state may employ a set of interventionist tools: taxation, subsidies, monopoly concessions, regulatory legislation, price controls, interest rates, and so on. A program of such interventions is sometimes referred to as a plan, but it is not planning in the original sense of the term or even planning as it now exists in the communist states.

PUBLIC OWNERSHIP

Except in time of war or other emergency, central planning cannot work without a high degree of public ownership. Presumably, the central plan requires investment decisions other than those that private owners would spontaneously make; otherwise, there would be no need for the plan. Implementing the plan requires coercive threats against owners to make sure they do as instructed. If a whole new class of potential criminals is not to be created, it seems more reasonable for productive property to be publicly owned, thus obviating conflicts between the plan and property rights.

Common ownership can be achieved in a number of ways. In the Third World it can be built directly onto existing communal traditions. If a peasant village already holds grazing, timber, or water rights in common, collective ownership of the surrounding arable land may not be a drastic step. Another approach to common ownership is the voluntary co-operative, which lends itself to organizing either producers or consumers. A great many co-operatives—credit unions, wheat pools, housing co-ops—already exist in Canada, where they function as part of the market economy, but they could also be integrated into a socialist economy. Another possibility is for the workers themselves to own their factory or other workplace. A variant of socialism known as *syndicalism* (from the French *syndicat*, "association") takes this approach. A fully syndicalist economy has never been tried, but there are elements of syndicalism in the Yugoslavian version of socialism, where workers' councils have some say in the running of enterprises. Although these options are interesting and important, common ownership in the mainstream of socialism has meant state ownership. Socialization or *nationalization* of property has implied a takeover by the state, which owns and administers it as agent of the people. This ownership can be direct, as in the case of the Canadian armed forces, which are operated as a government department under ministerial supervision, or indirect, as in the case of Air Canada and Canadian National Railways, which are Crown corporations owned by the state but operating more or less autonomously under a board of directors.

The Soviet Union represents state ownership carried out consistently. The state owns all factories, railways, retail stores, publishing houses, schools, hospitals, and so forth. It also owns all natural resources and all land, which it may lease to projects such as collective farms or housing co-operatives. Private ownership is almost wholly confined to consumer goods. Some other communist states have not gone quite this far. In Poland there is still an independent peasantry, as most farm land has never been nationalized. But the general principle of state ownership is dominant in Eastern Europe, China, North Korea, Vietnam, and Cuba. However, where market-inspired reforms have been introduced, as in Hungary and China, private ownership of small enterprises such as restaurants, boutiques, and personal service businesses is sometimes allowed.

Social democracy retreated long ago from a commitment to complete nationalization. The Regina Manifesto, while exempting farms from public ownership, called for nationalization of the entire financial industry, transportation, communications, electric power, "and all other industries and services essential to social planning."[76] These latter would have included many firms in primary industries. The logic of the list was that these industries represented "the commanding heights of the economy."[77] All other businesses, whether in manufacturing, wholesaling, retailing, or personal services, need access to credit, transportation, communications, energy, and natural resources. If government owned and controlled these indispensable industries, it would be able to compel or induce other industries to work toward politically chosen goals. Manufacturing firms, for example, could be lured to locate in depressed areas by offers of low-interest loans or cheap transportation.

EQUALITY OF CONDITION

One of the attractive goals of socialism has been to reduce the material inequality that is part of a market economy. This inequality is unseemly to socialists, and they have sought to overcome it through a planned economy and public ownership of property. However, it is easy to call for equality of condition but much harder to state precisely what it means. We differ so much in our aptitudes, needs, and desires that it would be absurd to say that we should all have the same number of shoes or the same number of square metres of housing.

One approach, which was discussed in Chapter 10, is equality of opportunity: using the state to make sure that everyone can have certain chances in life but allowing individuals to keep the rewards of their own efforts. This social democratic idea, now widely accepted by reform liberals, fits in well with the contemporary welfare state, which is supposed to educate us as children and protect us against contingencies as adults. Its "landing net" will allow us to bounce back from sickness, accident, or unemployment but will not in itself guarantee a very desirable standard of living. We have to achieve that on our own initiative.

A related approach to equality is to reduce the range of inequality by raising the floor and lowering the ceiling. Extremes of wealth and poverty would vanish, but some variation would still remain. This partial egalitarianism is widely accepted today, not just by socialists but also by reform liberals and many others who have no definable ideology. It can be attempted as an intervention in the market system by progressive taxation, redistribution, and the abundant services of the welfare state. Or, in the Soviet style of planned economy, it can be done by setting wages and salaries on an egalitarian basis.

Yet the whole business is not as straightforward as it seems. Progressive taxation, if pushed too far, may become a disincentive to productivity because more effort may be spent avoiding taxes than competing effectively in the marketplace. The progressive income tax seems to have reached a ceiling in most Western countries, but the Soviet model has pitfalls of its own. By some statistical indices, the communist states seem to have equalized living standards remarkably; published data on incomes show smaller differentials between manual workers and professionals than exist in the West; and of course, large pools of capital in private hands have been abolished. However, statistics do not tell the whole story because communist systems have significant forms of non-monetary privilege. High officials of the Communist party, as well as leading scientists, athletes, managers, and artists, have access to special housing and shopping, can often avoid waiting lists for things such as automobiles, and receive the privilege of foreign travel.[78]

The most provocative analysis of this inequality comes from the Yugoslav communist Milovan Djilas. Once a high official in party and state, he has become ideologically like a social democrat. He has argued that communism as practised in Eastern Europe is the very opposite of a classless society.[79] Its essence is that a "new class" of party officials and managers has created a privileged position for itself, stemming not from owning property, but from dominating the state.

The ultimate in equality is still the Marxian slogan, "From each according to his ability, to each according to his needs." This noble sentiment expresses the operating principle of a happy family, where parents can assess the needs and abilities of their children—but could an entire society of adults be like one family? If we let people assess their own needs and contributions, it is likely that the former will be estimated on the high side and the latter on the low. It seems hard to avoid the need for a central authority to decide such questions (as, indeed, parents are almost all-powerful in relation to their children). But if this is true, it casts serious doubt on the withering away of the state, something that is also supposed to occur in the highest stage of communism. Who except those who run the state could adjudicate the disputes about abilities and needs that would arise under Marx's famous slogan?

SELFLESSNESS

The discussion in the preceding paragraph assumes that human behaviour will remain self-interested. The situation would be different if selfishness were caused only by the effects of a market economy, which encourages people to put their own interests first. Socialists have often assumed that whereas conflict is typical of capitalism, co-operation would be typical of a socialist system. However, to oppose co-operation to conflict is a little misleading. Spontaneous order depends upon co-operation voluntarily achieved through mutual pursuit of self-interest. A planned economy calls for co-operation directed from above. The important question is not whether we should have co-operation, for obviously we must; it is whether mutual co-ordination or authoritative direction is a more effective means of achieving it.[80] One does not have to accept the philosophically questionable doctrine of a fixed human nature to realize that there is an enormous inertia in society consisting of customs, traditions, and usages inherited from the past. Both genetic evolution and cultural change are aspects of human existence, and neither takes place according to governmental timetables.[81]

Furthermore, it is debatable whether human behaviour can be so easily altered by a change in government. In contrast to socialism, both liberalism and conservatism accept human beings as they are, with all their flaws, and seek to understand the resulting social order. They assume that society is, and will always be, composed of different groups in conflict with one another. The most they hope to do is contain that conflict within a peaceful framework, not abolish it altogether. To the extent that socialists in the twentieth century have retreated from some of their earlier and more visionary expectations about planning, public ownership, and equality, they have also become pessimistic about an easy, quick change in human tendencies.

GOVERNING

We have sufficiently discussed the differences between communists and social democrats in their approach to obtaining power. The distinction between constitutional and unconstitutional means also carries through to governing the socialist state. Social democrats in their rapprochement with liberalism have adopted the constitutional philosophy of the limited state and the rule of law, which was originally a liberal creation. Communists use constitutionalism as a means of achieving power but have not demonstrated any abiding attachment to it. And indeed, the Leninist principle of democratic centralism, when made the working theory of the state, seems incompatible with liberal constitutionalism.

Communist states are more than mere absolute or unlimited governments, of which the world has seen many, because central planning and state ownership of the means of production put the entire economy at the disposal of the government. This produces such an unparallelled concentration of power that a new term, totalitarian, has had to be invented to describe the resultant system (see Chapter 17). This expansion of the state has posed thorny problems for the ideologists of Marxism-Leninism. Marx's dictatorship of the proletariat was, to be sure, an absolute, unlimited government, but it was clearly a transitional device, even if Marx did not say how long it would last. Marx, a classically educated man, adopted the term dictatorship from the Roman *dictator*, who was appointed for six months at a time to guide the state through emergencies. The dictatorship of the proletariat was supposed to preside over the dissolution of social classes and thus make itself unnecessary; a permanent dictatorship of the proletariat would be a contradiction in terms.[82]

Soviet thinkers now maintain that the Soviet state is "a state of the whole people." In the words of Nikita Khrushchev to the twenty-second Congress of the Communist party of the Soviet Union (1961):

> With the victory of socialism and the country's entry into the period of full-scale communist construction, the working class of the Soviet Union has on its own initiative, consistent with the tasks of communist construction, transformed the state of proletarian dictatorship into a state of the whole people. That, comrades, is a fact unparalleled in history! Until now the state

has always been an instrument of dictatorship by this or that class. In our country, for the first time in history, a state has taken shape which is not a dictatorship of any one class, but an instrument of society as a whole, of the entire people.[83]

This solves one problem but creates another because it contradicts Marx's view that all states are means by which one class rules over others. Ideology cannot conceal the fact: contrary to the expressed intentions of the early socialists, implementing their ideology has exalted, not abolished, the state.

13   Nationalism

The nation, it will be remembered, is the specific type of political community that evolved from feudal Europe and now exists in the modern world. The decline of universal institutions—Catholic church and Holy Roman Empire—coupled with the erosion of parochial or regional loyalties to manor, village, city, or province, produced large aggregates of people sharing a common identity. The nation, having arisen in Western Europe, has now become the model of community for the rest of the world as well.

Nationalism, at the level of emotion, is a feeling of loyalty to the nation, a recognition of ties with other members of the group. The pride Canadians feel when a Canadian wins a medal at the Olympics or the sense of recognition that Canadians experience when they happen to meet in a foreign land are manifestations of nationalism. Writing about the *polis*, Aristotle said that "friendship . . . seems to hold states together."[84] Nationalism is the equivalent of friendship in communities that are so large that we can never actually know more than a tiny proportion of the other members. A common identity in the nation helps us care about people with whom we are unacquainted.

These experiences of identity and loyalty are fostered by a sort of national mythology, stories about the common history and destiny of the nation. The model for such national myths is the historical self-awareness of the Hebrews, who might be taken as the prototype of all nations. Their understanding of themselves as a Chosen People, endowed by God with a mission to perform for the betterment of humanity, recurs in the myths by which other nations justify their existence. Nations do not have a single myth or story, but rather a complex mythology or set of stories existing at several levels from folklore up to deliberate creations of intellectuals writing history in order to further national consciousness.

A fine example of the latter is the book by Monseigneur Laflèche, Bishop of Trois-Rivières, *Quelques Considérations sur les rapports de la société civile avec la religion et la famille* (1866). Laflèche wrote that "Providence has allotted each and every nation its own mission to fulfil."[85] The French-Canadian people were a nation among the human family of nations, with their homeland in the valley of the St. Lawrence. Their special calling was

> basically religious in nature: it is, namely, to convert the unfortunate infidel local population to Catholicism, and to expand the Kingdom of God by developing a predominantly Catholic nationality.[86]

Laflèche's sketch of the history of French Canada emphasized missionary work among the Indians. Now that that period was largely past, the new calling was to be a devout Catholic enclave in Protestant North America, setting an example that might lead others to Rome. Catholic faith would be reinforced by adhering to the French language. The whole ideology is well suited to preserving the identity of a minority by intertwining their language, religion, and customs into a protective whole.

Laflèche did not create French-Canadian nationalism; rather, he articulated historical symbols to express more clearly what the people already felt. His myth entered the wider mythology to which many other writers also contributed. Of course, the mythology changes over time. Today the religious formulation of Laflèche would not express very well the aspirations of French-Canadian nationalists, who are more likely to speak about the unique value of their culture. But the underlying idea is still the same—that the nation has a special role to play in the drama of human history.

The national mythology of English Canada is much more diffuse than that of French Canada because the community itself is less well defined. English-speaking Canada is not a single entity, but an alliance of several communities founded in different circumstances. Massive immigration has further complicated an already complex situation. However, one continuing theme in the interpretations Canadians give of the meaning of their collective existence is that to be Canadian is not to be American. Initially, of course, there was no Canada and no Canadian identity, only several British colonies in North America sharing the experience of ideological rejection of the American Revolution. Indeed, they were largely populated by the descendants of people who had left the United States in 1776 or shortly thereafter. The union of these separate colonies was impelled less by positive feelings of friendship for one another than by fears that if they remained separate, they would inevitably fall into the orbit of the United States.

Not surprisingly, statements about the meaning of Canada almost always involve a comparison with the United States. In the nineteenth century and much of the twentieth, these comparisons usually interpreted Canada as a more conservative, orderly, and peaceful country than the United States. Common themes of self-congratulation were the superiority of constitutional monarchy over democracy, the British tradition of social deference, an orderly frontier protected by the North West Mounted Police, and generous treatment of Canada's native peoples. Today the topics of comparison are different, but the mental process is much the same.[87] Canadians repeatedly stress that they are fortunate to have less crime than the United States, less racial hostility, a more pristine natural environment, and a smaller burden in international politics. Again, it is obvious that the structure of Canadian national mythology serves to protect the group's distinctiveness by discouraging absorption into a larger neighbour. The logic of the situation compels both English- and French-Canadian national mythologies to be defensive in nature.

The character of American nationalism differs from both Canadian nationalisms. The American national identity rests upon the political ideas that animated the revolution of 1776. Americans have ever since that time interpreted themselves as participants in a social experiment of vast importance to all humanity. They are testing the limits of liberty. As Thomas Jefferson wrote in 1802:

> It is impossible not to be sensible that we are acting for all mankind; that circumstances denied to others, but indulged to us, have imposed on us the duty of proving what is the degree of freedom and self-government in which a society may venture to leave its individual members.[88]

American national mythology plays endlessly on the theme of freedom and interprets everything else in relation to it. Democracy, which was first introduced in the United States, is not just majority rule, and capitalism is not just the organized pursuit of wealth; both are the means by which a free people conducts its affairs. The Declaration of Independence, the constitution, and the Bill of Rights are not just political documents; they are sacred texts for the inspiration of all humanity.

This characteristic of American national mythology perhaps helps explain why American ventures in international politics so often tend to become crusades. Freedom itself is at stake in contests with other nations. Woodrow Wilson brought the United States into World War I "to make the world safe for democracy." Franklin Roosevelt interpreted American participation in World War II in a similar way. The rivalry with the Soviet Union is not just an exercise in power politics; it is the defence of the "free world." These slogans are entirely serious to Americans, even when they amuse or bewilder other nationalities.

The point, of course, is not that one nation's myths are false while another's are true. It is that each nation worthy of the name has a mythology that supports its national identity by lending meaning to its collective history. Without such a source of meaning, the nation, which is ultimately a psychological reality, could not exist. Space has permitted only a brief look at a few examples, but similar myths will be found for all nations.

This means that nationalism is not a single ideology. The details of each nationalism are unique because each nation is unique. However, there are common factors in the structure of belief because the national mythologies serve similar purposes for the various nations. Most broadly, nationalism is "the making of claims in the name, or on behalf, of the nation."[89] The claims commonly take the form of two propositions.

LOYALTY TO THE NATION

Loyalty to the nation should transcend other loyalties, such as allegiance to one's family, region, or ethnic group. The nation is taken to be the primary social group that outranks all others. This presupposition is so deeply entrenched today that we do not often recognize its significance. Why, for example, are economic statistics kept on a national basis? In fact, economic relationships do not necessarily coincide with national sentiments. To say that the unemployment rate in Canada is 11 per cent obscures the fact that in some parts of Alberta it may be 13 per cent and in some parts of Ontario 7 per cent. What the national figures mean is rather unclear, yet they are religiously computed. Similarly, athletes can compete in the Olympic games only as members of a national team; they cannot represent themselves, towns, or sponsoring clubs. Yet sport has intrinsically as little to do with the nation as does economics.

QUEST FOR THE NATION-STATE

The nation and the state should coincide in the nation-state. This is not a universal belief of nationalism. The traditional posture of French-Canadian nationalism, for example, was defence of the French-Canadian nation within the Canadian binational state, which in practice often meant heavy emphasis on provincial autonomy. But the demand for the nation-state tends to recur. Thus French-Canadian nationalism has become separatist since the early 1960s. Interestingly, former premier Lévesque once defended separatism by saying that it was "natural" for a nation to aspire to statehood. The word natural reflects the predominance of the nation-state in contemporary thinking.

Opinion about the inevitability of the nation-state is divided. Because authority depends on legitimacy and freedom on authority, John Stuart Mill argued that a free society is in the long run only possible in a nation-state. He wrote in *Considerations on Representative Government* (1861):

> Free institutions are next to impossible in a country made up of different nationalities. Among a people without fellow-feeling, especially if they read and speak different languages, the united public opinion, necessary to the working of representative government, cannot exist.[90]

Mill feared that one nation would always end up by coercively oppressing others within a multinational state. National antagonism would require such a strong government that individual freedom would be impossible. The contrary opinion was maintained by Mill's younger contemporary, Lord Acton (1834–1902), who wrote that "those states are substantially the most perfect which, like the British and Austrian Empires, include various distinct nationalities without oppressing them."[91] The existence of different nationalities was a positive blessing because it provided a bulwark against too much state domination of society. Smaller nations within the state, fearful that the government would be controlled by the larger nations, would be reluctant to assign too many functions to the central authorities. Things such as education or social insurance programs would tend to remain with local governments or perhaps even in private hands.

Acton's beliefs greatly influenced the political thought of Pierre Trudeau and formed the philosophical basis of his linguistic and constitutional policies, which had the intention of making Canada a pluralistic state in which neither French nor English would feel oppressed by each other. Trudeau's vision of Canada as a culturally pluralistic state was expressed in his often-quoted essay "The New Treason of the Intellectuals":

> Without backsliding to the ridiculous and reactionary idea of national sovereignty, how can we protect our French-Canadian national qualities? . . . We must separate once and for all the concepts of state and of nation, and make of Canada a truly pluralistic and polyethnic society. Now in order for this to come about, the different regions within the country must be assured of a wide range of local autonomy, such that each national group, with an increasing background of experience in self-government, may be able to develop the body of laws and institutions essential to the fullest expression and development of their national characteristics.[92]

These two general concerns of nationalism, loyalty to the nation and the quest for the nation-state, manifest themselves in a bewildering complexity of phenomena. We may at least draw attention to a few of the typical situations in which we speak of nationalism.

1. A tribal, ethnic, or racial minority seeks to establish its credentials as a nation in order to assert itself as a group. Thus the Dene of Canada claim to be the Dene Nation, the Métis call themselves "The New Nation," and Indian bands are now calling themselves "The First Nations." In both these instances, nationalism is joined to a demand for self-government within Canada, not the establishment of a sovereign nation-state.

2. A national minority seeks to separate from the state that now rules it in order to establish a nation-state, as shown by separatist movements in Quebec or among the Welsh and Scots in Great Britain. Sometimes the minority would have to separate from two or more states, such as the Basques, who are now ruled by France and Spain, or the Kurds, who are divided among Turkey, Iraq, Iran, and the Soviet Union.

3. A national majority that controls the government uses its political power to suppress, assimilate, or expel minorities that do not fit the image of the nation-state. In the early 1970s, the African states of Uganda, Kenya, and Tanzania drove many from among their substantial East Indian minorities to emigrate. They were vilified as alien exploiters who had received from the British colonialists an unfair position of economic advantage.

4. A nation-state lays claim to fragments of territory on its borders on grounds that they constitute a historical part of the nation. The constitution of the Republic of Ireland (Eire) specifically mentions the six counties of Ulster (Northern Ireland) as forming part of its national territory. The government of Ireland does not press its claim by force at the moment, but it hopes that some day, circumstances will bring about the unification of Ireland under its control. Similarly, the preamble to

the 1978 constitution of the People's Republic of China states: "Taiwan is China's Sacred Territory. We are determined to liberate Taiwan and accomplish the great cause of unifying our motherland."[93] The technical name for this sort of claim is *irredentism*.

5. A large and powerful nation creates an empire by imposing itself on its neighbours. German nationalism between the two world wars began with irredentist claims to territory that had once been part of the German Empire but had been taken away at the Treaty of Versailles, such as the Sudetenland in Czechoslovakia. From there it went on to demand *Lebensraum*, "living space," by subjugating the peoples of Eastern Europe, such as Jews, Gypsies, Slavs, and Magyars. Thus nationalism can transcend the nation-state to build a multinational empire under the rule of the dominant nation.

6. The nation-state tries to insulate itself from external influences that are perceived as threatening in some way. This could mean blockading ideas, as in censoring foreign publications or jamming broadcast signals. It could also mean erecting barriers against the movement of goods, such as import quotas or protective tariffs, when they are believed to stimulate production at home. A particularly important form of nationalism involves the attempts of national governments to exert control over multinational corporations operating within their boundaries. The National Energy Program announced by the government of Canada in the fall of 1980 is a case in point. It was supposed to allow Canadians to "seize control of their own energy future through security of supply and ultimate independence from the world oil market."[94] Canadian-owned companies were to be given preference over foreign-owned firms. The state oil company, Petro Canada, was to acquire one and probably more of the Canadian subsidiaries of multinational firms. The government was to play a more active role in guiding the industry toward what are alleged to be Canadian purposes. These were strong measures by Canadian standards, although they did not approach steps often taken elsewhere, such as confiscating corporate assets without compensation. The rule of law in a fundamentally liberal country such as Canada puts very real obstacles in the path of economic nationalism.

This last point brings up the relationship of nationalism to other ideologies. History shows that one can be a nationalist while simultaneously being liberal, conservative, or socialist. The reason is that nationalism has a different fundamental concern than the other three ideologies. They all range about the question of what the role of government in society is, whereas nationalism addresses itself to the question of what the proper limits of the political community are. We can imagine three French nationalists agreeing that France ought to be a sovereign nation-state "une et indivisible" but adhering otherwise to conservative, liberal, or socialist views about the functions of government. The relationship between nationalism and other ideologies is not merely a matter of random chance but is structured, as

Hans Kohn has shown, according to the course of historical development in the last two centuries.[95]

Initially, nationalism and liberalism seemed to be natural allies. Great Britain, the first modern nation to emerge, was also the home of liberal constitutionalism. The United States, the first "new nation," was constituted in 1776 in a reaffirmation of the principles of the Glorious Revolution. In France the concept of the nation was discovered and proclaimed in 1789 as part of the liberal freedoms enunciated in the Declaration of the Rights of Man and of the Citizen. The political situation in the first half of the nineteenth century strengthened the assumption that nationalism and liberalism were two sides of the same coin. Nationalism meant chiefly the liberation of small European nations from rule by large empires: the Irish from the British Empire, the Czechs from the Austro-Hungarian Empire, the Greeks from the Ottoman Empire, the Poles and Finns from the Russian Empire. With the notable exception of Britain, these empires were based on traditional authority, not on legal constitutionalism. Those who struggled for national emancipation had to struggle at the same time for liberal goals, such as elected parliaments, freedom of the press, and religious toleration. It was assumed that the peoples of the earth, once liberated from alien rule, would compose a family of nations living peacefully and freely side by side.

The alliance between liberalism and nationalism reached its peak in 1848, when there was a wave of attempted revolutions across Europe, all having the same goal of creating liberally governed nation-states. But the empires were able to reassert themselves, not least by playing off the different nationalities against each other, and the liberal nationalist dream did not become reality.

Liberal nationalism continued to exist after 1848, but it was increasingly displaced by a more militaristic, state-oriented kind of nationalism. The national unification of Italy and Germany, long a goal of liberal nationalism, was achieved in 1861 and 1871 respectively less by liberal methods of voluntary agreement than by military conquest. The new nation-states almost immediately began acquiring colonial empires, especially in Africa, where Britain and France, which had long possessed overseas empires, also joined in. Even the United States, which had always been critical of European imperialism, acquired overseas colonies—Puerto Rico, Cuba, the Philippines—in a war with Spain (1898). By the end of the nineteenth century, nationalism had come to imply much less the liberation of small nations than the imperial aggrandizement of powerful ones. Numerous writers extolled the virtues of military service and loyalty to the state. This was also the period when racial theories became allied with nationalism. Writers of the various large nations justified their policies of imperial expansion by claiming biological superiority for Anglo-Saxons, French, or Germans. The "coloured races" had to be ruled for their own good as well as that of humanity in general.

Anti-Semitism also became a political factor during this period. Jews, who lived dispersed in many European states, were attacked as alien elements in the national community. The German composer Richard Wagner wrote:

The Jew speaks the language of the nation in whose midst he dwells from generation to generation, but he always speaks it as an alien. . . . Our whole European art and civilization, however, have remained to the Jew as a foreign tongue; for, just as he has taken no part in the evolution of the one, so he has taken none in that of the other; but at most the homeless wight has been a cold, nay more, a hostile on-looker.[96]

One of the most important expressions of this mood of anti-Semitism was *The Protocols of the Elders of Zion*, a forged document first published in 1903 and afterward often reprinted.[97] It purported to prove that there was a secret Jewish conspiracy to degrade and enslave the entire world. Jewish achievements in science, international finance, and the socialist movement were interpreted not as isolated events, but as part of a calculated ploy to gain ascendancy over the Gentiles. The *Protocols* were to have a fateful influence upon Adolf Hitler later in the twentieth century. The myth of an international Jewish conspiracy continues to lead a subterranean existence, surfacing into public view from time to time, as in 1985, when Ernst Zundel and Jim Keegstra were tried in Canada for fomenting hatred against Jews. Both were best known for asserting that the Holocaust—the murder of about six million Jews during World War II—never took place and was a creation of Jewish propaganda. This assertion was based on the underlying notion that there existed a supremely powerful Jewish conspiracy that could perpetrate such a massive hoax upon the world.[98]

As a significant example of how deep-seated nationalist thinking had become, European Jews reacted to this wave of anti-Semitism by developing their own form of nationalism. Zionism taught that the Jews would never achieve respect until they became a nation-state. The Jewish population must be gathered onto a single territory under the control of a sovereign Jewish state. An early Zionist, Theodore Herzl, demanded in 1896 that his "people without a land" be given a "land without a people."[99] Many Jews left Europe, Asia, and Africa in the twentieth century to settle in Palestine, leading to the creation of the Jewish state of Israel. Because Palestine was scarcely a "land without a people," the result has been the displacement of many Palestinians and chronic warfare between Israel and its Arab neighbours.

The aggressive nationalism of the late nineteenth and early twentieth centuries culminated in World War I, with Britain, France, Russia, and Italy arrayed against Germany, Austria-Hungary, and Turkey. At first, the outcome of this bloody war seemed a revival of liberal nationalism. The Treaty of Versailles dismembered the empires that had ruled Central and Eastern Europe and replaced them with nation-states equipped with liberal constitutions. Poles, Czechs, Hungarians, Lithuanians, Finns, and others emerged with their own states for the first time in history. But nationalism and liberalism soon parted company. Each of these new "nation-states" had important national minorities, such as the Germans in Czechoslovakia or Hungarians in Romania. Nationalistic conflict and irredentism raised the temperature of politics to the point where individual freedom seemed of small moment compared to the status of the national group. In the 1920s and 1930s, constitutional government was overthrown in almost all these new states of Europe, from Italy and Germany eastward. Nationalism took on an even more aggressive appearance as the new ideology of fascism.

It is not easy to describe *fascism* briefly, for it was intimately bound to conditions in Central Europe in these years *entre deux guerres*. In many of these countries, a communist takeover, as had occurred in the Russian Empire in 1917, seemed a very real possibility. Liberal constitutionalism appeared unable to combat this threat or deal with post-war inflation and unemployment. The alternative of fascism was created by Benito Mussolini, who had been an ardent socialist but who had rallied to the support of Italy in the Great War. Afterward, Mussolini began a political movement with a unique mixture of ideological themes. Rejecting liberal individualism and constitutional government was paramount. There would no longer be a private sphere of life exempt from governmental intrusion. The state was exalted as the highest expression of the nation, war extolled for bringing "all human energies to their highest tension and setting a seal of nobility on the peoples who have the virtue to face it."[100] The symbol of the movement, which also lent it its name, was the *fasces*, a bundle of sticks that had been a Roman symbol of authority. The sticks represented the power of coercion—beating—while the fact that they were bound together symbolized the unity of the nation. For the third time, Italy would emerge as the leader of humanity. After the Rome of the Caesars and the Rome of the Popes would come the "Third Rome," the "Rome of the People." To these nationalist motifs Mussolini added elements of socialism. The state would not nationalize property but would guide the economy for collective purposes. From Lenin, Mussolini learned that an elite, disciplined party could seize power in a constitutional state and maintain its hold thereafter by ruthlessly suppressing opposition. Conspicuously absent were the egalitarian ideals of social-ism, except inasmuch as everyone was equally exhorted to follow the charismatic leadership of *Il Duce*.

Hitler's doctrine of National Socialism was similar to Mussolini's fascism, except that he substituted German for Italian nationalism. His goal was the *Dritte Reich* (Third Empire), a new German empire to succeed the medieval Holy Roman Empire and the empire Bismarck created in 1871. Hitler also added a heavy dose of anti-Semitism, which had not been part of Mussolini's doctrine. Similar ideologies sprang up elsewhere in Europe. Their adherents came to power in Spain, with the help of Italian and German intervention, and became influential in Central European countries, such as Hungary and Romania.[101]

Fascism is extremely difficult to categorize. The fact that it is certainly not liberal has led some to regard it as a form of conservatism. Indeed, it did play on conservative sentiments by promising to prevent the triumph of communism. But its futuristic symbols, such as the Third Rome or Third Reich, express an attitude quite foreign to the conservative reverence for continuity with the past. Fascism was in fact a promise of radical reform, a conscious break with the past to produce what Mussolini called "Fascist man." On balance, fascism is probably best understood as an extreme form of nationalism, incorporating certain elements of socialism to strengthen the state and playing on conservative fears of communism. Although some writers seek to apply the label fascist to contemporary military and anticommunist regimes, such as South Korea, Chile, and the Philippines, we feel that European fascism was so much a unique product of historical circumstances that it is better to restrict the term to Hitler, Mussolini, and others, to regard it as a specific phase of nationalism rather than a separate ideology.

The aftermath of World War II has brought a historical period in which nationalism is truly a worldwide force. The British, French, Italian, Portuguese, American, Dutch, and Japanese colonial holdings have all attained independence, leaving the Russian Empire, surviving as the Soviet Union and its sphere of influence, as the last of the great multinational empires. The world is now a society of nation-states, even if many of the new nations are still rather tentative aggregations of tribal, ethnic, and regional groups. The most important new manifestation of nationalism in the post-war period has been the struggle of these new nations for independence. In Vietnam, Algeria, Angola, and Mozambique, for example, the colonial power was reluctant to surrender its sovereignty and did so only after a prolonged war of "national liberation."

In the Third World the mentality and symbolism of national liberation is still strong. Political sovereignty has been achieved, but most of the new nations are economically precarious. They commonly blame their low standard of living not only on the colonial past but also on what they perceive as continuing economic domination by the capitalist nations of the Western world, especially the United States. Not surprisingly, because they believe their problems are caused by the market system, many of the new nations have turned to socialism, as described in Chapter 12.

However, with some exceptions, they are not turning to orthodox communism. Many leaders in the Third World reject both the capitalist and the communist models as blueprints for rapid social, economic, and political change. Their criticism is that capitalist and communist solutions were devised for situations and experiences unlike those in developing nations today. The authoritarianism of communism stifles the initiative and innovation so desperately needed to stimulate development, while the lack of governmental intervention in capitalism enables the rich in developing nations to maintain a stratified society with little or no social or economic mobility. Developing nations, they argue, must seek their own solutions to their problems of development. Celso Furtado, an exiled Brazilian economist, is critical of communist methods.

> Historical experience has demonstrated that whenever a revolution of the Marxist-Leninist type has been imposed on a complex social structure—as in the case of certain European countries—socialism as a form of humanism

becomes perverted. As there is no possibility of converting an open society into a dictatorship without creating a climate of frustration, there is a deterioration of social values. Since the dictatorial regime does not permit the individual to play his proper part in society, a series of social myths is put forward in order to replace genuine human values. Thus, material development can take place at the same time that the dictatorship is consolidating itself upon principles which are the antithesis of humanistic revolutionary ideals.[102]

Eduardo Frei, former president of Chile (1964–1970), perceives a flaw in the capitalist system.

There is something that we should understand. Capitalism as a system dehumanizes the economy, although, in its first stage, it meant an enormous expansion of economic development and the creation of wealth. Yet there is no doubt that it tended to concentrate economic power in a few hands, to allow the great monopolistic powers to control the market so that, by a fierce dialectical process within its own structure, it led to the disappearance of economic freedom. In the productive process, it separated labor from management and, more than that, from the concept of property and the exercise of that right.[103]

Both men seek indigenous solutions to their problems of development in some form of non-communist socialism.

Concrete manifestations of this socialist nationalism are nationalization of the subsidiaries of multinational firms or heavy regulation of their business activities, attempts to cartelize production of essential commodities sold on world markets, demands for higher levels of foreign aid with no strings attached, and proposals for an international income tax by which the Third World could claim as a matter of right a share of the wealth of the more advanced nations. Such proposals are often summarized under the heading of the "new world economic order" demanded by representatives of the Third World. This vision seemed almost plausible in the heyday of OPEC in the late 1970s. If Third World oil producers could bring the West to its knees, why not Third World producers of bauxite or bananas? But by the mid-1980s, it was obvious to everyone that OPEC no longer controlled the price of oil and that no equivalent cartels were in the offing.

The alliance between nationalism and socialism may prove itself very long-lasting because the two ideologies have an important affinity: both see the state as a central institution. For socialists it is the planner of society and for nationalists it is the expression of national identity, whereas for liberals and conservatives it is a limited instrument with special purposes. Socialist and nationalist uses of the state are not incompatible and, indeed, can reinforce each other. Nationalization of a multinational corporation may be advertised as an assertion of sovereignty as well as a benefit to the local working class. A sign that the link between socialism and nationalism may prove durable is that it is not confined to the impoverished nations of the Third World. In many wealthy nations, too, the socialist left is the most nationalistic part of the political spectrum. In Canada the New Democratic party prides itself on its nationalism, while the Parti Québécois is a social democratic as well as a nationalist party. In Britain the left wing of the Labour party was, and still is, opposed to participation in the European Economic Community on the grounds that membership in this free-trade association hinders the British government's ability to introduce measures of socialist reform at home. In Greece the socialist government of Andreas Papandreou has threatened to withdraw from both NATO and the EEC.

This rapprochement between nationalism and socialism is mildly ironic because the early socialists had little use for the nation-state. Marx sympathized with the national aspirations of the Irish and the Poles not for their own sake, but because national liberation would weaken the political system that helped maintain capitalism. Marx believed that all states, including nation-states, would ultimately disappear. The socialist parties of the Second International also had an antinationalistic outlook. They believed the aggressive nationalism of their day distracted from the true issue of the class struggle. But the worldwide proliferation of nation-states in this century is a political fact to which ideologies must adjust if they are to survive at all. Socialists have managed to make the transition by focussing on the state in preference to those parts of the original socialist doctrine that anticipated the passing away of the state as a form of political existence.

14   Left, Right, and Centre

Are ideologies related to each other in a systematic way such that we could array them along a single dimension? One such common classification depends on the distinction between *left* and *right*. Many observers accustomed to using these terms agree on the following construction of the political spectrum:

Left		**Centre**		**Right**	
Communism	Social Democracy	Reform Liberalism	Classical Liberalism	Conservatism	Fascism

Although this spectrum corresponds to common perception, it is not easy to say precisely what it means. Is the left for, and the right against, change? That simplistic explanation will hardly do, for everything depends on who is in power. In the communist state, classical liberalism is an ideology of radical change. In the Western constitutional democracies, both communism and fascism represent radical change. Freedom is not much help either. All ideologies, even fascism, claim to be for freedom, but they define it in different ways. Invoking democracy does not solve the problem because the democratic centralism of Marxism-Leninism is really just as antithetical to popular government as fascism is.

Considering the circumstances under which the words left and right first began to be used as political labels sheds some light on the subject. The custom arose shortly after 1789 in the French National Assembly. Those factions that favoured retaining substantial powers for the monarchy, such as appointing judges and vetoing legislation, sat on the right of the Speaker of the Assembly. Those who wanted the monarch reduced to a purely symbolic figure and elected representatives of the people to exercise all political power sat to the left of the Speaker. The basic issue was popular sovereignty. The extreme left held that all political power emanated from the people, the extreme right believed that political power was conferred by God on the monarch through heredity, and the centre sought a compromise or balance of these two principles.[104]

This political difference between left and right was soon overlaid by an economic dimension as socialism assumed a prominent role in European politics. The term left was applied to those who favoured equalizing property through political action. More profoundly, socialists proposed replacing the impersonal market process, which is not under the control of any identifiable person or persons, by a system of planning that is under political control. Socialism thus extends popular sovereignty from the political to the economic sphere.

The ambiguities of left-right terminology arise from this double origin. Advocates of popular sovereignty do not inevitably favour socialist planning; they may be sincerely convinced that the market principle will in the long run be more beneficial to ordinary working people. It is also not inevitable that advocates of socialist planning support popular sovereignty with equal warmth, for the desires of the real, existing people (as opposed to the hypothetical, reformed people) may obstruct the plan. Thus the political and economic left often coincide but need not necessarily do so.

In contemporary usage, the economic factor seems to predominate, though the political is still in the background. Going back to our common sense listing of ideologies on the left-right spectrum, we can now interpret them approximately in terms of the meanings of equality that have been discussed. Let us now redraw the spectrum, adding concepts to represent the various forms of equality and inequality that the ideologies claim as their own.

Left	**Centre**		**Right**		
Equality of Condition	Equality of Opportunity		Equality of Right	Aristocracy	Hierarchy
Communism	Social Democracy	Reform Liberalism	Classical Liberalism	Conservatism	Fascism

This picture could be seriously misleading without appropriate qualifications. Communists advocate long-run equality of condition in the sense of the equality of happiness that would be produced by implementing the motto "From each according to his ability, to each according to his needs." In the short run, they claim to equalize conditions somewhat but not absolutely. Social democrats and reform liberals are not exclusively wedded to equality of opportunity. Their use of the progressive income tax as a levelling measure is also an approach to equality of condition. The classical liberal commitment to equality of right is not too problematic in this context, but the conservative position easily causes confusion. Early conservatives such as Burke saw a hereditary aristocracy as a socially useful institution. Twentieth-century conservatives no longer defend the hereditary principle but may argue that the wealthy perform some of the same useful functions as a hereditary aristocracy—philanthropy, public service, and so on. Obviously, this position shades into classical liberalism; the difference is only a matter of whether one emphasizes the equality of universal rules or the unequal results arising from them. Finally, fascists tended to think of hierarchy not as social transmission through legal inheritance, but as biological transmission of racial qualities. For Hitler, Germans were a "master race" (*Herrenvolk*); Jews were "subhuman" (*Untermenschen*).

This is the most absolute type of inequality that can be imagined because there is no conceivable way of altering it. Fascists also completely rejected the constitutional principle of rule of law, which is another formulation of equality of right.

This underlying dimension of egalitarianism is not an absolute scale of measurement that allows us to assign a precise value to an ideology from any time or place. "Leftness" is not a measurable attitude like height or weight. However, it does make a limited amount of sense to say of two ideologies at a certain place and time that one is to the left or right of the other. The same applies to the adherents of ideologies. Thus it is reasonable to say that in recent Canadian politics, the NDP, as a party of social democracy, is usually to the left of the Liberal party. Yet the difference should not be exaggerated. Prime Minister Louis St. Laurent said of the CCF, the predecessor of the NDP, that they were only "Liberals in a hurry." A long list of quasi-socialist measures, such as national health insurance and a publicly owned oil company, were proposed by the CCF/NDP and ultimately legislated by the Liberal party. Similarly, the Liberals, as a reformist party, are generally to the left of the Progressive Conservatives, but again there is much overlap. During the national election campaign of 1984, Conservative leader Brian Mulroney proclaimed that medicare was a "sacred trust," even though it had been created by a Liberal government. The Conservatives might have been less enthusiastic in the first instance about the various programs of the welfare state, but they seem reluctant to dismantle them once they exist.

Note that except for fascism, we have not attempted to place nationalism on the left-right scale. As explained in the preceding section, nationalism has at different times been allied with liberalism, conservatism, and socialism. Commitment to the nation-state does not automatically dictate a position on issues of equality. In time of war, for example, normal political differences are suspended. Parties of the left and right often come together in a coalition "government of national unity" to prosecute the war effort. This shows that support for the nation is on a different level than normal political issues. When the threat to the nation is past, the distinction between left and right reasserts itself and governments of national unity soon fall apart, as happened in France and Italy after World War II.

It cannot be emphasized too much that the left-right spectrum is unidimensional, while ideologies are multidimensional—that is, they are concerned not only with inequality and equality but with many other political values as well. For example, it would be possible to map ideologies on a continuum according to their views on the scope of state control of society.

Maximum			**Minimum**
Communism	Social Democracy	Classical Liberalism	
Fascism	Reform Liberalism	Conservatism	Anarchism

Communists and fascists favour the total identification of state and society. Social democrats and reform liberals espouse a theory of active government regulation and intervention, but they do not wish to subject all of society to control by the state. Conservatives and classical liberals desire a very limited state to carry out certain restricted functions, enabling society to evolve according to its own laws. Anarchists believe that society can exist without any government at all.

This classification is as valid as the conventional left-right spectrum, but it also expresses another aspect of the reality of ideologies and thus does not coincide with the left-right spectrum. To speak of left and right is a useful shorthand way of referring to ideologies as long as its limitations are kept in mind. Left and right are only convenient labels; they are no substitute for a detailed understanding of a point of view. Difficulties quickly become apparent when we try to apply the notion of a left-right continuum to concrete issues. As examples, let us look at several issues from economics, politics, and society.

Among economic issues, the left-right spectrum fits very well the debate surrounding progressive taxation. Those furthest to the left are the most vociferous in their desire to "make the rich pay," as the Communist party of Canada puts it. Those in the middle accept the principle of progressive taxation but may worry whether the marginal rate is so high as to interfere with productivity; they wish the state to act in a redistributive way but not to "kill the goose that lays the golden eggs." Those on the right reject progressive taxation in favour of proportional taxation; thus it was not wholly surprising that the Conservative government of Saskatchewan announced in 1985 that it would run a small experiment with a flat-rate tax scheme. The issue of taxation can be readily mapped onto the left-right continuum because the underlying question is one of egalitarianism.

The fit is not so snug with another current issue, deregulation of passenger air travel. A priori, one might think that the market-oriented right would favour free competition in air travel, the moderate centre would accept a degree of regulation (for example, government approval of service and fares), and the left would favour comprehensive regulation or even public ownership of this essential service. While this distribution of views is found in intellectual discussion, it is overlaid by another pattern arising from the effects of decades of regulation. Air Canada and Canadian Pacific Air were long protected from competition by smaller carriers. Thus both corporate giants, one publicly and one privately owned, have protested against deregulation, which makes it possible for smaller airlines to offer cheaper fares and new routes. Interestingly, the deregulation initiative began when Liberal Lloyd Axworthy, generally considered a left or reform liberal, was minister of transport. The same patterns have been visible in the United States, where deregulation began under President Carter and was opposed by the large airlines that had prospered under the old regime. Thus airline deregulation is typical of many economic issues where vested interests distort the expected alignment of positions on the left-right continuum.

In the political sphere, left and right are most clearly distinguished in the international context, where the United States and the Soviet Union contend for influence in the Third World. Attitudes toward, say, the Nicaraguan revolution can be readily organized along this dimension. The right views the Sandinista regime in Nicaragua as an extension of Soviet influence and a threat to capitalist hegemony in the Western hemisphere. The left sees the Nicaraguan revolution as an example of national liberation from imperialist domination.

However, the situation becomes confusing when one moves beyond this single dimension of international conflict between socialism and capitalism. The Nicaraguan regime has done many things that would surely be criticized by the democratic left if done in Canada. It postponed elections for five years after the revolution and then held an election in which the opposition was severely handicapped. It censors all media of mass communication. It has organized a comprehensive system of neighbourhood surveillance, like that in Cuba, and has built up by far the largest armed forces in Central America. This situation reflects the earlier noted discrepancy between the older conception of the left as popular self-government and the newer conception of it as egalitarianism.

On so-called social issues, the left seems to favour a position of individual libertarianism—abortion on demand, legalization of marijuana, abolition of movie censorship—whereas the right seems to uphold traditional standards of morality. But this seeming unidimensionality exists only where the extreme left is weak in liberal democracies, as in North America. Communists and other revolutionary leftists are in fact rather puritanical in their outlook on many moral questions. Marijuana and other mind-altering drugs are rigorously forbidden in communist countries, as are many mildly obscene books and movies that would hardly raise an eyebrow in the West. Again, freedom of individual choice is not a high priority for the revolutionary left.

Even within the foreshortened spectrum of opinions existing in Canada, designations of left and right become blurred on many social issues. Pornography, for example, is opposed by an oddly assorted coalition of Christian conservatives and radical feminists. The feminists, who stand to the left on economic issues such as equal pay for work of equal value, believe that pornography degrades women when it pictures them as objects of sexual violence and hence demand that the state override individual taste. Other feminists, in contrast, uphold the traditional libertarian outlook of the democratic left.

Even with all these nuances and exceptions, the terms left and right are convenient designations for ideological tendencies. Most of the inconsistencies disappear if we restrict their application to stable constitutional democracies when the extreme right and extreme left are weak or non-existent. Under these conditions, left and right stand for relatively coherent ideological positions—reform liberalism/social democracy versus classical liberalism/conservatism.

Notes

1. Lyman Tower Sargent, *Contemporary Political Ideologies*, 4th ed. (Homewood, Ill.: Dorsey Press, 1978), p. 3.
2. Philip Converse, "The Nature of Belief Systems in Mass Publics," in David Apter, ed., *Ideology and Discontent* (Glencoe, Ill.: Free Press, 1964), pp. 206–261.
3. Karl Marx, *A Contribution to the Critique of Political Economy* (1859), in Lewis S. Feuer, ed., *Marx and Engels: Basic Writings on Politics and Philosophy* (Garden City, N.Y.: Doubleday, 1959), p. 44.
4. Karl Mannheim, *Ideology and Utopia* (New York: Harcourt, Brace and World, n.d.). First published 1936.
5. Jeremy Bentham, *An Introduction to the Principles of Morals and Legislation* (1789), in Jeremy Bentham and John Stuart Mill, *The Utilitarians* (Garden City, N.Y.: Anchor Books, 1973), p. 73.
6. Karl Marx, "Introduction to the Critique of Hegel's Philosophy of Right" (1843), in T. B. Bottomore, ed., *Karl Marx: Early Writings* (New York: McGraw-Hill, 1964), p. 44.
7. Pierre Berton, *The Smug Minority* (Toronto: McClelland and Stewart, 1968), pp. 42–43. Reprinted by permission of McClelland and Stewart.
8. Bertrand de Jouvenel, *Sovereignty: An Inquiry into the Political Good*, tr. J. F. Huntington (Chicago: University of Chicago Press, 1957), pp. 247–259.
9. John H. Schaar, "Equality of Opportunity and Beyond," in J. Roland Pennock and John W. Chapman, eds., *Equality*, vol. IX of *Nomos* (New York: Atherton, 1967), p. 242.
10. Neil Nevitte and Roger Gibbins, "Neoconservatism: Canadian Variations on an Ideological Theme?" *Canadian Public Policy* 10 (1984), p. 388.
11. John Locke, *The Second Treatise of Government* (Indianapolis: Bobbs-Merrill, 1952), p. 5.
12. Ibid., p. 76.
13. Ibid., p. 114.
14. Carl L. Becker, *The Declaration of Independence*, 2nd ed. (New York: Random House, 1942), p. 8.
15. J. Salwyn Schapiro, ed., *Liberalism: Its Meaning and History* (New York: Van Nostrand Reinhold, 1958), p. 129.
16. John Locke, *A Letter Concerning Toleration*, 2nd ed. (Indianapolis: Bobbs-Merrill, 1955), p. 18.
17. Schapiro, *Liberalism*, p. 126.
18. Ibid., p. 129.
19. John Stuart Mill, *On Liberty* (Indianapolis: Bobbs-Merrill, 1956), p. 13.

20. Adam Smith, *The Wealth of Nations* (Chicago: University of Chicago Press, 1976), vol. I, pp. 477–478.

21. See especially Milton and Rose Friedman, *Free to Choose* (New York: Harcourt Brace Jovanovich, 1970); and Friedrich A. Hayek, *The Constitution of Liberty* (Chicago: University of Chicago Press, 1960).

22. David Hume, *A Treatise of Human Nature* (1739), cited in James Moore, "Hume's Theory of Justice and Property," *Political Studies* 24 (1976), p. 108.

23. Friedrich A. Hayek, *Law, Legislation and Liberty*, 3 vols. (Chicago: University of Chicago Press, 1973–1979), vol. I, pp. 35–54.

24. Smith, *The Wealth of Nations*, vol. II, pp. 208–209.

25. The discerning reader will understand that the streetlight is a collective good because streets are publicly owned. If the streets were turned over to an entrepreneur who could find an appropriate way of charging for their use, he or she could furnish lighting as part of the overall service.

26. John Stuart Mill, *Principles of Political Economy*, vol. II of *Collected Works of John Stuart Mill* (Toronto: University of Toronto Press, 1965), p. 207.

27. T. H. Green, "Liberal Legislation and Freedom of Contract" (1881), in John R. Rodman, ed., *The Political Theory of T. H. Green* (New York: Appleton-Century-Crofts, 1964), pp. 51–52.

28. Friedrich A. Hayek, ed., *Capitalism and the Historians* (Chicago: University of Chicago Press, 1954).

29. Kenneth Minogue, *The Liberal Mind* (London: Methuen, 1963).

30. John Kenneth Galbraith, *The New Industrial State* (Boston: Houghton Mifflin, 1967).

31. Neil H. Jacoby, *Corporate Power and Social Responsibility* (New York: Macmillan, 1973), ch. 6.

32. The *Globe and Mail*, November 13, 1984, p. B1.

33. John Kenneth Galbraith, *The Affluent Society*, 3rd rev. ed. (Boston: Houghton Mifflin, 1976).

34. Jouvenel, *Sovereignty*, p. 139.

35. W. G. Runciman, *Relative Deprivation and Social Justice* (sponsored by The Institute of Community Studies, London: University of California Press, 1966).

36. The best critiques are Jouvenel, *Sovereignty*, ch. 9; and Hayek, *The Mirage of Social Justice*, vol. II of *Law, Legislation and Liberty*, ch. 9.

37. Friedman and Friedman, *Free to Choose*, p. 306.

38. Michael Oakeshott, *Rationalism in Politics and Other Essays* (London: Methuen, 1962), p. 169.

39. W. L. Morton, "Canadian Conservatism Now" (1959), in Paul W. Fox, ed., *Politics Canada*, 3rd ed. (Toronto: McGraw-Hill, 1970), p. 233.

40. A similar train of excesses followed the overthrow of the Shah of Iran in 1979. Burke's views on sudden, revolutionary change are not merely of historical interest.

41. Edmund Burke, *Reflections on the Revolution in France* (Indianapolis: Liberal Arts Press, 1955), p. 99.

42. Gordon W. Allport, *The Nature of Prejudice* (Reading, Mass.: Addison-Wesley, 1954), p. 20.

43. Ibid., p. 9.

44. Edmund Burke, "Letter to Sir Hercules Langrische on the Catholics" (1792), cited in Russell Kirk, *The Conservative Mind* (Chicago: Henry Regnery, 1960), p. 52.

45. Burke, *Reflections on the Revolution in France*, p. 110.

46. Clinton Rossiter, "Conservatism," in David L. Sils, ed., *International Encyclopedia of the Social Sciences* (New York: Macmillan and The Free Press, 1968), vol. III, p. 294.

47. Edmund Burke, "Thoughts and Details on Scarcity" (1795), cited in C. B. Macpherson, *Burke* (Oxford: Oxford University Press, 1980), p. 58.

48. Rod Preece, "The Political Wisdom of Sir John A. Macdonald," *Canadian Journal of Political Science* 17 (1984), p. 479.

49. E. S. Savas, *Privatizing the Public Sector: How to Shrink Government* (Chatham, N.J.: Chatham House, 1982), ch. 6.

50. George Gilder, *Wealth and Poverty* (New York: Basic Books, 1981).

51. Today's classical liberals, feeling the need for a distinctive name, often call themselves libertarians. An example in Canada is the journalist Barbara Amiel, who advocates the free market while opposing censorship and restrictive drug legislation. See her book *Confessions* (Toronto: Macmillan, 1980).

52. Acts of the Apostles 4:32–33.

53. J. L. Talmon, *The Origins of Totalitarian Democracy* (New York: Praeger, 1960), pp. 167–247.

54. John Anthony Scott, ed., *The Defense of Gracchus Babeuf* (New York: Schocken Books, 1972), p. 68. Copyright 1967 by University of Massachusetts Press.

55. Ibid., pp. 62–63.

56. Mark Holloway, *Heavens on Earth: Utopian Communities in America 1680–1880*, 2nd ed. (New York: Dover, 1966).

57. Karl Marx, "Introduction to the Critique of Hegel's Philosophy of Right," pp. 58–59.

58. Karl Marx, "Economic and Philosophical Manuscripts" (1844), Ibid., p. 132.

59. Ibid., p. 124.

60. M. M. Bober, *Karl Marx's Interpretation of History*, 2nd ed. (New York: W. W. Norton, 1965), ch. 12.

61. Friedrich Engels, "Socialism: Utopian and Scientific" (1892), in Karl Marx and Friedrich Engels, *Selected Works* (Moscow: Progress Publishers, 1968), p. 432.

62. Karl Marx and Friedrich Engels, *The Communist Manifesto* (Harmondsworth: Penguin, 1967), pp. 104–105.

63. Karl Marx, "Critique of the Gotha Programme" (1875), in Lewis S. Feuer, *Marx and Engels*, p. 119.

64. Karl Marx and Friedrich Engels, *The German Ideology* (Moscow: Progress Publishers, 1968), p. 45.

65. On anarchism see James Joll, *The Anarchists* (London: Methuen, 1964).

66. James Joll, *The Second International* (London: Routledge and Kegan Paul, 1955).

67. Alfred G. Meyer, *Marxism: The Unity of Theory and Practice* (Ann Arbor: University of Michigan Press, 1963), pp. 122–126.

68. Lenin's seminal work on party organization is *What Is to Be Done?* (1902). On democratic centralism see Alfred G. Meyer, *Leninism* (New York: Praeger, 1962), pp. 92–103.

69. V. I. Lenin, *Selected Works*, 3 vols. (Moscow: Progress Publishers, 1967), vol. I, p. 680.

70. Michael S. Cross, ed., *The Decline and Fall of a Good Idea: CCF-NDP Manifestoes 1932–1969* (Toronto: New Hogtown Press, 1974), p. 19.

71. Ibid., pp. 33–42.

72. Julius K. Nyerere, *Nyerere on Socialism* (Dar es Salaam: Oxford University Press, 1969), p. 42.

73. Cross, *The Decline and Fall of a Good Idea*, p. 19.

74. Information supplied by Dr. R. C. Keith, Political Science Department, University of Calgary.

75. Research Committee of the League for Social Reconstruction, *Social Planning for Canada* (Toronto: University of Toronto Press). First published 1935. The League for Social Reconstruction was an intellectual study group founded in 1932 on the model of the British Fabian Society. It was not, strictly speaking, affiliated with the CCF, but members of the LSR were usually CCF activists.

76. Cross, *The Decline and Fall of a Good Idea*, p. 20.

77. The Waffle Manifesto (1969), in Ibid., p. 45.

78. David Lane, *The End of Inequality? Stratification Under State Socialism* (Harmondsworth: Penguin, 1971); and Mervyn Matthews, *Privilege in the Soviet Union* (London: George Allen & Unwin, 1978), ch. 2.

79. Milovan Djilas, *The New Class: An Analysis of the Communist System* (New York: Praeger, 1957).

80. Charles E. Lindblom, *Politics and Markets: The World's Political-Economic Systems* (New York: Basic Books, 1977). Lindblom adds a third alternative, exhortation, which does not seem to be even close to the other two in long-term effectiveness.

81. Charles J. Lumsden and Edward O. Wilson, *Promethean Fire: Reflections on the Origin of Mind* (Cambridge, Mass.: Harvard University Press, 1983).

82. See Richard N. Hunt, *The Political Ideas of Marx and Engels* (Pittsburgh: University of Pittsburgh Press, 1974), vol. I, ch. 9.

83. N. S. Khrushchev, "Report on the Program of the Communist Party of the Soviet Union, October 17, 1961," in *Documents of the 22nd Congress of the CPSU* (New York: Crosscurrents Press, 196l), vol. II.

84. Aristotle, *Nicomachean Ethics*, 1155a.

85. Ramsay Cook, ed., *French-Canadian Nationalism: An Anthology* (Toronto: Macmillan, 1969), p. 95.

86. Ibid., p. 98.

87. Seymour Martin Lipset, "Canada and the United States: The Cultural Dimension," in Charles F. Doran and John H. Sigler, *Canada and the United States* (Englewood Cliffs, N.J. and Scarborough, Ont.: Prentice-Hall, 1985).

88. Letter to Joseph Priestley, June 19, 1802, cited in Saul K. Padover, ed., *Thomas Jefferson and the Foundations of American Freedom* (Princeton, N.J.: D. Van Nostrand, 1965), pp. 120–121.

89. Edward A. Tiryakian and Neil Nevitte, "Nationalism and Modernity," in Edward A. Tiryakian and Ronald Rogowski, *New Nationalisms of the Developed West* (Boston: Allen & Unwin, 1985), p. 67.

90. John Stuart Mill, *Considerations on Representative Government* (Chicago: Henry Regnery, 1962), p. 309.

91. Lord Acton, "Nationality" (1862), in Gertrude Himmelfarb, ed., *Essays on Freedom and Power* (New York: The Free Press, 1949), p. 193.

92. Pierre Elliott Trudeau, *Federalism and the French Canadians* (Toronto: Macmillan, 1968), pp. 177–178.

93. Edward McWhinney, *Constitution-Making* (Toronto: University of Toronto Press, 1981), p. 206.

94. Government of Canada, Energy, Mines and Resources, *The National Energy Program—1980* (Ottawa: 1980), p. 2.

95. Hans Kohn, ed., *Nationalism: Its Meaning and History*, 2nd ed. (Princeton, N.J.: D. Van Nostrand, 1965).

96. Richard Wagner, "Judaism in Music" (1850), Ibid., p. 165.

97. On the *Protocols* see Norman Cohn, *Warrant for Genocide*, 2nd ed. (New York: Harper & Row, 1969).

98. The most elaborate exposition of "Holocaust revisionism" is Arthur Butz, *The Hoax of the Twentieth Century* (Brighton: Historical Review Press, 1977).

99. Kohn, *Nationalism*, p. 75.

100. Benito Mussolini, "The Doctrine of Fascism" (1932), in Department of Philosophy, University of Colorado, *Readings on Fascism and National Socialism* (Denver: Alan Swallow, n.d.), p. 15.

101. A convenient overview of fascism is Eugen Weber, *Varieties of Fascism* (New York: Van Nostrand Reinhold, 1964).

102. Reprinted in Paul E. Sigmund, ed., *The Ideologies of the Developing Nations*, rev. ed. (New York: Praeger, 1967), p. 415.

103. Ibid., p. 384.

104. David Caute, *The Left in Europe since 1789* (New York: McGraw-Hill, 1966), chs. 1 and 2.

Vocabulary

episteme
doxa
ideology
personal freedom
limited government
equality of right
consent of the governed
classical liberalism
reform liberalism
laissez faire
equality of condition
equality of opportunity
property franchise (suffrage)
spontaneous order
organization
free riders
collective goods
redistribution
welfare state
justice
social justice
progressive tax
intervention
conservatism
neoconservatism
deregulation

privatization
socialism
utopian socialism
proletariat
alienation
bourgeoisie
scientific socialism
dictatorship of the proletariat
First International
anarchism
Second International
democratic centralism
communist
Third International
Comintern
Cominform
social democrats
planning
syndicalism
nationalization
nationalism
irredentism
fascism
left
right

PART THREE

Forms of
Government

15   Classification of Political Systems

The review of ideologies completed in Part Two leads naturally to the study of forms of government. Ideologies are not just abstract ideas; they reflect the experience of people who live under one form of government or another. This experience may express itself ideologically as acceptance of a form of government, rejection of it, or proposals for modification. Also, as Marx saw, ideology is at least partially determined by social milieu, of which government is an important part. Finally, ideology is a determining factor of government because it sets up goals toward which people strive. Liberals, for example, try to fashion governmental machinery to enhance individual freedom, however they may define it, while socialists enhance the power of the state through central planning and nationalizing industry. Hence government and ideology are reciprocally related, each being both cause and effect of the other. Part Three of this book examines the chief forms of government in relation to the ideological climate of the late twentieth century.

Before one can understand a complicated set of facts, one must be able to classify them, sort them into groups based on their position along some dimension. This process of organizing factual information about governmental systems produces broad schemes of classification usually known as *typologies*. Once such typologies are formed, knowledge progresses by formulating and testing generalizations about the similarities and differences of the various categories.

One of the oldest, and still one of the best, typologies of governments dates back to the founders of political science, Plato and Aristotle. They classified governments with two questions in mind: Who rules? and In whose interest? Their answer to the first question was simple: rule can be exercised by a single person; by a minority, which they called "the few"; or by a majority of the whole people, which they called "the many." The second question, concerning whose interests are served, is more difficult and requires a longer answer.

Plato held that there are two basic ways in which rule may be conducted: lawfully and lawlessly. Either the governors may be bound by constitutional rules that they are not free to set aside, or they may rule according to unchecked whims and emotional desires. The first possibility corresponds to what we have called the rule of law, the second to the rule of men. In the words of Aristotle:

> He who bids the law rule may be deemed to bid God and Reason alone rule, but he who bids man rule adds an element of the beast; for desire is a wild beast, and passion perverts the minds of rulers, even when they are the best of men. The law is reason unaffected by desire.[1]

Aristotle added that rule by law is in the general interest of the entire community, whereas arbitrary rule represents exploitation of the ruled for the special interest of the governors. He also pointed out that rule in the common interest tends to be seen as legitimate, giving rulers authority that the ruled obey voluntarily, while selfish government does not seem legitimate to those who are oppressed and therefore has to be sustained by coercion and fear. In sum, we have two great kinds of regimes: lawful authority seeking the common good and lawless coercion seeking private interest. Combining these two dimensions of "who" and "how" yields a sixfold typology, illustrated in Figure 15.1.

A *monarchy* for Plato and Aristotle was a regime in which sovereign authority was vested in one person who ruled within the laws of the *polis*. Its corrupt counterpart was a *tyranny*, in which one person ruled arbitrarily. An *aristocracy* was a system in which political power was held by a restricted class, usually people of wealth and noble ancestry, but that class ruled in the general interest under law. An *oligarchy*, in contrast, was a regime where the wealthy class holding power used its position to exploit the impoverished and powerless multitude. *Democracy*, in the Greek sense of the term, was also an exploitative form of government in which the many used their political power to obtain for themselves the wealth of the rich. It was the rule of the common people unchecked by legal restraints. The positive counterpart of democracy was *polity*, which today we might call constitutional democracy. This word is derived from *polis*, the Greek word for "city-state." It expresses the idea that the rule of the many is good only if it is exercised within a fixed constitutional framework that prevents the majority from oppressing minorities. It represents the balance of public and private interests through the political process.

This raises the more general point that to the ancient Greek philosophers, democracy or popular government was not necessarily a good thing. Any lawful

FIGURE 15.1

Platonic/Aristotelian Typology of Government

	How is Rule Conducted?	
	Lawful (in the common good)	Lawless (in private interest)
Who Rules?		
One	Monarchy	Tyranny
Few	Aristocracy	Oligarchy
Many	Polity (constitutional democracy)	Democracy

regime was preferable to any lawless one. The question of numbers, though not unimportant, was secondary to the question of lawfulness. This insight—that who rules is less important than how rule is conducted—has been seriously jeopardized by the twentieth-century habit of speaking of democracy as something good in itself. Plato and Aristotle would have said that while a polity or constitutional democracy was a good form of government, unchecked democracy was only mob rule, no different in principle from tyranny or oligarchy. The nineteenth-century writers Alexis de Tocqueville and John Stuart Mill made the same point when they expressed the fear that democracy could become a "tyranny of the majority."[2]

Plato and Aristotle have left us a heritage of emphasis upon the rule of law, yet paradoxically, Plato believed there was an even higher form of rule. In his famous book *The Republic*, he sketched the ideal of rule by a *philosopher-king*. This would be a man so pre-eminent in wisdom and moral virtue that he could rule by personal judgment rather than by the constraint of law. He would not be arbitrary or oppressive because his philosophic wisdom would protect him from the temptations of power. The people would consent to this form of rule because it would be in their own interest. Plato never completely renounced his belief in the philosopher-king, but his later works show he was rather pessimistic about the possibility of finding such a man. Thus, given the imperfections of humanity, he and his pupil Aristotle shifted to the notion of law as the best political solution likely to be attained. Rule of law is second best in terms of what might be imagined, but best in terms of what human beings, with their limited knowledge, can probably achieve. Yet the image of the philosopher-king, ruling disinterestedly above law in the common good, has never ceased to haunt history. It has often reappeared in the guise of various "benevolent dictators," who have not felt it necessary to be confined by law.

One other important point must be made. Aristotle was always concerned to point out that the conflict between the few and the many was as much one of wealth as of numbers, for in practice the many are usually poor in comparison to the wealthy few. The besetting vice of democracy in his view was for the majority to use the power of the state to confiscate the property of the wealthy minority, while the parallel failing of oligarchy was for the wealthy few to manipulate the laws to bring about easier exploitation of the masses.

Aristotle's preference was for a polity or constitutional democracy that protected property rights by law. In a sense, polity is a compromise between the two bad governmental forms of democracy and oligarchy. If both the wealthy and the poor, the few and the many, hold a share of power in the state, but neither faction is supreme, they can check each other. Thus, in a negative way, we come back to the desired situation of rule of law because the counterpoised factions watch each other to make sure that neither begins to manipulate the laws to its own selfish advantage. However, Aristotle also pointed out that the balance would probably be unstable if society were polarized into camps of extreme wealth and poverty. It would be best to have a large middle class, which in a sense would unite numbers and property within itself. Such a class, though not itself rich, would have a stake in protecting the property of the rich; for if the rich could be despoiled, the middle class itself might be next. Aristotle's words have lost none of their wisdom even after 2,300 years:

> Great then is the good fortune of a state in which the citizens have a moderate and sufficient property; for where some possess much, and others nothing there may arise an extreme democracy, or a pure oligarchy; or a tyranny may grow out of either extreme.[3]

This classical typology of the six forms of government was the beginning of political science and is still useful today, but it is not the only approach to classification. Indeed, there can never be a definitive or final typology because classification depends on which aspect of reality we wish to emphasize. As forms of government undergo historical modification, schemes of classification change with them. The remainder of Part Three uses three different typologies that correspond to three aspects of government in the twentieth century.

First, we distinguish among governments according to the relationship between state and society on which they are based. The three categories that appear in this classification are totalitarian, authoritarian, and liberal-democratic. Second, we distinguish among governments according to the relationship between the executive and legislative powers of government. The chief distinction here is between parliamentary and presidential systems. Third, we classify governments according to their degree of centralization or decentralization. This was not a major concern of Plato and Aristotle because they thought of government chiefly in the context of the small, independent *polis*; but it is a big problem for the large states of modern times. The major categories in this context are the unitary state, devolution, federalism, and confederation.

Our three classifications are not mutually exclusive, but they can be applied together for a multidimensional description of any particular government. Thus Canada would be described as a liberal-democratic, parliamentary, and federal state; Indonesia would be authoritarian, presidential, and federal; and Albania would be totalitarian, parliamentary, and unitary. There are inevitably many borderline cases that tend to straddle categories: Mexico has certain aspects of both the liberal-democratic and authoritarian state; France has a unique combination of parliamentary and presidential systems; federalism in the Soviet Union is in practice largely overridden by the dominance of the Communist party. Even though all typologies involve intermediate or ill-fitting cases, we can use these classifications as a first approach to the phenomena we wish to study.

16   Liberal Democracy

Democracy seems to be one of the few unquestioned terms in today's world. Virtually every government claims to be democratic; certainly, Canadians claim to have a democratic system. And when we criticize government, it is often for not being democratic enough. But democracy was not always so popular. Its universal acceptance stems only from World War I, fought, in the famous words of Woodrow Wilson, "to make the world safe for democracy." Opinion was divided in the nineteenth century, and before that, almost everyone who had ever written anything on politics was sceptical about democracy.

Democracy in itself is simply a technique, a way of making certain decisions by accepting the will of the majority. For us it becomes a legitimate form of government only when it is united with the traditional Western ideals of constitutionalism, rule of law, liberty under law, and the limited state. And conversely, it is not the only legitimate form of government. Britain and the Dominions, such as Canada, became fully democratic early in this century when universal adult suffrage became a part of constitutional democracy. Prior to this century, they had often been well governed as constitutional monarchies. Although only a relatively small number of people could vote, aristocratic rule was not always considered oppressive. Our current democratic government carries on British constitutionalism while bringing the common people into the political realm.

The most basic conceptual problem today is that the two dimensions of the "how" and the "who" of government have become blurred in the single term democracy. Current usage in the Western world seems to mean not only majority rule but also a condition of freedom in which a limited state respects people's rights. Freedoms of speech, religion, and so on are commonly identified as democratic liberties. To make the issue even cloudier, democracy outside the Western world usually means government allegedly *for* the many, but conducted by a ruling elite, such as a communist vanguard party or a military junta, with few constitutional limitations on the state. This raises so many problems that we will restrict ourselves for the moment to a discussion of the Western conception of democracy, in itself no easy task. As one writer has stated:

> In the nineteenth century, democratic government was seen mainly in terms of equality of political and legal rights, of the right to vote, to express differing political opinions and to organise political opinion through political parties, of the right of elected representatives to supervise or control the activities of the government of the day. Today, much more stress is laid upon the need for the State to guarantee to everybody certain economic and social rights, involving the elimination of educational and social inequalities.[4]

Over the past century, the concept of democracy has been expanded. It has now come to imply freedom, encompassing political and social rights, as well as the rule of the many.

Brief reflection is enough to show that these two dimensions are quite different and that there is no intrinsic connection between them. Freedom is made possible only by the rule of law, which minimizes arbitrary coercion in favour of universal submission to equal laws. Yet the rule of the many, as Aristotle saw, may or may not be lawful. Specifically, a majority might take away the property, language, or religious rights of a minority unless the majority itself is restrained by the constitution. Democracy inherently requires freedom only in the limited and partial sense that a certain amount of political freedom is necessary if people are to choose officials. They must have a chance to nominate candidates, discuss issues, cast ballots, and so on. But beyond this necessary minimum, democracy in other realms of life could be quite oppressive. From now on, we will speak of a constitutional or *liberal democracy* to denote a system where the majority chooses rulers who must govern within the rule of law. This is exactly what Plato and Aristotle meant by polity.

The term liberal democracy must be carefully interpreted. It refers to liberalism in the broadest sense without distinguishing between classical and reform liberalism. Whatever their disagreements about laissez faire, social justice, redistribution, or government intervention, classical and reform liberals are united in their support of constitutional procedure, the limited state, and a private sphere of personal freedom. Liberal democracy, based on this common ground, is broad enough to encompass different experiments in economic policy. The moderate form of socialism that we have called social democracy is also compatible with liberal democracy as a system of government. The limited amounts of nationalization, central planning, and egalitarianism advocated by social democrats are subordinated to majority rule and respect for constitutional procedure.

Communism, on the other hand, is not compatible with liberal democracy. The Leninist theory of democratic centralism, when converted into the operating philosophy of the communist state, does not allow political freedom or the right of constitutional opposition. (Thus Marxist-Leninist governments refer to themselves as *people's democracies* to differentiate their form from liberal democracies of the Western type.) The uncontested elections that have always been the hallmark of communism in power are sharply different from the practice of liberal democracy. It is a good question whether a non-Leninist, but still thoroughgoing, socialist ideology could be combined with liberal democracy. Complete nationalization and central planning concentrate so much power in the hands of the state that the temptation for rulers to act arbitrarily might be overwhelming.

Liberal democracy can be briefly defined as a system of government in which the people rule themselves either directly or indirectly through chosen officials, but in either case subject to constitutional restraints on the power of the majority. This definition can be expanded by examining four operating principles of liberal democracy: equality of political rights, majority rule, political participation, and political freedom. Let us look at these individually.

EQUALITY OF POLITICAL RIGHTS

Equality of political rights means that each person has the same right to vote, run for office, serve on juries, speak on public issues, and so forth. Political rights are obviously a matter of degree, and it is only in this century, with women and racial minorities attaining these rights, that full equality has been approached in most Western systems. There is no hard and fast line to determine how much political equality is "enough" for democracy to exist, but universal suffrage of free adult males has usually sufficed in the minds of most observers.

By this criterion, the United States was the first democracy of modern times. Equality of political rights was not attained all at once—the constitution of 1787 left the determination of the franchise to the discretion of the several states. In the first decades of the nineteenth century, the states one by one adopted universal manhood suffrage, with the important exception of slaves in the South. The emancipated slaves were theoretically enfranchised after the Civil War, but many were prevented from voting by various tactics until the 1960s. Women received the vote at a single stroke by the Nineteenth Amendment to the constitution (1920).

Great Britain was somewhat behind the United States in attaining equality of political rights. At the opening of the nineteenth century, there was still a restrictive franchise that allowed only about 200,000 male property owners to vote in elections for the House of Commons. The three parliamentary Reform Acts of 1832, 1867, and 1884 gradually extended the franchise to include the middle class and the more prosperous elements of the working class. The remaining men, as well as women over thirty, received the vote in 1918, and in 1928 women were admitted to the suffrage on equal terms with men. The growth curve of the British electorate is illustrated in Figure 16.1.

The expansion of the franchise in Canada is more difficult to describe because it has been intricately involved in federal-provincial relations. Prior to 1885, qualifications to vote in parliamentary elections were determined by the provinces. In that year, Sir John A. Macdonald pushed a uniform Electoral Franchise Act through Parliament because, among other reasons, he did not like the tendency of the provinces to abolish the property franchise. The Act of 1885 established a moderate property qualification that remained until 1898, when the government of Sir Wilfrid Laurier returned the franchise to the provinces. Most property qualifications disappeared around that time.

From 1898 to 1917, the provinces controlled the federal franchise, but they could not disenfranchise particular groups of people. If a man could vote in provincial elections, he could also vote in federal elections. In other words, the provinces could not, through legislation, single out individuals or categories of individuals and deny them the right to vote in federal elections. In 1920, with the passage of

FIGURE 16.1

Number of Persons Having Right to Vote per 100 Adults

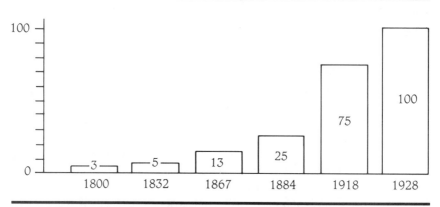

Source: J. Harvey and L. Bather, *The British Constitution*, 2nd ed. (London: Macmillan, 1968), p. 51.

the Dominion Elections Act, the federal government resumed control of qualifications for voting in federal elections. Qualifications for voting in provincial elections remained the responsibility of the provincial governments. Some women were admitted under special wartime conditions to the federal franchise in 1917, and in 1918 women over twenty-one gained the right to vote in federal elections. Provincially, they were enfranchised first in Manitoba in 1916, but not until 1940 in Quebec.[5]

Although each country's history is unique, the general pattern in the Western world has been step-by-step extension of the franchise, with adult male suffrage being reached at the end of the nineteenth or beginning of the twentieth century. Women were given the vote in most countries during or shortly after World War I. Switzerland was one exception: women gained the right to vote in federal elections in 1971 and even later in some cantonal (provincial) elections.

Since World War I, suffrage laws have continued to expand by lowering the voting age or enfranchising special minority groups, such as native peoples living on reservations. Today the franchise can hardly be extended further in most countries except by giving it to children, aliens, prisoners, and inmates of insane asylums. The right of all these groups to vote may well be litigated under s. 3 of the Canadian Charter of Rights and Freedoms: "Every citizen of Canada has the right to vote in an election of members of the House of Commons or of a legislative assembly . . ." An effort to restore the franchise to inmates of federal penitentiaries has already been launched under this section.[6] We have reached virtually the end of a process that has transformed the vote from a trust exercised by property owners or heads of families into a universal right for adult citizens.

MAJORITY RULE

Majority rule is the normal working principle of decision making in democracies. It can be derived logically from the prior principle of political equality. If each vote is to be counted equally, the decision of the majority must be accepted.

Yet in some circumstances, democracies depart from majority rule. Election to public office in Canada, Britain, and the United States is normally by *plurality* rather than *majority*. The candidate with the largest single total is declared victorious, even if it is less than the 50 per cent plus one that constitutes a majority. This is an easing of the majority criterion, done for purposes of economy. If candidates to office were always required to receive a majority, there would have to be an expensive series of run-offs to reduce the candidates to two; for only then could it be guaranteed that a plurality would also be a majority of votes cast. On the other hand, the majority requirement is sometimes raised, for example, to three-fifths, two-thirds, or three-fourths and is known as a *qualified majority*. This is done to protect the rights of minorities. Because a qualified majority is obviously harder to obtain than a simple majority, it is more difficult for the larger party to act against the rights of the smaller.

The qualified majority is a constraint on democracy, enacted in the spirit of the rule of law. It is used in most modern democracies in the process of constitutional amendment, on the assumption that the fundamental laws of the state are so important that they should not be easily altered by a simple majority. A constitutional amendment in the United States, after being passed by two-thirds of the Senate and House of Representatives, must be ratified by three-fourths of the states. In Canada the custom of the provinces consenting to amendments to the Constitution Act, 1867 that affect their rights was recognized by the Supreme Court in its September 1981 decision on patriation of the constitution, and the process was institutionalized as part of the Constitution Act, 1982. Amending most parts of the constitution requires ratification by the Senate and the House of Commons plus the legislative assemblies of "at least two-thirds of the provinces that have, in the aggregate, according to the then latest general census, at least fifty per cent of the population of all the provinces." On certain matters of fundamental importance, such as existence of the monarchy, consent of all the provinces is required.[7]

A variation of the qualified majority is the *concurrent majority*, sometimes used in the legislature of the old united province of Canada (1840–1867). An attempt was made for laws to receive a majority of votes from representatives of both Canada East (Quebec) and Canada West (Ontario). This was supposed to hinder the two regions, one English and one French, from oppressing each other. A special form of the concurrent majority is *bicameralism*, the practice of dividing the legislature into two chambers. The requirement that a bill be passed twice is meant to be a safeguard against precipitous action. Prime Minister Macdonald called the Canadian Senate "the sober second thought in legislation." He also supported the requirement, entrenched in Section 23(4) of the Constitution Act, 1867, that a senator's "Real and Personal Property shall be together worth Four thousand Dollars over and above his Debts and Liabilities," a substantial amount at that time. According to Macdonald:

> A large property qualification should be necessary for membership in the Upper House, in order to represent the principle of property. The rights of the minority must be protected, and the rich are always fewer in number than the poor.[8]

The Senate no longer plays the role Macdonald envisioned for it, but its existence demonstrates the principle that liberal democracy sometimes accepts restraints on the will of popular majorities in order to protect potentially unpopular minorities in their legal rights. A decision requirement of *unanimity* would be the ultimate in protecting minorities, for then no one could be required to do anything against his or her will. But the practical task of getting unanimous agreement is so formidable that political systems have had to settle for a qualified or concurrent majority as a restraint on popular powers.

POLITICAL PARTICIPATION

Democratic institutions are founded on mass participation. The two great varieties of democracy, which differ in the nature of this participation, are *direct democracy*, the only kind known to the ancient world, and *representative democracy*, or indirect democracy as it is sometimes called, the predominant form in modern times.

In the democratic city-states of Greece, the highest authority was the assembly of all male citizens. Executive officers were either elected by this body or chosen by lot, a procedure that was considered superbly democratic because it gave everyone an equal chance to serve. In either case, terms of office were very short, usually a year or less. Citizens were paid to hold office and even to attend assembly meetings so that poverty would not prevent participation.

Assembly-style direct democracy must face two obvious problems. One is the practical difficulty of assembling more than a few thousand persons to discuss public issues. Direct democracy was just barely possible in the Greek city-state, but how could it exist in the modern nation-state? Another question concerns the quality of decisions made by large meetings, where emotional rhetoric and demagoguery easily sway votes. The democracy of Athens destroyed itself by enthusiastically voting for a disastrous military campaign against Syracuse. The best minds of antiquity, such as Plato and Aristotle, were so unimpressed with direct democracy in action that they turned decisively against it.[9]

Representative democracy seems to transcend both objections. It overcomes the obstacles of population and distance, and it provides the means for choosing rulers whose talent is presumably superior to that of the people at large. These rulers are then kept in check and made to serve the majority through the machinery of elections. A ruler elected for life would be effectively insulated from the popular will. Hence democracy requires regular elections that those in power cannot indefinitely postpone.

The rationale of representative government was clearly stated as early as 1825 by James Mill, the first important political philosopher to come out in favour of what we would today call democracy. "The people as a body," he wrote, "cannot perform the business of government for themselves."[10] What is required, therefore, is to create a system of "checks" that will induce rulers to act for the general benefit. These checks are established by electing representatives of the community for a limited period. Limiting the duration of rule is, according to Mill, "an old and approved method of identifying as nearly as possible the interests of those who rule with the interests of those who are ruled."[11]

It cannot be emphasized too strongly that democratic elections do not and cannot decide questions of policy. Citizens vote for a representative but do not make policy decisions; elected representatives make public decisions for the society. Citizens probably agree with some opinions of their favourite candidates and disagree with others. Furthermore, neither voters nor candidates can have any clear idea of the shape of the future. Politicians are notorious for breaking campaign promises, not because they are especially dishonest, but because things look different a year or two after the election, particularly when they have the vantage point of public responsibility. Elections are much more like a post mortem inquest than a decision about the future. If the voters know they are dissatisfied with the past record of the incumbent government, they have the chance to install another government. It is not much, but we believe it is enough to keep representative democracy working.

Even if the assembly form of direct democracy is not suitable for large states, there are certain other mechanisms of direct democracy that can be used to supplement representative democracy.

The *referendum*, also called *plebiscite*, is citizen approval of legislation after an issue is referred by a legislative body to the voters.[14] It is widely used in Switzerland and in the United States by some states and cities. It is sometimes used in Canada, as in the 1980 referendum in Quebec on sovereignty association. In some provinces it is part of the provincial and local governmental process. Seven provincial plebiscites have taken place in Alberta since 1915, most of which involved liquor sales. In the most recent referendum, 1971, a majority of voters supported daylight-saving time. It should be noted that Canadian referendums are only advisory, with the actual decision being reserved for Parliament or the provincial legislature. Attachment to parliamentary sovereignty explains this reluctance to let the referendum become more than a consultative device.

In Switzerland, on the other hand, the vote in a referendum legally determines the legislative outcome of an issue. The French president can also call a national referendum on an issue, the outcome of which is binding. President de Gaulle (1959–1969) used this power on six occasions as a way of circumventing a legislature that would not co-operate with his policy proposals. While this power remains with French presidents, it has seldom been used since 1969.

The British government, in the parliamentary tradition, has used the consultative referendum to clear the air on decisive issues. In 1975 the Labour government, for the first time, called a national referendum on membership in the European Economic Community. The Conservatives in 1972 had decided on membership, but many Labour party members remained opposed to the decision. In 1975 Prime Minister Harold Wilson's Labour government used the referendum in the hope of laying the matter to rest. British voters in fact endorsed membership by slightly more than a two-thirds majority. In March 1979, the referendum was used in Scotland and Wales as a way of deciding the issue of devolution. Voters in Scotland and Wales rejected proposals for regional assemblies. This vote was a blow to nationalists in both regions.

A second element of direct democracy is the *initiative*. A specified number of voters (the number is spelled out in a constitution, statute, or city by-law) signs a petition requiring governmental action on a particular issue. That action may be that the legislative body enact the proposal outlined in the petition or that it submit the proposal to voters in a referendum. A referendum originates in the legislative body and goes to the electorate, whereas an initiative moves from the people to the legislature.

In Switzerland, for example, 50,000 votes can initiate action on an issue. The initiative has also been a frequently used device in the state of California. The famous Proposition 13 was committed to a state-wide referendum in 1978 as a result of an initiative signed by 1.5 million voters. The voters proceeded to endorse a forced limit on local property taxes, which naturally was unpopular with politicians, but very popular with the electorate.[15]

A third element of direct democracy is the *recall*, when voters in a constituency remove their elected representative from office. The practice was a populist reform introduced in the United States at the turn of the century. Its purpose was to rid the constituency of representatives dominated by political machines. Provisions for recall usually require a petition by a substantial proportion of the electorate in a constituency, and a successful recall vote requires at least a simple majority of those voting. These provisions are designed to protect representatives from a minority of voters who may not like a particular stand. Recall is used in cities and states in the United States, but less frequently today than in the 1920s. Voters in Wisconsin introduced a recall of Senator Joseph McCarthy in 1954, although it was unsuccessful.[16] An interesting episode involving the recall took place in Alberta during the first Social Credit government (1935–1940). Premier Aberhart had the legislature pass a recall act as part of a reform package, but he then had the act repealed when a petition for his own recall was circulated in his constituency.

These elements of direct democracy are the subject of much dispute. Usually they are not popular with legislators—especially initiatives and recall. It is often argued that they involve more emotion than reason. Except in Switzerland, they are used infrequently by governments at the national level. Between 1945 and 1980, for example, 169 national referendums were held in Switzerland, compared to a total of only 75 in 20 other democratic countries.[17] They still, however, offer a way for citizens to participate formally in the public decision-making process and can represent a very real check on public officials. As institutional devices, they are indeed a way of combining some of the virtues of direct democracy with representative democracy; public responsibility moves momentarily from elected representatives to the people. Their popular appeal stems perhaps from some inherent desire for direct democracy.

Public opinion polls also play an important advisory role today in all democratic countries. A democratic enthusiast will periodically remind us that it is now technically possible to wire all citizens into one computer system and let them decide all questions of public policy. But even if such a non-stop referendum were possible, it is doubtful that it would be a good idea. Complex questions of public policy need the attention and deliberation of informed minds and time for digesting different views. Representative democracy is not just a second-best substitute for direct democracy, made necessary by the size of modern states; it is a mechanism for trying to find the wisdom essential to good government.

Democratic participation extends considerably beyond electing representatives. It also includes attempting to influence the formulation of public policy by expressing ideas publicly or making submissions to elected representatives. Governments today usually go through an elaborate exercise of consultation with the public before major legislation is passed. A general policy statement may be published, followed by a draft of the statute. There are often public hearings at which interested parties express their views. In fact, participation has expanded so much in recent years, particularly at the level of local government, that it is sometimes subject to criticism on the grounds that it unduly slows decision making and offers too much influence to vocal and well-organized minorities.

It is not unusual for governments, even when they possess a strong parliamentary majority, to withdraw or modify policy proposals in the face of public criticism. When the Progressive Conservatives proposed partially de-indexing pensions for the elderly in the budget speech of April 1985, they were surprised at the broad support within many sectors of the populace for retaining full indexation. In this and many other cases, public reaction to draft legislation has led to eventual modifications. Public participation and consultation is an ongoing process in democratic government; elections merely punctuate the process and change the participants.

POLITICAL FREEDOM

Meaningful participation is possible only if political freedom prevails. Unfree participation or directed mobilization of the masses is characteristic not of genuine democracy, but of totalitarian pseudo-democracy. An infallible test for political freedom is the legitimacy of opposition. Freedom is meaningful only if it extends to those who think differently from those in authority. Freedom only to agree is no freedom at all. If freedom does not exist, public support or opposition is only speculative, and this lack of knowledge can become a convenient device for manipulative rulers. At the same time, the opposition in a liberal democracy must operate within the rule of law. Resorting to unlawful means of action, such as conniving with foreign powers or preparing an insurrection, is not compatible with political freedom in a liberal democracy.

Political freedom has numerous aspects: the right to speak freely, even to criticize the government; the right to form associations, including political parties, which may oppose the government; the right to run for office; and the right to vote without intimidation and choose among more than one candidate for office. Without these rights, democracy might be "for the people," but certainly not "by the people."

Extensive and important as it is, political freedom is only a part of the whole range of personal freedoms. For instance, it does not include the right to own property or the right to use one's chosen language. It is quite possible for very wide political freedom to co-exist with, and even be the cause of, reduced freedom in other areas. To take an example from Quebec: all citizens have full political freedom in that province, but in the years 1977–1983, before the Parti Québécois government amended its language legislation, businesspeople were not allowed to put signs on their buildings in any language other than French. In this instance, the majority used its political freedom to reduce the linguistic freedom of minorities.

This small but not unimportant example highlights a general problem of constitutional democracy: can the power of the majority be restrained by law so that it does not use its political freedom to take away other freedoms of unpopular minorities? The tension between democracy and the rule of law is shown in this passage from Xenophon, one of the pupils of Socrates. The quotation describes a proposal in the Athenian assembly—the democratic gathering of all male citizens—to arrest certain alleged enemies of the regime.

> Great numbers cried out that it was monstrous if the people were to be prevented from doing whatever they wished. . . . Then the Prytanes [the executive committee of the assembly], stricken with fear, agreed to put the question—all of them except Socrates . . . he said that in no case would he act except in accordance with the law.[18]

Socrates was ultimately put to death by a democracy that ignored the rule of law and heeded only its own will.

The classical fear of democracy, voiced by Aristotle and echoed by countless other writers, is that the many would use their political power to expropriate and distribute the wealth of the few. In the words of John Adams, second president of the United States:

Debts would be abolished first; taxes laid heavy on the rich, and not at all on the others; and at last a downright equal division of everything be demanded and voted.[19]

In fact, the record of liberal democracy does not bear out this gloomy prediction of a dramatic clash between rich and poor, probably because in those countries where liberal democracy has been successful, society has not been polarized into extremes of wealth and poverty.

A more realistic danger for liberal democracy arises from the interest group competition that is endemic to modern democratic politics. The freedom and participation that are part of liberal democracy encourage the formation of organized groups who try to promote the interests of their members. Universal suffrage and majority rule imply a necessity for politicians to appeal to these groups in order to build electoral coalitions. In return for their support, these groups often demand concessions or privileges from government that are contrary to the general interest. Manufacturers demand import quotas and protective tariffs; unions work for laws on collective bargaining and picketing to promote their ability to extract concessions from employers; the organized professions seek rules of licensing and accreditation to keep out "unqualified" practitioners; dependent groups like pensioners or welfare recipients agitate for higher transfer payments. Democratic politics may consequently degenerate into an auction in which state power is in effect sold to the highest bidder to be used for group advantage. Over time, the result may be an accumulation of restrictions and special privileges contrary to the spirit of liberal democracy.[20]

Something like this was foreseen in the last century by Tocqueville, who predicted that democracy might bring about a novel form of despotism, not cruel and violent, but "regular, quiet, and gentle." His words are reminiscent of some of the less attractive features of the welfare state:

> It covers the surface of society with a network of small complicated rules, minute and uniform, through which the most original minds and the most energetic characters cannot penetrate, to rise above the crowd. The will of man is not shattered, but softened, bent, and guided; men are seldom forced by it to act, but they are constantly restrained from acting: such a power does not destroy, but it prevents existence; it does not tyrannize, but it compresses, enervates, extinguishes, and stupefies a people, till each nation is reduced to be nothing better than a flock of timid and industrious animals, of which the government is the shepherd.[21]

ELITES

A serious criticism of representative democracy is that it is elitist. It is true that by definition, representative democracies are a form of elite rule, if by *elite* we mean "a minority of the population which takes the major decisions in the society."[12] But to understand the place of political elites in modern politics, one must understand the difference between elites in Western societies and elites in traditional societies. Although traditional elites were a very small segment of society, they played an enormous role. An interlocking and related group of families dominated the social, economic, and political life of a society. In most instances they owned large estates, and their children inherited all the wealth and responsibilities that went along with their status.

Traditional societies were highly stratified; that is, there was a large gap between the elite and the masses. This simple, dichotomized society was perpetuated as the children of the elite inherited their positions, while opportunities for the masses were restricted. There was little if any social mobility between the elite and the masses.

In all Western societies, this situation has gradually been transformed. The Industrial Revolution broke the hold of the landed aristocracy and created new sources of wealth and employment; mass education created opportunities for many in the lower classes; guilds and unions helped improve working conditions and wages for artisans and workers; urban centres served as the base for dynamic marketing systems; and new attitudes about equality and freedom led to more participatory politics.

Modern society is characterized by a large middle class, not by a polarization between wealth and poverty. Opportunities for education and jobs have become extensive, creating a great deal of social mobility between classes. Politics is charged with new sources of authority and legitimacy. In short, the old dualism of the traditional society has given way to a very complex and dynamic modern social order.

Correspondingly, the old idea of a traditional elite was replaced by the concept of pluralism. New elites began to spring up and challenge the agrarian aristocracy. An industrial elite, a commercial elite, a financial elite, a military elite, and even a political elite emerged with wealth and power, posing a threat for the old guard with its roots in the land. In modern societies, elites do not disappear; rather, they become more numerous and more diverse. Marxists tend to deny that modern changes have really affected societies that much. They still see a simple dichotomy— the rulers and the ruled. The two-class situation dominates their frame of reference; in other than socialist societies, rulers are thought to exploit the masses. But other observers recognize that modern societies, and modern politics, have become pluralistic. As the French author Raymond Aron has written:

> . . . democratic societies, which I would rather call pluralistic societies, are full of the noise of public strife between the owners of the means of production, trade union leaders and politicians. As all are entitled to form associations, professional and political organizations abound, each one defending its members' interests with passionate ardour. Government becomes a business of compromises.[13]

In democracies, those who aspire to rule must build a power base. They must first of all be chosen by the electorate, and if they are to remain in office, their policies must be responsive to the needs of some coalition of groups. Contemporary theorists of democracy emphasize the competition of these diverse elites. They see the representative system as an instrument for ensuring that no elite can attain power divorced from the desires of the ordinary people. If elections are doing their job, then there is not necessarily a contradiction between liberal democracies and elite rule.

In sum, a liberal-democratic political system is one in which, on the basis of universal adult suffrage, citizens select their governors (representatives); these representatives are responsible to the electorate through periodic elections; individual or group opinions can be discussed freely without fear of retaliation by public officials or private individuals; a legal opposition is free to criticize; and an independent judiciary resolves disputes between citizens, between citizens and government, and between levels of governments. If this seems excessively long for a definition, it is because it is not easy to characterize in a few words a form of government that seeks to reconcile the two dimensions of freedom and majority rule.

How many contemporary governments can be called liberal democracies? Restricting judgment to the years after World War II, there would be universal agreement to include in this category Japan, Israel, Australia and New Zealand, the United States and Canada, and the nineteen countries of non-communist Europe, although qualifications must be made about Portugal, Spain, Greece, and Turkey. The first two emerged only in the 1970s from long periods of authoritarian rule; Greece was under a military dictatorship from 1967 to 1974; and a military government was proclaimed in Turkey in 1980 when the country seemed on the verge of civil war. In Latin America Costa Rica, Venezuela, and perhaps also Mexico and Colombia have experienced some years as liberal democracies. In 1980 the military returned Peru to civilian control, as occurred in Argentina, Brazil, and Uruguay in 1984; Chile, which at one time was a democracy, has remained under military rule since 1973. In the Caribbean one could count Jamaica and perhaps some of the medley of smaller islands. In Africa many attempts were made to form liberal democracies at the time of decolonization, but virtually all have been overthrown. South Africa proceeds by majority rule among the white community, but that is only a minority of the whole population, and even its political freedom is rather circumscribed. Democracy still exists in the new state of Zimbabwe, although Prime Minister Robert Mugabe has repeatedly declared his intention of creating a one-party state. Apart from Japan, India is the only major democratic power in Asia. Making allowance for borderline cases, three dozen is a reasonable approximation of the number of liberal democracies in the world—between 20 and 25 per cent of the sovereign states and approximately 30 per cent of the world's population.

Numerous explanations have been advanced for the obvious fact that liberal democracy has taken root and flourished almost exclusively in Europe and countries such as Canada, New Zealand, and Israel that are inhabited chiefly by people of European extraction. Transplantation to non-European societies has been extremely difficult, though the examples of Japan and India show that success is possible. No single explanation adequately deals with all cases, but there are several that throw some light on the question. We can somewhat artificially divide these explanations into economic, social, and political.

Aristotle already saw the relationship between constitutional democracy, or polity, and property. Democracy would quickly degenerate into class war if society was polarized along economic lines. This polarization is a fact of life in much of the Third World, where there is a small class of landlords and industrialists, a large class of peasants and labourers, and no significant middle class. In such a situation, the left is always tempted to use democracy as a means of confiscating and redistributing, while the right strives to maintain its position by manipulating elected politicians or resorting to military rule. This overheated climate, akin to and sometimes engendering civil war, does not produce the popular consensus that liberal democracy requires.

In social terms, liberal democracy is a political expression of a society that has undergone the transition from traditional to legal authority. This transition took place in Western Europe, frequently accompanied by violent revolutions, in the eighteenth and nineteenth centuries. Stable liberal democracy did not emerge until after many years of conflict. It is perhaps premature to think that liberal democracy can exist in societies that are presently in the throes of such a momentous transformation.

Finally, the political rivalry between the world's great powers intensifies the difficulties of democracy. Neither the United States nor the Soviet Union willingly loses an ally or a client state. The Soviet bloc gives massive military and economic aid to left-wing dictatorships, such as those in Ethiopia and South Yemen. It also assists insurgent movements in countries such as El Salvador and secretly supplies money, arms, and technical advice to terrorist groups around the world, even when they do not follow orthodox communism. Terrorist disruption of liberal democracy is an effective means of paving the way for a communist-led revolution. The United States, for its part, bolsters many non-democratic regimes, such as South Korea and the Philippines, as long as they remain anticommunist, and has sometimes connived to overthrow democratically elected governments that have become dominated by the left. Such external intervention tends to destroy the moderate centre ground upon which, as Aristotle saw, democracy must rest.

17   Totalitarianism

Aristotle defined tyranny as "the arbitrary power of an individual which is responsible to no one, and governs all alike . . . with a view to its own advantage, not to that of its subjects, and therefore against their will."[22] Montesquieu (1689–1755) said much the same thing when he defined *despotism* as one man ruling through fear without regard to law.[23] These and other definitions of tyranny or despotism always point to certain similar and interrelated characteristics:

1. Rule is arbitrary and not bound by law.
2. Rule is exercised in the interest of the rulers and not in the common interest.
3. Rule is based on coercion and fear.

These ideas are logically interlocked. People willingly submit to authority if it is exercised under genuine laws that are universal rules of conduct, binding government and citizens alike for the common good. If these conditions are not met, fear must substitute for voluntary compliance.

Note that the essence of tyrannical rule appears in the "how" of government, not in the "who." It is not a question of numbers. A single individual who rules under law is a constitutional monarch; someone who rules arbitrarily, according to caprice, would be called a tyrant.

Montesquieu's most famous book, *The Spirit of the Laws* (1748), gives an unforgettable description of despotism:

> When the savages of Louisiana are desirous of fruit, they cut the tree to the root, and gather the fruit. This is the emblem of despotic government.[24]

What he meant is that tyranny or despotism is the direct application of force to human affairs, disregarding the internal laws by which society is structured. It is the exaltation of the tyrant's will above all else. Like cutting down a tree to harvest the fruit, it may achieve some immediate result, but it destroys the social order by subordinating all human relationships to fear.

Tyranny is nothing new. There is little to be added to the description and analysis of it given by classical authors such as Plato, Xenophon, and Aristotle. But many scholars argue that the twentieth century has witnessed a new form of despotic rule: *totalitarianism*. The word was coined by Mussolini to describe his system of government. He epitomized his views in a speech in 1925: "Everything in the state, nothing outside the state, nothing against the state."[25] The term was soon accepted by the Nazi regime in Germany, applied by external observers to the Stalinist regime in the Soviet Union, and extended to the People's Republic of China under Mao Zedong. The concept does not include sundry dictatorships, both of the right and of the left, such as Pinochet of Chile, Mobutu of Zaire, or Marcos of the Philippines.

In a perceptive analysis of the way modern political leaders can manipulate the masses, use political organization and the power of the state, and apply ideology and terror, Hannah Arendt notes that

> totalitarianism differs essentially from other forms of political oppression known to us such as despotism, tyranny and dictatorship. Wherever it rose to power, it developed entirely new political institutions and destroyed all social, legal and political traditions of the country.[26]

Totalitarianism as a term was most commonly used immediately after World War II. Its use has become somewhat less frequent as Hitler and Mussolini have faded from public memory, as the Soviet regime has moderated in some respects after Stalin's death in 1953, and since communist China, fearful of the Soviet Union, has been improving its relations with the rest of the world. Naturally, communists have never accepted the term, which equates them with fascists; they regard it as a piece of capitalist propaganda. They prefer to emphasize alleged resemblances between Western democracies and fascist dictatorships.

The term totalitarian is thus a contentious one. It has been enmeshed in Cold War polemics, and some scholars have held that the concept is propaganda—that it has existed more in the minds of analysts who were either anticommunist or antifascist than as a classification for real political systems. President Ronald Reagan and members of his administration often use the term to describe communist systems, or systems such as that in Nicaragua, that appear to be moving toward communism. As the term is still used by politicians, journalists, and scholars in the West, it deserves serious analysis.[27]

Hannah Arendt restricts the term totalitarian to a small number of regimes that combine an all-powerful political leader and an almost Messianic sense of historical mission. Distinguishing features of such a system are a revolutionary movement that is in accord with "nature" or "history" and the use of terror as an essential tactic to maintain the momentum of a society on the move. The leader uses systematic terror as a means of keeping the entire populace off balance, of atomizing individuals. Arendt describes this use of terror:

> Under conditions of total terror not even fear can any longer serve as an advisor of how to behave, because terror chooses its victims without reference to individual actions or thoughts, exclusively in accordance with the objective necessity of the natural or historical process.[28]

In Arendt's analysis, the arbitrary use of terror on any and all segments of the population becomes an institutionalized way of preventing the development of political forces opposed to the leader's vision of a new society.

Carl Friedrich and Zbigniew Brzezinski present a broader concept of totalitarianism as a set of interrelated characteristics, a "syndrome" or "pattern of interrelated traits":

> an official ideology, a single party typically led by one man, a terroristic police, a communications monopoly, a weapons monopoly, and a centrally directed economy.[29]

Rearranging these characteristics slightly and adding some related ones, we would list eight elements of the totalitarian "syndrome." One or more of these elements may be found individually in other forms of government, but it is their union and interrelationship that constitute totalitarianism.

ATTEMPT TO REMAKE SOCIETY

Central to totalitarianism, distinguishing it from simple tyranny, is the attempt to remake society on a grand scale, to produce a condition of utopian perfection. These blueprints for the future are usually considered a part of the official ideology. Communists, for example, claim to be working toward the "classless society" and the "withering away of the state." This transformational view of history is enshrined in the Soviet constitution, whose preamble asserts that the Soviet Union is now "a developed socialist society," which is "a logically necessary state on the path to communism."[30] Hitler envisioned a "new order" in which the German "master race" would create a new empire (Third Reich) that would "last a thousand years." Mussolini proclaimed the age of the "Third Rome" in which modern Italy, following the Roman Empire and the Roman papacy, would again lead the world to new heights of civilization. Although the communist and fascist visions of the future differ from each other, they share common features. Both are sweeping, radical, and, above all, *monistic*, reducing everything to a single factor—class (communism), race (Nazism), or state (Mussolini's fascism). This monism gives rise to terror as a principle of government because pluralistic society must be forcibly remoulded to fit the monistic image. Thus the enormous scale of violence arises that has marked totalitarianism. Hitler liquidated six million Jews and a half million Gypsies as inferior races. In the 1930s, Stalin eliminated millions of *kulaks* (independent peasants) by famine and deportation. Between 1975 and 1979, the Khmer Rouge may have killed one-quarter to one-third of the population of Kampuchea (Cambodia). The Cambodian doctor who lived through this horror and went on to win an Oscar for his role in *The Killing Fields* has said that the appalling brutality exhibited in this movie was much less than the reality. At the time of the "Great Leap Forward" (1958), a disastrous attempt to industrialize China almost overnight, Mao characterized totalitarianism in an unforgettable way:

> Apart from their other characteristics, China's 600 million people have two remarkable peculiarities; they are, first of all, poor, and secondly, blank. . . . A clean sheet of paper has no blotches, and so the newest and most beautiful pictures can be painted on it.[31]

Society, to vary the metaphor, is conceived as raw material to be moulded by the state according to ideological design.

ONE-PARTY STATE

One single, mass political party penetrates all aspects of state and society: army, schools, trade unions, and so forth. This disciplined party, controlled from above, co-ordinates all sectors of society. Churches, universities, unions, and government departments may be formally distinct from one another, but the leaders of all institutions are either members of the party or acceptable to it. All other political parties are outlawed, as in the Soviet Union, or carefully manipulated in a common front, as in East Germany and Poland. In neither case is real opposition tolerated.

This "leading role of the party" is a central tenet of communism. The Soviet Union intervened in Czechoslovakia in 1968 because it feared that the Communist party was losing its monopoly of political power. Reforms and experiments are tolerated only as long as the party's position is not threatened. The proclamation of martial law in Poland in December 1981 occurred after the Solidarity labour movement began to speak of nominating its own candidates for election to public office. Martial law was revoked only after Solidarity was effectively driven underground.

Rejecting political pluralism is linked to the transformation of society. If, as in Mao's metaphor, a picture is being painted, the artist must be in control of the materials and cannot allow another artist to sketch a rival conception on the same canvas. The fundamental difference between totalitarianism and liberal democracy is the assumption that society is united in a single, common project directed by the party through the state. In contrast, the liberal democrat sees society as the field in which individuals and groups pursue projects of their own choosing.

ALL-POWERFUL LEADER

At one time, it seemed that the domination of the party by an all-powerful, charismatic leader was an integral part of totalitarianism. But Mussolini, Hitler, Lenin, Stalin, Mao Zedong, Ho Chi Minh, and Tito have passed away without leaving replacements of comparable stature. The only totalitarian leaders today who might be called omnipotent or charismatic are Kim Il Sung of North Korea and Fidel Castro of Cuba. It may be that charismatic leadership is a phenomenon of the early stages of totalitarianism, transmitting the energy necessary to seize and consolidate power. The routinization of charisma described by Max Weber in other contexts applies here as well, and after the death of the leader, power passes into the collective leadership of the party. There may be a reaction against the departed leader, as in the Soviet Union after Stalin's death in 1953, when a new generation of leaders criticized the "cult of personality" and vowed that it would never happen again. Or, as is now taking place in China, the memory of the leader may be revered and made almost mythical, but there is an effective break with many of his policies. In any case, the evidence is that totalitarianism seems able to carry on indefinitely without charismatic leadership.[32]

PSEUDO-DEMOCRATIC RULE
The leader and the party maintain their power by force but rationalize their rule with pseudo-democratic arguments. Hitler argued that he represented "the people" (*das Volk*) in such a special way that elections were unnecessary. Communism relies on Lenin's theory of democratic centralism. Elections take place, but the party nominates all the candidates. There is usually only one candidate per position, and voting is more ratification than selection. The role of an elected representative or party member is not to contest the policies of the leadership but to engender and maintain society's support for the leadership and its policies. In reality, new leaders are co-opted by powerful party members. Limited political pluralism may exist within the party as different factions contend for power, but it does not spill over into the public at large, which knows little of such intra-party contests.

Authoritarian regimes also use such pseudo-democratic devices to legitimize their authority. But pseudo-democracy is an intrinsic part of totalitarianism. Because society is being remade, it is important to create popular participation without allowing the people to change their rulers. Thus the curious situation arises that mandatory political participation, though ineffective and meaningless from a liberal-democratic point of view, is energetically promoted by the state. Voting is made a legal duty. Courses in political education in school and university are mandatory. Attendance at political meetings and discussion groups is encouraged or even required. Parades and demonstrations are arranged as needed for specific purposes. In contrast, authoritarian regimes are usually happiest if their subjects stay out of politics and refrain from criticism.

CONTROL OF COMMUNICATIONS
The totalitarian state seeks to monopolize the flow of ideas. This means that the physical bases of communication—newspapers, radio and television stations, publishing houses—are owned and/or completely controlled by the state. Pre-publication censorship is rigidly enforced to ensure that public statements follow what communists call the "party line." Even photocopying machines are considered a potential threat, and in Eastern Europe access to them is carefully restricted. Foreign books, newspapers, and magazines are not sold freely, but are confined to special libraries used by trustworthy researchers. With the means of mass communication so much under state control, dissenting opinions can circulate only by word of mouth or by the painful process of dissidents typing and retyping—what the Russians call *samizdat*, "self-publication."

The purpose of this control of communications is to support an official ideology. Political doctrine is espoused by the totalitarian state in much the same way as other states in the past have had an official religion. Fascism or Marxism-Leninism is taught in the schools and otherwise made the only publicly acceptable system of belief, while competing ideologies are subject to persecution.

An important aspect of totalitarianism is the extension of ideology from a political doctrine to an all-encompassing system influencing other areas of reality, even the fine arts and natural sciences. Because of Albert Einstein's Jewish origin, the Nazis rejected the theory of relativity as "Jewish science" and did not allow it to be taught in German universities. Jewish works of art and literature were likewise banned. In the Soviet Union in the 1930s, an obscure agronomist named T. D. Lysenko attracted Stalin's attention with the Lamarckian theory of the inheritance of acquired characteristics, which had been otherwise discredited. Lysenko promised a shortcut to breeding better strains of wheat and cattle; instead of the patient work of selective breeding over generations, it was necessary to nourish only one generation exceptionally well and let it pass on its vigour to its progeny. This doctrine was officially ratified by the Central Committee of the Communist party in 1948 and was not discredited until after the fall of Nikita Khruschev in 1964. It dealt Soviet agriculture a blow from which it has never fully recovered. In China the expansion of ideology merged with the charismatic leadership of Mao Zedong to produce the almost magical "thought of Chairman Mao":

> The thought of Mao Tse-tung is the sun in our heart, is the root of our life, is the source of all our strength. Through this, man becomes unselfish, daring, intelligent, able to do everything. . . . The thought of Mao Tse-tung trans- forms man's ideology, transforms the Fatherland.[33]

USE OF TERROR

Totalitarian rule is supported by the terroristic activities of a special *political police* (for example, Hitler's Gestapo or the Soviet KGB). Such a political police reports directly to the leader and is under no legal restraint. It may use intimidation, arbitrary arrest, torture, and execution. It infiltrates other coercive agencies of the state, such as the regular police or the armed forces, to ensure their compliance. Canadians and Americans have no experience with a political police. The RCMP and the FBI perform security and counter-espionage functions among their many responsibilities, and anyone accused of political crimes is tried in the normal courts and sentenced to confinement in normal penitentiaries. A true political police operates as an empire in itself, maintaining its own prisons, mental hospitals, and labour camps. It is outside the supervision of the courts and other legal agencies of the state.

Authoritarian regimes also use political police, and their methods may be equally grim. But there is a difference in the scale of operations. Tyrants usually single out political opponents for mistreatment, whereas totalitarian regimes may use the political police against almost anyone. This is a logical consequence of remaking society. Anyone who does not wholeheartedly embrace the state-sponsored monistic society of the future is a political opponent. The difference could be formulated this way: in a liberal democracy, the main political crime is to attempt or advocate the violent overthrow of the government; in an authoritarian regime, even criticism or peaceful opposition becomes a political crime; in a totalitarian state, literally any word or action that suggests less than complete commitment to the regime can become cause for detention by the political police.

SUBORDINATION OF LAW TO THE STATE

Law is the tool of the totalitarian state, which pushes legal positivism to its extreme. Law is only what the state says, and it may speak differently tomorrow. Law is subordinate to the state, not the other way around; there are no rights in the proper sense of the term, for rights exist only under law.

In the enthusiasm of the first years after the October Revolution, Soviet theorists held that law would disappear altogether in a communist society. Enforceable rules of conduct were required because of the antagonisms of class society, but they would no longer be necessary in the classless society of the future. These early notions were long ago replaced by the concept of *socialist legality*, which is a particular form of legal positivism. The state should follow regularized procedures in dealing with citizens. These legal norms, however, arise not from an existing consensus in the present society but from the desired shape of the hypothetical future society under construction. Because the state, guided by the party, is the only legitimate interpreter of the goal of evolution, it is for all practical purposes the source of all law.

One manifestation of this is the status of constitutional documents in totalitarian states. All the communist states have constitutions that spell out civil liberties in admirable terms. What could be clearer than article 45 of the Chinese constitution: "Citizens enjoy freedom of speech, correspondence, the press, assembly, association, procession, demonstration and the freedom to strike, and have the right to 'speak out freely, air their views fully, hold great debates and write big-character posters.'"[34] In fact, periods of freedom of speech have been announced several times in China with great fanfare, as in Mao's "Hundred Flowers" campaign of 1957 ("Let a hundred flowers bloom, let a hundred schools of thought contend") or after Mao's death in September 1976, when the new leadership suggested the virtue of "four freedoms." In each case, the state intervened to suppress discussion when it threatened to become critical.

PLANNED ECONOMY

The totalitarian state meticulously controls a planned economy. This may entail public ownership, as in communism, or state supervision of private enterprise, as in Nazi Germany and fascist Italy, where each state took a vigorous role in setting prices and production quotas. A controlled economy is a necessity to the totalitarian state. It cannot allow a liberal economy, in which each individual or group pursues private interests and co-ordination is left to the process of reaction and interaction, something Adam Smith called the "invisible hand." Individual interests and purposes must be subordinated to the imposed purpose of social transformation.

This helps explain the position of labour unions in totalitarian states. All such states foster unions by making membership compulsory, but they are not autonomous associations of workers. Leadership is controlled by party members, and collective bargaining in the Western sense does not take place. The union is a control by the state over the workers, rather than an expression of the workers' own interests. This is not surprising because in any economy, labour is the most important factor of production. If the state could not set wages or otherwise direct labour, central planning would be meaningless. Therefore the emergence in Poland in 1980 of the Solidarity union as an autonomous force, no longer directed by the government, was an event of the highest significance. The government of General Jaruzelski reacted in December 1981 by declaring martial law, which restricted the activities of Solidarity. Then in October 1982, all unofficial unions were banned, re-establishing the supremacy of the Communist party and demonstrating the reluctance of the leadership to accept relatively autonomous organizations in society. Incipient economic pluralism is not compatible with the inner logic of the totalitarian state. It is not in the short run as obvious a threat to the state as the Prague Spring of 1968, but in the long run, it is hard to imagine how totalitarianism can co-exist with a free labour movement.

Totalitarianism, then, makes use of the vastly improved technical apparatus of rule that has become available in this century. Innovations in mass communication make it possible to saturate the population with propaganda to an unprecedented degree. Inventions in weapons and forms of organization allow coercion on a novel scale. Totalitarianism is in one sense a bigger and better despotism, a utopian impulse for a perfectly harmonious society, implemented by the most up-to-date means of despotism. But it differs from authoritarianism in the importance of ideology and the single-minded urge to remake society.

Many aspects of the totalitarian syndrome can also be found in other types of systems. For instance, there are many governments today that practise terror as a means of supporting a leader. The most recent Argentine military regime (1976–1984) was brutal at times in its treatment of the "opposition." Was this treatment not worse than the way many totalitarian regimes treat their citizens? But violence in itself is not necessarily a mark of a totalitarian system. As in many schemes that involve classification, a number of factors must be present that together form a particular method of organizing political rule.

The common denominator of totalitarian systems is that the political leaders have a tremendous will to change significantly the nature of the society, mobilize the people in order to achieve change, and use indiscriminate force against those who might oppose the change. This seems to be the telling difference between totalitarian and authoritarian dictatorships. Authoritarian dictators usually try to .void extensive changes. Indeed, change is considered disruptive and should be avoided or at least carefully administered. The totalitarian regime, on the other hand, is much engrossed in a vision of achieving a new destiny for the society. The means to this end is rapid and pervasive change. Thus, in spite of costs, the compelling drive to change in order to attain a utopian social order is the mark of a totalitarian system. The distinction between authoritarian and totalitarian features should be more explicit after discussing authoritarian systems in the next chapter.

Recognizing that there may be some disagreement about this list, we submit the following as instances of totalitarianism: Hitler's Germany (1933–1945) and Mussolini's Italy (1922–1943); the Soviet Union, especially but not only under Stalin (1924–1953); certain Marxist-Leninist states closely allied to the Soviet Union, but not subject to direct control, such as North Korea and Vietnam (which has its own satellites of Laos and Kampuchea); the People's Republic of China, particularly when Mao Zedong was in full control (1949–1976); Albania; and perhaps the most brutal government of the twentieth century, Kampuchea under the Khmer Rouge (1975–1979).

The Soviet satellites—Poland, East Germany, Czechoslovakia, Hungary, Romania, Bulgaria, Afghanistan, and Mongolia—pose a special problem of classification. Their governments, formed more or less closely on the Soviet model, are in many ways totalitarian. But they remain in power only because of Soviet military pressure and support and would probably collapse if this support were withdrawn, as shown by Soviet military repression of popular movements in East Germany in 1953, Hungary in 1956, Czechoslovakia in 1968, and currently in Afghanistan. Thus these satellite governments are more a phenomenon of great-power imperialism than of a true totalitarian impulse within society. Other cases that are difficult to classify are Yugoslavia, whose regime is considerably more relaxed than that of the other communist states, or African states, such as Ethiopia and Mozambique, whose governments espouse the goals of Marxism-Leninism but may lack the technical capacity to fully implement them. The regimes mentioned in this paragraph would probably be considered totalitarian under the "syndrome" approach of Friedrich and Brzezinski, but not under Hannah Arendt's narrower definition, which emphasizes continued terror on a large scale.

Great despotisms of the past had relatively simple aims: to rule and perhaps to conquer. Rulers acted ruthlessly to achieve those aims; but outside that sphere, subjects were left largely alone as long as they showed no signs of opposition. This is still generally true of authoritarian regimes. Although ordinary citizens may at times be caught up in events, systematic persecution is usually reserved for political opponents. But in Hitler's Germany, Stalin's Russia, and Pol Pot's Kampuchea, whole categories of citizens were eliminated because there was no place for them in the new order; and all citizens were subjected to massive changes in their lives.

Having said all this, it is important to note that totalitarianism in practice, at least in the Soviet Union and its client states, has given rise to curiously conservative regimes. After the hostile classes are liquidated and the social order is remade, what remains is a society subject to pervasive and paternalistic supervision by the state. First-time travellers in Eastern Europe are liable to think they are caught in a time warp. Fashions in clothing, hairstyles, television, movies, magazines, recreation, and consumer goods seem slowed down and behind trends in the Western world. The "routinization of charisma" leaves a society heavily burdened with bureaucracy and dependent on the outside world for most of its innovations.

18   Authoritarianism

More than a hundred contemporary states would not fit comfortably into the categories of either liberal democracy or totalitarianism. The most common word used to describe these regimes is authoritarian. In a way, the term is ambiguous, for authority is a universal aspect of politics and is as much a part of liberal democracy as of the so-called authoritarian governments. The concept *authoritarianism* implies authority that may or may not rest on wide popular support but that is not put to the test of free elections. Another problem in speaking of authoritarian regimes is that the category includes such a wide diversity of types. Some regimes are civilian (Syria), others military (Guatemala); some are secular (Iraq), others avowedly religious (Libya); some are capitalistic (South Korea), others socialistic (Tanzania).

We cannot pursue all these differences here, but we will draw a distinction between right-wing conservative regimes that interpret their mission as protecting society from harmful (usually communist) influences and left-wing revolutionary regimes that claim to be building some sort of new society, usually socialist. Current examples of the former are Chile, Nigeria, Paraguay, South Korea, and Taiwan; of the latter, Tanzania, Libya, Iraq, and Nicaragua. As well, there are some regimes that are ideologically centrist, like Kenya or Ecuador.

There are important similarities across the political spectrum in the way authoritarian government is conducted. All assume that the peaceful but still very real conflicts that occur within liberal democracy are too costly and divisive. Centrifugal social forces must be held together—coercively, if necessary.

RIGHT-WING AUTHORITARIANISM
Drawing heavily upon the example of Spain under Franco (1936–1975), Juan Linz has developed a model of the right-wing authoritarian system of government that emphasizes the following characteristics: limited political pluralism; no elaborate or guiding ideology; no extensive political mobilization; and leaders exercising power within ill-defined yet predictable limits.[35] One might add to these a movement toward statism and the dominant political role of the military.

In most right-authoritarian systems, there is no idea of a classless society or a master race. A substantial degree of social pluralism is tolerated. As the society grows more complex, a variety of organizations—business associations, labour unions, churches, peasant groups, and so on—can function with a minimum of interference by government. In fact, an authoritarian regime may use these organizations to help achieve such goals as producing certain goods and services or generating political support. These segments of the population can survive as entities as long as they offer political support or at least remain politically neutral. If, however, they become too critical of government policy or suggest a change in political leadership, they are expendable.

Authoritarian systems do not have an elaborate blueprint for utopian order. While the authoritarian ruler always advocates economic development, there is usually no doctrinaire plan for a total transformation of the society to achieve this growth. Rather, economic development—the most common objective—is defined in terms of doing more of what is already being done and doing it within the existing structures of society.

Brazil under twenty years of military rule is a case in point. State-directed capitalism was the order of the day for the Brazilian military, who ruled from 1964 to 1984. Their objective was to achieve rapid economic development by managing a mixed economy. Indeed, Brazil made significant advances when one views the overall growth rate. While the picture changed somewhat during the last ten years because of slower growth and inflationary pressures, progress in the first decade of military rule was dramatic, with growth averaging about 10 per cent per year. These impressive statistics must be qualified, however, by Brazil's very uneven economic growth. Sectors that were growing prior to 1964 became even more dynamic. But regions where poverty was extensive, such as the north-east, were bypassed by the new prosperity. Moreover, many of the opponents of the regime were repressed if they objected to the military's plan of action. In effect, Brazil became a classic case of the "trickle-down theory"—where an infusion of capital benefitted the already prosperous segments of the economy, but very little spilled over into the marginal sectors.

Another characteristic of the authoritarian model is the fact that there is no great drive to mobilize the society to achieve utopian ends. In Chile, for example, all political parties are banned; the military government does not even maintain a party of its own, so great is its distaste for mass participation in politics. Mobilizing large numbers of people can nurture political instability; it breaks down old patterns of living and creates new institutions. Unless the effects of these changes can be channelled or contained, they can be disastrous for a political leader. This is one of the primary reasons for the elaborate controls imposed by totalitarian leaders. Few authoritarian leaders are willing to risk the consequences of drastic change. On the contrary, most cling to the stability of the status quo. However, they may undertake certain reforms, particularly in the interest of economic efficiency. South Korea has redistributed much agricultural land from large landowners to smaller peasants, and the late Shah of Iran confiscated large landholdings of the Islamic clergy. Improvements in non-political areas, such as technical education, are also not uncommon in conservative authoritarian regimes, but reform generally stops short of upsetting the balance of political power.

Rightist authoritarianism, even though broadly opposed to socialism, often leans toward *statism*. Rulers are usually unwilling to leave the process of economic development entirely to the private sector. While they may not impose state ownership of the economy, they do see the state as a principal instrument for expanding the production of goods and services. The state becomes the driving force, influencing wages, employment, investment, development, and management of natural resources and international trade. This particular role of the state seems to be a significant characteristic of many authoritarian systems. Yet such a generalization is subject to certain qualifications. There are numerous authoritarian governments that have used their concentrated political power to impose many, if not all, aspects of a market economy. Examples are Taiwan, South Korea, Kenya, Brazilian military governments, and Chile. The last case is particularly instructive.

In 1973 a military revolt overthrew the socialist government of President Allende. The government of General Pinochet has subsequently reversed many of Allende's socialist policies, most notably in the monetary field, where rampant inflation has been reduced by applying conservative economic theories. Relative monetary stability has improved the climate for business investment, yet the military government has no intention of reversing the nationalization of the copper industry undertaken by Allende's regime. This proves the general rule that authoritarian leaders are often eclectic with respect to ideologies. They choose ideas from several sources rather than making a commitment to a doctrine as a whole. In this sense, their approach remains statist, for the ultimate choice of policy is determined by the needs of the rulers rather than being left to spontaneous social evolution.

Finally, the military in right-wing authoritarianism in many cases emerges as the dominant institution. Given its weapons and organizational ability, the military can intimidate institutions such as political parties, interest groups, and the courts. Because authoritarian leaders have to rely on coercion rather than popular support, the military becomes the decisive force in a struggle for power. It often promises a return to civilian rule and occasionally keeps the promise; but more often the date of free elections is repeatedly postponed until it recedes into the indefinite future. However, civilian rulers such as President Marcos of the Philippines can also retain their hold on power as long as they keep the loyalty of the military.

Three Latin American military regimes pose interesting cases. In Argentina (1976), Brazil (1964), and Uruguay (1973) the military ousted elected civilian governments. In each case, they accused the civilian politicians of sowing economic chaos and pledged economic stability and development through efficient management. In 1984 each regime took steps to return its government to elected civilians. Interestingly, the economy in each case was in no better shape than it had been when the military seized power. These examples do not support the "efficient authoritarian" hypothesis; generals, like other mortals, seem to have no quick fixes for complex problems of economic development.

LEFT-WING AUTHORITARIANISM
Leftist authoritarian regimes seem very different, at least at first glance. They have an official ideology, usually some variety of socialism other than orthodox Marxism-Leninism, combined with a strong element of nationalism. Tanzania has Nyerere's

ujaama socialism—a blend of British Labour ideology and indigenous African traditions. Iraq and Syria, though mortal enemies to each other, both profess *ba'ath* (Renaissance) socialism. In Libya Colonel Kadaffi has propounded a unique mixture of revolutionary socialism and Islamic fundamentalism. His *Green Book* rivals the *Little Red Book* of Chairman Mao as prescribed ideological reading for a whole nation. Another example is the "revolutionary humanism" of the early years of the left-wing military regime that ruled in Peru from 1968 until it voluntarily relinquished power in 1980:

> The Peruvian Revolution is an autonomous process of development for changing the political, economic, and social system of the country, and ending our capitalist and oligarchic state of underdevelopment and submissiveness to interests of imperialism, and it is intended to construct a social democracy in which all Peruvians will be able to contribute through full participation in the exercise of social power in a truly sovereign national community.
>
> The Peruvian Revolution is defined as *Nationalistic* or Independent and ideologically it is rooted in a Revolutionary Humanism clearly in opposition to dogmatic and totalitarian systems of social exploitation. Therefore, it rejects the capitalist and communist systems.[36]

Though they differ in detail, the ideologies of all these regimes project a fundamental social transformation, and revolution is a word used in all public discussion. In certain other ways, too, they seem more totalitarian than authoritarian, at least at the rhetorical level. Political mobilization of the masses is a continuing theme, as are central control and planning of the economy under the guidance of a vanguard party.

Perhaps the difference between these left-authoritarian regimes and true totalitarianism is one of degree rather than kind. If they lived up to their stated goals, they might well become totalitarian. But their revolutions have not been as thoroughgoing or single-minded in the pursuit of utopian goals; they have compromised more with present reality and allowed more autonomy for groups as long as they avoid opposition to the leadership. In Iraq the influence of the old leading families has been much reduced but not entirely broken. A lot of property and land still remains in private hands. The intransigent ethnic minority of Kurds has been tamed but not utterly destroyed as a political force. Tanzania has promoted communal ownership of land by tribe or village, which is not the same as true state ownership.

An interesting rule of thumb for distinguishing left-authoritarian from totalitarian states is that legal emigration is readily possible. The totalitarian state, regarding its people as almost a natural resource, keeps them home by all means, unless it decides to expel groups of malcontents. Then there are likely to be spasms of forced emigration when people are virtually driven out, compelled to leave all their possessions behind, as has happened in Cuba and Vietnam. In contrast, legal emigration under stable procedures is possible in countries such as Algeria and Iraq.

Lacking the full intensity of totalitarian regimes, left-authoritarian governments in practice often resemble right-authoritarian ones. Some social pluralism is tolerated as long as it does not become politically dangerous. Police terrorism is used chiefly to retain power rather than induce social change. The rigours of central planning are softened by bribery and corruption. Lip service is paid to ideological goals, but the government does not enforce a monopoly of ideas. Foreign travel and reading foreign publications allow some ideological diversification.

Whether of the left or right, authoritarian leaders tolerate little or no opposition and may do almost anything to remain in power. In virtually every case, they reject the principles of liberal democracy—or the "capitalist state," a more popular phrase. They say the liberal democracies of the West are inefficient for the needs of developing nations striving for economic change. They argue that these democracies promote factions and that a faction-ridden society cannot attain the mass "unity" required for development.

There is, no doubt, a great deal of truth in these criticisms. Liberal democracies are clumsy in their response to crisis and slow to implement specific public policies when they must consider a variety of interests. On the other hand, the alleged efficiency of authoritarian rulers is often illusory. Their statist mentality often leads them to impose on society vast projects that are no more productive than the pyramids of the Pharaohs. Or they may embark on reckless international adventures, such as Argentina's attempt to take the Falkland Islands from Britain by force in 1982 and Iraq's invasion of Iran in 1981. When only one will is obeyed, the chances of dramatic error are heightened. The presumed inefficiency of a liberal government is in the long run actually one of its virtues. By fragmenting power, it allows many projects to compete with each other. Some will inevitably fail, but diversity increases the likelihood that solutions will be found to the unexpected problems of the future.

While liberal democracies have worked well for most Western societies, they are not easy processes to manage, and it may take a certain democratic tradition to make them work. The fact remains, however, that they are not designed to run efficiently. Internal checks are built into them to impede a takeover by the "man on horseback." The processes are set up in such a way that a political leader cannot set a blind course and refuse to hear criticism or consider alternative action. What seems like inefficiency in the short run may be in the long run the most efficient method of governing in an ever-changing and unpredictable world.

Evidence of this comes from the relatively short period of power enjoyed by many authoritarian rulers, even those who initially ride a tide of popularity into office and use various tactics to try to maintain popular support. In Argentina Juan Peron founded the Peronista party, whose legacy remains today. Sukarno organized a "Guided Democracy" in Indonesia as a new form of government that he hoped would generate mass appeal. And Kadaffi today uses Islamic evangelism to encourage support for his system. Leaders like this are frequently charismatic, or they articulate goals (mostly economic) that have mass appeal. In time, however, the people's enthusiasm wanes as they are unable to perform economic miracles. Time seems to erode initial support for authoritarian dictators, and to remain in power they begin to rely more on coercion than popular support. Ultimately, they are often overthrown by a sudden *coup d'état* organized by an oppositional faction within the military or the ruling party. In many authoritarian systems, most notably Bolivia, the coup d'état has been virtually institutionalized as a means of changing officeholders, playing a role analogous to elections in a liberal democracy. The system remains authoritarian, but at least there is rotation of personnel at the top.

Those who enjoy the advantages of liberal democracy are often quick to condemn authoritarian governments for the way they treat their citizens. However, in many societies, particularly in the Third World, liberal democracy may not be a realistic possibility for all the reasons discussed at the end of Chapter 16. In such situations, authoritarian regimes, repressive as they may be, seem to have at least one advantage over totalitarian governments, which cannot admit any standard of criticism higher than the will of those who control the state. Authoritarian regimes, precisely because they do not aspire to totally dominate the course of transforming society, are sometimes improved or overthrown by internal forces. They also, occasionally, show traces of responsiveness to criticism from outside. These internal and external factors mean that change is possible. But no totalitarian regime has yet been overthrown except by external conquest, as happened in Italy, Germany, and Kampuchea. Thus to those concerned with promoting liberal democracy, the distinction between authoritarian and totalitarian states is not merely an academic matter, but an important guiding principle in world politics; for it seems more likely that an authoritarian state, rather than a totalitarian one, can be transformed into a liberal democracy.

19   Parliamentary and Presidential Systems

Of the many possible ways of organizing the apparatus of representative government, the two most important models are the parliamentary and presidential systems. From their common origin in British government of the seventeenth and eighteenth centuries, both have now become worldwide, found even in societies that owe relatively little to Anglo-American traditions. They exist not only in a true sense in liberal democracies but also as a veneer in many authoritarian or totalitarian systems, as a pretext for creating an aura of legitimacy.

An explanation of the difference between the parliamentary and presidential systems requires an understanding of the principle of *separation of powers*, a doctrine that has a long history in political science. All governments, no matter how they are organized, have to perform certain functions and exercise certain powers. The most common approach to these powers is to divide them into three: the legislative, executive, and judicial powers of the state. The *legislative* power makes general laws of conduct for members of the community. They include matters of private law, such as rules against theft and murder, as well as public law, such as rules governing voting, military service, and paying taxes. The *executive* power does not make general rules but administers the particular resources that are at the disposal of the state. The executive commands the army created by the legislative power, and raises and spends taxes that have been legislatively authorized. This entails making, instead of universal rules, many discretionary decisions, such as where to locate a post office or military base. In private law, the executive power enforces rules of conduct by administering police forces and prisons to ensure that laws are obeyed. The *judicial* power, different from both of the above, resolves particular conflicts that arise when laws are not obeyed or when there is disagreement about what the law means.

Early liberals such as John Locke argued that these powers of state should be distributed among different hands, not concentrated in one institution, like the monarch, because they weakened the temptation to abuse power arbitrarily. Locke wrote that "in all moderated monarchies and well-framed governments the legislative and executive power are in distinct hands."[37] In its simple form, this view tends to equate one power with one branch of government that specializes in it. In his *Spirit of the Laws* (1748), Montesquieu analysed British government in this way. He wrote that Parliament constituted the legislative branch, the monarch and ministers the executive branch, and the courts the judicial branch. The separation of powers into distinct branches of government was, in Montesquieu's opinion, the secret of the excellence of the British constitution, which made Britain the freest and most enviable country of Europe. Thus the doctrine of separation of powers has become an integral part of liberal thinking, providing a structural and legalistic way of limiting the power of government.

Although certainly true in part, Montesquieu's analysis was oversimplified. He overlooked the fact that the courts had a large share of legislative power because the common law evolved through their decisions. This was not deliberate "making" of law as in the case of Parliament, but it was equally significant as a source of rules of conduct. Even more important was that Montesquieu did not fully appreciate the custom, observed increasingly since the Glorious Revolution, that ministers of the Crown had to be members of Parliament, of either the Commons or Lords. This meant that the executive and legislative branches were more closely connected than Montesquieu seemed to think.

Since the publication of *The Spirit of the Laws*, British representative government has evolved in two different directions. In the United States, where at the time of the constitutional convention Montesquieu's philosophical authority was very great, the Americans retained institutions modelled on those of Britain but tried to separate the president and Congress more clearly than monarch and Parliament had been. This is the source of most contemporary presidential systems in which the separation of powers is still maintained. But in Britain and colonies such as Canada that stayed within the Empire, political evolution brought the legislative and executive branches closer together. In modern parliamentary systems, the executive (cabinet) and the legislature seldom function separately because of the practice of political party discipline (to be discussed below). We will discuss the parliamentary system first and then return to the presidential model.

THE PARLIAMENTARY SYSTEM

After the Norman conquest, all three powers of government were united in the king. Not only was he the "font of justice" and supreme military commander, he could legislate by royal proclamation. Parliament, which was first convened by Edward I in 1295, was not initially a legislative body at all. Apart from advising the king, its major function was to approve taxes necessary to support government. Over time, Parliament increased its power by refusing to grant revenue unless the king fulfilled its desires, drawn up in "bills," or lists of requests. This ancient practice is the reason a statute under consideration by Parliament is known today as a *bill*. Another reminder of this early period is that all legislation is still proclaimed by the queen or king "with the advice and consent" of Parliament. Though Parliament long ago captured legislative power, the verbal formula shows that it once belonged to the king.

Political evolution in Britain culminating in the Glorious Revolution brought about a separation of previously united powers. Parliament made itself a legislative body and also created an independent judiciary by forcing the Crown, which appointed judges, to respect their tenure in office. The settlement of 1689, although it made Parliament supreme, still left considerable scope to the royal *prerogative* powers–those powers the monarch could exercise according to personal discretion. The monarch remained a true chief executive, able to appoint and dismiss officials, declare war, conduct foreign relations, command the armed forces, pardon convicted criminals, and (as a remnant of lost legislative power) refuse to assent to legislation.

Subsequent political evolution reunited the legislative and executive powers under the control of a new executive: the prime minister and Cabinet. At first this trend seemed to be a further victory of Parliament over the Crown, as the custom grew that ministers had to be members of Parliament and had to have the political support of a working majority in the House of Commons. This mechanism of *responsible government* allowed the Crown to act only on the advice of advisers who had the confidence of Parliament. Parliament, by the middle of the nineteenth century, appeared to have captured the executive power as it had previously captured the legislative. But it was not long until the new practice of *party discipline* showed that the Cabinet, and particularly the prime minister, were the real victors. As long as the followers of the prime minister in the House of Commons vote as directed, then executive and legislative powers are combined or fused, rendering the separation of powers ineffectual as a check. The check in a parliamentary system comes when the prime minister loses majority support and the opposition can withdraw confidence from the government.

After this brief historical sketch, let us look at the details of the contemporary British parliamentary system. The political machinery, referred to as the Westminster model, consists of the Crown, the Cabinet, the House of Commons, and the House of Lords. The Crown requests the leader of the majority party or majority coalition to form a government, consisting of Cabinet ministers from either House; they govern, supported by a majority in the House of Commons. If a majority party does not exist and there is no basis for a formal coalition, a party leader with a large block of seats is asked to form a government. Such a situation is referred to as a minority government, and this government is entitled to govern as long as a majority in the Commons supports it.

Parliament is a bicameral institution consisting of the House of Commons and the House of Lords. The Commons is organized in a pyramidal fashion. The prime minister, leader of the majority party, was originally thought to be *primus inter pares*–"first among equals." Now, however, he or she is much more: *the* first minister of Cabinet, *the* party leader, and *the* leader of government. Cabinet ministers of the governing party manage the legislative process with some co-operation from opposition parties. *Parliamentary secretaries* are elected members of the party chosen to help cabinet ministers carry out their duties as ministers of the Crown. They are serving a form of apprenticeship, being groomed for positions of leadership. Everyone who is not in the Cabinet is referred to as a *private member*, whether sitting on the side of the government or the opposition. They are the rank and file of the elected parliamentary members who are not part of the governing party leadership. Their influence is not substantial in the process; while they may introduce private members' bills, few of these bills are ever passed by Parliament.

The House of Lords consists of 1,062 members, most of whom are peers, but about 150 members usually conduct the business of this institution. Since 1958, distinguished men and women have been appointed to life peerages, and they constitute about one-quarter of the membership of the Lords, including most of those who are active in legislative work. The powers of the two Houses of Parliament were originally equal, but since the Parliament Acts of 1911 and 1949 were passed, the Lords have become subservient to the Commons. They may initiate and amend or revise legislation but cannot veto acts of the Commons. They may now delay bills for what amounts to approximately one year. Thus the parliamentary system has become today what some observers refer to as "cabinet government" or "prime ministerial government" because no one else—monarch, private members in the House of Commons, or members of the House of Lords—compares in power to the prime minister and Cabinet.

Our own Parliament developed within the British tradition as one of the first examples of a colony peacefully breaking away from a modern colonial power. Prior to 1867, colonial governors representing the Crown existed alongside locally elected legislatures. The Constitution Act, 1867 finally implemented Lord Durham's report of 1839, which had recommended the eventual union of Canada, Nova Scotia, and New Brunswick. At the national or federal level, one Parliament was created for all the colonies. This institution is a bicameral legislature containing two Houses—the Senate, with 104 seats, being the upper house, and the Commons, with 282 members, the lower house.

Except for the fact that Canada is a federal system, the Canadian Parliament operates in principle like the British. The queen or king of Great Britain is our *head of state*. The Crown's representative in Canada is the governor general, appointed by the monarch, according to a now well-established convention, on the advice of the prime minister. Lieutenant-governors appointed by the governor general, also on the advice of the prime minister, play the role of head of state in provincial governments. The monarch, governor general, and lieutenant-governors together represent the Crown in Canada. The prime minister, like the premiers of the provinces, plays the role of *head of government*.

The head of state normally does not exercise actual political power; he or she "reigns rather than rules." Most functions of the head of state are usually of a symbolic nature. These include (1) selecting or dismissing a head of government; (2) performing certain ceremonial functions, for example, greeting foreign dignitaries; (3) assenting to and proclaiming legislation; (4) appointing public officials such as judges; (5) dissolving Parliament and calling elections; and (6) exercising certain emergency powers when there is a leadership crisis or when government is deadlocked. Under normal circumstances, the representative of the Crown carries out these functions without making real prerogative choices. The monarch or governor general must take the advice of the Cabinet as long as there is a government in office. No executive action is taken without the signature of one or more ministers. Even in selecting a new government, the head of state normally has no real choice because the person appointed to be head of government has already been determined by the voters.

By constitutional convention, the political party with a majority of seats in the House of Commons is asked by the governor general to form the government of Canada. The prime minister then nominates other ministers of personal choice. Or, if there is no single party with a majority of seats, a party leader with the largest plurality of seats or with explicit or implicit support of other parties is asked to form a government. For example, in May 1979, the Progressive Conservatives were asked to form a government with 136 seats. They did not have the 142 seats needed for a clear majority, but they had more seats than any other party.

An interesting development occurred after the Ontario provincial election in 1985. The Progressive Conservative party, in power since 1943, held only 52 of the 124 seats in the provincial legislature after the April election. The Liberals held 47 seats and the New Democrats 25. Premier Frank Miller, who had been chosen party leader in January 1985 after William Davis resigned, continued to govern until defeated in the legislature. The Liberal and NDP opposition defeated the Tory government on a non-confidence motion in June 1985. David Peterson, leader of the Liberal party, then formed a government supported by the NDP. The government was not a coalition because no ministerial positions were allocated to the NDP. Rather, the Liberal and NDP parties entered an "accord," a written agreement that stated that for two years, the Liberals would not call an election and the NDP would not defeat the government on a non-confidence motion. There had been many previous examples of informal understandings in Canadian politics in order to support a minority government, but this was the first formal, written agreement.

In almost every case, the constitution dictates the actions of the Crown. In rare circumstances, there might not be a constitutionally clear course of action—for example, if a prime minister unexpectedly died in office and the party had not agreed upon a successor. Then the head of state might have to use discretion in asking someone to form an interim government until the majority party could sort out its affairs. In general, the Crown acts unilaterally only if a crisis immobilizes responsible political institutions. In time of emergency, there is a role to be played by the head of state. The exercise of prerogative power to meet situations of this kind has been one of the principal arguments of those who advocate retaining the Crown as an integral part of Canadian government.[38]

A case in point was the crisis that followed the U.S. intervention in Grenada in October 1983. Prime Minister Maurice Bishop had seized power in 1979, backed by the New Jewel Movement that initially enjoyed a great deal of popular support on the island. In October 1983 Bernard Coard, an official in the Bishop government, staged a coup d'état. Maurice Bishop was ousted and subsequently shot by forces supporting Coard. The United States then intervened militarily at the request of several neighbouring islands. With the prime minister dead and Bernard Coard in custody, Governor General Sir Paul Scoon assumed responsibility for governing the island and called national elections in 1984. Thus the head of state governed until the people had an opportunity to choose new leaders to form a government.

The second major component of our parliamentary system is the House of Commons. The House is to the machinery of government what the engine is to the automobile. The government of the day is formed mostly from the House. The leader of the majority party, or of a party that has a working majority by the support of other parties, becomes prime minister and normally chooses ministers from members of the House or the Senate. Technically, a prime minister may choose an individual who is not a member of either House to become a member of the Cabinet. The practice is rare, and when it does occur, that individual is expected to obtain a seat in the House or the Senate within a matter of months. Cabinet ministers, supported by members of this party, have legitimate and legal powers to govern as long as they can command the confidence of the House.

The third component of the Canadian parliamentary system is the Senate. Under the Constitution Act, 1867, the Senate must approve all legislation. Thus it has the power to veto but normally does not exercise that power. The Senate has not flatly refused a bill passed by the House of Commons since 1961. Even if it suddenly reasserted itself and did refuse a bill from the Commons, the government would not have to resign because the Cabinet does not require the confidence of the Senate as it does of the Commons.

However, short of exercising its veto, the Senate does have ways of differing with the House of Commons. It may, and often does, suggest amendments to bills, which the House often adopts. It may also delay legislation, as happened in early 1985, when the Senate took weeks to pass a borrowing bill that would normally have gone through as a routine matter. It appeared that the large Liberal majority in the Senate was trying to embarrass the new Conservative government. This episode caused Prime Minister Mulroney to announce that his government would seek a constitutional amendment to limit the Senate's powers in some way. At the time of writing, it is too early to know whether anything will happen.

Even without a constitutional amendment, it is clear that the Senate's power is greatly reduced in comparison to what was anticipated at the time of Confederation. One explanation for this diminished power is that the Senate is an appointed body. The governor general, on the advice of the prime minister, appoints members to the upper house, and this method of selection is considered less democratic than that of the people electing members of the House of Commons. The Senate is sometimes portrayed as a retirement home for politicians, an institution that allows a prime minister to pay political debts or get rid of political enemies. Whatever the truth of that portrait, the Senate is not totally without impact. Numerous amendments to bills have emerged from deliberations in the Senate, and Senate committees have made important alterations to legislative proposals. Perhaps less than it used to, the Senate offers a "sober second look" at legislation. Moreover, senators can be ministers of the Crown, and this is useful for putting someone in the Cabinet who does not hold a seat in the Commons. Also, it can give representation in the Cabinet to regions that elect no government members to the House.

An elected upper house with powers equal to those of the lower house can pose problems in a parliamentary system. In 1975 in Australia, for example, the House of Commons passed a money bill that the Senate refused to approve. The conflict evolved into a fiscal and constitutional crisis. The government under Prime Minister Whitlam would not budge, nor would the Senate. Finally, the Governor General, Sir John Kerr, exercised his prerogative and dissolved both houses (the Australian Senate is popularly elected). The prime minister was furious and accused the governor general of overstepping his powers and precipitating a constitutional crisis by permitting the upper house to bring down the government. In effect, the ensuing election resolved the political issue. Mr. Whitlam's government was defeated, vindicating the governor general to some degree.

There is general agreement that an upper house with equal power can obstruct legislative proceedings of a parliament. There is little agreement, however, on the value of the obstruction. Unitary parliamentarians often argue that the final say on bills should rest with a single house where representation is based on population. For these proponents, obstruction by another house is a violation of democratic parliamentary principles. On the other hand, federal parliamentarians often suggest that an elected second house, with representation based on region, should have an opportunity to veto bills of a lower house—especially when representation may reflect concentrations of population. This is the argument behind the "triple E" idea of Senate reform particularly popular in Alberta: an elected, equal, effective Senate to safeguard regional interests.

In order to understand the actual running of Parliament, one must understand the basis of the fusion of powers that characterizes the relationship between the executive and legislature. As Figure 19.1 shows, the prime minister is dependent on party members (or some coalition of parties) in the House of Commons and ultimately on the voters.

The system functions as follows. In elections, voters determine the balance of partisan power in the House of Commons. Three outcomes are possible. One party may win a majority of seats in the House, in which case its leader forms a *majority government*. Or, if no party wins a majority, the leader of one party, usually but not necessarily the largest party, may form a *minority government*. Such a minority government can stay in office only if the other parties refrain from defeating it. Finally, two or more parties may join forces to form a *coalition government*, dividing ministerial appointments between them; the leader of the larger coalition partner normally becomes prime minister. In all cases, the prime minister chooses

FIGURE 19.1

The Canadian Parliamentary System

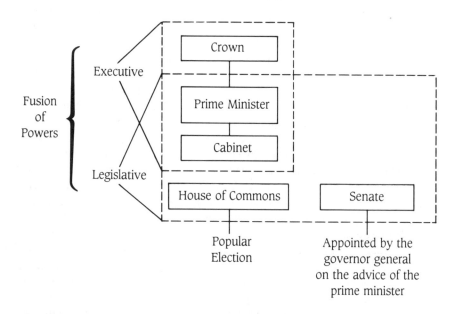

the other ministers, who are then officially appointed by the governor general. The latter may also dismiss them on the advice of the prime minister, although what usually happens is that the prime minister requests and receives a resignation from ministers whom he or she wishes out of the Cabinet. The prime minister and the Cabinet ministers, along with the Crown, form the executive. Some cabinet ministers are also assisted by parliamentary secretaries. Although they are specially appointed members of the House of Commons and are being groomed for later ministerial roles, they do not actually sit in the cabinet.

The Cabinet determines legislative priorities and sets the legislative agenda. Cabinet decisions supported by a majority in Parliament ultimately become the laws and public policies of the land. Cabinet ministers initiate almost all legislative proposals, using the civil service as a primary source of information and ideas. The Cabinet has been aptly called "a combining committee—a hyphen which joins, a buckle which fastens, the legislative part of the state to the executive part."[39] It is the institution that most clearly distinguishes the modern parliamentary system from the presidential form of government. It is a true collective decision-making body, although in many circumstances, votes are not formally taken. After extensive discussion, the prime minister states the sense of the meeting and summarizes the action to be taken. Once a course is set, the principle of *cabinet solidarity* prevents members from criticizing government policy in public, even though they may have private reservations.

Private members' bills, introduced by members of Parliament who are not ministers, may be numerous, but few are passed. Significant legislation is almost always initiated by Cabinet ministers. The prime minister and Cabinet, and the leader of the opposition and his or her chief advisers, are the principal figures in the parliamentary process, not the backbenchers.

Procedures involved in passing legislative proposals give the opposition an opportunity to criticize the government's position. The House functions within strict procedures and rules observed most of the time by all parties. These are enforced by a Speaker nominated by the prime minister, seconded by the leader of the opposition, and elected by the House. In Great Britain the Speaker becomes an impartial figure who completely withdraws from party affiliations, runs unopposed for re-election, and serves as Speaker until retirement from the House. In Canada the Speaker is supposed to conduct the affairs of the House impartially too, but the divorce from politics is not so complete. The Speaker runs unopposed; but if there is a change of majority in the House, the new government appoints another Speaker from its own ranks.

A proposed bill must go through three *readings*. After the first reading (an introduction of the bill's title), the text of the proposed legislation is printed and distributed to members. After the second reading, full debate occurs on the bill, with the opposition and government backbenchers having a specified time to question different aspects of it. It may then go to either a standing committee or a special committee of the House. *Standing committees* are permanent committees with membership proportional to party strength in the House. Examples include committees on agriculture, external affairs and national defence, and finance, trade, and economic affairs. Special or *ad hoc committees* are established to deal with specific problems. Examples include committees on employment opportunities for the 1980s and North-South relations. In the first session of the 33rd Parliament (1985), there were twenty-nine standing, special, and joint committees. Backbenchers can become involved in the legislative process by serving on parliamentary committees, but their power is limited because party voting prevails. The same party or coalition that forms the government and dominates the House also controls committee proceedings. Committees sometimes produce amendments to government bills but do not reject them altogether. The bill then goes through a *report stage*, in which the House receives the report of a committee and votes on any amendments it proposes.

If amended, the bill is then received and voted on by the House—this is the third reading. Normally, it is then introduced in the Senate, whose deliberations usually involve committee action. The Senate's version of the bill goes back to the House if changes are suggested. Under modern conditions, where the Senate does not oppose the House of Commons on matters of principle and functions chiefly as a source of technical amendments, it may finish its consideration of a bill before the Commons, so that suggested amendments may be incorporated by that House at third reading. A bill passed by the House and Senate then goes to the governor general for royal assent and proclamation. *Royal assent* means that the governor general signs the bill; *proclamation* means setting the date on which the new law will take effect. There is often a period of weeks or months, and occasionally even years, between royal assent and proclamation.

In this process, Cabinet members with support of their party determine what sort of legislation is passed. If the minister responsible for the legislation does not like the amendments proposed by the opposition on the floor of the House, in parliamentary committees, or in the Senate, they will probably be rejected. Again, the power of the prime minister and the Cabinet, supported by the party majority, represents a strong system of government.

Throughout the legislative process, the *opposition*—those parties that do not share ministerial appointments—criticize and sometimes win concessions from the government, even though it does not have the voting strength to make its views prevail. The government may feel that points raised by the opposition have merit or public support, and it may yield in order to avoid obstructive or disruptive behaviour.

In Canada and Britain the largest of the opposition parties is singled out as the *official opposition*, a position that gives it access to research funds and certain privileges during debate. The leader of the official opposition assigns party members to follow the activities of ministers with particular attention. For example, an agriculture critic among the opposition watches the minister of agriculture. The leader of the official opposition and these specialist critics may form a cohesive group known as the *shadow cabinet*. This leadership, supported by its backbenchers, is organized just as it is on the government side and is ready to assume office instantly if invited to do so by the head of state.

In the parliamentary process, the lifeblood of the government is party loyalty. Apart from having to hold an election at least every five years, the government's tenure of office depends on its ability to maintain a majority on the floor of the House of Commons. In other words, exercising governmental power hinges on the ability of the government to maintain the *confidence* of the House. Maintaining this confidence is rooted in the principle of responsible government, which makes the Cabinet responsible to the House of Commons. Every legislative proposal by government must go to the floor of the House. As long as these proposals are supported by a majority of those voting, the government enjoys the confidence of the House and is ruling "responsibly." In Canada, though not in all parliamentary systems, most votes on bills introduced by the government are considered the equivalent of confidence votes—that is, the government should win every vote and resign if it is defeated. Exceptions are made when the House decides that a particular motion is not to be treated as a confidence vote or when defeats occur under peculiar circumstances, such as an unexpected absence of a large number of government members from the House when a vote is taken. In these cases, a defeat of the government does not mean a loss of confidence.

The necessity to maintain a majority has led to the growth of party discipline in all parliamentary systems. A member's loyalty to the party generally takes precedence over personal views or loyalty to constituents. Party discipline implies that a member who does not support the party position on the floor of the House can be punished, even denied the opportunity to run under the party banner in a subsequent election. Contemporary Canadian practice allows MPs to deviate from the party line occasionally, but not too often, especially if it might unseat the government.

Recent developments in Great Britain have led observers to note some flexibility emerging in the party system. Government bills are being defeated more often, and these defeats no longer constitute grounds for the government to resign. In the period 1974–1978, governments (Labour and Conservative) were defeated 123 times in the House of Commons, compared with 11 defeats in the years 1945–1966.[40] In effect, more party members are "crossing over" to vote with the opposition on particular issues. On motions of non-confidence or bills involving finances, a defeated government must still resign. Absolute party discipline is giving way on certain issues but is still paramount when confidence is involved. Similar practices may arise in Ontario under the accord between the Liberals and NDP, which agrees to sustain the Liberal minority government in power; for the accord states that defeats for the government on ordinary matters are not to be treated as non-confidence votes.

One other deviation should be noted. Occasionally, the government may allow a *free vote* on certain bills that are controversial. In other words, all members of the caucus do not have to vote with the party; they are free to vote according to their conscience. The vote to retain abolition of capital punishment by the Canadian House of Commons in 1976 was allegedly a free vote, although behind the scenes, the Liberal leadership pushed its followers hard to vote for abolition. Free votes are rare in modern practice and never involve questions of raising or spending money.

Critics of the parliamentary system often complain that members do not have the freedom to vote their conscience or the will of their constituents. This is true if party discipline is effective, but it does not imply that *backbenchers*—those who are not in the Cabinet or the shadow cabinet and therefore sit on the rear benches in the House—have no influence on their party leadership. One primary function of the *party caucus* is to give party members this opportunity. The party caucus is a closed meeting of the members of a parliamentary party in the House and the Senate. Each party, the party forming the government as well as the opposition parties, has a caucus. At caucus meetings, backbenchers have an opportunity to question their own leaders and suggest alternatives to the leadership's policies. Thus the caucus is the time when MPs within a party can differ with each other and when the leadership can test the pulse of the party on particular proposals. Knowing that a majority position needs the support of backbenchers, party leaders must take into account the nature and strength of backbench opposition. In caucus meetings, an attempt is made to arrive at a consensus on issues. Unanimity seldom exists, so these meetings can be knock-down, drag-out affairs. However, once the issue is settled and goes to the House, all members are expected to support the government's position. Although it rarely occurs, backbenchers of a majority party can bring down a government. Therefore the government's own party provides an important check on political power.

A second check on government is the opposition. The development of an institutionalized practice of loyal opposition, in which one can legally challenge the government without fear of repression, is one of the significant achievements of liberal democracy. The rationale for an opposition is the liberal view that everyone has limited knowledge. No government or governor is infallible. The mighty make mistakes too, and there should always be an opportunity to air them in public.

The essence of the parliamentary process is the formal duel between the government and those forces unable to muster sufficient legislative seats to form a government. This opposition has three basic functions: to offer an alternative government, to offer alternative policies, and to question and call attention to controversial legislative proposals or governmental actions of any kind. If the opposition is in a minority, it cannot of itself defeat the government; but it does have important opportunities to object to legislation it opposes and to delay and obstruct legislative proposals it wants altered. Time is limited in the House, and parliamentary procedures protect the role of the opposition. Proceedings can be immobilized unless the opposition co-operates with the government. The "bell ringing" tactic, devised by the Progressive Conservatives in the last days of the Liberal government under Trudeau, is an example of what the opposition can achieve. The Conservatives simply refused to answer the bells announcing a vote. The government would have been legally correct to hold the vote anyway, but it feared public displeasure at voting without the opposition present. Such extreme tactics dramatically place an issue before public opinion. They lose their impact if used too often, but they can be effective if used sparingly. A government that tries to run roughshod over the opposition parties may succeed in passing a particular piece of legislation, but it may well find other aspects of its program jeopardized by delaying tactics.

A final check on the government is the electorate. At least every five years, voters have the opportunity to pass judgment on the record of the party in power. It is a reminder of the liberal-democratic principle that political power emanates from the people with the consent of the governed. Ideally, the check exercised by elections ensures that government legislation is responsive to the needs of people. Again, in the liberal tradition, there is an unwillingness to assume that government automatically acts in the best interest of its citizens. Checks are there when the unresponsive system needs prodding.

We have used the British and Canadian examples to describe the parliamentary system of government. While there are a number of structural differences between our process and that of Great Britain (federalism, for instance), the two systems exemplify the Westminster model. In other cases, the basic model has been modified to meet the needs of different political environments and frequently to strengthen the role of the executive, especially when it must face a politically fragmented legislative body. The parliamentary process is vulnerable to minority government; without a majority, governments may change frequently, causing political instability. In very few instances has Canada or Great Britain had to contend with the problem, but twentieth-century political history in Germany and France illustrates the point.

Under the Weimar constitution, adopted in 1919, Germany had something close to the Westminster model of parliamentary government. Representation in the legislative body was badly split between a number of political factions, so that no political party commanded a majority. Weak coalition governments, often depending on the support of extremist or splinter parties, were unable to deal effectively with political crises. Combatting the economic crash of 1929 proved too much for the system, with the result that the Third Reich was founded under Hitler in 1933. After World War II, the Germans modified the parliamentary system to overcome the problem of instability. The constitution of the Federal Republic of Germany (West Germany), known as the Basic Law, was adopted in 1949. The drafters of the document instituted what has been termed a positive or *constructive vote of confidence*. The chancellor is the chief executive officer of the government and forms a Cabinet. He or she is the leader of the majority party, or a coalition of parties making up a majority, in the Bundestag, the lower house of Parliament. The government can be defeated on a non-confidence vote in the Bundestag, but the vote defeats the government *only* if the chancellor's successor is chosen at the same time. In other words, a majority in the Bundestag can bring down the government, but not until that majority selects another government. This breaks with the British and Canadian custom of forming a new government after defeat on a non-confidence motion or any major piece of legislation.

The French people during the Fourth Republic (1946–1958) experienced a similar type of political instability. Numerous political parties were represented in the National Assembly, none of which could command a majority of the seats. Governments were founded on loose coalitions of parties whose tenure of office was usually short. In the constitution of the Fifth Republic (1958), General de Gaulle remedied the instability by modifying the political executive. In addition to the prime minister and the Cabinet, the French now have a president elected directly by the people for a seven-year term of office. The president is the actual head of government, not just a titular head of state. He or she appoints the prime minister, traditionally the leader of the majority party or the senior party in a coalition in the National Assembly. The president appoints the Cabinet, although the prime minister can propose names for the job. The National Assembly can still pass a non-confidence motion, or *vote of censure* as it is called, and defeat the government, but it can be exercised only once in a year. When the government is censured, only the prime minister and the Cabinet must resign—the president has been elected for a specified term of office. He or she then dissolves the National Assembly and appoints a new prime minister after elections.

Because the president remains in office in spite of government turnovers, the executive branch of government is stabilized; however, the value of this stability should be weighed against the possibility of deadlock. A French president may belong to one party, and a majority in the National Assembly may belong to another. This has not yet happened, but as of 1985, most observers expect that the Socialist-Communist alliance will lose its parliamentary majority in the impending election, leaving Socialist President François Mitterand to deal with a National Assembly dominated by opposition parties.

Modifications have also occurred in other systems where the parliamentary process is practised. Nevertheless, the basic principle of the system remains responsible government. A government is not entitled to govern unless it commands a working majority of the seats in the legislative body. Regardless of the way in which the machinery is adjusted, this principle remains essential to the parliamentary apparatus.

THE PRESIDENTIAL SYSTEM

The presidential system of government was first devised in the United States as an alternative to the monarchical system. It and the parliamentary system represent the two basic models for structuring modern governments.

While many countries use the presidential model, the way it is practised varies considerably. In some cases, it may be simply a guise for an authoritarian dictatorship. Or, like the parliamentary model, it may be adapted to fit particular needs. Nevertheless, the basic model is distinct; the principle of separation of powers and the lack of responsible government set it apart from the parliamentary system. The following discussion focusses on the United States as an example of presidential government in a liberal democracy. Important similarities exist with other liberal democracies, such as Venezuela or Costa Rica, which also have presidential systems. However, the description of American government is largely irrelevant to situations like South Korea or the Philippines, where presidential government is a façade for an authoritarian regime.

After 1776, the new United States reacted to its previous experience of a strong British executive by placing an extraordinary amount of political power in the legislative body. This was logical, given their suspicion of strong government exercised by the British Crown. They felt that the danger of abuse could be minimized if governors were elected and periodically held responsible to the people. These sentiments were demonstrated in the Articles of Confederation of 1781, the first constitution for the new republic, which made the executive almost non-existent. The legislatures of the several states were supreme. In time, however, it was realized that empowering an executive to initiate legislation and supervise the work of government was a necessary part of the governmental process. This fault was corrected with the adoption of the constitution in 1789. A president was made the chief executive officer of the government, answerable to the legislative branch in certain respects, but not dependent on it for continuation in office.

While the parliamentary system is known for the fusion of powers and Cabinet government, the presidential system is known for the separation of powers and the congressional committee system. The executive branch, although instrumental in the legislative process, is physically separated from the legislative branch. While the separation is real (each branch has veto powers), co-operation is required to pass legislation. In this system of government, the committees of both houses of Congress dominate the legislative process. Figure 19.2 depicts the presidential system of the United States, which is the oldest of its type and which has served as the model for presidential systems in Asia, Latin America, and the Middle East.

The customary term used to describe the presidential system, *separation of powers*, is somewhat misleading. James Madison, the chief draftsman of the American constitution, explicitly criticized the oversimplified view that the legislative, executive, and judicial powers of government ought to be absolutely separated among the distinct institutions or branches of government. In No. 47 of *The Federalist*, a series of essays written to persuade the American public to ratify the new constitution, Madison outlined the ideal of putting each power into the custody of a branch of government primarily concerned with it, while allowing the other two branches a secondary role in exercising it. This delicate balance of institutions would diminish arbitrary government by preventing unilateral actions. Neither the president, Congress, nor the courts would be able to follow a course of action very long without the co-operation of the other branches. A modern scholar has suggested that "separated institutions sharing powers" is a more apt description of the Madisonian system than "separation of powers."[41]

The president, elected by a national constituency for a four-year term, is both head of state and head of government. As head of state, he or she greets foreign dignitaries and performs other ceremonial functions. As head of government, he is the chief executive officer. The constitution grants the president powers that are on the whole rather similar to the ancient prerogative powers of the British monarch. Whereas these are now wielded by the prime minister with relatively little interference by Parliament as long as party discipline holds, presidential powers are hemmed in at every step by a Congress of which the president is not a member and on whose members he may exert influence, but not authority. Let us look at this complex balance of power in more detail.

The president has the power to appoint the highest officials of government, such as Cabinet secretaries, ambassadors, federal judges, and senior civil servants. But all these appointments must be approved by the "advice and consent" of the

FIGURE 19.2

The United States Presidential System

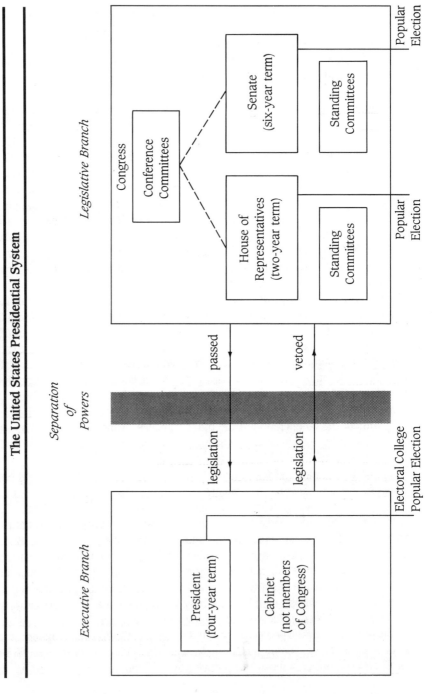

Senate, the upper house of Congress. A simple majority suffices. As chief executive, the president directs the manifold business of government yet is dependent for revenue on appropriations from Congress. He submits a budget to Congress, but that body can and does alter it freely. Congress also has the power to investigate the administrative activities of government in closed or public hearings.

The president is responsible for the general conduct of foreign affairs and, in particular, is authorized to negotiate treaties with other states. But these treaties must receive the "advice and consent" of the Senate, in this instance a qualified majority of two-thirds. Canadians were reminded in 1981 that the Senate can and does reject treaties when President Reagan had to withdraw a Canadian-American fisheries treaty because he could tell that the Senate would not ratify it.

The president is the commander-in-chief of the armed forces, but this coercive power is also subject to congressional limitation. The armed forces can be paid only with revenue voted by Congress, and a declaration of war requires approval in both houses of Congress. This constitutional provision has not been invoked since 1941 because the Korean and Vietnam wars were not declared by Congress; but public reaction against such expansion of presidential power makes this unlikely to happen again.

The president is elected by an electoral college, and because of the complexities of this method of voting, it will be explained briefly. Delegates to the constitutional convention of 1787 were of many minds. When a chief executive officer was finally agreed on, suspicions of presidential powers remained. Some delegates wanted the president to be elected by Congress. Others, fearing the demise of state power in the federal system, wanted the office to be chosen by state legislators. A few others considered a more radical move—direct election by all voters. An electoral college was the compromise. It was made up of a group of electors, supposedly upstanding and respected individuals of an independent mind, who would be chosen by state legislators and who would in turn formally elect the president. The number of electors from each state in the electoral college was determined by adding the number of representatives from the state in the federal House of Representatives (determined by the population of the state) to the number of senators (two). The total electoral college vote in the U.S. is now 538: 435 members of the House, 100 Senators (2 from each of the 50 states), plus 3 electors chosen from the District of Columbia.

During the electoral process itself, each state legislature selects its delegates to the electoral college. They then vote for a presidential candidate and mail their ballots to the Speaker of the House of Representatives. In the January following the November election, the Speaker counts the votes and officially declares the winner.

In fact, everyone knows the outcome of an election the night of the vote because members of the electoral college *usually* follow a constitutional convention—to vote according to the popular vote in the state. For example, New York has 41 electoral college votes, all of which went to Ronald Reagan in 1981 because the popular vote in the state was greater for Reagan than for any of his opponents. In the 1984 presidential election, Ronald Reagan received 58.77 per cent of the popular vote; Walter Mondale, 40.54 per cent. The electoral vote was much more one-sided. Reagan received 525 votes, whereas Mondale received only 13–10 from his home state of Minnesota and the 3 from the District of Columbia. The departure from proportionality arises from the convention of bloc voting by states. On rare occasions, this has also resulted in a candidate receiving more electoral votes than an opponent, even with a smaller proportion of the popular vote. If you can figure out how this can happen, you understand the system!

Congress, like the Canadian Parliament, is a bicameral legislature. There are 435 members of the House of Representatives, all elected in constituencies based on population. Each elected member represents a constituency called a congressional district. As in our own electoral system, the boundaries of these districts are redrawn periodically to reflect population shifts, and attempts are made to keep these districts approximately equal in size.

The term of office of a member of the House is two years. Unlike the parliamentary system, there is no provision for the government to call elections except on fixed dates. Election day in the United States is on the Tuesday after the first Monday in November. At that time, all elected officials at the federal and state levels, as well as many at the local level, are chosen. In contrast with the parliamentary system, holding elections on fixed dates prevents the president or the congressional leadership from controlling members by threatening to dissolve the House and make them face the people in an election.

The Senate is made up of one hundred members (two from each state) elected for a six-year term. Senators were originally chosen by state legislatures, but this process was changed in 1913 by the Twelfth Amendment to the constitution. Senators are now elected directly by voters in the states. At the constitutional convention in 1787, equal state representation in the Senate, as against representation by population in the House, was a compromise between the populous states, which wanted to emphasize numbers, and the thinly populated states, which wanted to emphasize territory, as the basis of representation. The Senate is considered the upper house and has more functions than the House of Representatives, notably confirming presidential appointments and ratifying treaties. All money bills, however, must originate in the House of Representatives; this is an imitation of the ancient British practice whereby revenue bills originate in the House of Commons.

Congress is the chief repository of legislative power; but as Congress checks the president in the executive area, so the president checks Congress in the legislative area. All bills passed by Congress are sent to the president, who then has three options: to sign the bill, at which time it becomes law; to not sign the bill (after ten days it becomes law without the signature); or to veto the bill. If this happens, the bill returns to both houses of Congress. If they pass the bill again with a two-thirds majority, they override the president's veto and the bill becomes law. Because this latter contingency is rather rare, the president's veto is usually final.

The president also has an important initiatory role in legislation. He or she cannot actually introduce a bill into Congress—that task must be performed by a senator or representative—but can have legislation drafted to submit to Congress, and in fact, a large majority of American legislation originates this way. However, it is subject to amendment as it goes through Congress, so that the final result may differ greatly from the original draft.

There are other important ways in which the presidential machinery of government differs from the parliamentary model. Neither the president nor the Cabinet secretaries may hold a seat in Congress. In fact, if the president chooses a member of the House or Senate to be a Cabinet secretary, the member must resign the congressional seat—an obvious contrast to the fusion between executive and legislature in the parliamentary system. The American Cabinet, furthermore, is not a collective decision-making body. The main relationship is between the president and the secretaries individually. Under some presidents, the Cabinet seldom or never meets as a group. The number of Cabinet secretaries varies with administrations, but the usual number is eleven or twelve.

Another essential feature of the presidential system is that there is no vote of confidence and thus no principle of responsible government. The tenure of office of the president and members of Congress is specified in the constitution. No matter how votes go on the floor of either House, there is nothing comparable to the non-confidence motion or the dissolution of Parliament. Once elected, the president is in office for four years, members of the House of Representatives for two years, and senators for six years (assuming they are not removed from office for misconduct). Because the executive is not responsible to the legislature, there is less need to practise party discipline. Party loyalty or solidarity is not crucial for survival. A member may choose to vote against the party's position on a bill and not be disciplined. In such a system, the individual's first loyalty is to conscience or the constituency, not the party.

This generalization admits of certain exceptions. Appointments to congressional standing committees are made along party lines at the opening of each session. If, for example, 60 per cent of the membership of a chamber is Democratic, the partisan division of members constituting committees would be 60–40, Democrats and Republicans. Party positions often, though not invariably, count in these committees. Still, the fact remains that the necessity for strong party ties that exists in the parliamentary system does not hold in the presidential system.

A final feature of the presidential system is the importance of the congressional committee system. The number of committees may vary slightly, but in the 99th Congress (1984–1986) there were twenty-one in the House and fifteen in the Senate. They represent the primary functions of most governmental organizations. Examples of committees in the House are agriculture, armed services, banking and currency, foreign affairs, veterans' affairs, and ways and means. Most of the committees of the Senate are similar in name and jurisdiction, except that there is a finance committee instead of a ways and means committee. These committees are in effect "little legislatures." After a bill is introduced in either House, it goes immediately to a committee. In most instances, if a bill is to reach the floor of either House, it must be approved by the committee.

Congressional committees, as opposed to the Cabinet in the parliamentary system, are the most powerful organizations for managing the legislative process. A bill that has been successfully reported out of committee usually passes on the floor of the House or Senate. Conversely, bills are easily kept bottled up in committee by influential members, such as the chairman of the committee or a powerful subcommittee. In the process, a great deal of trading off, or "log rolling," develops between committees in order to get legislation passed. Deals arise in committee that in the parliamentary system would be hidden in Cabinet proceedings.

Legislative committees also exist in parliamentary systems, but they are much weaker because they are controlled by members of the disciplined majority party, which in turn is controlled by the Cabinet. The Cabinet manages the legislative process and does not allow desired bills to die along the way. Committees serve as a forum for debate that sometimes produces minor or technical amendments, but rarely substantial changes.

A word must also be said about the place of the judiciary in the presidential system. Although the constitution does not mention *judicial review*–the power to declare legislation unconstitutional–the Supreme Court quickly claimed this role for itself and the lower courts. Judicial review means that the courts are not limited to judicial power in the strict sense of deciding conflicts under law; they also have in effect a veto power on legislation, which amounts to a share of legislative power. As well, they share executive power to the extent that they rule on the legality of administrative actions that are challenged. This power helps keep executive discretion within the bounds of law.

Court decisions are final in the short run, but in the long run, the judiciary is balanced by the other branches of government. Because judges must be appointed by the president and confirmed by the Senate, the political complexion of the courts can be changed gradually as retirements create vacancies on the bench. In 1985 several liberal members of the Supreme Court are clinging to office in spite of advancing old age; they correctly anticipate that President Reagan wants to replace them with more conservative judges. If vacancies do give Reagan a chance to alter the ideological composition of the Court, it will be one of the most important legacies of his presidency. Also, if the courts declare a piece of legislation unconstitutional, the Congress can introduce an amendment to the constitution. The amending process is a complex one: an amendment must be passed successfully by two-thirds of the members of Congress, then ratified by three-fourths of the state legislatures. Nevertheless, the amending process serves as a potential check on the judiciary by the legislative branch.

An important consequence of this system of "checks and balances," as the Americans call it, is that it gives the many interest groups of a pluralistic society marvellous opportunities to find friends in government. Cotton growers, to select an example at random, make a special effort to have good relations not only with the chairmen of the Senate and House agriculture committees but also with the chairmen and members of the subcommittees that deal particularly with fibre crops. Even if the president or a congressional majority has pledged to do something that may reduce the cotton growers' income—for example, end a price-support program—they may be able to hold their ground by persuading a strategically placed senator or representative to let the bill die a lingering death in committee. Or if a group cannot seem to make much headway with either Congress or the president, as was true of American blacks in the 1950s, it may turn to the courts to accomplish by litigation what it could not achieve by legislation. In the more narrowly focussed power configuration of the parliamentary system, there are not as many vantage points for influence outside the Cabinet.

It is apparent that the presidential system is highly decentralized, almost fragmented. Power, instead of being concentrated in the hands of a prime minister and Cabinet, is divided among many offices. The reason for this was explained by Madison in *The Federalist* No. 51:

> Ambition must be made to counteract ambition. . . . If men were angels, no government would be necessary. If angels were to govern men, neither external nor internal controls on government would be necessary. In framing a government which is to be administered by men over men, the great difficulty lies in this: you must first enable the government to control the governed; and in the next place oblige it to control itself.[42]

Separation of the legislative, executive, and judicial branches is one way of organizing government so as to "oblige it to control itself."

The models of the presidential form of government used around the world today are not carbon copies of the U.S. example. Structural as well as cultural factors influence the way in which forms of government work in different countries. In Mexico, for example, a very powerful president dominates all facets of the political process. Chosen for a six-year term (and not able to serve more than once), the president uses a powerful institution—the Institutionalized Revolutionary Party (PRI)—to control the governmental machinery and co-ordinate control of the Congress, the bureaucracy, the courts, and even the governments of the various Mexican states and municipalities. The president uses patronage, legislative programs, electoral intimidation, and coercion to persuade and cajole to achieve personal ends. The Mexican case might be considered an authoritarian president using a single dominant party as a power base.

On the other hand, a Brazilian president faces quite a different situation—both *de jure* and *de facto* powers are very different. Legally speaking, the powers of the president of Brazil are comparable to those of the president of Mexico. In fact, however, the president of Brazil must face a fragmented political party system, strong state interests supported by personal political followings, and a military with a tradition of intervening in the affairs of state. Under these conditions, Brazilian presidential politics are very different from Mexican presidential politics.

The success or failure of a presidential system does not necessarily ride on the constitutional arrangement alone. On the contrary, how the institutions in the system work depends on historical tradition, cultural and institutional factors, and even economic conditions.

It is a moot question whether the parliamentary system is preferable to the presidential system as a form of liberal democracy. It is indicative that those who live under one system and become critical of it usually wish to make it more like the other. For example, it is often said in Canada that the prime minister's power of appointment is too unrestricted and that there should be a body, like the American Senate, to confirm appointments to the bench or other high office. Or it is suggested that party discipline is too strict; members of Parliament should be free to vote according to their conscience or the wishes of their constituents. But in the United States, students of the presidential system often yearn for the coherence and leadership they perceive in the Westminster model. In 1980 the prestigious journal *Foreign Affairs* contained an article by Lloyd Cutler, legal counsel to then President Carter, that proposed modifying the American constitution to make it more like the parliamentary system. One of his ideas was that president, senators, and members of Congress should all serve simultaneous six-year terms and that the president should be allowed to dissolve Congress and call new elections once in a term of office.[43] Perhaps the conclusion is that "the grass is always greener." Once a system is solidly established, it has so much inertia and weight of tradition behind it that the benefit of a wholesale change is unlikely to be worth the cost, although piecemeal reforms may transfer to one system some of the advantages of the other.

Even if the net balance of advantages and disadvantages of the two systems is approximately equal, it is clear that they have different strengths and weaknesses, which can be summarized as follows:

Parliamentary

Strengths

1. With a majority, the government has the power to govern.

2. The non-confidence vote provides a check on the government.

3. The lines of responsibility for passage or defeat of legislation are clear. A voter can make decisions on the basis of party stance.

Presidential

Strengths

1. Separation of powers discourages concentration of power.

2. Checks and balances limit the power of branches of government.

3. Without party discipline, members can be constituency-oriented.

Parliamentary	Presidential
Weaknesses	*Weaknesses*
1. The system may be unstable if a majority is not obtained.	1. Separation of powers fragments the system, sometimes rendering it immobile.
2. The power of a government with a large majority is very great—possibly insensitive to public needs.	2. Voters cannot pin responsibility on any one party.
3. Because party loyalty is necessary, individual members may have to vote against their conscience or the wishes of their constituents.	3. Without a non-confidence vote, the electorate must wait for an election to unseat an unpopular president or members of Congress.

Overall, it might be said that while both are effective forms of liberal democracy, the presidential system is more liberal and the parliamentary system is more democratic. By "more liberal," we mean that the presidential system has more internal checks on the exercise of power, in line with the liberal fear of excessive state control of society. By "more democratic," we mean that the parliamentary system is a more effective means of expressing the will of the majority because it allows it to choose a government that can govern with relatively little hindrance from countervailing power.

This democratic potential of the parliamentary system raises problems for a country such as Canada in which forming a national majority is often hindered by regional or linguistic fragmentation. In such situations, the parliamentary system may confer tremendous power on the governing party, even though it represents not a true majority, but only the largest single minority. One of the recurrent themes of Canadian politics is protest by minorities who feel their rights have been ignored or curtailed by overwhelming parliamentary majorities. One thinks immediately of the demands of native peoples for self-government or the continual struggle of the Western provinces against Ottawa during the Trudeau years. Parallels at the provincial level are the attempts of Anglophones in Quebec or Francophones in Manitoba to assert linguistic rights against legislation supported by large majorities both in the legislature and in the public at large. These considerations lead to the discussion of the centralization and decentralization of government in the next chapter.

20   Unitary and Federal Systems

Governments can also be classified according to the degree of centralization that they exhibit. The two main types applicable to modern circumstances are the *unitary system*, in which a single sovereign government controls all regions of the country, and a *federal system*, in which sovereignty is divided between a central government and several outlying or constituent governments. Two other types of less practical significance are the *devolutionary system* and the confederal system, commonly called *confederation*.[44] The former is a variant of the unitary state, in which the central government creates regional governments but can override them as it wishes, even to the point of abolishing them. The latter is an inherently unstable arrangement in which sovereign constituent governments create a central government without sovereign power of its own.

These types can be arranged on a continuum of centralization as follows:

Sovereign States	Confederation	Federalism	Devolution	Unitary State
No central government	Central government exists, but sovereignty retained by constituent governments	Sovereignty shared between central and constituent governments	Constituent governments exist, but sovereignty monopolized by central government	No constituent governments

As in most other classifications, the types represent points on a continuum, and existing political systems may fall between types. One federal system, for instance, may be so centralized as to be scarcely more than a case of devolution, while another may be so decentralized that it amounts almost to a confederation. With this qualification in mind, let us discuss the major types.

THE UNITARY SYSTEM

In a *unitary system*, powers and responsibilities are concentrated within central governmental authorities. Constitutionally, the central government is sovereign. Minor constituent governments—municipal, county, or departmental—may exist, but their responsibilities are delegated by statute from the central government. Their functions are more administrative than legislative, and much of their revenue comes from grants from the central government. In a unitary system, no attempt is made to create provinces or states with specific powers established in a constitution. Great Britain has a unitary system of government, as do France, Colombia, Japan, Sweden, and most other contemporary states. In each case, a National Assembly, Congress, Parliament, or Diet has the responsibility for governing the entire nation. The power of local governments varies considerably, depending on the extent to which central authorities have delegated responsibilities of government and administration.

Devolution—the granting of governmental, including limited legislative, responsibilities to regional governments—is a step toward decentralization. Regional governments, however, are not entrenched in the constitution. They are created by statute of the central government and may be modified or abolished in the same way. An example would be the government of Northern Ireland from 1921 to 1972. Under the Government of Ireland Act of 1920, the British established at Stormont a Parliament with local responsibilities. This legislative body had a great deal of autonomy in its control of domestic matters such as housing, services, and public employment. The experiment was terminated in 1972 because violence between the Protestant majority and Roman Catholic minority rendered the society ungovernable.[45] The fact of termination demonstrates the utter dependence of regional governments on the central government in a devolved system. There was no constitutional barrier to the British Cabinet's unilateral decision to dissolve the Stormont Parliament and put Northern Ireland under the direct control of a secretary of state for Northern Ireland.

In the mid-1970s, there was a great deal of support for devolution in Scotland and Wales. Advocates suggested parliaments be formed, modelled on the example of Northern Ireland. The proposals were not implemented, however, because Scottish voters rejected devolution in an advisory referendum (1979). Scotland, incidentally, though it remains without a regional Parliament, is administratively distinct from the rest of Britain in several ways and also retains a unique legal system owing more to European civil law than British common law. There are many ways that regional differences can be accommodated within a unitary state.

THE FEDERAL SYSTEM

In a *federal system*, powers and responsibilities are divided between a federal (or national) government and outlying or constituent governments such as provinces, states, or cantons. The federal government, for example, may be responsible for minting money and raising an army, while constituent governments may be responsible for education and building roads. Constitutionally, sovereignty is divided between different levels of government instead of being concentrated in one government. Both levels of government are mentioned in a constitutional document, and neither can modify or abolish the other without its own consent. In reality, however, it is virtually impossible to divide powers neatly so that the responsibility of each government is absolute or totally independent of the other. Therefore overlapping jurisdictions, disputes, and joint efforts are commonplace in any federal system of government. The American constitution of 1789 created the world's first federal system. The model has since been imitated in Brazil, Mexico, Venezuela, Canada, Australia, Indonesia, India, the Soviet Union, Switzerland, and the Federal Republic of Germany.

The invention of federalism was precipitated by the inadequacy of confederation as a form of government. After winning its independence from Britain, the United States adopted in 1781 the Articles of Confederation, the first American constitution. The states retained sovereignty, and the federal Congress was little more than a meeting place for ambassadors of these state governments. Congress could not levy taxes, raise an army, regulate commerce, or enforce law within the states, nor was there a national executive authority. The general recognition in the country that this system could not last very long led to the constitutional convention of 1787. Another relevant example of confederation is the proposal for sovereignty association between Quebec and the rest of Canada, which, depending on the details of implementation, might not even reach the level of a confederation. According to the official proposal of the Parti Québécois, Canada and Quebec would be sovereign nations co-operating in selected areas. For example, there would be a common currency supervised by a central bank in which both partners would hold shares. But there would be no central legislature of any kind, not even one like the very weak American Congress of 1781–1789.

Because of its special relevance to Canadians, let us return to a more extended discussion of federalism. There are at least three primary reasons for the origin of federal systems. It has been said that "federalism is one way to resolve the problem of enlarging governments."[46] Federal systems are alternatives to large empires established by imperial force. Decentralization should allow far-flung regions to feel that not all decisions are made for them in a distant capital. Not surprisingly, most federal states are geographically large: Mexico, Australia, India, and so forth. A second reason is that federal systems are often established in diverse societies where a substantial degree of linguistic, religious, or cultural autonomy exists. This explains the existence of federalism in Switzerland, which is geographically small but linguistically and religiously diverse. Linguistic division is not a factor in the Federal Republic of Germany, but historical reasons have promoted federalism there. Because Germany was not fully united until 1871, some of the German *Länder* (states), such as Bavaria, were until relatively recently sovereign states and thus have important historical traditions of their own. Federalism can also accommodate this sort of diversity. In practice, large size and cultural pluralism often go together, so that federalism has a double *raison d'être* in countries such as India or Canada. A third reason is that federal systems provide one way of checking governmental power. By dividing powers between levels of government, absolute power is not concentrated within a single unit. The logic would be much the same as James Madison's justification of the separation of powers—obliging government to "control itself" by setting up the ambition of one group of politicians to counteract the ambition of another.

Writers on federalism also cite a number of other advantages of the federal system of government. A larger nation should have greater power with which to defend itself against foreign enemies. Also, the larger the nation-state, the greater the economies of scale. It should be cheaper to administer public services on a large scale, and costs can be spread among more people. Third, with governments located at a regional level, people should feel closer to the decision-making process, and conversely, these decision makers should be well aware of local needs and be able to respond to them. And finally, constituent governments can often establish innovative programs and policies aimed at particular problems. These experiments may be very valuable for the entire country once they are tested. Saskatchewan's health care programs, which go back to the 1930s, are a good example of an innovation tested in one province and later adopted across the country as the medicare program.

In spite of these advantages, as Garth Stevenson states, "One is tempted to conclude that both the arguments against federalism and the arguments in its favor can be as easily refuted as supported."[47] Duplicating levels of government creates expenses that may outweigh any economies of scale a federal union may achieve. While governments at the local or provincial level are closer to the people, there is no guarantee that they are any more responsive to local needs than a federal government.

It is obvious, however, that the division of sovereignty in a federal system reduces the power of the central government, thus taking away some of its ability to become oppressive. It is less obvious, but equally true, that the existence of two levels of government is a check on tyrannical tendencies in the constituent governments. This was brilliantly pointed out by Madison in his contributions to *The Federalist*. He showed that in a small democracy, there is a strong likelihood of some group gaining the upper hand and exercising a tyranny of the majority over minorities. A small jurisdiction is usually homogeneous in social composition, and this makes it easy for a majority to form. But in a large country, there is such a diversity of groups—farmers, workers, merchants, and so forth—that there are "in the society so many separate descriptions of citizens as will render an unjust combination of a majority of the whole very improbable."[48] A confirmation of Madison's theory occurred in Alberta in the 1930s when William Aberhart's Social Credit government, elected by a majority of debtors, passed laws against creditors that amounted to a confiscation of property. When the newspapers criticized him too harshly, Aberhart tried to impose a form of censorship on them. The federal government protected the rights of banks and newspapers by disallowing provincial legislation and exercising judicial review.

The situation with blacks in the American South is also a case in point, but from a different perspective. For almost one hundred years, state governments in the decentralized American federal system had been able to pass laws that discriminated against blacks. For instance, laws were passed limiting voting rights and segregating schools. By 1965, with the Supreme Court of the United States leading the way, the federal government was finally able to override the legal structure of racial segregation. The point is that in a decentralized federal system, power at the constituent level (in this case, the state level) can be used to restrict social, economic, and political rights of minorities. Although it took about a century and a lot of grief for blacks and some whites, Madison's idea of justice did prevail. Thus the genius of federalism is recognizing that power at any level is subject to abuse and establishing layers of government with enough power to balance each other.

Although each federal system must be uniquely adapted to the pluralistic conditions of its society, there are certain structural features that are universal, or very nearly so. First, there must be a written document that explicitly assigns powers to the two levels of government. It is hard to see how such complex and technical matters, which must be very clearly stated, could rest solely on tradition. In Canada Section 91 of the Constitution Act, 1867 grants power to the federal government, while Sections 92 and 93 spell out the powers of the provinces. Powers of the federal or national Parliament include, for example, control of trade and commerce, maintenance of a postal service, and responsibility for navigation and shipping. Provincial powers under Section 92 include control of the sale of alcoholic beverages, responsibility for marriage law, and management of hospitals. Section 93 makes provincial governments responsible for education "in and for each province"; this wording is open enough to allow the federal government to help support universities, whose research role transcends provincial boundaries.

The constitution of a federal system must also say something about *residual powers*, that is, those powers of government that are not specially enumerated in the text. No list of functions can ever be complete, if only because the future will present situations unforeseen at the time of drafting. In Canada residual powers were given to the federal government by Section 91 of the Constitution Act, 1867:

> It shall be lawful for the Queen, by and with the Advice and Consent of the Senate and House of Commons, to make Laws for the Peace, Order, and good Government of Canada, in relation to all Matters not coming within the Classes of Subjects by this Act assigned exclusively to the Legislatures of the Provinces . . .

In contrast, the Tenth Amendment to the American constitution took the opposite approach:

> The powers not delegated to the United States by the Constitution or prohibited by it to the States, are reserved to the States respectively, or to the people.

Practically all federal systems have bicameral legislatures in the central government, although in some the powers of the upper house have atrophied over the years. The rationale of federal bicameralism is to provide the provinces or regions with a special form of representation within the central government. This is suppposed to ensure that regional voices are heard in the capital and prevent regional interests from being overridden by a numerical majority in the nation. It is quite frankly a restraint upon the pure democracy of majority rule.

The Federal Republic of Germany is a strong example of federal bicameralism. The upper house or Bundesrat is composed of delegates chosen by and responsible to the governments of the *Länder*; the number of delegates is roughly proportional to the size of the *Land*. The central government is responsible only to the lower house or Bundestag, but the Bundesrat, unlike our own Senate, often exercises its power of refusing to pass legislation. The American Senate is another good example. Senators, now democratically elected, were once chosen by state legislatures. They still feel responsible for seeing that their states' interests are respected in Washington. Having two senators per state, regardless of the size of the state, guarantees equal state representation.

In comparison, we have a weaker form of federal bicameralism because the power of the Canadian Senate is limited. Section 22(4) of the Constitution Act, 1867 specifies a certain regional distribution of senators (twenty-four each from Quebec, Ontario, the Western provinces, and the Maritimes, six from Newfoundland, and one each from the Northwest and Yukon territories), but this distribution does not always make senators true provincial representatives. Senators are appointed by the governor general on the advice of the prime minister; this means that many would not view themselves as strong advocates of the provinces. It is not surprising that most of the recent proposals to reform the Canadian constitution concern changing the Senate to make it a stronger representative of provincial interests. Canada's upper house does not really do the job that equivalent bodies in most federal states perform; and this probably contributes to a feeling among provinces such as Newfoundland and Alberta that their interests are not effectively represented in Ottawa but are repeatedly overridden by the majority voting power of electors in Ontario and Quebec. On the other hand, many members of Parliament and some analysts of the Canadian federal system would argue that all provinces are represented in the House of Commons and that, regardless of whether the MP is on the government or the opposition side, this representation is adequate.

The weakness of regional representation in Ottawa has encouraged Canadian federalism to develop an "interstate" rather than an "intra-state" character.[49] Provincial governments have become the main advocates of regional interests and therefore deal with each other and with the federal government in quasi-diplomatic fashion. The most visible manifestations of this "executive federalism" are the periodic first ministers' conferences, which are conducted very much like international conferences with their public posturing, secret negotiations, communiqués, etc. These sessions are only the most apparent part of a ceaseless round of federal-provincial meetings at various levels among cabinet ministers, deputy ministers, and specialized officials. This cycle of negotiations and meetings occurs outside parliamentary government in Ottawa. There is nothing like it in other major federal systems such as Australia, the United States, or the Federal Republic of Germany.

In federal systems, constituent governments frequently clash with each other and with the national government, and the courts usually become the arbiters of such conflicts. Judicial review, the power to declare legislation unconstitutional, is a significant feature of most federal constitutions (with the exception of the USSR, where federalism is more apparent than real). It is an important way of keeping each level of government from overstepping its powers. Federalism makes the courts politically prominent, which they usually are not in a unitary state such as Great Britain. This in turn makes judicial appointments politically sensitive.

In the United States, Senate confirmation of presidential appointments to the bench helps raise the legitimacy of the federal judiciary in the eyes of the states; but in Canada judicial appointments are made by the governor general on the advice of the minister of justice, with the prime minister playing a special role by nominating chief justices of the various courts. There is no formal role for provincial governments or provincial representatives in Ottawa, although consultation sometimes takes place behind the scenes. As long as the highest Canadian appeals court was the Judicial Committee of the Privy Council, a special British court that heard appeals from the whole empire, the issue was not crucial to the provinces; for in fact, the Judicial Committee rendered a whole series of decisions favourable to the provinces in their disputes with Ottawa. But when appeal to the Judicial Committee was abolished in 1949, the Supreme Court of Canada, appointed solely by federal authorities, became the ultimate interpreter of Canadian law. Since that time, the provinces have increasingly desired some role in choosing judges, and the judiciary is frequently attacked as an instrument of federal policy.

Constitutional amendment is another contentious issue in federal systems. There must be some sort of balance between the two levels of government. If the central government can change the constitution at will without the consent of the constituent governments, the system is tantamount to devolution because the central government could modify or even abolish the constituent governments by unilateral constitutional amendment. Prior to 1982, the legal method for amending the Canadian constitution was for the British Parliament, acting on a joint address from the Canadian Senate and House of Commons, to change the British North America Act (as it was then called) as requested. In most but not all instances where provincial rights were affected, the federal government obtained the prior consent of all the provinces before requesting constitutional amendments. An amending formula was introduced as part of the Constitution Act, 1982. Under Section 38, amendments must be passed by the House, the Senate, and the legislative assemblies of two-thirds of the provinces that have at least 50 per cent of the population of all the provinces. This provision institutionalizes the federal and provincial governments' roles in amending the constitution and excludes Great Britain altogether. In the United States all constitutional amendments must receive approval from two-thirds of both houses of Congress and three-quarters of state legislatures. Again, this provides a balance of power between the central and constituent governments.

Finally, the Canadian system has a feature that is unusual in federal states: the ability of the central government to nullify legislation of the constituent governments, even when they are acting within their proper constitutional sphere. There are two mechanisms by which this can happen. In the first, known as *reservation*, the lieutenant-governor of a province can refuse royal assent to a bill and request advice from the federal Cabinet. In the second, known as *disallowance*, the federal Cabinet can nullify a provincial act within one year of passage, even though it has received royal assent from the lieutenant-governor of the province. These powers of the federal government were used frequently in the early years of Confederation but are now in abeyance. No provincial act has been disallowed since 1943, although use of the power has been threatened. In 1961 the lieutenant-governor of Saskatchewan reserved a bill without seeking prior advice from Ottawa, much to the embarrassment of the prime minister. Apart from that confused episode, this power has not been recently used. In practice, challenge in the courts seems to have replaced reservation and disallowance, even though both powers are still constitutionally alive. In the United States, as in most federal systems, there is no parallel to this constitutional dominance of the central government.

This review shows that Canadian federalism was originally so highly centralized as to border on devolution. The federal powers to appoint judges and senators, nullify provincial legislation, amend the constitution, and claim residual powers initially far outweighed the provincial powers. This was by design. The founders of Confederation could not ignore the American Civil War (1861–1865). Most believed that the American constitution had granted too much power to the states. Sir John A. Macdonald would have preferred a unitary state, then known as a *legislative union* (only one legislature for all of Canada); but he realized that some form of federalism was required to entice Quebec and the Atlantic provinces into association with Ontario. The solution that emerged was, legally, a strong central government with minimal concessions to the provinces.

The subsequent evolution of Canada has undone much of this work. Although there have been long cycles of provincial or federal gains, the overall trend has been that the provincial governments have improved their situation vis-à-vis Ottawa. Their access to direct taxation has provided a strong revenue base. Their ability to exploit natural resources, which Section 92 of the Constitution Act, 1867 assigns to provincial control, has made several provinces financially independent of Ottawa.

Curiously, American political evolution has gone in the other direction. In the United States power has shifted toward the federal government. International crises—two world wars, the Cold War, and the Korean and Vietnam wars—and the "nationalization" of domestic issues, such as racial disparities and inflation, have tended to focus all eyes on Washington in the search for solutions. The role of the federal government totally overshadows the role of any state or group of states in its ability to confront national issues. An abstract reading of the American and Canadian constitutions would seem to show that American states are far more powerful than Canadian provinces, but this is in fact a highly distorted picture of the current reality.[50] The constitutional allocation of residual powers, to the federal government in Canada and to the states in the United States, has had little long-run, practical effect.

While federal systems have enabled large nation-states to be built, they have not provided the cure for all political ills. Indeed, separatist movements have plagued many countries with a federal form of government. The Civil War in the United States was fought over the South's right to secede from the Union. Separatist feelings have run strong in many Mexican states. Nigerians from the north and west fought Biafrans in order to keep their territory intact, and separatists in the Parti Québécois still vow to establish sovereignty in Quebec. A small but vocal minority of Western Canadians also feels separatism is the only way of escaping the political power of Ottawa.

A basic problem with all federal systems is establishing a workable balance acceptable to all levels of government. It was once believed that a central government was best suited to cope with national problems. Over the last sixty years, there has been a trend toward centralizing power at the national level, partly because governments have expanded their functions to meet economic crises and have become involved in international conflicts. Today, however, many individuals argue that outlying governments can deal with citizens best, and there seems to be a lot of appeal for the thesis that "small is beautiful."

But it would surely be simplistic to overemphasize either level of government at the expense of the other. In most federal systems, there is currently a combined attack on problems: federal, provincial, and local governments may provide funds for education, share costs in developing transportation systems, and aid in providing cheaper housing. These efforts, sometimes described as "co-operative" federalism, may better characterize the actual workings of the majority of federal systems today. In spite of functional co-operation, one should not lose sight of the fact that in most federal systems, continuous struggles exist between levels of government, struggles over power and financial resources. These disputes are an inherent part of the federal form of government. And Canada today suggests how difficult it is to resolve them.

Notes

1. Aristotle, *Politics*, iii, 16, in Richard McKeon, ed., *The Basic Works of Aristotle* (New York: Random House, 1941), p. 1202.

2. John Stuart Mill, *On Liberty* (Indianapolis: Bobbs-Merrill, 1956), p. 7; and Alexis de Tocqueville, *Democracy in America*, ed. Andrew Hacker (New York: Washington Square Press, 1964), p. 102.

3. Aristotle, *Politics*, iv, 11, p. 1221.

4. Dorothy Pickles, *Democracy* (London: B. T. Batsford, 1970), p. 11.

5. Terence H. Qualter, *The Election Process in Canada* (Toronto: McGraw-Hill, 1970), p. 9.

6. *Attorney General of Canada et al. v. Robert Gould*, [1984] 5 C.R.D. 325.30–02.

7. The Constitution Act, 1982, ss. 38, 41.

8. Speech of October 11, 1864, in Joseph Pope, ed., *Confederation* (Toronto: Carswell, 1895), p. 58.

9. J. A. O. Larsen, "The Judgment of Antiquity on Democracy," *Classical Philology* 49 (1954), pp. 1–14.

10. James Mill, *An Essay on Government* (Indianapolis: Bobbs-Merrill, 1955), p. 66.

11. Ibid., p. 70.

12. Geraint Parry, *Political Elites* (London: George Allen & Unwin, 1969), p. 30.

13. Raymond Aron, "Social Structure and the Ruling Class," *British Journal of Sociology* 1 (1950), p. 10, quoted in T. B. Bottomore, *Elites and Society* (Harmondsworth: Penguin, 1966), p. 115.

14. For a number of discussions of the referendum, see David Butler and Austin Ranney, eds., *Referendums* (Washington, D.C.: American Enterprise Institute, 1978).

15. Alvin Rabushka and Pauline Ryan, *The Tax Revolt* (Stanford, Calif.: Hoover Institution, 1982).

16. Particulars of the initiative, referendum, and recall can be found in J. A. Corry and Henry J. Abraham, *Elements of Democratic Government*, 4th ed. (New York: Oxford University Press, 1964), pp. 410–422.

17. Arend Lijphart, *Democracies* (New Haven, Conn.: Yale University Press, 1984), p. 202.

18. Cited in Friedrich A. Hayek, *Law, Legislation and Liberty*, 3 vols. (Chicago: University of Chicago Press, 1973–1979), vol. III, p. 1.

19. John Adams, "A Defense of the American Constitutions" (1787), in George A. Peek, ed., *The Political Writings of John Adams* (Indianapolis: Bobbs-Merrill, 1954), p. 148.

20. On this theme see two widely discussed books: Samuel H. Beer, *Britain Against Herself: The Political Contradictions of Collectivism* (New York: W. W. Norton, 1982); and Mancur Olson, *The Rise and Decline of Nations: Economic Growth, Stagflation, and Social Rigidities* (New Haven, Conn.: Yale University Press, 1982).

21. Tocqueville, *Democracy in America*, p. 316.

22. Aristotle, *Politics,* iv, 10, p. 1219.

23. Baron de Montesquieu, *The Spirit of the Laws* (New York: Hafner, 1949), p. 26.

24. Ibid., p. 57.

25. Giorgio Pini, *The Official Life of Benito Mussolini* (London: Hutchinson, 1939).

26. Hannah Arendt, *The Origins of Totalitarianism*, 2nd ed. (New York: World Publishing Co., 1958), p. 460.

27. One of the first analyses of totalitarianism was Carl J. Friedrich and Zbigniew K. Brzezinski, *Totalitarian Dictatorship and Autocracy*, 2nd ed. (New York: Praeger, 1965). A more recent work is Waldemar Gurian, "The Totalitarian State," *The Review of Politics* 40, No. 4 (October 1978), pp. 514–527.

28. Arendt, *The Origins of Totalitarianism*, p. 467.

29. Friedrich and Brzezinski, *Totalitarian Dictatorship and Autocracy*, p. 21.

30. Edward McWhinney, *Constitution-Making* (Toronto: University of Toronto Press, 1981), p. 190.

31. Stuart R. Schram, *The Political Thought of Mao Tse-tung* (New York: Praeger, 1963), p. 253.

32. On this subject see Richard Lowenthal, "Beyond Totalitarianism?" in Irving Howe, ed., *1984 Revisited: Totalitarianism in Our Century* (New York: Harper & Row, 1983), pp. 209–267.

33. Robert Jay Lifton, *Revolutionary Immortality* (New York: Random House, 1968), p. 73.

34. McWhinney, *Constitution-Making*, p. 210.

35. Juan J. Linz, "An Authoritarian Regime: Spain," in Erik Allardt and Stein Rokkan, eds., *Mass Politics: Studies in Political Sociology* (New York: The Free Press, 1970), p. 255.

36. *La Prensa* (Lima), February 26, 1975.

37. John Locke, *The Second Treatise of Government* (Indianapolis: Bobbs-Merrill, 1952), p. 91.

38. Frank MacKinnon, *The Crown in Canada* (Toronto: McClelland and Stewart, 1976).

39. Walter Bagehot, cited in R. MacGregor Dawson and Norman Ward, *The Government of Canada*, 5th ed. (Toronto: University of Toronto Press, 1970), p. 168.

40. See John E. Schwarz, "Exploring a New Role in Policy Making: The British House of Commons in the 1970s," *The American Political Science Review* 74,

No. 1 (March 1980), pp. 23–27; and Jon B. Johnson, "Testy U.K. Backbenchers cloud the patriation issue," the *Globe and Mail*, February 25, 1981, p. 7.

41. Richard Neustadt, *Presidential Power*, 2nd ed. (New York: John Wiley & Sons, 1964), p. 42.

42. Alexander Hamilton, John Jay, and James Madison, *The Federalist* (New York: Modern Library, n.d.), p. 337.

43. Lloyd N. Cutler, "To Form a Government," *Foreign Affairs* 59 (Fall 1980), pp. 126–143.

44. Canadian Confederation (with a capital C) is an example of federalism. The general term confederation (with a small c) is an abstract concept of political science not particularly associated with Canada.

45. Vernon Bogdanor, *Devolution* (New York: Oxford University Press, 1979), ch. 3.

46. William H. Riker, *Federalism: Origin, Operation, Significance* (Boston: Little, Brown, 1964), p. 2.

47. Garth Stevenson, *Unfulfilled Union: Canadian Federalism and National Unity* (Toronto: Macmillan, 1979), p. 23.

48. Hamilton, Jay, and Madison, *The Federalist*, p. 339.

49. Alan Cairns, "From Interstate to Intrastate Federalism," *Bulletin of Canadian Studies* 2 (1979), pp. 13–34.

50. An excellent comparison of federalism in Canada and the United States can be found in Roger Gibbins, *Regionalism: Territorial Politics in Canada and the U.S.* (Scarborough, Ont.: Butterworths, 1982).

Vocabulary

typology	responsible government
monarchy	party discipline
tyranny	parliamentary secretary
aristocracy	private member
oligarchy	head of state
democracy	head of government
polity	majority government
philosopher-king	minority government
liberal democracy	coalition government
people's democracy	cabinet solidarity
plurality	reading
majority	standing committee

qualified majority
concurrent majority
bicameralism
unanimity
direct democracy
representative democracy
referendum
plebiscite
initiative
recall
elite
despotism
totalitarianism
monism
political police
socialist legality
authoritarianism
statism
coup d'état
separation of powers
legislative
executive
judicial
bill
prerogative

ad hoc committee
report stage
royal assent
proclamation
opposition
official opposition
shadow cabinet
confidence
free vote
backbenchers
party caucus
constructive vote of confidence
vote of censure
separation of powers
veto
judicial review
unitary system
federal system
devolution
confederation
residual powers
reservation
disallowance
legislative union

PART FOUR

The Political Process

21   The Political Process and Political Culture

In Part One we discussed politics in abstract terms. We associated it, for example, with authority, allocating values, and reconciling disputes. In Part Four we want to move from the level of abstraction to the level of concrete reality and be much more specific about the political process. Our objective is to explain the process of politics as an institutionalized process for making public decisions, so that politics becomes a vivid and concrete idea in the mind of the student.

The task may be easier said than done. While all of us know that the process exists and that it works, it is still difficult to describe it in precise terms. The *political process* is a complex activity of making public decisions for a society. The process can be seen, first of all, as a group of structural institutions (or components). Interest groups, political parties, executives and legislatures, the courts, and so forth are integral parts of this process. But describing components and explaining their roles is only the beginning. Politics is the interaction of all components in devising public laws and policies acceptable to individuals in society. It is also the selection and rejection of rulers, dissent and opposition, as well as support and consensus. Indeed, devising a successful course of action that can withstand the scrutiny of public dialogue is an art that requires a particular intuitive sense. It is probably true that the greater the freedom in society, the greater the participation in politics; and the greater the participation in politics, the more complex the political process. It is, then, a challenge to be able to understand this dynamic aspect of public life in an open society.

There is in all societies an endless and ongoing political process that makes public decisions in response to claims and counterclaims from elements of that society. This political process produces not only decisions but also patterns of accommodation, support, and resistance to these decisions. The process can be conceived as a system. In the cybernetic sense, a system is a connected set of functions that converts inputs into outputs and feeds the results back as data for a future round of decision making.[1]

An explicit application of systems analysis to politics was made by David Easton in a well-known book, *A Systems Analysis of Political Life* (1965). In its simplest form, Easton represented the political system as a process of authoritative decision making,[2] illustrated in Figure 21.1. Politics is likened to a systematic flow. Specific inputs (demands and supports) are generated in society. Demands are what people would like government to do for them; supports are the approbation they bestow on a government they consider legitimate. These demands and supports are transformed or converted into outputs: laws and policies. This conversion takes place in

FIGURE 21.1

The Systematic Flow of Politics

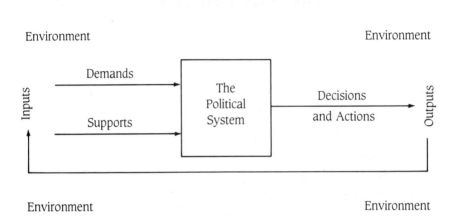

Easton's "black box," or the political system, which is made up of the various branches and layers of government. It is called a black box because at this point, we are not concerned with the internal mechanisms by which conversion is accomplished; we are just noting that conversion occurs and are trying to situate it in a systematic context. The box is black because we do not yet look inside it. The impact of laws and policies on society takes place through feedback that generates new demands and supports. Easton's work was one of the first applications of the phrase *political system*, now used extensively in the political science literature to refer to the process of government and politics in any nation-state.

A rather similar approach was taken in the influential book of Gabriel Almond and G. B. Powell, *Comparative Politics* (1966).[3] They also adopted the fundamental notions of input, conversion, output, and feedback. However, they provided a more detailed analysis of the conversion process in the modern democratic state that is at the same time compatible with traditional conceptions of political science, such as the separation of powers into legislative, executive, and judicial branches. They pointed to six important *structures* that carry out necessary functions: interest groups, political parties, the mass media, legislatures, executives, and the judiciary. The corresponding *functions* in the political process are interest articulation (making the position of the group known), interest aggregation (combining the positions of a number of interests), communication, making laws, administering laws, and adjudicating disputes.

In our model of politics, Figure 21.2, politics is portrayed as a process in which information flows from left to right. Beginning with the plural society (one composed of many interests), it becomes a process for converting political inputs—demands,

FIGURE 21.2

The Political Process

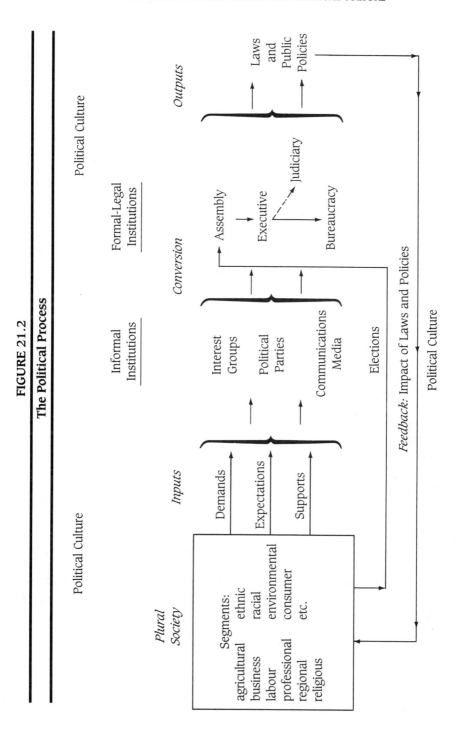

expectations, and supports—into political outputs—laws and policies. Institutions, both formal and informal, interact to achieve this conversion and produce laws and public policies. Feedback allows the system to adjust spontaneously to ever-changing conditions as outputs are evaluated and give rise to new inputs.

In society, conflicts inevitably develop among groups with different interests, goals, and expectations. For example, farmers may demand low freight rates in order to gain an advantage in the agricultural export market. At the same time, railways may be seeking higher freight rates to cover increasing costs. Freight rates in Canada are regulated by the federal government and must be reviewed periodically amid the pressures of various interests, conditions, and circumstances such as inflation and regional development. Any decision is an output that affects the various groups. Even a decision to postpone a decision is in effect an output that ratifies the present structure of freight rates.

Not all political activity by individuals and groups is necessarily conflict-oriented; numerous actions undertaken by individuals and groups support the political process. Taxes are paid and speed limits are observed. Complying with authority is very important to maintain an orderly society. In fact, without this voluntary behaviour, the entire process would become oppressive. The point is that political behaviour of individuals and groups involves both demands and supports. People usually pay taxes voluntarily. If, however, taxes go beyond what people consider a just proportion, they may demand tax reductions or refuse to pay.

Public participation by individuals and groups in the political process follows certain patterns. Most of it is organized around a set of intermediate institutions linking people and their governors: interest groups, political parties, and the communications media. These are frequently referred to as the *informal* institutions of government. While they are an integral part of the process, they are informal (as opposed to formal-legal) because they are not established by a constitution. Yet they have power because they tend to co-ordinate and channel the activities of people in a concerted way. The development of these intermediate institutions has facilitated participation by large numbers of people in the modern political process.

Other institutions are *formal-legal* because they are created explicitly by a constitution, which provides the rules of the political game. One of the primary functions of a constitution is to grant power to various institutions that formalize laws and policies for a society. These institutions include elected assemblies, executives, and the judiciary. A final formal-legal institution is, of course, the election—the means by which members of a society choose their governors and show their opinion of past performance. The activities of these formal-legal organizations are the most visible aspect of the political process.

Another important topic is political culture, which hovers somewhat mysteriously on the fringe of Figure 21.2. *Political culture* is a name to designate the way in which the political system is inserted into a larger social reality of beliefs, attitudes, values, and norms.

Observers have long noticed that different people of the world possess what might be called traits. The Chinese, for example, are thought to be industrious and to maintain close family ties. People of Latin origin are said to be very emotional in speech and actions. North Americans are probably more egalitarian in their outlook than any society, yet they are materialistic and achievement-oriented. Such traits are considered part of the traditions of a society; they reflect national character. In one of the better studies conducted on cultural traits, Thomas Sowell examined the culture of ethnic groups after immigration to the United States. The Chinese, for example, became known for their "endurance and frugality." These characteristics carried over into younger generations as they participated in activities in the New World. As children, they were "better behaved and more hard-working." All this led to a high percentage of people from Chinese immigrant communities who entered the professions, and by 1959, their average income had surpassed the U.S. national average.[4]

Anthropologically, one might refer to these traits as part of culture. Culture in this sense refers to the total living patterns of a people: the place of the family, the role of religion, the influence of climate, the nature of the economy, and the politics. Culture has become an umbrella term reflecting institutional arrangements as well as the attitudes, beliefs, and values that accompany them. That part of a total culture that reflects a people's orientation to politics is known as *political culture*,[5] a collection of attitudes, beliefs, values, and norms that people have developed toward government and politics.

Popular stereotypes, sometimes embodying a good deal of truth, exist about different political cultures. Germans, for example, think of themselves as being, and are thought by others to be, very respectful of public authority. While such a generalization is interesting and perhaps true, it cannot explain all of German politics. For one thing, it is rare indeed that a whole nation can be grouped within a single political culture.

Recent studies using the methodology of public opinion research reveal that most societies possess a number of political cultures. In a five-nation study, Gabriel Almond and Sydney Verba established three basic types of political cultures: parochial, subject, and participatory.[6] The parochial culture is manifested in people who do not expect any positive action from government. Perceiving government as a police officer and tax collector, they wish to keep as much distance as possible between themselves and the authorities. Moreover, they do not expect individual participation in politics; they consider that a game for the upper classes. Those classified as subjects do expect some positive action from governments. Perhaps influenced by the revolution of rising expectations, they may anticipate a school for the community, a dam to develop an irrigation system and expand crop production, or a paramedical unit for the village. While those who are part of a subject culture increase their expectations, they still do not see themselves involved in politics. The questions of where to put schools, dams, and medical teams will be decided by people with power and influence. Finally, the participatory culture is manifested in individuals who have high expectations about governmental actions *and* expect to participate in politics. This participation may involve choosing political leaders or attempting to influence political action. A participatory political culture is an integral part of liberal democracy.

Political culture is a complex term because it represents the psychological dimension of politics.[7] It exists in the minds of individuals, providing a way of orienting relationships with government and the political process. Because it includes attitudes, beliefs, values, and norms regarding government and politics, political culture also encompasses one's political ideology, containing notions about what government is and what it ought to be. An example might help to clarify the relationship between political culture and political ideology. Belief in individual freedom is a fundamental part of the political culture of the Western world. At the same time, within the ideology of liberal democracies, we not only value individual freedom but also believe that maintaining it should be a primary goal of governments. Freedom of political action is the basis on which individuals and groups can become involved in the political process. Without political freedom, there would be little opportunity to participate in politics. Thus the liberal-democratic ideology is an integral part of our political culture.

By way of contrast, an observer of Latin American politics has noted that political systems there are influenced by Iberic-Latin traditions (culture).[8] These traditions include, among other things, accepting a society that is hierarchical, stratified, and authoritarian. These social traits seem to produce a political culture that is not conducive to the ideology of liberal and participatory democracy. Latin American politics is often characterized as being class-based, authoritarian, paternalistic, and elitist.

It is difficult to establish the exact connection between political culture and the political process. One way of visualizing this connection is offered by Gabriel Almond, who suggests that the political process is "embedded" in the political culture.[9] Attitudes and beliefs individuals hold about government and politics influence at every step the interaction among the elements of the political process.

If political culture refers to political attitudes and beliefs that influence the process of politics, the transmission of this culture is very important. The means by which a political culture is transmitted from generation to generation is known as *political socialization*.[10] A number of socializing agents, such as the family, schools, peer groups, communications media, the workplace, and contact with government itself, transmit the beliefs and values so important to regularizing patterns of living in a society.

Socializing new generations with values and beliefs is not a tidy process that always occurs in an orderly way. Political culture is not a static concept because beliefs and values are forever changing. There may be a significant conflict between generations in a society over which values or beliefs should be revered. Such a conflict can lead to the disintegration of order, or it may be contained by maintaining public dialogue, without which politics is reduced to mere coercion. Public discussion is the means by which different social groups articulate their interests and demand governmental action. Thus we come back to social pluralism as the source of inputs for the political system. The next chapter looks at interest groups as an extension of this pluralism.

22   Interest Groups

It is convenient to think of the political process beginning with the articulation of demands for action by particular social groups, usually called interest groups. An *interest group* is defined most simply as a collection of individuals who pursue common political goals.[11] It represents people who band together to accomplish specific objectives. Because groups exert political pressure to achieve ends, they may also be called *pressure groups*. Obviously, not all groups are political; people may organize for any number of reasons. There are social groups such as bridge and dance clubs, sports clubs, community associations, and professional organizations such as a bar association. Most of these voluntary organizations never become involved in politics; however, if they do, they become interest groups in the political process. As such, they facilitate popular participation in politics. They offer individuals an opportunity to become involved in the complex process of politics by co-ordinating political activities. Interest groups are thus informal political institutions linking people and government. Politics is an endless cycle because there are always new demands, generated by different interests, with which government must deal.

Note that interest groups do not seek to control the entire machinery of government. They merely seek to influence the outcome of the political process because they desire certain legislative or policy objectives. Organizations that go further and seek to actually control governments are political parties. Interest groups may work with political parties and may even become affiliated with them, as in the relationship between the New Democratic party (NDP) and the Canadian Labour Congress (CLC). However, parties and interest groups are conceptually distinct, even if their activities sometimes overlap.

The function of groups in politics is to articulate the interest of their members in order to obtain desired outputs of laws and policies. Interest groups seek to achieve their ends by persuading public officials. Developers may try to influence a city council's decision on planning or zoning; labour unions may try to influence the federal Cabinet on collective bargaining legislation; conservation organizations may seek to influence public policies toward national or provincial parks. In each case, citizens with a common goal band together in an effort to shape legislation that they believe affects their lives.

Increased activity by interest groups is a significant development in the political process over the last fifty years. Reasons for the increase are many, including extension of the franchise and increased education for most of society, which has produced a more articulate public. The growth of interest groups participating in politics has become a phenomenon common to all Western democracies.

This does not mean that prior to the 1930s, no interest groups functioned in politics. The Canadian Pacific Railway, for example, has long been a strong force behind transportation legislation. Industrialists occupying Cabinet posts have maintained the business viewpoint in government. Farmers, labour union members, and teachers have always tried to influence public decisions. But the change in the last fifty years is that many more groups have organized to achieve political ends. In a 1978 article in the *Financial Times of Canada*, it was suggested that "probably more than 200 associations, firms and individuals"[12] attempt to influence legislation in Ottawa. Well-known examples of major interest groups are the Canadian Manufacturers' Association, the Canadian Labour Congress, the Canadian Federation of Agriculture, and the Canadian Teachers' Federation. But many lesser-known groups now feel it imperative to work with government, including the Canadian Amateur Softball Association, the Canadian Crafts Council, the Canadian Veterinary Medical Association, the Dairy Farmers of Canada, the Canadian Federation of Students, the National Council of Women of Canada, the Navy League of Canada, and the Professional Association of Foreign Service Officers. Senior citizens' groups are a recent example of an interest organization formed to achieve an end: when Finance Minister Michael Wilson proposed partially de-indexing old age pensions in his 1985 budget, seniors across the country mobilized to pressure the government until the proposal was dropped.

Ottawa is not the only Canadian city to feel the proliferation of interest groups. In provincial capitals and even at the municipal level, interest groups are becoming an integral part of the political process. Many community or neighbourhood associations become politically active when city councils consider by-laws or otherwise make decisions that have an impact on their section of the city. As one writer has suggested, interest groups have become "creatures of mass political behavior."[13] With governments becoming more involved in all facets of social life, more groups are trying to influence the direction of legislation. Thus the proliferation of interest groups is directly related to the extraordinary expansion of the role of the state in the twentieth century.

Within the scope of this activity, how do we classify interest groups? One standard typology is the fourfold division of anomic, associational, institutional, and non-associational groups.[14]

ANOMIC GROUPS

Anomic groups form spontaneously in response to specific issues. If, for example, an official from a foreign country visited Ottawa and individuals happened to be opposed to government policies in that country, an organization might be formed to protest the visit. Demonstrations might occur at an airport or at meetings the official attended. A group organizes in response to a specific visit, its position is made known, but after the visit there is little reason for the organization to continue. Anomic groups may attract temporary publicity, but they are usually of little real importance, except that they may be manipulated by more durable organizations with ulterior motives. The Soviet Union, for example, has long used the World Peace Council, whose key leaders are always communists, to influence the amorphous "peace movement" in Western nations. Without realizing it, members of an anomic group may be pawns in someone else's game.

ASSOCIATIONAL GROUPS

Associational groups, in contrast, have a continuing formal organization and seek to articulate the interests of members over long periods of time. Labour, farm, business, and professional groups are examples. They have the opportunity to marshal the various resources of the group over time in order to achieve their ends. They are often the political arm of an organized group that already exists for other reasons, such as a trade union or professional association. This extra-political base, when it exists, is a vital source of workers, revenue, and continuity. An important theoretical analysis by Mancur Olson has shown that for many would-be interest groups, the costs in time and money of organizing for political actions outweigh the expected benefits to be gained by lobbying. When a group is already organized for other reasons, its incremental costs of entry into the political system are much lower. The theoretical prediction that pre-existing associations, like labour unions and professional associations, should be formidable pressure groups seems to be born out empirically.[15]

INSTITUTIONAL GROUPS

Institutional groups are organizations closely associated with government that act internally to influence public decisions. Public service unions and the military establishment are good examples. While these people are a part of government and are in theory politically neutral, they too have interests that they articulate by seeking to achieve specific ends. The expansion of government-service activities has made these institutional groups far more numerous and influential than they used to be. Like associational groups, they have the advantage of continuity and permanent organization.

There are certain associational groups that, according to this classification, might almost be labelled institutional because of their close association with governments – mostly through financial ties. Indian, Métis, and Inuit associations are examples, as would be the Consumers' Association of Canada and the Advisory Council on the Status of Women. In each case, all or part of the funding required to maintain the organization comes from the public purse. This tie raises questions about independence. Can the groups expect to look after the interests of their members when their very existence depends on government? Similarly, can government be expected to fund organizations and still scrupulously refrain from attempting to influence their policies? Such government funding tends to blur the lines between private and public spheres of activity. But with all its obvious pitfalls, it is a fact of increasing importance in pressure group politics.

NON-ASSOCIATIONAL GROUPS

Non-associational groups are made up of people who feel close to others on the basis of class, religion, race, culture, or some other criterion. They are without formal association, yet politically they may sometimes be considered as a unit. French Canadians, Protestants, Catholics, and Westerners are examples. Seldom do these people function as a coherent political group, but they are often considered a political force. The term *latent groups* that is sometimes applied to such blocs captures their significance. Even if a large number of people with a common interest are not formally organized, politicians recognize that they might, under appropriate circumstances, form an effective organization. Realizing the possibility, politicians would be foolish to completely ignore the interests of such latent groups.

Groups seek to influence laws and policies by *lobbying*. The term is derived from the practice of individuals and groups in the past seeking to talk to MPS and Cabinet ministers in the lobby of the British House of Commons. The term now expresses the many different methods interest groups use to influence public decisions. Lobbying takes many forms: arranging an interview with a Cabinet member, submitting a brief to a royal commission or parliamentary committee hearing, writing letters to MLAS, advertising in newspapers to generate public pressure over an issue, and offering "gifts" of different kinds to public officials. In every case, the objective is the same: to influence governors or the public so that they will be favourably disposed toward an issue.

Lobbying has become a normal part of today's political process. While it carries a certain derogatory connotation, many public officials admit that they depend on lobbyists as a source of information. Normally, elected officials depend on members of the administration or bureaucracy to supply the facts required for a political decision. But many legislators argue that the administration has its own views and biases or may not have all the information pertinent to a decision, so that depending on lobbyists for a range of views has become a recognized part of politics.

An important question in this regard is why some groups are more influential in their lobbying than others. What makes an interest group powerful? A number of factors have been suggested: size and cohesion of the group, wealth, organizational abilities, leadership, and the nature of an issue. Let us examine each factor in turn.

Numbers cannot help but count in democratic politics, so legislators have to listen when groups claim a large membership. This is why groups often try to expand their membership, hoping for more political influence. But numbers do not tell the whole story. Organized labour, for instance, represents one of the largest segments of our society. If it voted as a bloc, it could elect whomever it wanted in many constituencies and probably lobby better than any opponent. But organized labour has never operated as a fully cohesive body in Canadian politics. Therefore numbers must be qualified by the amount of cohesion within the group.

Another adage in politics is that money talks—it requires financial resources to put together an effective interest group. Hiring a lobbyist or lobbyists, maintaining an office, advertising, and even holding meetings all mean the group must have funds on which to draw. A group such as the National and Provincial Parks Association of Canada may want to undertake an advertising campaign across the country in order to make citizens aware of the value of parks, but putting ads in newspapers in major metropolitan centres is an expensive undertaking. Thus the availability of financial resources can be a big factor in the activity of a group.

Without organizational capacity, little gets done, so organizations enable large numbers of people to act in concert. It requires organizational skills to use the human resources of a large group effectively and translate the emotional feelings of people into action. If individuals feel taxes are too high, little may be gained by *ad hoc* and sporadic complaints to public officials. On the other hand, if individual responses are co-ordinated within an organized "taxpayers' revolt," they can be directed in a more efficient way. An organization can capitalize on diffuse emotion by focussing it in the public arena.

Another factor is leadership. Leaders can inspire and direct the activities of the members, whether it be writing letters, donating money, or appearing at public hearings. Leadership is often the difference between an effective and an ineffective political organization.

A final factor is the nature of the issue itself. The issue must have broad appeal to legislators and the public, or there is little chance of obtaining results in politics. If issues have little identification with basic values and beliefs, they are not apt to be very popular. One example is the communists' advocacy of public ownership of property in North America. There is probably no place in all the world where communists have made less headway than here. One explanation for this is that the tradition of private property is nowhere stronger than in Canada and the United States. Ownership of private property and its protection seems to be a fundamental tradition of these governments. It is clear that groups advocating issues that run counter to ingrained traditions are not apt to get very far with public officials or the public.

All of these factors may influence the power of a particular group. Combining as many of them as possible is perhaps the best strategy for becoming an effective interest group. Provincial medical associations are an example. While their numbers are few, they have a strong voice in government. They have almost unlimited financial resources, excellent organizational abilities and leadership, and a very cohesive group. This combination has made them effective lobbyists on the political scene.

Let us make some general observations about the place of interest groups in contemporary liberal democracies. First, there is a correlation between interest group activity and the guarantee of political freedom in a society. Without the constitutional guarantee of free speech, a free press, and the right to assemble, the political activities of interest groups would be seriously jeopardized. Governments seldom cherish criticism, and a good portion of an interest group's activities involves criticizing proposed or existing laws and policies. Without immunity from reprisal, there would be considerably less enthusiasm for this type of public participation. Even in our own relatively free society, there are accusations of governments withholding vital information and cases of governments using intimidation.

Second, interest group activity may be considered good "therapy" in the participatory society. While all groups do not achieve all their ends in the political process, it appears that a sufficient number do attain some of their goals. The theory of group politics is that because individuals can become involved in politics and enough groups do achieve some of their ends, confidence in the participatory political process is reinforced. Thus group politics may underscore the individual's belief in the legitimacy of the system. To deny the group an opportunity to participate in politics would undermine the legitimate operation of the system.

An increase in the activity of interest groups is a fact, but it is also a fact that only a small number of people in groups become activists. Are non-participants, those not affiliated with an interest group, excluded from the benefits of public decisions? As mentioned above, this is not the case because the unorganized still have "potential" for organizing and therefore constitute "latent" interests.[16] In other words, when public officials distribute benefits through the political process, they cannot afford to bypass these individuals totally. The unorganized are still voters, and they have the potential to become organized into effective groups.

Problems with interest group politics point up a fundamental dilemma inherent in the liberal-democratic process. While political freedom has nurtured a great deal of interest group activity, there is no assurance that this furthers the public interest of a society.

Interest group activity is closely interwoven with a distributive conception of politics. According to this view, politics represents an exchange. Voters render their support (votes) to politicians; politicians in turn enact programs and policies in the interests of those groups who support them. Although this is undoubtedly an accurate account of much that occurs in the politics of liberal democracy, it is hard to view it without concern. Liberal democracy as a form of government rests ultimately on the notion of universal laws applying equally to all citizens. It is this general equality before the law that justifies equal political rights for all citizens. But aggressive interest group activity easily becomes a pursuit of special privileges inimical to equality before the law. Manufacturers of certain products lobby for protective tariffs to prevent consumers from buying cheaper foreign products. Organized labour uses collective bargaining legislation to win for itself benefits denied to the rest of the work force. Organized farmers use their political power to influence government to set up marketing boards to raise prices in their favour. As one special interest group succeeds in its objectives, other interests may be stimulated to organize themselves for entry into the lobbying contest. If this process continued over many decades, a society of equal law could transform itself into a society of entrenched privilege, with each interest group jealously defending its special prerogatives.

A related phenomenon is the tendency to politicize issues. Once groups learn that they can use government to their particular advantage, a pervasive tendency develops to look for political rather than economic or social solutions to problems. For example, owners of declining industries, faced with severe competition from foreign producers, may seek protective tariffs and quotas rather than looking for new outlets for their capital. Similarly, the work force of such industries may pressure government to save their jobs by propping up the faltering company or even nationalizing it. What were once economic matters decided in the market-place can become political issues decided by a preponderance of power. If it injects government into all areas of life, such politicization can jeopardize the fundamental liberal concept of the limited state.

The problem of special interests in politics is sometimes seen as a threat to liberal democracies. Legislators at all levels of government have voiced the concern that powerful lobbying by special interests can dominate the process of distributing public goods and services. In a sophisticated argument, Mancur Olson suggests that small but cohesive organizations with a single purpose have a great deal of capacity for influencing public officials. Moreover, the goals of these groups often run counter to the national interest, creating problems such as economic ineffi-ciencies. Privileges granted to these interests may in fact lead to a decline in the well-being of a national economy.[17] It may be, then, that interest group politics is not the innocent and equitable distribution of public benefits that some have thought it to be.

Political thinkers at the dawn of the democratic era were acutely aware of these problems. Rousseau went as far as wishing to outlaw organized groups:

> But when cabals and partial associations are formed at the expense of the great association, the will of each such association, though *general* with regard to its members, is *private* with regard to the State. . . . It is therefore of the utmost importance for obtaining the expression of the general will, that no partial society should be formed in the State, and that every citizen should speak his opinion entirely from himself.[18]

His view was that individuals, taken singly, could exercise their political responsi-bilities in the spirit of what he called the "general will," that is, thinking of the good of the whole community, but that the formation of groups fostered a selfish spirit of particular advantage.

Rousseau's diagnosis was undoubtedly shrewd, but his remedy of banning private associations was extreme and perhaps totalitarian in its implications. James Madison suggested a more moderate approach in *The Federalist*, where he discussed interest groups under the eighteenth-century name of *faction*:

> By a faction, I understand a number of citizens, whether amounting to a majority or minority of the whole, who are united and actuated by some common impulse of passion, or of interest, adverse to the rights of other citizens, or to the permanent aggregate interests of the community.[19]

Madison clearly saw that factions could not be banned without destroying liberty itself. His remedy (which Rousseau had also accepted as a second-best solution) was to promote the existence of a great number and variety of factions, so as to maintain an approximate balance or equilibrium among them. This is a fundamentally defensive strategy that hopes that a drive for special privilege by one group will generate contrary political pressure from other groups who stand to be adversely affected.

The recent proliferation of interest groups in liberal democracies seems to fit Madison's view. However, his defensive strategy will not work unless there is a consensus that legalized privilege is to be combatted and that equality under general laws is the aim of public policy. If these beliefs are lost from the political culture, the dynamic of interest group competition may serve to erect new sanctuaries of privilege rather than tear them down.

23 Political Parties

Political parties are an essential feature of politics in the modern age of mass participation. In democratic governments, they enable society "to translate majority rule into fact."[20] In totalitarian or authoritarian governments, they are used to help the government maintain its hold on power. In either case, political parties are an important link between government and the people.

In historical terms, political parties are a rather recent phenomenon, evolving with the extension of the franchise. In the eighteenth century, the Tories and Whigs dominated the British Parliament as political clubs of the upper class. They had little in the way of strong connections with the general population. But as the Reform Acts of 1832, 1867, and 1884 extended the suffrage to most adult males, these clubs were transformed to accommodate the influx of voters, and the Conservative and Liberal parties were formed. The tendency toward greater mass participation continued with the development of the Labour party in the late nineteenth century as a party of the working class. By the 1930s, it had replaced the Liberals as the principal challenge to the Conservatives, leaving the Liberals a third and minor party in the British system.

Political parties perform so many tasks in the political process that it is difficult to establish a simple definition. However, Joseph LaPalombara's working definition can serve as a point of departure:

> A political party is a formal organization whose self-conscious, primary purpose is to place and maintain in public office persons who will control, alone or in coalition, the machinery of government.[21]

These organizations are not usually part of the formal-legal machinery of government. In most Western nations, they do not derive power from the constitution. Any power they have depends on how the electorate responds in elections. However, there is an increasing tendency in many countries for political parties to be drawn into the formal sphere of government. In Canada, for instance, donations to parties are tax deductible, while party finances are regulated by government and subject to disclosure laws. The very success of parties as informal institutions is pushing them toward formal-legal status.

The first and most important goal of the political party in a democratic system is electoral success. Winning an election legally enables the party to dominate the governmental machinery and enact some of the proposals to which the party is committed. Electoral success short of victory may enable the party to participate in a coalition government and thus achieve at least some of its aims.

A number of other roles complement the primary objective of taking power. A political party provides the vehicle through which a candidate is chosen to run for public office. One may choose to run as an independent, but by far the most candidates for public office are selected by party machinery. A related role is to influence voters during campaigns. A great deal of the work of a party organization goes toward trying to get voters to support a particular candidate.

At the governmental level, the party organizes legislative proposals in the assembly. This work is done for the most part by elected party members supported by administrative officials. Obviously, in a parliamentary body of 282 members, as in Canada, or 650, as in the United Kingdom, there must be some organization. The Cabinet of the governing party determines which legislative proposals are to be considered, drafted, debated, and passed.

The party also provides contact between elected members and the public, so political parties are an intermediate institution between people and their government. Government officials can maintain contact with people through party organizations. While the bulk of party activity occurs at election time, this continuous interchange between people and government can be an important function of the party.

Finally, the political party provides a training ground for political leaders. The party ranks become the primary base from which political leaders are recruited. Party workers in constituency organizations often choose to run for office, and if elected, they may work their way from the back benches to a ministerial post.

The most important function of the democratic political party is the *aggregation of demands*. Interest groups articulate a great many things they would like government to do, but it is never possible to perform all of them, particularly because many of the demands are mutually incompatible. For example, organized consumer groups may demand that import quotas on shoes be abolished, while manufacturers may wish import restrictions to be increased. The political party provides a forum in which these conflicting interests may be at least partially reconciled into a coherent program.

In authoritarian or totalitarian systems, parties also aggregate demands to some extent, although because of the lack of political freedom, this function must take place behind the scenes. Specialists in Soviet politics often suggest that the externally monolithic façade of the Communist party conceals squabbling factions representing interests such as the military or agriculture. More obvious is the totalitarian party's function of promoting support for the regime. The party is used as an instrument of government to enhance popular acceptance of public policy. To this end, the party co-ordinates publicity in the mass media, organizes meetings and demonstrations, and carries out persuasion through its cells in workplaces.

It must be remembered that we are speaking of political parties generally. Not all parties perform all of the above roles, and the roles may be played in different ways. For example, the role of political parties in the Canadian system is changing. They remain the primary vehicle by which most politicians are recruited, and they continue to mobilize the electorate at election time. But their function has changed in the area of policy formation. Most policy proposals come from the governmental executive: the prime minister, his or her personal advisers, other Cabinet members, and the administration. The work of developing policy proposals is not so much the effort of the party as it is of the senior people working for members of Cabinet. Many of these individuals do not belong to a party organization. Thus while local, regional, provincial, and national party organizations meet and make policy recommendations to the party leadership, policy proposals that emerge from the government may not reflect interests at the grass-roots level of the party. For this reason, most analysts now agree that the role of political parties in the legislative process has declined. As will be discussed in Chapters 27 and 28, the executive and bureaucracy are now more influential in managing the legislative process.

Because parties differ considerably from one another, it is necessary to have a scheme of classification. Without pretending to be definitive, the following typology captures some of the main types: the pragmatic, ideological, interest, personal, and movement parties.

THE PRAGMATIC PARTY

One of the more common types in Western societies is the *pragmatic party*, a term derived from the word pragmatism. The dictionary defines pragmatism as a philosophy of action in which "trust is . . . tested by the practical consequences of belief."[22] In other words, a pragmatist is one who is concerned with truth as encompassed not in a doctrine, but in the consequences of how something will work. A pragmatic political party is concerned primarily with programs that the public views as solutions to problems. The pragmatic party gears its campaign promises not to beliefs founded on doctrine, but to programs it believes have the greatest appeal to the public. They are thus open to the criticism of having no principles and "moving with the wind." Their programs are said to reflect nothing more than a cynical desire to achieve power. Such parties have enjoyed a high degree of success in the Anglo-American world. Examples of pragmatic parties are the Progressive Conservative and Liberal parties in Canada and the Democratic and Republican parties in the United States. Twenty years ago, the Conservative and Labour parties of Britain would also have been called pragmatic; but in recent years, the Conservatives have moved much further to the right than they once stood, while the Labour party was largely taken over by its left wing between 1978 and 1983, causing some of the pragmatic elements to form a breakaway Social Democratic party. Joined by a few dissatisfied Conservatives and having formed an electoral alliance with the Liberal party, the Social Democrats appear to be giving the Labour party a race for second place behind the Conservatives. In the 1983 election, they received 26.1 per cent of the popular vote and 23 seats. Labour, on the other hand, received 28.3 per cent of the popular vote and 209 seats.

When pragmatic parties compete with one another, they characteristically make overlapping proposals, even to the extent of borrowing each other's ideas. For example, when Prime Minister Trudeau imposed a three-year program of general wage and price controls in 1975, he was implementing an important part of the Conservatives' platform from the election of 1974, even though he had ridiculed the idea during the campaign. Again, when the Conservatives were in power briefly in 1979 and were attacked by the Liberals over high interest rates, they responded that these stemmed from international factors beyond their control. In 1981, when the Liberals were again in power, they responded to Conservative criticism of high interest rates in exactly the same way.

THE IDEOLOGICAL PARTY

The *ideological party*, in contrast, puts more emphasis on ideological purity than on the immediate attainment of power. The ideology of the party is even more important than winning elections. Such parties are criticized, of course, for their inflexibility. Often they put doctrine before the wishes of the voters, convinced that in time, voters will come around to their way of thinking. The Communist party is a good example of an ideological party, as are socialist parties and even some social-democratic parties. On the right, ultraconservative parties may be as doctrinaire as any on the left. Occasionally, ideological parties become less doctrinaire and more pragmatic in their desire to win elections, as exemplified in the well-publicized debate in the 1960s within the New Democratic party between the Waffle group (which felt the party stance should be more ideological) and a pragmatic wing of the party.

THE INTEREST PARTY

Another type of party is the *interest party*. Here we find people with a common interest converting their group into a full-fledged political party, running candidates and attempting to obtain power. Such a group feels it can best achieve its ends by acting as a party rather than trying to influence existing parties, but its narrow basis of support makes it hard to win control of the state. In Australia the Country party began as a farmers' party. There have also been peasant parties in Eastern Europe and Latin America. In Scandinavia industrialists have formed conservative parties. And in Great Britain the Labour party began as an interest party focussing on the welfare of the working class. Labour is now the largest single group in British society, and if all workers supported the Labour party, it would easily win every election. Workers, however, have never voted as a bloc. Thus the party has had to become more pragmatic to expand its appeal to other segments of society and keep pace with the Conservatives. The NDP is sometimes considered to be the voice of Canadian labour. While it is more closely aligned to trade unions, voting studies show that labour does not support the position of the party wholeheartedly. Even in unions that are formally affiliated with the NDP, only about one-third of the rank and file vote NDP in federal elections.[23] In a sense, the NDP is a cross between an interest party and an ideological party. Generally speaking, an interest party will have trouble becoming a serious contender for power unless it broadens its appeal and clientele, but in so doing it will cease to be an interest party.

There is vigorous debate about the respective merits of pragmatic, ideological, and interest parties. Some believe that pragmatic parties contribute to the stability of the political system. Pragmatic parties cover the waterfront, so to speak, in their response to demands by groups in society. These political parties endeavour to include something for everyone in their platform. They appeal to diverse groups— employers and labour unions, farmers and consumers, conservationists and developers. Its advocates see the pragmatic party as a mechanism for aggregating interests, blunting the lines of cleavage in a pluralistic society, and producing political stability.

Those who advocate the virtues of interest and ideological parties argue differently. They approach the problem from the standpoint of representation. They are quite critical of the pragmatic party, suggesting that by making broad appeals to all groups, the party platform becomes diluted and meaningless, so that nobody is really represented. Interest and ideological parties, on the other hand, offer an opportunity to make platforms very specific by catering to a single interest or a group with a defined ideology. Political parties of this type have an opportunity to offer voters a clear choice, and elected members have a responsibility to a specific clientele. But what is made up in representation could be lost in stability. The advocates of the pragmatic party suggest that interest and ideological parties tend to intensify cleavages in society rather than reconcile them. Moreover, if these parties are not willing to compromise at the legislative level, little is accomplished, and governmental instability and inaction could result.

In actual fact, both pragmatic parties and interest or ideological parties have shown themselves capable of aggregating interests and reconciling conflict. In the Anglo-American model of pragmatic parties, the resolution of conflict takes place *within* the party. Labour, business, and agricultural organizations come to some sort of compromise with the government of the day, which is almost always formed by a single party. In contrast, in democracies where coalition governments of ideological or interest parties are the norm, interest reconciliation takes place *among* parties. Parties do not have to surrender their principles internally, but they have to make compromises to keep a coalition cabinet in power. This illustrates the general principle that the necessary functions of the political process may be accomplished in quite different ways in different systems. Any successful political system must resolve conflicts of interest among different social groups; but this task can be carried out within parties, among parties, or by other institutions in the governmental process. The method may not matter very much as long as the job is done. The advantage of conceptualizing politics as a process is that it makes one sensitive to relationships of this type because one is led to look at the functions of institutions in their relation to other institutions, not just to study their form or structure.

THE PERSONAL PARTY

Another type of party is the *personal party*, which is founded around a single, influential political leader. After World War II, supporters of Charles de Gaulle formed the Gaullist party, which became the strongest political force in France after de Gaulle established the Fifth Republic in 1958. Support for his party, called the Union for the Defence of the Republic (UDR), enabled de Gaulle to be elected president in 1958 and 1965. The Gaullists, under a variety of party names, survived the general's retirement in 1969 and today represent a coalition of moderate conservatives. Juan Peron of Argentina also developed a political party from his personal following. His supporters elected him president in 1946 and 1951. Peron, however, was removed from office after a coup d'état in 1955. The Peronista party, although fragmented, remains a significant political force in Argentina, showing that personal parties need not always die with their founders.

Jomo Kenyatta of Kenya was one of the chief architects of KANU—Kenya African National Union. KANU provided a base of support for Kenyatta, who attempted to use the political party to integrate Kenya's many tribal groups. Will the influence of the personal party transcend the founder and remain a political force, as has been the case in France and Argentina? Kenyatta died in 1978, but like de Gaulle, his party has remained the dominant force in Kenya. In the 1985 elections in Zimbabwe, Robert Mugabe dreamed of establishing his Zimbabwe African National Union–Patriotic Front (ZANU-PF) as the single party under which racial and ethnic groups would be united. While his party received approximately 76 per cent of the vote, the whites heavily supported former Prime Minister Ian Smith, and the Matabele tribe voted for their leader, Joshua Nkomo. This ethnic and racial polarization may make it difficult for Prime Minister Mugabe, even though he has a majority of seats, to make his personal party totally dominant.

THE MOVEMENT PARTY

The *movement party* is a political movement that evolves into a party apparatus. A movement is an organization that aims at profound social change, such as achieving national independence, but does not itself aspire to govern. A movement sometimes becomes a party when the prestige that accompanies successfully achieving its original goals makes it a logical choice to take over the government. The Congress party in India is a good example. The Indian National Congress, organized in 1885, became the instrument by which Indians sought independence from the British colonial system. The party became the focus of nationalist feeling throughout India and mobilized popular pressure against the British. After achieving independence in 1947, it became the dominant political force in the federal Parliament, a position that it has since maintained, except for the brief interlude of 1977–1979 when it was out of power.

Political party systems also influence the manner in which parties carry out their roles. There are basically three types of party systems: one-party, two-party, and multi-party systems.

THE ONE-PARTY SYSTEM

There are two types of one-party systems: the true *single-party* and the *one-party-dominant* systems. Single party means there exists but one party in the political system, and no political alternative is tolerated. The Communist party system is the classic example. The communists, at least the Moscow and Peking varieties, suggest that the existence of more than one party is the antithesis of a classless society. Political opposition and political alternatives are only parts of a capitalist system. Where political leaders are building a utopian order according to an ideological blueprint, political opposition becomes heresy. Under such conditions, any political alternative is prohibited. There are also a great many non-communist single-party systems, found for example in Tanzania and Iraq.

In the one-party-dominant state, a single political party dominates the political process without the official support of the state. While a number of minor parties offer political alternatives, the electorate usually votes overwhelmingly for the dominant party. The Institutionalized Revolutionary Party (PRI) of Mexico is an example. After the Mexican Revolution began in 1910, a fierce struggle occurred during which many leaders, such as Pancho Villa and Emiliano Zapata, fought to gain control of the national government. Plutarco Calles consolidated power in the late 1920s and developed a party organization that in time emerged as the PRI. The party today claims to stand as a symbol of the ongoing revolution. Critics, on the other hand, suggest that the party is more institutionalized than revolutionary. Opposition is not outlawed, but the PRI maintains power by clever use of the state apparatus, especially through patronage and corruption.

Finally, there are situations where one party is dominant politically without either overt or covert use of the state machinery to support its position. For whatever reason, voters seem content with a single party for long periods of time. The Democratic party dominated the American South for a century after the Civil War. In Canada the province of Alberta has had the curious habit of endorsing one party for long periods, then suddenly turning to another. Since 1905, no party in Alberta, having once formed a government and then lost an election, has ever returned to power.

THE TWO-PARTY SYSTEM

A *two-party system* exists when two parties are credible contenders for power and either is capable of winning any election. The United Kingdom and the United States are normally cited as examples, but neither is literally a two-party system.

In Britain the Conservatives and Labour are challenged by the Liberals and now by the Social Democrats, who have broken away from Labour and the Conservatives. In the United States the last thirty years have seen numerous third parties, such as the Progressives, States Rights Democrats, Socialist Workers, Communists, and American Independents. In Britain and the United States, however, it is rare when one of these third parties gains enough popular support to threaten the two major parties. Thus when we speak of a two-party system, we mean that the victory at the polls is likely to go to the Conservatives or Labour, or to the Democrats or Republicans, even though minor parties may also contest the election. When third parties do experience success at the polls, pragmatic parties adjust their policies and programs to try to accommodate the criticism that led to this success.

In Canada the Liberals and Conservatives have dominated the political process since Confederation. Yet the NDP, formed in 1961, has been a consistent challenger, winning between 15 and 20 per cent of the popular vote and on two occasions enough seats to affect the balance of political power. Canada could perhaps be called a *two-party-plus system*, a slightly vague term that implies that while only two parties are likely to be able to form a government, there are one or more other parties that are large enough to affect the balance of power.[24] The Federal Republic of Germany has been in this situation for many years: the Christian Democratic and Social Democratic parties are so evenly matched at the polls that the small Free Democratic party determines who will govern by throwing its parliamentary weight to one side or the other.

The two-party system is widely praised as a source of political stability, especially in a parliamentary system where Cabinets must maintain the confidence of the elected assembly. The two-party system is likely to yield majority governments that can hold office for a respectable length of time. Less certain is the common argument that a two-party system serves the interests of voters by offering them a clear choice between two responsible aspirants to power. Parties in two-party systems are often highly pragmatic, so that for long periods of time their platforms may greatly resemble each other and voters may have little choice among political principles. American and Canadian politics are like this at most elections. On the other hand, the situation may be even worse if a two-party system becomes ideologically polarized, as in contemporary Britain. Society is subjected to bouts of stop-and-go, off-and-on policy as two parties with widely different views alternate in power. The resulting uncertainty can be devastating to economic life. All of this is not to say that the two-party system is necessarily any worse than the multi-party alternative, only that it is not as obviously superior as newspaper editorials in the Anglo-American democracies often maintain.

THE MULTI-PARTY SYSTEM

In the *multi-party system*, there are three or more political parties with a realistic chance of participating in government. In most cases, the parties are either interest parties or ideological parties, which consider the position of their clientele a first priority. Sweden is an example of a multi-party system. From left to right on the political spectrum, the political parties are the Communists, Social Democrats,

Liberals, Agrarians, and Conservatives. While party supporters cannot be identified absolutely, the Communists and Social Democrats are generally backed by workers and intellectuals, the Liberals by professionals and bureaucrats, the Agrarians by farmers, and the Conservatives by businesspeople and professionals.

Cabinet instability is common in the parliamentary system if there are many parties. When representatives are drawn from a number of parties, majority governments are difficult to come by, and coalition governments may become the norm. If the parties in a coalition government hold to principle and refuse to compromise, the government will likely change frequently. This was the case in the Fourth Republic of France in the 1950s, when there were thirteen governments in one period of eighteen months. The same is true of Italy, which has had more than forty governments since World War II. The example in Ontario will be interesting to follow. Will the Liberals and NDP be able to stabilize politics with their 1985 accord, or will they break ranks and go for an election? The situation is not the norm in Canadian politics and may offer a period of interesting and lively multi-party politics.

However, as is usually the case, generalizations do not universally apply. Instability does not occur in all multi-party systems. The multi-party systems of Denmark, Norway, and Sweden, for example, have at certain times experienced durable coalitions that cannot be characterized as unstable. The difference has an interesting and logical explanation. Italy and Portugal have large extremist parties of both left and right persuasions. Some of these parties are fundamentally opposed to the constitution and, hence, are not acceptable coalition partners; this restricts the number of possible coalitions. When a working partnership between parties breaks down, there may be no alternative to re-establishing it, unless perhaps the Cabinet is replaced. The result is a game of political musical chairs in which Cabinets succeed each other with monotonous regularity. In contrast, the Scandinavian countries have not had large extremist parties. All the important parties are acceptable coalition partners, so there is more room to manoeuvre and create durable coalitions.

One additional point should be made. Political parties have developed along with increased public participation in politics, and they have helped legitimize mass democracy. This does not mean that all political parties are mass organizations with every voter holding a membership; on the contrary, in most Western societies, the actual number of party members is very small. In Canada less than 5 per cent of the voting population belong to any federal or provincial party. Moreover, most of those who do are in the middle- and upper-middle-income brackets, are the most educated in society, and generally feel they have a great deal at stake in the political process. For this reason, political parties have been criticized as elitist or oligarchical organizations that represent not the masses, but the social and economic elite in the society. Indeed, if one examines a sociological profile of party activists, the criticism may seem valid. Oligarchies of a kind do run political parties.

Nevertheless, there is another side to the issue. The charge of elitism conveys the idea of a group closed off from the rest of society by restricted membership. This simply is not the case with political parties in most Western democracies. While there may be only a few militants and they may represent the upper echelons of society, the doors of party organizations are not closed. On the contrary, anyone who pays the nominal membership fee is welcomed with open arms, and anyone who hints that he or she will volunteer for party work is quickly inundated with tasks. The ranks of political parties are filled by a few middle-class activists because they are the ones who choose to become involved. A great deal of political apathy exists in our society. Many individuals simply may not have an interest in the mundane tasks that accompany political party membership. In most cases, the individual reward or payoff of party work is relatively small in comparison to the effort involved. Thus one needs either a special liking for such work or a special material interest, such as that of lawyers or public relations experts who may hope to profit from future government patronage if they can help their party into power.

This open membership can be contrasted with the more disciplined and closed political party in communist systems, where a different idea of party membership exists. The society is striving to achieve communism, and the party is the vanguard responsible for attaining this end. Lenin envisioned the Marxist-Leninist party being made up of the faithful and responsible for maintaining revolutionary fervour among the masses. It was never intended to be a mass organization open to all. But in fact, it has now become an organization filled with careerists, individuals who have made the party their vehicle for attaining better jobs and greater government responsibility.

The difference in membership between totalitarian and democratic parties is logical in view of the rather different roles they play in their respective political systems. The democratic party, which is primarily a vehicle for the aggregation of demands, is open to all who are willing to press their claims; but precisely because membership is open, it is not surprising to see the party dominated by those interested in working to achieve their ends through this organization. The totalitarian party, which is more an instrument of social and economic mobility within the government apparatus, must regulate membership to ensure that the aggregation of interests remains subordinate to the larger goal of social transformation.

24　Communications Media

The term *communications media* refers to newspapers, magazines, pamphlets, and books (print media) as well as radio, television, recordings, and films (electronic media). The media are not political institutions in the same way as interest groups or political parties. Both of the latter have an overt political purpose—to influence or control government—while the ostensible purpose of the media is to inform or entertain. However, as means of communication, they have such important ramifications for the political process that we must consider them an integral part of it. They are vital transmission channels for both articulating demands and expressing support.

Most individuals involved in newspapers, radio, and television will deny that their work is political. Their job, so they claim, is reporting facts, political events, and circumstances without political bias. Indeed, their work may not be political in the sense that it reflects a partisan bias (although editorials often do reflect a partisan bias, and even selecting what events are to be reported may reflect a bias). The point we are suggesting is that the media are a political institution, not necessarily by supporting particular parties, but as a link between people and government. The media provide the basis for public discussion of issues. Not only do they report political happenings, but they also provide the means for individuals, groups, and government to state a position that can be aired before the public. Thus in terms of the total political process, the media become an essential vehicle facilitating communication on public issues.

One often takes the political importance of the media for granted. However, it must be remembered that newspapers have existed for only about two centuries, and the electronic media are much more recent. Representative government, having been established before the age of mass media, was originally based on face-to-face contact between a representative and electors, who were few in number. The representative was personally known to almost all who voted. The election was held by a show of hands at a meeting of all electors convened for that purpose. Rival candidates would be present at this meeting to speak before the vote was taken. This method of election persisted well into the nineteenth century, until the democratic expansion of the franchise so increased the numbers of those who participated in politics that it became impossible for representatives and electors to know each other personally. Images conveyed by the mass media have almost entirely replaced this human contact. The consequences for democratic government are complex and cannot be fully discussed here, but it is apparent that representative democracy as we know it could not possibly exist without the mass media.

Political communication through the media takes many forms. On one hand, governments use the media to transmit information to the public. A prime minister or president may call a press conference or choose to address a national audience via radio or television. Press agents of important ministers make news releases available on particular issues, and governments may use the media as a way of informing people of public hearings or notices of petitions for rezoning. Some of this flow of information is purely factual, but much of it contains implicit or explicit pleas for support of government policy.

Members of society also rely on the media to communicate information to governments. Letters to the editor can show support for or opposition to specific policies. Interest groups of various kinds frequently use media advertising as a vehicle for taking their case to the public. Individuals may contribute articles, stories, and interviews, all having a political slant. And the media as an institution are central to the electoral process. Political parties and candidates communicate their platforms and stands on issues through the media.

In each of the roles described above, the media are more or less neutral channels for communicating messages initiated by others, either governments or members of the public. Much more important than either of these roles is the way the media actively create the world of political information, opinion, and symbolism—for example, to some degree in the open partisanship of editorials, where explicit stands are taken. However, people have minds of their own and do not necessarily think as they are advised by media editorials. This was shown by the Canadian general election of 1980, in which most of the large metropolitan daily newspapers, except the *Toronto Star*, supported the Conservatives rather than the Liberals, yet the latter won handily. More important than editorializing is the "objective" task of factual news reporting. Reporters strive for objectivity, but like the rest of us, they work within intellectual and emotional constraints of which they may not be fully aware.

Investigating how the ostensibly factual world of reported news is affected by the views of those who report it and the structure of the media that convey it is an important study in itself. Here we can only give an example. Consider mass public demonstrations that are supposed to be spontaneous manifestations of demand or support. Most of these are actually carefully staged events depending on the co-operation of the mass media. Organizers invite newspaper and television reporters well in advance. A study of American news media reports that in the 1960s, when there were many demonstrations against the Vietnam War, "experienced organizers [even] scheduled demonstrations to fit the schedules of camera crews."[25] The reporters likely come because mass demonstrations provide an interesting subject. Photographs and film footage are taken of the most rousing events: singing, dramatic speeches, shouts of affirmation, violent clashes with the police. Interviews are held with the demonstrators' representatives, who have prepared messages they wish conveyed to the public. When it is all over, newspapers and television present to the public the news of an event in which the mass media themselves were the most important participants. A recent case in point was the reporting of demonstrations in 1984 against the Cruise missile tests at Cold Lake, Alberta. Perhaps because the tests were conducted during the winter, and during the week when it is difficult to organize a crowd, there were more journalists than protesters. Nonetheless, the event was reported as newsworthy. The reality of the news cannot be grasped without understanding how demonstrators and media manipulate each other for their own purposes.

Another way the media shape political reality is through their investigative or watchdog activities. With the help of the opposition, reporters can often uncover inconvenient facts that governments or powerful interest groups would like to suppress. The most famous recent example of this activity is, of course, the Watergate affair, in which American reporters uncovered the misdeeds of officials in President Nixon's administration, leading to his resignation in 1974. This episode elevated the media to new heights of prestige. Yet it must be pointed out that no president had ever enjoyed worse relations with the mass media for most of his political career than Richard Nixon. How much was the enthusiasm to uncover the secrets of his administration based on personal dislike rather than an impartial desire to inform the public? It is clear that reporters knew, or should have known, of some rather serious violations of law or propriety in the administrations of earlier presidents, yet they chose to suppress them or at least not report them with great vigour.[26] The power of the press to vilify an elected official deserved more serious analysis than it generally received in the wave of self-congratulation after Watergate.

From examining the functions of the media, let us pass to some structural questions. One obvious comment is that most of the media, while well adapted to continuously reporting a flow of news, do not involve themselves in a thorough discussion of issues and background. In many countries, therefore, one or two newspapers have emerged as particularly important in politics because they provide good coverage and analysis. In Britain almost everyone involved in government or seriously observing it reads the London *Times* and/or the *Guardian*. Letters to the editor of the *Times* are often carefully thought-out statements by important people meant to be read by other important people. The paper in general serves as a handy means of communication among the political elite of the country. In France *Le Monde* and *Le Figaro* are read in the same way. In the United States the *New York Times* and the *Washington Post* have this position in national politics, although many other papers are of regional importance. But Canada does not really have the equivalent, except for *Le Devoir* in the province of Quebec. In English Canada no single paper is read by virtually everyone seriously interested in government, although the Toronto *Globe and Mail*, by using satellite technology, seems to be emerging as our national newspaper. It is the only newspaper in Canada that can be purchased in every province and territory. The absence until now of a truly national newspaper may have contributed to the fragmentation of Canadian political culture. Politicians and leaders in other walks of life in different parts of the country often lack a common frame of reference and fund of information that might be supplied in part if they were reading the same newspaper.

Another important structural question is ownership. The print media – newspapers, magazines, publishing houses – took shape in the eighteenth and nineteenth centuries, when the socialist idea of state ownership had not become influential. Today, although these media receive government subsidies in some countries, in the Western world they are still almost entirely in private hands· and are run as profit-making businesses. Governments do not license or otherwise regulate them, except for enforcing laws against libel, pornography, false advertising, and the like. Underlying this arrangement is the classical liberal philosophy of serving the public good through the competition of private actors following their own interests.

The recent trend toward concentration of ownership poses difficult problems for the classical liberal model. Newspapers, magazines, and publishing houses are now often owned in chains by large corporations. In Canada most English-language metropolitan daily newspapers are owned by either the Southam or the Thomson chains. When the number of owners is drastically reduced, and when the owners are mostly large corporations, does a free market of ideas in the mass media still exist? The situation was dramatized in 1980 when Southam and Thomson simultaneously shut down competing newspapers in Winnipeg and Ottawa, leaving each city with only one paper. The effect was as if a market-sharing agreement had been signed to give one city to Thomson and the other to Southam. As a result, the federal government appointed a royal commission on newspapers, chaired by journalism professor Tom Kent. When the commission reported on July 1, 1981, it maintained that the concentration of newspaper ownership in Canada could limit the free flow of ideas. Its recommendations included establishing a Canada Newspaper Act, under which ownership restrictions would be spelled out and existing concentrations could be broken up. The "Catch 22" of this solution is that the free press is to be guaranteed by a government that, under new powers, might itself inhibit the operation of a free press. To date, while bills have been introduced, no government has acted on the recommendations, and legislation seems unlikely to be forthcoming.

The major argument against government involvement in the newspaper business is that concentration of newspaper ownership, at least at its present level, does not threaten the free market of ideas. There are still several important independent newspapers, although the largest of these, the *Toronto Star*, announced a partial merger with Southam in the summer of 1985. Also, even if a city has only one local daily, its inhabitants can still receive news from a multitude of other sources: papers from other cities, weekly magazines, radio, and television. The question is exactly analogous to the debate over government regulation of oligopolies, which was touched on in the discussion of liberalism.

The electronic media, born as they were in the twentieth century when public ownership is a powerful idea, have been involved with government almost from the start. In many European countries, such as England, France, and Germany, radio and television are dominated by public corporations. Private enterprise is permitted in some cases but is restricted to a secondary role. In the United States private ownership is the rule, but unlike the print media, it is subject to government licensure. Canada combines both models. There are publicly owned English and French networks of radio and television stations (such as the CBC and Radio-Canada), but they do not dominate the market, which consists mostly of privately owned, governmentally licensed stations. Advocates of public ownership argue that a network supported by taxes rather than advertising revenue allows it to examine news and public affairs in greater depth—an argument that surely has some merit. On the other hand, if a government-owned network dominates the market, there is a powerful temptation to manipulate news coverage, although satellite television is making this more difficult today. Perhaps there is something to be said for the Canadian arrangement that provides the benefits of a subsidized, non-profit system without giving it so much power as to endanger the free market of ideas.

Outside the liberal democracies, almost all mass media, whether print or electronic, are owned and/or controlled by the state. In totalitarian systems, the mass media are quite frankly an instrument used by the state to transform society. Communication with the masses is considered too important to be left to independent organizations in society and thus must be totally controlled. In the Soviet Union, for example, *Pravda (Truth)* is the official organ of the Communist party, and *Izvestia (News)* is the official organ of the state. Like all other newspapers and magazines, they are owned by the state and are subject to pre-publication censorship.

Authoritarian states also supervise the mass media, but not quite to the same extent; their chief concern is usually to ensure that the government is not criticized in public. Criticism may result in imprisonment or exile of writers or closure of newspapers, journals, and radio and TV stations. Independent units of the media may exist and operate as long as their political reporting is neutral or complimentary to the government. In both totalitarian and authoritarian systems, the media are considered more a means of generating support for the regime than articulating demands by the public. As the late Forbes Burnham, former prime minister of Guyana, said in 1975, the media must become "an agency for pushing the development of the nation in the context of Government policy."[27]

There is at present an important clash taking place between the liberal-democratic and totalitarian-authoritarian perspectives on the mass media, under the slogan of a "new world order of information." The initiative has come from governments of Third World countries who are unhappy about the way they and their countries are portrayed in the Western news media. They complain particularly about the international news agencies (Associated Press, United Press, Agence France-Presse, and Reuters), which are controlled by consortia of private media owners in the Western world. They claim that Western coverage, which in effect means international coverage, is usually biased against the socialist or statist policies of Third World governments. At a series of international conferences on this subject, proposals have been put forward to constrain the Western media in various ways, from licensing of journalists to subsidies by Western governments to allow the Third World to set up its own news agency. Developing nations have had the enthusiastic support of the Soviet Union and its allies at these conferences but have met strong resistance from representatives of Western governments and media organizations.

We believe it is vital to liberal democracy to maintain the principle of private ownership of the media and independence from government control. There is much truth in the old adage, "Freedom of the press belongs to him who owns one." The system of private ownership allows discontented groups, who do not find their views represented in existing media outlets, to found their own. Government ownership of some outlets, as in Canada and other liberal democracies, does not jeopardize this freedom as long as the overall context is not one of public control. But we do not see how the inherently controversial business of news and information can be reduced to the level of a government utility, like water or sewerage, without stifling free expression of opinion. To this date, the only free communications media the world has known have operated in systems where government refrained from complete ownership and control.

25   Elections and Electoral Systems

Electing public officials is central to liberal democracy. As a technical device, it provides a way of changing rulers without resorting to bloodshed—no small accomplishment in itself, although hereditary selection has also achieved the same thing. More profoundly, competitive political elections are the basis of democratic legitimacy. The opportunity to participate in choosing rulers confers on the participants an obligation to obey the laws made by those who are chosen because they act as agents of the public. Citizens are presumed to consent to laws to the extent that they have participated in choosing the lawmakers. Disagreeing with the substance of decisions made does not normally provide sufficient reason for disobedience because periodic elections mean there will soon be an opportunity to vote for someone else who may be willing to alter the disliked rule or policy. Replacing traditional with legal authority means the collapse of traditional theories of obligation based on the will of God or inherited position; democratic elections provide an alternative theory of obligation compatible with the legal conception of authority.

Within the context of the political process, elections are best interpreted as a form of voter reaction. Because elected governors must answer to the public in a future election, the assumption is that they will rule responsively. In other words, elected officials would like to be re-elected and, therefore, will enact laws and policies that meet current desires. As the philosopher John Plamenatz put it, "Elections are important not only for what happens at them but for what happens because of them."[28]

In a simpler world, public officials might be elected with a mandate to do certain things and thus implement popular desires in a direct and unambiguous way. In that case, elections could be considered a mechanism for articulating demands. However, as was pointed out earlier, elections are actually more of a post mortem investigation of the record of those in office, whose actual performance may have had little to do with promises made when they were last elected. If voters like what has happened, they can vote for a continuation; if not, they can vote for a change, without being fully sure what the alternative will be. Elections are thus an ingenious mechanism for coping with an uncertain and ever-changing future. Elected rulers are allowed periods of creativity in which they seek to cope with the unexpected problems that are always presenting themselves, after which the voters decide whether they will be allowed to continue their efforts. Dealing with dilemmas gradually as they appear is a more supple procedure than trying to work out far in advance the answers to problems that may never arise in their expected form. The greatest strength of liberal democracy may well be the sophistication of its institutions linking the rulers and the ruled, among which elections are paramount.

For elections to provide this link, at least three conditions must be present. First, elections must be periodic. Usually their frequency is specified in a constitution and ranges from two years (the House of Representatives in the United States) to seven years (the president of France). The point is that elections must be institutionalized. They must not be called at the whim of a head of government or cancelled so that an individual can rule for life. Elections must be regular and reasonably frequent if they are to be effective in a democratic system. As voters evaluate political outputs, they may change their choice of governors. If that opportunity is taken away, the democratic system will lose its grounds for legitimacy, as will any process that is deprived of the opportunity for effective response.

Second, there must be opportunity to run for office; this gives voters a choice. If restrictions are placed on who can run for office, then elections are not playing a democratic role in the political process. There has been a great deal of discussion about whether elections in one-party systems might be considered democratic. If within the party there is a rigid process for selecting candidates and this process is controlled by a small party elite, there is little competition for public office and little choice for voters. On the other hand, there are those who argue that the one-party system can be democratic if there is competition among factions within the party. If the party nomination process is relatively open, there may be a choice of candidates. But the choice in this case is made by party members, not all voters, so this process is democratic only in a very restricted sense.

A third factor required in elections is a high degree of political freedom. If freedom of speech or the press is limited, the primary function of the campaign is altered, and voters do not have an opportunity to make decisions on the basis of full information. Restricting political freedom inhibits the role of the electoral process.

Even after elections were established as a way of selecting rulers, various devices have sometimes limited mass participation. The property franchise, for example, required an individual to own a specified amount of assets before being allowed to vote. Poll taxes paid as a prerequisite for voting also limited the participation of the poor. Age and extensive residency requirements have been manipulated to influence voter turnout, and literacy requirements are still used in many developing nations to restrict full participation in elections. This is especially true where educational opportunities are limited. Another obvious device was sexual discrimination, which, until the turn of this century, barred half the population from voting lists. As discussed earlier, the long-term trend of liberal democracy has been to erase or minimize these restrictions.

In totalitarian and authoritarian governments, elections have little or nothing to do with the give and take between rulers and the ruled, but rather are means of mobilizing support for the regime. Voters ratify lists of selected candidates, often under threat of penalty for not participating in the election. Token opposition is sometimes permitted by authoritarian regimes, when they have a firm grip on the situation, as a way of enhancing the external legitimacy of the electoral result. Incidentally, this function of mobilizing support for the government also attaches legitimacy to elections in liberal democracies. National elections are quasi-sacred occasions in which the participants reaffirm their commitment to constitutional procedures. This comparison of liberal-democratic to authoritarian or totalitarian elections again shows how seemingly similar institutions actually perform quite different functions in different systems.

An election is a complex procedure, and not all countries use the same methods to conduct them. A bewildering variety of electoral systems has been tried at one time or another. We describe some of the more common kinds below and point out a few of the consequences of the different types on the democratic process.

THE FIRST-PAST-THE-POST SYSTEM

The *first-past-the-post system* is familiar from its use in Britain, Canada, and the United States. In its simplest form, one candidate is to be elected in each constituency, and each elector has one vote to cast. The winning candidate is the one who receives a plurality of valid ballots. If there are only two candidates, the winner automatically gets a majority; but if there are several candidates who split the vote fairly evenly, the winner's plurality may be far from a majority.

The first-past-the-post electoral method is a natural partner to the two-party system because it does not distort electoral results when there are only two candidates. A plurality is also a majority, and the democratic criterion of majority rule is unambiguously satisfied. For this reason, many writers on politics enthusiastically endorse the first-past-the-post method. However, when social cleavages are such that a two-party system cannot be maintained, adhering to the first-past-the-post method of election can have disturbing consequences.

For one thing, it allows candidates to be elected without a majority. This was an important factor in Chile, when President Allende, having won the presidency in 1970 with only about 36 per cent of the vote, embarked on a radical course of action that met important opposition, finally culminating in a coup d'état. His position would surely have been stronger (though not necessarily impregnable) if he had had a majority behind him.

It also penalizes small parties. A party may win 20 per cent of the popular vote but hardly any seats. The one exception to this is small parties that are regionally concentrated, as the Social Credit was in Quebec or the NDP is in Saskatchewan. But voters in general quickly learn not to waste votes on small parties that have little chance of electing candidates. Thus the system discourages the formation of new parties. Furthermore, it magnifies the result of relatively small shifts in the popular vote. An increase in a party's popular vote from 50 to 60 per cent of the total will produce a landslide in parliamentary seats. For example, between 1980 and 1984, the federal P.C. popular vote went from 37.4 to 49.96 per cent, while seats increased from 103 to 211. This sort of result may occur with the first-past-the-post method even in a two-party system, but it is particularly drastic in multi-party situations, when fragmentation of the opposition can give the governing party an artificially and enormously inflated strength in the elected assembly.

Particularly in ethnically segmented societies, these technical consequences of the first-past-the-post method can lead to the permanent underrepresentation of minorities. During the years of the Stormont Parliament, the Catholics of Northern Ireland were about one-third of the population, but they never came close to winning one-third of the seats in the Assembly. Electoral districts were *gerry-mandered*,[29] so that Catholics almost everywhere found themselves a minority outvoted by a Protestant majority. Such long-continued underrepresentation can destroy the legitimacy of government in the mind of the aggrieved minority.

The Run-Off System. Two variations of the first-past-the-post system have been devised to ameliorate its drawbacks. One is the *run-off system*, which resembles the first-past-the-post, except that the winner must obtain a majority of votes cast. If a multiplicity of candidates prevents a majority, additional rounds of balloting are held. Trailing candidates are successively dropped until someone obtains a majority. This system is used to elect party leaders at conventions in Canada and the United States. The candidate with the lowest total is dropped after each ballot, and voting continues until someone obtains a majority. This device ensures that the ultimate winner has a majority of the votes cast on the final ballot and helps preserve party unity. To have a party leader chosen by less than a majority would likely prove divisive before too long.

In the French Fifth Republic, a somewhat similar system for parliamentary and presidential elections has been adopted. There are, however, only two ballots. Trailing candidates are not automatically dropped, but during the interval between ballots, parties are allowed to form coalitions in the constituencies. When a coalition is formed, one or more candidates withdraws in favour of the other(s). Because it is possible for more than two names to be on the final ballot, the system is not technically a run-off; but in practice it functions like one by strongly rewarding those who make coalitions and penalizing those who do not.

The system was introduced into France by General de Gaulle in 1959 to encourage the numerous small parties to form coalitions in order to win majorities. De Gaulle envisioned it as a step toward a two-party system. After being used for more than twenty years, we can say that it has had an influence in that direction but has not been able by itself to do the job. Coalitions have been formed and broken repeatedly because of personal rivalry or difference of ideology. The presidential and parliamentary elections of 1981 resulted in spectacular victories for the Socialist party of President Mitterand, aided to a degree by the communists. Although co-operation among parties continues, there is no sign of the mergers that could create a two-party system. It seems that technical changes in the electoral system are not in themselves powerful enough to overcome the social cleavages that produce a multi-party system.

The Preferential or Alternative Ballot. Another variation is the *preferential* or *alternative ballot*, which attempts to capture information not only about voters' first choices but also about their second, third, and further choices. Electors are given a form on which they rank candidates according to their order of preference. If only two candidates are running, this system operates just like a run-off or first-past-the-post. But three or more candidates change the picture radically. Voters' first preferences are tabulated on the first count. If no one has a majority, the lowest candidate is dropped and a second count is taken. The candidate's votes are distributed to the other candidates according to the second preferences expressed on the ballots. The process continues until a majority is reached. The objective of the preferential ballot is similar to that of a run-off: to ensure that the victor has majority support. The difference is that the preferential ballot collects the necessary information in advance and thus dispenses with further rounds of balloting. In a sense, it is a condensed run-off system.

The major example of the preferential ballot at the present time is in Australian parliamentary elections. However, it was widely used in the past in provincial elections in Western Canada; Alberta, British Columbia, and Manitoba experimented with it at various times. It was sometimes introduced to try to reduce the influence of extremist parties. The reasoning runs as follows: most people are moderate in opinion, and their views tend to cluster toward the middle of the political spectrum. Radical parties may have a following, but they are unlikely to obtain a majority when second and third preferences are added in. The argument is plausible, but in practice, the results of the preferential ballot have sometimes been unpredictable. For instance, it was introduced into British Columbia in 1952 by the Liberals in order to hurt the CCF, whose fortunes were then on the rise. To everyone's surprise, the next election was won by the new Social Credit party, which no one had thought to be a serious contender for power. Perhaps the lesson is that electoral methods, like all political institutions, should be based on general principles, not opportunistic attempts to help or harm a specific party.

PROPORTIONAL REPRESENTATION

Proportional representation is the second great type of electoral system. It is designed to provide representation for a broad spectrum of interests in a constituency. Proportional representation is accompanied by multi-member constituencies. The vote of a constituency becomes a reflection of not a single majority, but a number of minorities (depending on the number of representatives selected). Representation is proportional to the vote of major interests in a constituency.

John Stuart Mill was the first important political thinker to popularize proportional representation (he favoured the quota system, which is discussed later). He thought that the first-past-the-post system, which was then and still is used in most of the Anglo-American democracies, gave too much power to the triumphant majority, which might then abuse the rights of minorities. He preferred proportional representation precisely because it would assure the representation of various minorities. He wrote in *Considerations on Representative Government*:

Because the majority ought to prevail over the minority, must the majority have all the votes, the minority none? Is it necessary that the minority should not even be heard? In a really equal democracy, every or any section would be represented, not disproportionately, but proportionately.[30]

There are two forms of proportional representation—the list system and the quota system (sometimes called the Hare system after its inventor, Thomas Hare). Both have the same aim: to ensure that representatives are elected in numbers proportional to the share of votes that their parties receive in the balloting. Both always make use of multi-member constituencies. Israel, for example, is one giant constituency with 120 representatives. Or a country may be divided into small constituencies, each electing, for example, ten or twelve candidates.

The List System. The *list system* is the easier of the two to grasp. The elector votes not for individuals, but for parties. Each party has a list of as many candidates as there are positions to be filled. If a party gets x per cent of the popular vote, then the top x per cent of its list is declared elected. This system gives great power to the party leaders, who determine the candidates' positions on the list. Being high on the list of a major party is tantamount to election; being low on the list of any party is tantamount to defeat. Barriers are usually inserted against tiny parties, such as the requirement of a minimum of 5 or 10 per cent of the popular vote in order to get any seats at all.

The list system is used in one form or another in almost all of Western Europe, except Ireland, Britain, and France. It is sometimes combined with other systems, as in West Germany, where some representatives are chosen by proportional representation and others by a first-past-the-post method.

The Quota System. In the *quota system*, candidates are listed individually on the ballots, and electors vote for them as individuals rather than just indicating a party list. The method of voting is preferential—the elector ranks the candidates from first to last, according to the number of positions to be filled. A formula establishes the quota of votes required to win, and the victors' surplus votes are transferred according to lower preferences. The following formula is widely used:

$$\frac{\text{Total number of valid ballots}}{\text{Number of seats} + 1} + 1 = \text{Quota}$$

In a constituency with four seats and 100,000 valid ballots cast, the quota would be:

$$\frac{100,000}{4 + 1} + 1 = 20,001$$

Any candidate receiving 20,001 or more first preferences would be elected immediately. The remaining positions would be filled by counting procedures that take account of second and lower choices. These procedures are complex and vary in different systems. Suffice it to say that they produce a more or less proportional result without endowing the party leadership with the extraordinary power given it by the list system. The quota system is presently used in the Republic of Ireland. One may speculate that if proportional representation was ever brought to North America, it would be the quota rather than the list system because the latter is incompatible with our tradition of decentralized political parties.

Many debates have been held about proportional representation since Mill stated his case. The main arguments may be listed as follows:

Pro
1. Every vote counts; there are no wasted votes, which there inevitably are in the winner-take-all system.
2. It is a more democratic system, for it ensures minority representation in the precise ratio of minority votes.
3. It is mathematically accurate.
4. Every politically active group of any size, with very few exceptions, has some representation in the legislature.
5. It provides greater freedom of choice for voters and thereby raises their interest in the body politic.
6. It tempers the domination of political machines.
7. It eliminates the evils of gerrymander because there are no districts to be gerrymandered.

Con
1. It creates splinter parties; it balkanizes the party structure.
2. It encourages bloc voting and extremism.
3. It is divisive; it renders compromise extremely difficult, if it does not eliminate it entirely.
4. Majority government—government by a single political party with a majority of seats in the legislature—is usually impossible to attain; hence, PR militates against government stability.
5. It actually centralizes control by political parties by strengthening party machines.
6. It is mathematically confusing to the voter.
7. It weakens the intimate contact with the constituency that is possible under single-member district systems.[31]

Proportional representation in both forms tends to favour the existence of small parties, at least those able to exceed the minimum number of votes required to have any seats at all. It is not necessary to come anywhere close to a majority to attract voters, as in a first-past-the-post situation. A party only has to be able to retain the support of its loyalists. Thus PR tends to encourage relatively small or medium-sized interest or ideological parties—for example, a Catholic party, a farmer's party, a worker's party, an employer's party. Such allegiances can be stable over long periods of time, and this can create a distribution of representatives in the assembly that changes very little from election to election. This is the contemporary situation in most European states.

When this occurs, and when no single party commands a majority, the result must be prolonged coalition government. This in itself is not a bad thing, though it is alien to the British tradition. It can work well, as it has in most Scandinavian countries; but in cases such as Italy, where the presence of large extremist parties severely limits the choice of coalition partners, the Cabinet may be unstable.

Proportional representation has often been attacked for encouraging the proliferation of parties, thus balkanizing politics and making majority government impossible. The criticism is not without force. But it is often true that social cleavages exist that will produce a multi-party system regardless of the electoral method. In these circumstances, proportional representation is a way of keeping civil peace by allowing all significant minorities to feel represented. A first-past-the-post system might extinguish the smaller parties and leave certain minorities permanently underrepresented.

One school of thought holds that proportional representation in some form or other would be a beneficial innovation in Canada.[32] The NDP has officially taken this position, and when Pierre Trudeau was prime minister he toyed with the idea, though he did not make a strong commitment. The source of concern has been the regional polarization of the country after decades of Liberal party dominance: the Conservatives have won very few parliamentary seats in Quebec and the Liberals very few in the four Western provinces. Usually each party has gained a significant minority of the vote in the region, but the first-past-the-post electoral system has prevented those votes from being turned into seats.

The data in Table 25.1 show that between 1962 and 1980, the Conservatives never came close to proportionality between seats and popular vote in Quebec. The Liberals did so only once in the West, in 1968, when an unusual surge of popularity for Trudeau put the Liberals in a position where the first-past-the-post system did not work against them. Although not shown in the table, the New Democratic party faced similar problems in much of the country. Usually the NDP won 15 per cent or more of the popular vote, but rarely did it have more than 10 per cent of the seats in the House of Commons.

The federal election in 1984 changed the picture considerably. The Progressive Conservatives received their highest popular vote since 1958 (when they won 53 per cent), and for the first time since 1891 they won more than 50 per cent of the vote in Quebec, where they took 58 of the 75 seats (see Table 25.2).

TABLE 25.1

Seats and Popular Vote

Year	Percentage Conservative Votes in Quebec	Percentage Conservative Seats in Quebec	Percentage Liberal Votes in West	Percentage Liberal Seats in West
1980	12.4	1.3	23.4	2.6
1979	13.3	2.7	22.6	3.9
1974	20.1	4.0	29.2	19.4
1972	17.5	2.7	27.6	8.6
1968	21.1	5.4	41.7	39.6
1965	21.3	10.7	27.0	11.4
1963	19.6	10.7	28.4	14.3
1962	29.8	18.7	25.3	8.6

TABLE 25.2

Election Results 1980 and 1984 (Seats and Popular Vote)

	Liberals	Progressive Conservatives	NDP
1980	147 (44%)	103 (32.4%)	32 (19.8%)
1984	40 (28%)	211 (49.96%)	30 (19%)

The results seemingly destroyed the argument that under the existing electoral system, the Conservatives could not penetrate Quebec. There voter switching was translated into seats. But the overall results point up the predictable effect of the single-member constituency and first-past-the-post system. Significant discrepancies exist between popular vote and seats. The Liberals received 28 per cent of the popular vote, but only 14.2 per cent of the seats; the P.C.s, 49.96 per cent of the popular vote and 74.8 per cent of the seats; and the NDP, 19 per cent of the popular vote and 10.6 per cent of the seats.

The election of 1984 has at least temporarily undercut the movement for proportional representation in Canada. Yet the arguments are still interesting to consider. Advocates of proportional representation argue that it would ensure that more of the elected Conservatives would be from Quebec and more of the Liberals from the West, and this would presumably foster a healthier, less polarized political climate in Canada. The argument is plausible, although the study of systems behaviour shows that a change in one element in an ongoing system often does not have the predicted consequences. Other elements quickly react to altered conditions, creating a new equilibrium that is virtually impossible to predict. Concretely, a change in electoral laws would set off a whole series of other changes: new strategies by parties, new voter perceptions and behaviour, and so forth. This is not to argue against change as such, merely to point out that it is almost always wrong to see in one factor the sole cause of the existing condition of a system and to believe that manipulating that factor will readily produce a desired result. If systems analysis has shown anything, it is that political systems are far more complex than that.[33]

26   Representative Assemblies

According to liberal democratic theory, the representative assembly should be the central institution for converting political inputs into outputs. Through the mechanism of elections, the sovereign people have delegated to the assembly their power to rule—that is, to make decisions about public business. In the political system, these decisions constitute conversion. Conversion, which takes place in the elected assembly, meets the standard of democratic legitimacy because it is performed by representatives of the people.

This ideal picture, which attributes central importance to the assembly, must be severely qualified in reality because a great deal of decision making also occurs in the executive and judicial branches of government; this decision making is often beyond the effective control or supervision of the assembly. However, we will discuss the assembly first because of its special importance in the theory of liberal democracy.

The most prominent function of the democratic assembly is to legislate, so much so that representative assemblies are commonly referred to as *legislatures*. This terminology is misleading, however, for two reasons: modern assemblies do much more varied work than just legislate, and at least in parliamentary systems, they have lost effective control of the content of legislation; this control has passed into the hands of the executive. In the parliamentary system, as described in Chapter 19, the assembly's role is now mostly to discuss and publicize measures drafted by the executive; party discipline ensures that the outcome of voting is seldom in doubt. In presidential systems that are genuine liberal democracies and not just façades for authoritarian rule, the assembly retains greater control of legislation, though even there it generally reacts to executive initiatives.

Second, the assembly ensures that the business of government is carried out by the executive branch: that laws are enforced, taxes collected, roads paved, and so forth. The assembly cannot itself perform such tasks, but it can cause them to be performed, investigate the performance, and debate the results. Responsible government is the chief mechanism in the parliamentary system by which the assembly retains some control over the business of government. The highest executive officers of the state must be members of the assembly, must be answerable to their colleagues in the assembly for the conduct of business, and must retain the confidence of a working majority. Members of the assembly may ask questions of the executive, request disclosure of documents, or even conduct special investigations into governmental business. Assemblies in presidential systems do not have such intimate ties with the executive, but they possess other powers of control, such as the ability to alter budgets. In various ways, all democratic assemblies seek to influence the administration of public business.

Other functions of the assembly can be more briefly described. One is local representation. Different interests or regions of the community are represented in the legislative assembly by constituency representatives. As representatives, they provide a vital link between people and government by speaking for the interests of their constituents. Another function is to provide opposition. Members of the assembly who are not on the government's side of the House criticize policies and programs so that the government cannot sweep issues or incidents under the rug. At the extreme, the organized opposition within the assembly is even ready to offer an alternative government. Thus changes in power can take place without an interregnum of confusion.

Assemblies play two additional roles, one educational and one involving socialization. The work of an assembly must be educational—debates and discussions must draw the public's attention to certain issues. And the fact that assemblies do attempt to wrestle with public problems means that the institution can become an agent for socialization. The workings of the institution can be the grounds on which individuals form opinions, attitudes, and beliefs about the nature of the governmental process.

As the scope of state activity has expanded in this century, it has placed greater limitations on what the assembly can accomplish by itself. During the period of classical liberalism, when government was relatively small, the assembly could debate most legislation at length and monitor all the administrative activities of the state. But the welfare state has grown so large that this is impossible today. Hence there has been a trend in all countries toward greater responsibility of the executive at the expense of the assembly.

This tendency is particularly noticeable in parliamentary systems. Through party discipline, the modern Cabinet exercises a high degree of control over the majority caucus and thus over the assembly as a whole. Under these conditions, individual members of the assembly have little effective control over legislation and particularly over governmental revenues and expenditures. The assembly still links the executive to the electorate, but it has lost much of its power to initiate legislation. This is less true in presidential systems, where the assembly is not so subject to party discipline; but even in the United States, which probably has the most independent assembly of all important democracies, political observers have repeatedly commented on how the president's power has grown at the expense of the power of the Congress.

The decline of assemblies, an idea popular among political scientists, has perhaps not been fully grasped by public opinion. Many naive views still exist about how assemblies work. People often visualize the elected assembly as the focal point at which all issues are raised, debated, and voted upon. Visitors to Ottawa or the provincial capitals frequently express disillusionment when they see a single speaker talking to an almost empty House. The fact is that much of the work of the assembly is done elsewhere: in the parliamentary system by Cabinet, bureaucracy, caucus, and parliamentary committees; in the presidential system by Cabinet, bureaucracy, and congressional committees. Full debates from which significant decisions follow are rare. In most cases, full debates come after most of the wrinkles have been ironed out of legislative proposals and compromises have been struck. In effect, the assembly is putting its stamp of approval on a bill that has already been subjected to a great deal of discussion and scrutiny.

It would be impossible for the entire assembly to handle all the intricate details required to work out a compromise between conflicting interests. This is why the executive is responsible for preparing most of the assembly's business and carrying out the administrative details of bills the assembly passes. But again, the executive must have the support of a majority of members of the assembly before establishing laws or policies. To that extent, the assembly retains real power in the conversion part of the political process.

The long-term decline of the assembly relative to the executive arm of government has an interesting structural correlate in the decline of bicameralism. Many assemblies today are at least nominally bicameral, as shown by the following list:

Country	Lower House	Upper House
United Kingdom	House of Commons	House of Lords
Canada	House of Commons	Senate
United States	House of Representatives	Senate
Japan	House of Representatives	House of Councillors
Federal Republic of Germany	Bundestag	Bundesrat

The basic argument for bicameralism, as discussed in Chapter 16, is the liberal idea of fragmenting power. One house is supposed to supply a check upon the ambitions of the other.

Unicameral assemblies are less common—they exist, for example, in Denmark, Finland, New Zealand, Tanzania, and all the Canadian provinces. These institutions are more apt to be used in homogeneous societies or in societies where a deliberate attempt is made to avoid fragmenting a government when the society is already divided along cultural, regional, or racial lines. It is also argued that a single assembly is a more efficient way of representing the popular will.

The most common tendency has been for upper houses to atrophy rather than be abolished outright. They do not fit well with either the logic of majoritarian democracy or the machinery of responsible government. The experience of the Canadian Parliament is typical of that of many countries. Generally speaking, the only upper houses that have been able to retain their vitality are in presidential systems, such as the United States, or in federal parliamentary systems, such as the Federal Republic of Germany. In the former instance, senators are elected by the voters of the states; in the latter, they are appointed by the *Land* governments. In both instances, they represent important and durable interests of particular regions of the country. This principle, which in the end comes down to protecting the minority rights of different regions, has been able to maintain itself against the democratic legitimacy of majority rule. In contrast, other ways of choosing a second chamber, such as heredity (House of Lords) or appointment as a reward for service (House of Lords, Canadian Senate) provide these bodies with little force in a direct conflict with democratically elected lower chambers. However, the expertise of an appointed body can make it a legitimate source of technical amendments to legislation.

REPRESENTATION

Discussing representative assemblies makes it necessary to re-examine the basic concept of representation.[34] The word *representation* has three different meanings, all of which are relevant to political science:

1. A representative may be a symbol—that is, a sign by which something else is known. A flag or national anthem may be said to represent a country.

2. A representative may be an agent who is empowered to act for a principal, as a lawyer represents a client in the courtroom. In a similar sense, city councillors, MLAS, and MPS are representatives because they are agents who act on behalf of their electors, who are the principals.

3. One is sometimes said to represent a group if he or she shares some of its typical characteristics. At the collective level, a subset of items is said to be a representative sample if it accurately reflects selected characteristics of the universe from which it is drawn. For example, one might say that the House of Commons is not truly representative of the Canadian people because only a handful of its members are women, whereas more than half of the adult population is female.

We will not be further concerned here with representation in the symbolic or sociological sense. Our concern is with the latter two meanings because either may affect the way one views the role of representatives. Representation is almost a universal fact of politics. Any system except the smallest and simplest direct democracy requires that some people act for others. And questions inevitably arise about whether the agents reflect the salient characteristics of their principals.

Theories of representation are as varied as theories of legitimacy. Authoritarian and totalitarian governments of all sorts generally claim to represent their people in some way that does not need to be tested by competitive elections. Communist governments claim to represent the forward motion of history, and so on. We will confine ourselves here to discussing kinds of representation relevant to a free society in which citizens actually choose those who rule in an indirect democracy. Representation in a free society is an attempt to express the "will of the people" if we understand by that phrase not the whim of any fleeting majority, but the enduring desire of the people to be well and justly governed. Even in this limited situation, one can distinguish several types of representation.

There are four different ways in which agents may represent those who elect them to a representative assembly. Three concern the individual representative; the fourth concerns representatives as a collective body. To put it another way, representatives may play any one of four different roles.

Trustees. The role of *trustee* demands that representatives rely on their personal judgment of what is in the best interest of the community. The people elect them and may refuse to re-elect them if they do not like what they do; but in the meantime, the representatives act independently. This theory was given its classic formulation in 1774 by the famous British parliamentarian Edmund Burke in a speech to the electors of Bristol: "Your representative owes you, not his industry only, but his judgement, and he betrays, instead of serving you, if he sacrifices it to your opinion."[35]

Party discipline in parliamentary systems has largely destroyed the role of trustee. Canadian MPS are free to use their own judgment only in rare free votes or behind-the-scenes attempts to influence the party leaderships. However, Cabinet members might be considered trustees to the extent that they deliberate to determine policy positions that are then imposed on backbenchers. City councillors may act as trustees because parties do not normally function at that level in Canada. American senators and members of Congress may also act as trustees because party discipline is rather weak.

Delegates. Representatives are *delegates* if they subordinate their own views to those of their constituents and act as instructed by them. This form of representation is sometimes called the mandate role—elected members must vote according to a mandate from their constituents. Party discipline largely excludes this role, along with that of trustee. But city councillors often act as delegates when they vote in accordance with the wishes of their ward on issues such as locating roads and granting building permits. American representatives often act as delegates. A famous example was Senator William Fulbright of Arkansas, who, although he privately claimed to be an integrationist, voted against civil rights bills because of the wishes of the majority of his constituents. The delegate model is also used in many private associations, such as trade unions, political parties, and churches, where representatives chosen to attend national conventions go armed with specific instructions.

Note that the delegate model requires representatives to pursue the special interests of their constituents, not the general good of the community. This is a limitation that suggests that representatives cannot always be delegates. There are occasions when the general interest must be paramount over sectional concerns and representatives must rise above the desires of their electors.

Party Members. Representatives who are *party members* may vote and act simply as loyal members of their caucus, following the instructions of the leadership.

Party discipline has made this the dominant form of representation in parliamentary systems in the twentieth century. However, it is only a minor feature of American politics and does not apply at all to non-party systems, found in most municipal governments. The party model assumes that the policy of the party takes account of the general interest as well as special interests. In a sense, the party leadership act as trustees, using their own judgment and drawing on their own conscience to determine what is best for the community. Thus the notion of trusteeship appears somewhere in each of these three models. It is a logical requirement of concern for the common good but not necessarily a position appreciated by the electorate. Burke, for example, was voted out of office after his speech at Bristol.

The Microcosm. Whether a system uses one, two, or all three of these roles, a qualitatively different question is bound to arise: are the representatives similar to those they represent? Do they reflect the characteristics of race, language, religion, gender, class, income, occupation, and so forth that are found in the population at large? There is a common feeling today that representatives must be similar to their constituents in order to have their best interests at heart. English-speaking constituents would probably not trust a body made up of solely French-speaking representatives, or vice versa. We can call this the *microcosm* theory—a governing body should be a miniature replica of those it represents. John Adams, the second president of the United States as well as a political philosopher, wrote two hundred years ago that the representative assembly "should be in miniature an exact portrait of the people at large. It should think, feel, reason, and act like them."[36]

Obviously, the microcosm theory cannot be applied too literally; there is an infinity of characteristics that might be considered politically relevant. It is impossible to get a working body of reasonably small size that will have just the right proportions of all conceivable characteristics. But it can be given a more sensible interpretation. While exact proportionality is not important, no significant group of people should be left without a voice. This ties in well with the view of Bernard Crick, discussed in Chapter 1, that politics involves the conciliation of minorities. For example, the precise proportion of French- and English-speaking judges on the Supreme Court of Canada is not critical, but it is important that there be some of each. A more complex example is the Canadian Cabinet. In choosing ministers, the prime minister usually tries to have about three-fourths Anglophones and one-fourth Francophones, including Anglophones from inside Quebec and Francophones from outside Quebec. In addition, the prime minister wants to have at least one minister from each province, as well as at least token numbers of women, native peoples, ethnic groups, and so forth. It is a complicated balancing act whose purpose is twofold: to allow all significant groups to be heard and convince the population that no sector has been omitted from consideration. Image is as important as reality.

This principle of microcosmic representation was well illustrated in Prime Minister Mulroney's first cabinet. He nominated 40 ministers: 13 from Ontario, 11 from

Quebec, 11 from the West (Yukon 1, British Columbia 2, Alberta 3, Saskatchewan 2, Manitoba 3), and 6 from Atlantic Canada (New Brunswick 1, Nova Scotia 2, Newfoundland 1, Prince Edward Island 1). He thus managed to represent all provinces and one territory, while achieving a balance of geographic regions more or less proportional to population. Because of the composition of the Conservative caucus, he was not able to appoint francophones from outside Quebec, but he did have two Quebec anglophones in the Cabinet. He also had six women, an all-time high for Canada.

Each of these four models of representation has its own strengths and weaknesses. Trustees are a bit removed from popular pressure and can thus take a more independent view. Remember the free vote on capital punishment in the House of Commons: MPS voted to abolish it, even though public opinion polls showed that most people wanted to reinstate the death penalty. While the trustee role offers an opportunity for independence, it may also offer an opportunity for representatives to vote their own narrow biases. Conversely, the closeness to public opinion, which is the delegates' virtue, may blind them to a long-range appreciation of the public interest. Party discipline restricts representatives' initiative, but it tends to produce a more coherent and intelligible set of policies than the other models do. One of the reasons why local politics is so hard to understand is that councillors act individually as delegates and/or trustees but not cohesively as identifiable groups. Finally, the microcosm theory has its own special problem: it clashes with efficiency. The person with the right external characteristics of race and religion may not be the most able person for the job.

Perhaps there is no simple answer to these problems. It may be that all modes of representation are useful in varying circumstances, and together they may compensate for each other's drawbacks. However, regardless of what may be best in some abstract sense, the tendency of development in parliamentary democracies is clear. The roles of trustee and delegate have declined, while the party member role and the microcosm idea have expanded. These latter two are more compatible with the expanded power of the executive that is typical of the modern state.

27   The Executive

Broadly speaking, the executive branch of government includes not only highly visible officials, such as a prime minister or president, but also the many anonymous officials who labour in the civil service. We will discuss the latter group in the next chapter under the heading of administration; here we will confine our attention to those at the top of the executive pyramid—to those officers of state who are in some sense politically responsible and not theoretically neutral public employees. This category includes the head of state, the head of government, the ministry or Cabinet, and the personal advisers or assistants to these officers. We shall refer to these people as the *political executive*.

Although we have previously discussed the head of state and head of government at some length, we have said relatively little about other ministers. In Britain the *prime minister* selects about seventy MPs to become ministers. These MPs—the *ministry*—head the departments and agencies of the administration. About thirty of these ministers are designated *Cabinet* ministers, that is, close advisers to the prime minister who sit together as a committee to supervise the business of government. Ministers who are not in the Cabinet do not share this responsibility. In Canadian practice, all ministers are in the Cabinet, so that the terms ministry and Cabinet are synonymous in this country.

As government has become a larger service agency, the size of Cabinets has increased. A century ago, Sir John A. Macdonald could make do with a dozen members in his Cabinet; today Canadian Cabinets have three dozen or more members, and provincial governments may be almost as large. Prime Minister Mulroney's first Cabinet contained forty ministers. Such size necessitates internal organization.

Modern Cabinets are now divided into a number of specialized committees, each of which may deal with a number of related areas, such as foreign policy and national defence. Ministers who sit on the specialized committees naturally tend to have a bigger voice when an issue in their domain is discussed by the whole Cabinet. It is also important to have some way of keeping the many concerns of Cabinet in balance and establishing priorities among them. The Liberals recognized the problem and initiated the Royal Commission on Financial Management and Accountability (the Lambert Commission), which reported in 1977. Both the Progressive Conservatives (elected in 1979) and the Liberals (1980–1984) accepted the Commission's findings and reorganized the Cabinet structure. The most significant change was organizing the Cabinet into five committees, the dominant one being the *Priorities and Planning Committee*. It includes the prime minister and from twelve to sixteen of the key ministers. It has become the nerve centre of the

Cabinet, determining the direction of the government as well as being the last word on financial expenditures.

Provincial premiers may simply canvass the opinions of an informal circle of advisers within the Cabinet, such as the "Patio Clique" that was reputed to dominate the Alberta Executive Council under Premier Lougheed in the 1970s. In all cases, the modern Cabinet is not just a collection of three dozen equal people, but a highly structured body with an internal hierarchy. Political executives in a liberal democracy do much the same as executives in any organization—they manage the business of the enterprise. The business of the political executive has two major aspects: to initiate policy proposals for the assembly and supervise the administration of laws passed by the assembly.

The first function is a necessity. A session of Parliament would never end if the entire body had to develop its own policy proposals, debate these proposals, consider amendments, and vote on the final version. Thus the executive formulates legislative proposals to be submitted to the entire assembly. In parliamentary systems, of course, the executive goes even further and actually controls the deliberations of the assembly.

Administering laws once passed is also the responsibility of the executive. Ministers run different departments according to particular areas of responsibility. A minister of agriculture, for example, is responsible for all federal activities that fall under the department of agriculture. This may involve keeping trained agricultural agents in the field, running experimental farms, providing loans to farmers in special situations, and keeping statistics on farm production. The same applies to departments of fisheries, transport, and labour. The minister, and the Cabinet collectively, are responsible to the House (and ultimately to the people) for the business of their departments.

It should be noted again that structural differences exist in parliamentary and presidential executives. Because the executive and the legislature in the parliamentary process are fused, all ministers answer directly to the House for the work of their departments. Managing legislation through the House, in committees, and so forth is the responsibility of the Cabinet. In the presidential system, the president and Cabinet secretaries are not members of the legislative assembly because these institutions are separated. While the executive formulates policy proposals, it depends on party leaders and committee chairmen to manage the flow of legislation.

Chapter 26 mentioned that the power of the executive has been growing at the expense of the assembly. As governments increase their activities in society, much of the burden of these activities falls to the executive. When governments expand their regulatory role, extend social programs, and generally spend more money on services, the ultimate decision to do all this remains with the legislature. But the executive must formulate proposals and administer them once they are passed. This expanding responsibility has, today, placed political executives in the limelight. When people clamour about jobs, inflation, the balance of payments, foreign ownership of industries, or more public support for education, they aim their comments at the executive. Conversely, when governments seem to accomplish something, the executive is the first to take the credit.

In addition to preparing legislation and supervising its administration, the roles of the executive include performing symbolic and ceremonial functions, providing party and national political leadership, making government appointments, such as to the judiciary and regulatory agencies, and exercising military power. The expanding role of the political executive has influenced the governmental process in two important ways. There has been a dramatic growth in the administrative arm of government. Administrative departments, agencies, boards, and commissions have increased in number and size in order to carry out the government's additional responsibilities. This growth is manifested in the size of the civil service at the federal, provincial, and municipal levels. In addition, there has developed a very significant organizational tier that advises the government. While these advisers are part of the executive, they are separate from the traditional civil service. These personal advisers to the prime minister and Cabinet are important not in terms of numbers, but in terms of their influence on the governmental process.

In Canada the legislative process is managed by four key executive organizations: the Cabinet (primarily the *Priorities and Planning Committee*), the *Prime Minister's Office* (PMO), the *Privy Council Office* (PCO), and the *Treasury Board*. All are instrumental in initiating policy proposals and attempting to marshal support for them. The Cabinet is composed of ministers who manage administrative departments of government. Seldom does the Cabinet as a whole conduct public business; usually it receives and accepts recommendations from the various Cabinet committees. The Priorities and Planning Committee is the apex of this procedure, a super-committee made up of strategic ministers, such as the finance, energy, and external affairs ministers and the president of the Treasury Board. The Committee is the control centre of the government.

The Prime Minister's Office came into its own under the Trudeau governments, and it has also been used extensively by Mr. Clark, Mr. Turner, and Mr. Mulroney. The PMO consists of eighty to one hundred individuals with technical and political expertise. They include personal secretaries as well as advisers on special topics, such as trade relations, energy matters, and economic problems of the different regions of the country. These people are hired and fired by the prime minister, serving at his or her pleasure and without the career security of civil servants. They are individuals on whom the prime minister relies for information about particular problems facing the government. Marc Lalonde, for example, was a friend of Mr. Trudeau's who served in the PMO before being elected to the House of Commons and being appointed a minister of the Crown. Mr. Mulroney has drawn upon old friends from university days at Laval and from industry to assist him in the PMO.

The Privy Council Office was intended to help the government co-ordinate strategy in developing policy proposals. The *Privy Council* itself is made up of all present Cabinet ministers, former Cabinet ministers, and other individuals on whom the government would like to confer special honour. The Cabinet is its active part and acts in its name, while the Privy Council as a whole does not meet. In the words of R. MacGregor Dawson:

> The Privy Council . . . performs no functions as a Council, despite the fact that it is mentioned a number of times in the British North America Act as an advisory body to the Governor. Such functions have been assumed by that small portion of the Council which constitutes the Cabinet of the moment.[37]

The Privy Council Office, however, is very much alive as the secretariat to the Cabinet. Employing more than three hundred people, it is responsible for establishing overall government priorities and co-ordinating the process by which these priorities are achieved. There are various sub-organizations within the PCO, one of the most important of which is responsible for federal-provincial relations.

The Treasury Board, separate from the department of finance since 1967, is responsible for effective management of government administration. Its powers include fiscal matters as well as management skills and techniques. It consists of a special committee of Cabinet, chaired by a minister known as the president of the Treasury Board, and of course assisted by a large bureaucracy.

Organizations such as the PMO, PCO, and Treasury Board are known as *central agencies*. They do not themselves provide services to the public; rather, they are instruments by which the prime minister and Cabinet attempt to manage the entire public service. Which organizations play the key role in the process depends to a great extent on the style of the prime minister. Mr. Trudeau, for example, relied heavily on the PMO and then the PCO to assist the executive in setting the agenda for parliamentary sessions. Mr. Mulroney seems more inclined to use the Priorities and Planning Committee of Cabinet to set the agenda of his government.

It is difficult to depict this managerial arrangement because different organizations may have more or less influence, depending on the prime minister or the issue. Formally, however, the lines of responsibility are as follows:

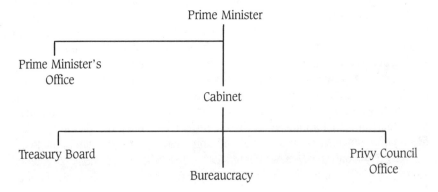

This process has displaced the old direct relationship between the prime minister, the Cabinet, and the bureaucracy and has provided a counterforce to the growing permanent bureaucracy. At the same time, however, it has led critics to suggest that ministers of the Cabinet and senior bureaucratic officials, such as deputy ministers and assistant deputy ministers, have taken a back seat to the prime minister's personal advisers. Critics contend that the central agencies have given the prime minister an inordinate amount of power in the legislative arena. With the support of the PMO and PCO, the prime minister can dominate the process by which public policy proposals are developed and priorities to them assigned. The expansion of these organizations reinforces the argument that the collegiality of Cabinet government is giving way to "prime ministerial" government, which is highly focussed on the person of the prime minister. Comparisons are sometimes drawn between the contemporary role of the prime minister, with a phalanx of personal advisers in the PMO and PCO, and that of an American president, with an admittedly much larger White House staff. The comparison is worrisome because the president does not control Congress to the extent that the prime minister controls Parliament. Thus the latter's power may be relatively unchecked.

Two mechanisms were traditionally supposed to make the assembly ultimate master of the political executive in a parliamentary system. Under the principle of *responsible government*, the Cabinet is collectively responsible to the House. The prime minister and the Cabinet as a whole cannot rule without the majority support of the popularly elected branch of the assembly. But we have seen how party discipline has weakened, if not completely destroyed, the meaning of responsible government.

The second great check on the political executive was a minister's individual responsibility to the assembly for the conduct of the business of the departments within that *portfolio*. Under the doctrine of *ministerial responsibility*, should there be a serious problem in a department (such as dishonesty or gross incompetence), a minister should offer to resign. This idea developed in the age of smaller government, when it was reasonable to assume that ministers could keep in touch with everything being done by their underlings. It is somewhat unrealistic to expect the same today, given the far-flung activities of departments that may have thousands of employees and budgets of billions of dollars. Thus ministers in Canada today do not usually offer their resignations unless they are personally implicated in a breach of trust, even if the opposition demands that they step down. Although not frequent, the process does work. Over the past seven years, at least six ministers (three Liberal and three P.C.) have resigned Cabinet posts because of questionable activities. However, in all cases, the cause of the resignation was some personal action of the minister. For example: Liberal Solicitor General Francis Fox forged the signature of his girlfriend's husband in order to help her get an abortion (1978); Conservative Minister of Defence Robert Coates acted indiscreetly by visiting a strip bar while on a junket to West Germany (1984). There are no recent examples of ministers accepting responsibility for, and resigning because of, misconduct or bad judgment among the career civil servants in their departments.

Although ministerial responsibility and responsible government have both lost some of their effectiveness, the assembly still has the power to inquire, expose, and accuse. Ministers do not wish to appear in a bad light, even if their jobs are not immediately threatened—their long-run political future could be at stake. Thus most executive functions are tempered by regard for the assembly. In spite of the trend toward executive power, an interdependency between the executive and the assembly remains. Checks on the executive exist today as they always have. And as long as the process operates by the rules that enable the checks to work (vote of confidence, caucus, popular election), the power of the executive, while great, is not absolute.

28   The Administration

The modern state requires a large administrative apparatus to implement its legislative and policy outputs. The assembly and the executive would be powerless without the support of a massive *administration* (used here interchangeably with the term *bureaucracy*). This latter term has acquired many negative connotations of delay, inflexibility, and red tape; but it has a particular and indispensable meaning in social science. Its etymological sense of the "rule of offices" hints at its meaning. It designates a particular kind of social structure for carrying out organized work, a structure that has a number of characteristics:

1. The work is divided into impersonal roles or offices that may be filled by different persons as the need arises. Bureaucracies always have job descriptions to ensure that the positions are stable over time.

2. These positions tend to be specialized, which is another way of saying there is a high degree of division of labour.

3. This specialization demands a career commitment from employees because complex roles can be learned only through long experience.

4. Careers are protected by some form of job security or *tenure*. This usually means that employees can be dismissed only for designated cause.

5. Positions are filled by *merit recruitment*, which normally means competitive examination. The opposite is recruitment by *patronage*, which means jobs are distributed according to kinship, friendship, or personal favour.

6. Ideally, the bureaucracy is supposed to be a neutral instrument in the hands of those who command it because it is organized as a hierarchy, with authority flowing down from top to bottom.

The bureaucratic form of organization is not confined to government. The Roman Catholic church and many large corporations are examples of private bureaucracies. In fact, although bureaucracies were known in ancient empires, such as Rome, Egypt, and China, they have been perfected and widely used by Western states only in recent times. The absolute monarchs created bureaucratic armies, but government administration did not become bureaucratic in general until the late nineteenth and early twentieth centuries. The principle of merit recruitment was not really accepted in Canada until the Civil Service Act of 1908 was passed.

A well-functioning bureaucracy has many advantages that have caused the form to be so widely adopted. Ideally, it exhibits honesty, impartiality, stability, predictability, and a measure of competence. It may be short on imagination and innovation, but presumably these qualities can be found elsewhere in the political system. In theory, it should be politically neutral, responding to directions emanating from the assembly and political executive, but not itself making political decisions. As we shall see, this last expectation is not wholly realistic, so that the bureaucracy must be considered an independent element in the conversion phase of the political process, not just a passive adjunct to the political executive. Moreover, because the bureaucracy tends to become the home of many institutional pressure groups that pursue their self-interest simultaneously with performing public business, it is also an important source of demands on the political system.

The bureaucracy has two fundamental roles in the governmental process: it advises the political executive, and it administers laws and policies enacted by the assembly. For instance, at the request of the minister of justice, the department may prepare for Cabinet a set of legislative alternatives on the issue of capital punishment. Or the minister of Indian affairs and northern development may have that department, in consultation with Indian and Inuit groups, explore the various ways that recognition of land claims can be handled by the government. In its administrative role, the bureaucracy is responsible for distributing family allowance cheques and veterans' pensions, staffing customs and immigration offices in Canada and abroad, monitoring environmental conditions, and performing a myriad of other tasks in the modern welfare-service state. The bureaucratic structure is enormously complex (organization charts are available from the government of Canada).[38] If one counts the number of people working directly or indirectly for the federal government in departments, agencies, boards, Crown corporations, and the military, the total is over five hundred thousand. If one includes provincial and municipal employees, the figure is over one million people—about 12 per cent of the labour force.[39]

Figure 28.1 illustrates the basic principle of control of the public service in a parliamentary system—responsibility of the bureaucracy to the political executive and through it to the elected assembly. Each department is headed by a minister of the Crown. Quasi-independent agencies and boards, such as the Immigration Appeal Board and the National Parole Board, as well as Crown corporations, like Air Canada and the Bank of Canada, are not directly under ministerial authority but must report to a minister. If the operations of such a commission or Crown corporation do not please the Cabinet or assembly, different personnel may be appointed or legislation may be introduced to change the body's terms of reference. The underlying principle is hierarchical control and responsibility, modelled on a pyramid of authority emanating from the sovereign.

The term *Crown corporation* is unique to Canada, but public corporations can be found in almost every nation-state. They are numerous in Great Britain. The greatest wave of nationalization of key resource and transport industries occurred after World War II. From 1946 to 1951, the Labour government created the National Coal Board, the British Railways Board, the National Bus Company, the National Freight Corporation, the British Gas Corporation, and the British Steel

FIGURE 28.1

Canadian Public Administration

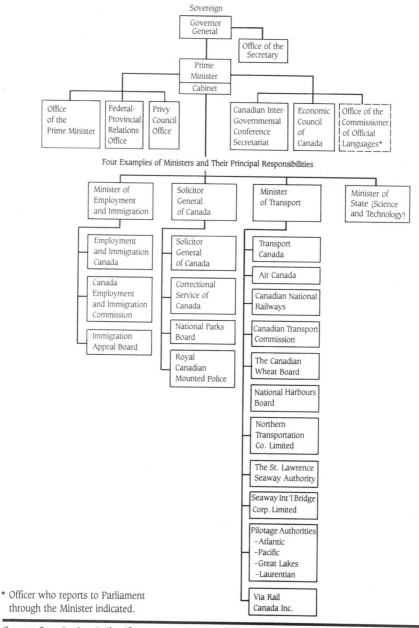

* Officer who reports to Parliament through the Minister indicated.

Source: Organization & Classification Division, Treasury Board Secretariat, December, 1981.

Corporation. From 1971 to 1977, the government acquired a number of ailing industries: Rolls Royce, British Leyland, British National Oil Corporation, British Shipbuilders, and British Aerospace. In 1976 nationalized public corporations "accounted for 9.6% of GNP and 6.9% of employment."[40] Public corporations in the United States are more apt to be public utilities—for example, electric companies—managed by an independent commission. These are also usually authorized under state law. AMTRAC, the combined national railway passenger service, is a public corporation responsible to the federal government. In all cases, the public corporation, as an alternative to the conventional civil service, is supposed to offer more business flexibility while still retaining an ultimate link to the political executive.

Note that all forms of public bureaucratic control differ intrinsically from bureaucratic control in the private sector. Private bureaucracies are to some extent a check upon each other, because corporations compete for dollars and churches for souls; but what is to restrain the public bureaucrats who wield the authority of the state? When government provides a non-monopolistic public service, competition provides some control, as for the CBC or Canadian National Railways; but most governmental services are monopolistic, so that the competitive model is by definition inapplicable. What remains is the model of authoritative hierarchy and responsibility.

Following the British parliamentary tradition, Canada has tried to control the public service by ensuring that it is firmly subordinated to Parliament, as illustrated in Figure 28.2. The theory of the Canadian system is that all executive power emanates from the Crown. The Crown acts only through ministers, who are in turn accountable to the House of Commons for their actions. These ministers supervise the machinery of government under their respective portfolios and thus share responsibility for supervising the entire public service. The bureaucracy, as a hierarchy, is supposed to respond to direction from above. Thus popular sovereignty is ultimately served, and the public service is kept a servant of the people, not its master.

Ministers are politicians, not specialists in the business of their portfolios. They seldom serve in any one position long enough to build up much expertise, and in fact, many prime ministers deliberately rotate their ministers to prevent them from becoming too identified with a particular aspect of government. *Deputy ministers*, in contrast, are not politicians, but usually career civil servants (or perhaps administrative experts brought in from the private sector). The prime minister appoints deputy ministers, and this gives him an important lever of control over the public service. Deputy ministers have reached the apex of the bureaucratic career, presumably having been promoted for competence. They run their departments, issuing instructions through assistant deputy ministers down the whole chain of command. They are also supposed to offer advice to their ministers, explaining what is or is not administratively feasible. Because of this high responsibility, deputy ministers serve at the pleasure of the Crown and can be dismissed at any time; but it is Canadian practice not to fire deputy ministers very often. They may

FIGURE 28.2

Subordination of Bureaucracy to Parliament

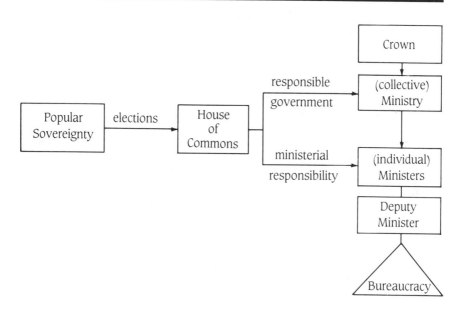

be transferred from one department to another, but they are seldom released unless they have been politically indiscreet. This is in sharp contrast to the American custom, in which an incoming president makes wholesale changes in the top ranks of the federal civil service.

In theory, Canadian civil servants are supposed to be politically neutral and able to work under a minister of any party. In 1984–1985 Mr. Mulroney's government dismissed very few ranking civil servants, a surprise after so many years of Liberal government appointments. The new government did, however, initiate an extensive retirement program for senior civil servants as a way of renewing the administration.

The Canadian model of administrative control assumes that there is a clear distinction between politics and administration. Politics is supposed to be the realm where goals are set and the choice between options is made. Administration is supposed to be the realm where settled policy is carried into effect. Politics is the business of ministers; administration, of deputy ministers; and the latter are clearly subordinate to the former. But this assumption is only partially true. Politicians in power depend on information and expert advice from the public service. These administrative officials, with knowledge and experience, wield a great deal of power in the political process. Their position may overshadow that of elected officials who are not expected to have technical expertise. Civil servants can make or break legislative proposals. Furthermore, even when legislation is adopted, the public service must put it into effect. Much may depend on the way a law is put into practice. Modern legislation is only a broad framework whose impact becomes clear as administrative decisions accumulate.

For all these reasons, many observers of politics fear that too much power is vested in the public service and that its subordination to Parliament is not as effective as it should theoretically be. A number of experiments have been tried in recent years in order to combat this tendency. As mentioned above, prime ministers have greatly enlarged their personal staff in the Prime Minister's Office and the Cabinet staff in the Privy Council Office in order to be less dependent on the regular public service for advice. The federal House of Commons has appointed an independent *auditor general* to review the annual expenditures of the public service. The public accounts committee of the House is now chaired by a member of the opposition to give it great latitude in investigating possible administrative misuse of funds. Nine of ten provinces have appointed an *ombudsman* to deal with complaints of individual citizens who feel that bureaucrats have not treated them properly. Typically, the ombudsman does not have the authority to grant relief to a complainant, but the power to investigate and expose may be enough to goad the bureaucracy into taking another look at the matter.

These and other reforms may all do something to reduce the power of the public bureaucracy and make it accountable to politicians—and ultimately to the people. Yet it is doubtful whether any true solution to the problem is in sight. The mechanisms of parliamentary control of administration were developed in an era of small government. If people want a large service-oriented state that does a great deal for them, they will have to live with a powerful bureaucracy—the only means by which such a state can deliver the services people demand of it.

Even the most casual observer of government knows that its bureaucratic agencies, once created, are rarely dissolved, and most seem to grow inexorably despite changes in the political complexion of the Cabinet. There appears to be a logical reason for this tendency toward growth. We must assume that public servants, like other individuals, are self-interested—they seek success and advancement in their chosen careers. Advancement in a bureaucratic structure means supervising more people, running more programs, spending a larger budget, delivering more services. Thus those who work within any bureaucracy have powerful incentives to work to expand their own organization.

This tendency is equally strong in private and public bureaucracies, but there are stronger countervailing tendencies in the former than in the latter. Business corporations cannot pursue growth to the neglect of profitability; expansion for its own sake leads to lower rates of return on investment, declining dividends on shares, falling prices in the stock market, and possibly even bankruptcy. The existence of market competition, to the extent that it is effective, disciplines the internal tendencies of the bureaucracy toward expansion for its own sake. But public bureaucracies, which rarely compute profit and loss and usually enjoy a monopoly position, lack this countervailing force. This immanent tendency toward self-aggrandizement must be checked by political resistance—most often a shortage in the public treasury. The internal incentive structure of public administration means, therefore, that the political masters of the bureaucracy continue to receive advice favouring the growth of the welfare-service state.[41]

We must think realistically of the assembly, executive, and bureaucracy as partially co-operating, partially conflicting centres of power in the political process. Constitutionally, the assembly appears to have the last word because a majority of its members can pass or defeat legislation. But the bureaucracy, with its information and expertise, can set the terms of legislative debate. Facts can be marshalled in order to impose the bureaucracy's preferences on the Cabinet or assembly. Again, the executive can call on its own special resources of party discipline, information, and constitutional authority to impose its will on the bureaucracy or the assembly. The question of dominance is perhaps misleading because power relations change according to circumstances and issues under consideration. It is more important to grasp the interaction of assembly, executive, and bureaucracy and see how that interaction can serve social needs in the conversion phase of the political process.

29 The Judiciary

The rule of law is a cornerstone of civilized life in society. Institutionalized rules (laws), applied equally, restrict the public authority or private persons from arbitrarily using power. An extension of the rule of law is a system of courts—institutions that adjudicate disputes under law. We will look at the courts first as a legal institution, then as part of the political process.

Adjudicating disputes between individuals, between individuals and the state, and between different levels of government within the state takes place within the boundaries of a single country. But there are also disputes involving two or more states, and individuals or corporations and other states, that concern breaches of international law. Such disputes may be brought before the International Court of Justice, but its decisions are not binding because it has no power to enforce its decisions; it depends on voluntary compliance. Our discussion will not look further at this international dimension of courts; we will confine ourselves to the framework of domestic law and court systems.

There is no single model for a system of courts. Each country seems to adopt a structure of courts in response to particular needs. For instance, court systems vary in federal and unitary states. In a unitary system, there is normally a single set of laws written by the central government and a single system of courts administering justice. In a federal system, where laws are made by different levels of government, there may be a tier of courts with jurisdiction at each level: federal courts, with responsibility for federal laws, and provincial or state courts, for provincial or state laws. Moreover, specialized courts may be established to deal with specific laws. Tax, labour, family, and juvenile courts are examples that can be found in many different countries.

British courts are an example of court organization in a unitary state. There is one unified structure in which all judges are appointed by the Crown on the advice of the prime minister and/or Lord Chancellor. The highest court of appeal is the House of Lords, but by custom the whole House does not hear cases. This work is left to a special committee of Lords with legal expertise. An interesting feature of the British system is that there are separate courts for criminal and civil matters, although appeals from both divisions go ultimately to the Law Lords.

The American system makes an interesting contrast to the British because federalism has had such a strong impact on the organization of American courts. As shown in Figure 29.1, there is a dual system of courts. Disputes under federal law go before a system of federal courts whose judges are appointed by the president subject to the advice and consent of the Senate. In addition, each of the fifty states maintains its own system of courts, culminating in a state Supreme

FIGURE 29.1

The American Court System

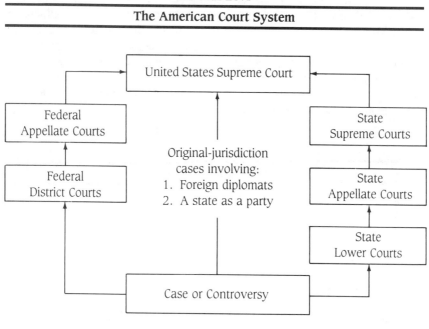

Source: Adapted from Kenneth Prewitt and Sidney Verba, *An Introduction to American Government*, 2nd ed. (New York: Harper & Row, 1976), p. 354.

Court. There is great diversity among these systems: in some, judges are appointed by the state governor; in others, they are popularly elected. Although federal and state courts are organizationally distinct, they are not wholly isolated from each other. For one thing, many cases can go to either a federal or state court because federal and state laws overlap. Kidnapping, for example, which is an offence in all states, also becomes a federal crime if state lines are crossed, so that an accused kidnapper can be tried in either system. Another feature linking the systems is that the federal Supreme Court exercises *appellate* jurisdiction over the Supreme Courts of the states if federal questions are involved.

The Canadian arrangement falls between the British and the American. Figure 29.2 shows that the system is fundamentally unified. The Federal Court of Canada deals with certain specialized matters of federal administrative law: claims against the Crown, taxation, customs duties, immigration, etc. Apart from these exceptions, all cases are heard in the provincially organized courts at one level or another. The provinces maintain their own *provincial courts* for matters such as small claims and minor criminal offences. The judges of the *superior courts* are all appointed by the governor general on the advice of the prime minister or minister of justice. However, federalism plays a role by allowing each province to organize its superior courts in a distinctive way. Provinces also provide the support personnel and services required by the courts. Canada thus has an interesting compromise between the unitary and federal approaches to court organization. The federal government's monopoly on appointment creates uniform interpretation, but the power of the provinces to organize the provincial and superior courts as they wish means that this interpretation is applied to diverse local conditions.

FIGURE 29.2

The Canadian Court System

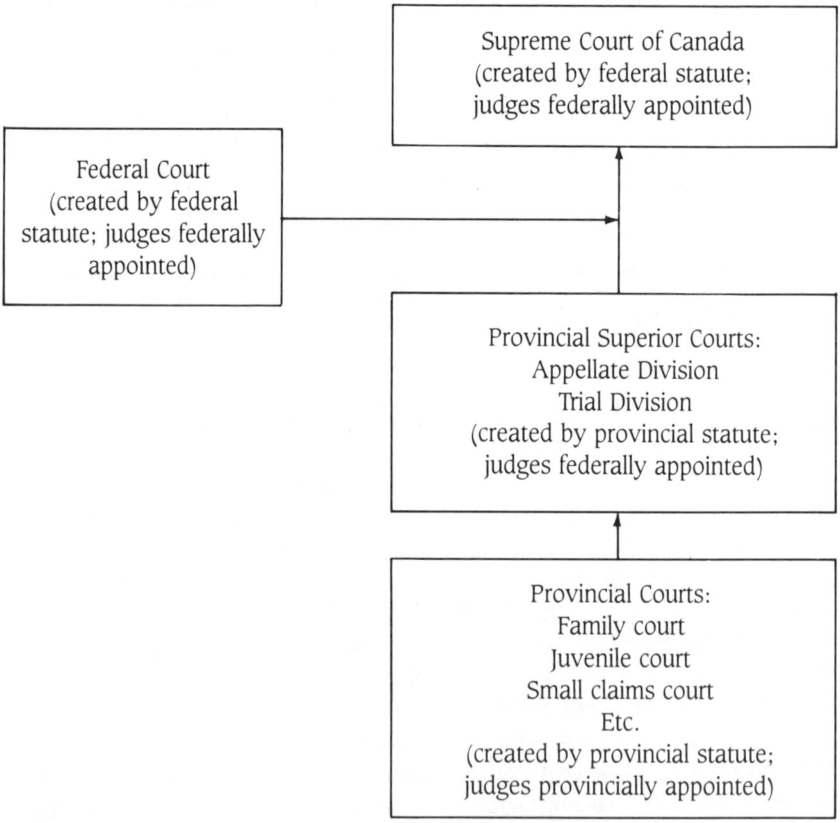

Source: Adapted from Gerald L. Gall, *The Canadian Legal System* (Toronto: Carswell, 1977), pp. 99–100.

The apex of the Canadian court system is the Supreme Court of Canada, which is the highest court of appeal. This does not mean that every appeal is heard by the Supreme Court, because the justices may refuse to hear a case, allowing the lower court's decision to stand.

The Supreme Court has not always been the highest court of appellate jurisdiction. Before 1949, court decisions could be appealed to the *Judicial Committee of the Privy Council* in Britain, the highest court of appeal for the British Empire. Removing the Judicial Committee's appellate jurisdiction over Canadian cases was another step in Canada's gradual emancipation from British institutions of government. The Supreme Court is made up of nine justices, of whom one is the chief justice. Three of the justices must be from Quebec, a stipulation that reflects a peculiarity in the Quebec legal system. While other provinces rely on the British common law tradition, Quebec has its own *code civil* for civil law matters.

The professed object of a court system in a liberal democracy is to administer justice equally to all citizens. Unequal treatment before the law means a violation of one of the fundamental principles of liberal democracy. Here we can mention some of the main considerations that determine whether equality before the law is realized in practice.

The first problem is the judiciary's independence from direct political interference; this can be guaranteed in a number of ways. Tenure in office (serving "during good behaviour") means that judges cannot be discharged except for violation of law or gross impropriety of conduct. In the United States, Congress is constitutionally barred from lowering judges' salaries while they are in office (although neglecting to grant periodic raises may have the same effect in an inflationary age). In spite of such safeguards, politicians may still try to influence judges, either by public criticism or more subtle private communications. Instances of both occurred in Canada in the 1970s, leading to resignations from the federal Cabinet. Judicial independence, probably the single greatest institutional support of the rule of law, is something that can never be taken for granted.

A second problem is the courts' efficiency. Cases before the courts must be handled expeditiously. It can be a tragedy to hold individuals in custody over a long period of time awaiting trial. The court system, like many other public services, is expensive, and providing enough courtrooms, judges, and penal institutions is often a cost people do not want to shoulder. Nevertheless, clearing the docket of its backlog of cases maintains people's respect for the judiciary.

A third problem is imposing equal punishment for the commission of the same crime. The sentencing practices of judges have been a matter of debate for many law reform commissions. There is no way to guarantee that judges in Halifax or Toronto, or even two judges in the same city, will apply the same penalty for similar crimes. Penalties written into the law contain some latitude, and for a good reason. Judges may take account of particular circumstances surrounding a crime, and their interpretations of the severity of a crime vary greatly. We will undoubtedly never find uniformity when punishing violators of the law, but there must be some common denominator, or again, the system will be questioned.

A final problem involves the cost of obtaining justice in the court system. Hiring the time of a lawyer, especially a good one, is an expensive proposition and may be beyond the means of many people. Because of this, our legal system is criticized for having a double standard—one for the rich and one for the poor. However, this criticism is at least partly met by providing free or low-cost legal services through legal aid.

In spite of their neutrality in partisan politics, the courts play an important role in the political process. Their decisions about cases sometimes have the same effect as legislative outputs from the assembly or policy outputs from the executive or bureaucracy. Of course, most cases that come before the courts do not have such sweeping implications; they merely require applying a known body of law to a particular situation. But occasionally, there may seem to be no precedent that really applies to the case, or perhaps the dispute hinges on the interpretation of the wording of a statute. In both instances, the court's decision, as it becomes a precedent for subsequent decisions of other courts, is a source of law just as effectively as if a statute were passed or amended.

For example, Section 24 of the Constitution Act, 1867 allows "qualified persons" to be appointed to the Senate. When Prime Minister Mackenzie King wanted to appoint Emily Murphy of Edmonton to be the first woman in the Senate, it was not clear whether the words "qualified persons" included women. The result was the celebrated "Persons Case," finally decided in 1929 by the Judicial Committee of the Privy Council, which held that women were persons within the meaning of the statute.[42] The case was political in at least two ways: because it changed law and policy to allow women to sit in the Senate, it was virtually the equivalent of a constitutional amendment; it also signalled a remarkable victory for women as a group and helped lead to subsequent improvements in their status.

The interpretive power of the courts in a liberal democracy, coupled with their relative independence from the assembly and the executive, make them an attractive alternative for interest groups that lack influence with other decision-making institutions. The way in which American blacks, in organizations like the NAACP, used the courts to overturn segregation is well known. In Canada native peoples' associations have tried, so far with ambiguous results, to use the courts to validate aboriginal claims that Parliament and Cabinet have not been willing to recognize. In Manitoba the trivial matter of a parking ticket became the case of *Forest v. the Queen*, leading to the ruling that Manitoba, established as an officially bilingual province by the Manitoba Act (1870), must publish all its statutes in both English and French—an extraordinary victory for the Francophone minority of that province that could never have been won in the legislature.[43]

Interest groups now work out strategies of litigation as calculatingly as they lobby the assembly for legislation. Perhaps the most advanced in this direction in Canada is the Canadian Advisory Council on the Status of Women, which has produced a report outlining a strategy of "systematic litigation."[44] It calls for the establishment of a legal defence fund to sponsor cases of interest to organized feminist groups. The "four basic steps" of systematic litigation are:

(1) defining a goal in terms of the desired principle of law to be established; (2) plotting how the principle of law can be established from case to case in incremental, logical and clear steps; (3) selecting winnable cases suitable for each stage taken to achieve the goal; (4) consolidating wins of each stage by bringing similar cases to create a cluster of cases in support of the principle established.[45]

With such approaches to litigation, interest group politics now clearly embraces the judiciary as well as the other branches of government.

The most spectacular political role of the courts is *judicial review*. Essentially, judicial review is a court ruling on the constitutionality of legislation. The concept was mentioned in the discussion of federalism in Chapter 20 because disputes often arise in federal systems, where legislative powers are granted to different levels of government. The distribution of powers is frequently not absolutely clear, or there may be overlapping responsibilities, so that jurisdictional disputes invariably arise between levels of government.

A current Canadian example is the ongoing dispute over television broadcasts conveyed via satellite. The federal government has traditionally regulated the communications industry through the Canadian Radio-television and Telecommunications Commission (CRTC). Provinces, on the other hand, have been given the power to govern in matters of culture and education. Theoretically, if the federal government legislates in the area of culture and education, the provinces could challenge the constitutionality of the legislation, and the courts would have to rule. By the same token, if provincial governments legislate in the area of communications, the federal government might challenge the constitutionality of such attempts. The provinces claim that television broadcasts are a cultural issue, while the federal government claims that national standards must be established to control foreign communications signals.

Judicial review exists in both Canada and the United States, as in most federal systems, but it has historically been carried much further in the United States than in Canada. One reason is the British tradition of parliamentary supremacy. Canadian judges, educated in this tradition, were reluctant to say that an assembly may not legislate as it wishes. The main use of judicial review was for the courts to decide which assembly, provincial or federal, possessed legislative power under the Constitution Act, 1867. Having decided which is the appropriate legislature, the Canadian courts seldom used judicial review to challenge legislative wisdom. A second factor was the presence in the United States of a constitutional Bill of Rights, which put limits on what any legislature, state or federal, could do.[46] This entrenched document made the American courts more self-confident in ruling legislation *ultra vires*.

This particular role of the courts, called *judicial activism*, has been a feature of American politics throughout the last half century. In the 1930s, the Supreme Court initially ruled much of President Roosevelt's New Deal legislation unconstitutional. In one period from 1935 to 1937, the Court held twelve acts of Congress *ultra vires*. There was then a sudden shift in the Court's decisions after the president threatened to "pack" it by expanding its size and appointing members who shared his ideology of reform liberalism. In this instance, judicial activism favoured the ideological right, but it can be used equally to forward the aims of the left.

The U.S. Supreme Court was particularly active from 1954 to 1969, when Earl Warren was chief justice. The Warren Court struck down racial segregation, compelled the states to draw constituency lines to approximate "one man one vote," greatly enhanced the rights of those accused of crimes, legalized abortion on demand, outlawed prayer in public schools, and in many other ways wrought unprecedented changes in the social fabric of the United States. When courts begin to decide so many questions of policy, they have plainly become politicized institutions, offering a unique way of making public decisions. There is in all of this a difficult question of democratic theory, for judges, after all, are appointed, not elected. Is it compatible with the idea of representative government to have so many questions settled by appointed officials who serve for life and never have to confront the voters?[47]

With the adoption in 1982 of the Charter of Rights and Freedoms as part of our constitution, the role of the judiciary in Canada began to change. Judicial activism is gradually becoming a part of our legal process. The guarantee of individual rights and freedoms now depends on the constitution and the courts' protection of these enshrined principles. In effect, except where the "notwithstanding" clause intervenes (s. 33 of the Charter), the constitution, not federal or provincial parliaments, becomes sovereign. This fundamental change in constitutional law in Canada will by no means work itself out overnight. Individuals are beginning to use the courts to challenge the constitutionality of particular federal or provincial laws. The courts, not legislatures, now become responsible for reconciling these disputes.

The reason for adopting the Charter, it was explained to the Canadian public, was to advance toward the ideal of rule of law in a liberal democracy—it would prevent governments, no matter how strong their majority support, from violating the rights of individuals or minorities. While this rationale is undoubtedly true, there is another aspect of the Charter that cannot be overlooked: it involves a large transfer of decision-making power from governments and legislatures to courts.

The rights enunciated in the Charter are necessarily described in such broad language that they become meaningful only through judicial interpretation. To take one example, s. 10 of the Charter reads in part:

10. Everyone has the right on arrest or detention . . .
(b) to retain and instruct counsel without delay and to be informed of that right . . .

The *Therens* case, decided in 1985 by the Supreme Court of Canada, hinged on the precise meaning of "detention."[48] After having an automobile accident in Moose Jaw, Saskatchewan, Therens was requested by a police officer to go to the police station to take a breathalyzer test. (To refuse this request is itself a violation of the Criminal Code.) Therens complied and was later prosecuted for driving while impaired. At the trial, Therens's counsel moved for dismissal of the breathalyzer evidence because the police constable had not informed Therens of his right to retain counsel. The legal question, ultimately decided in the affirmative by the Supreme Court, was whether being asked to go to the police station to give a breath sample amounted to "detention."

A related question was whether the evidence might be introduced anyway, even though it had been obtained in violation of s.10(b). Section 24(2) of the Charter states:

> . . . the evidence shall be excluded if it is established that, having regard to all the circumstances, the admission of it in the proceedings would bring the administration of justice into disrepute.

Again, the courts were required to interpret abstract words. The Supreme Court upheld the view of the lower courts that to admit such evidence would bring the administration of justice into disrepute.

The point here is not whether the decision was right or wrong, but where decision-making power is located. Parliament, in providing for check-stop procedures under the Criminal Code, had not explicitly said that those requested to "breathe into the box" should be informed of their right to retain counsel. But by interpreting the generalized language of the Charter, the courts have now laid down this rule, which is just as binding as if it had been legislated by Parliament.

From its proclamation on April 17, 1982 to the time of writing in mid-1985, the effects of the Charter have been felt largely, though certainly not exclusively, in the field of criminal law. Most frequently litigated have been rights such as security against unreasonable search or seizure and the right to counsel. Numerically, the main groups using Charter arguments in the courts have been those accused of driving while impaired and selling illegal drugs.[49] Because the courts obviously have great expertise in criminal law, the transfer of decision-making power from government and Parliament has not seemed problematic. Outside the criminal law field, only a few Supreme Court decisions based on the Charter have thus far had broad consequences. That will undoubtedly change after the proclamation on April 17, 1985 of the "equality rights" section of the Charter:

> 15. (1) Every individual is equal before and under the law and has the right to the equal protection and equal benefit of the law without discrimination and, in particular, without discrimination based on race, national or ethnic origin, colour, religion, sex, age or mental or physical disability.

Federal and provincial statute books contain literally thousands of clauses authorizing differential treatment based on the criteria in s. 15(1). To mention only a few examples: one generally has to be sixteen to obtain a driver's licence and eighteen to vote; publicly supported athletic competitions are usually divided into classes by sex; physically and mentally handicapped children are subject to special treatment of many kinds in the public schools. In the past in Canada, legislatures and administrative authorities made the rules governing such situations, but now the courts will inevitably be drawn into deciding whether particular rules or policies are discriminatory. In the long run, the effects of the Charter will profoundly transform the Canadian political process.

30 The Political Process: A Case Study

Conceptualizing the process of politics is useful if it provides a framework within which political phenomena can be studied. In this final chapter, we will show how the ideas and concepts developed in Part Four can help our understanding of difficult political issues. The particular issue on which we focus is the health of the forest products industry in New Brunswick and Nova Scotia.

For decades, economic growth in the four Atlantic provinces has lagged behind that of Central Canada and the Western provinces. Stagnant economies in the region were one reason for the adoption of federal equalization payments—a program designed to transfer federal revenue to "have not" provinces so that their citizens could enjoy public services equal to those enjoyed in other provinces. Therefore, when a key industry of the region, such as fishing or forestry, experiences problems, the effect on the well-being of the province is profound. The political culture of the region consequently encourages a positive attitude toward measures that will increase employment and business activity.

The forest industry is vital to both New Brunswick and Nova Scotia. In New Brunswick forestry, along with wood and paper manufacturing, combine in a $500 million industry, making up just over 20 per cent of the provincial gross domestic product (GDP). In Nova Scotia they are a $260 million industry, constituting approximately 10 per cent of the provincial GDP.[50] In Nova Scotia the industry is said to employ, directly or indirectly, 24,000 workers;[51] in New Brunswick, 35,000.[52] When the spruce budworm infestation hit in the early 1950s, the natural reflex was to do almost anything necessary to maintain jobs in this critical sector of the economy.

The spruce budworm is a small insect that feeds on the new growth of coniferous trees. Moths lay the eggs, and when the worms are hatched they can, over a period of years, defoliate a forest. Worm infestations seem to appear in approximately twenty- to thirty-year cycles. They were observed in the nineteenth and early twentieth centuries, but damage was not as important then. For example, in New Brunswick

> 50 years ago, the annual production of sawn lumber at better than 300 million fbm was only moderately less than it is today at 400 million fbm. However, the production of newsprint in those days was only 20,000 tons; in 1980 it will be 600,000 tons, an increase of 30 times. Softwood pulp production 50 years ago was 175,000 tons; today it is more than 1.1 million tons, an increase of more than 6 times. Hardwood pulping was unknown in New Brunswick in 1930, but today it exceeds 450,000 tons, or twice as much as the total output of softwood in those former days.[53]

Obviously, there is a great deal of pressure on forests today. The forest industry must have large areas on which to draw to sustain its yield of this renewable resource, but problems with the budworm could easily lead to a shortage. This is why government and industry have used chemical sprays to check the infestation.

New Brunswick was infested first, in 1952, and spraying was introduced. DDT was the common compound used at that time. By 1967 it was realized that certain of its ingredients were harmful to wildlife, and other chemicals were applied. The government of New Brunswick, as well as the forest industry, thought throughout this period that spraying was essential to save the forests.

Not all individuals in the province agreed. Citizens' groups opposed to spraying began to form, mobilizing popular support for their cause. The Concerned Parents' Association argued that evidence existed linking health problems to spraying. A high incidence of birth defects and cancer was cited as common to areas where spraying was concentrated. As well, the group noted research suggesting that Reye's syndrome might be caused by chemicals in the sprays. Its argument was that as long as doubt existed about the effects of spraying, it should be halted.

Individuals concerned about the problems associated with spraying tried to use the media to build support for their cause,[54] but they confronted a problem peculiar to New Brunswick. The K. C. Irving family has accumulated extensive holdings in both the wood products and the news media industries. The conglomerate is said to control eleven million acres of forest land and own controlling interest in every English daily newspaper in the province.[55] It also owns radio and television stations. Environmentalists trying to organize to oppose government policies on spraying were frustrated by what they felt was unequal access to the media. They felt that it was impossible to mobilize opposition when it was difficult to get their information before the public. Media coverage, however, did appear in newspapers and national journals such as *Maclean's*, and in 1982 CBC's "Sunday Morning" broadcast a special program on the possible effects of chemical spraying.[56] Thus the pluralism of the larger Canadian society was used against local concentrations of almost monolithic power.

In spite of these attempts to mobilize popular support, government and industry stuck to their position and continued to spray. They argued that spraying was absolutely essential to check further defoliation of the forests.[57] However, the Department of Natural Resources in New Brunswick experimented with different chemical mixtures and established non-sprayed buffer zones between populated areas and spray areas in order to reduce the chances of adverse consequences. The position of government officials and the wood products industry was that as long as no concrete evidence linked sprays with health hazards, economic arguments dictated the necessity of spraying.

In Nova Scotia the heaviest concentration of budworm infestation was in Cumberland and Colchester counties and on Cape Breton Island. The issue came to a head in the mid-1970s. The industry advocated spraying, but the government decided that spraying would not be permitted on either Crown or private land. Rather, the idea was to let the forces of nature work and hope the budworm's natural cycle would run its course over a short period of time. Also, with federal government assistance, a program was started by which dead trees would be harvested as soon as possible. The government was gambling on the hope that the budworm cycle would be short-lived and confined to one area of the province.

In 1981 the Department of Lands and Forests in Nova Scotia announced the spraying of limited areas to check the spread of the budworm. Its rationale was that in the Cape Breton highlands, for example, 78 per cent of the balsam fir was "dead or dying," as was 34 per cent of the spruce.[58] Nevertheless, the decision to spray was a blow to environmentalists, who thought Nova Scotia officials were sympathetic to their cause. In fact, many of the conservationists had anticipated a decline in the spread of the budworm, thus arguing that it was not necessary to spray on the downside of the cycle.

An issue related to insecticide spraying, and perhaps more controversial, has been the use of herbicides in reseeded areas of both provinces. After forests are cut, new stands of timber are cultivated by either natural reseeding or planting seedlings. New stands of small coniferous (softwood) trees must compete with rapidly growing deciduous (hardwood) trees and underbrush such as berries. The forest industry uses herbicides to spray this latter foliage in order to give the softwood trees a better start in their first few years of growth. Electrical power companies also use herbicides to kill the foliage under power lines.

This practice has become very controversial in New Brunswick and Nova Scotia because of the chemicals used. Many of the herbicides contain 2,4-D, 2,4,5-T, and some amount of dioxin, considered a deadly chemical. This compound is better known as Agent Orange, used by the United States military as a defoliant in Vietnam. In the last few years, the chemical has been banned in Sweden, the United States, and the provinces of British Columbia, Saskatchewan, and Ontario.

Naturally, there has been a reaction to the use of this herbicide. The Concerned Parents' Association in New Brunswick and the Coalition Against Pesticides in Nova Scotia have marshalled campaigns to halt the spraying. In Nova Scotia a group of landowners banded together in the spring of 1983 to seek a court injunction against all spraying. Again, their argument was that sprays were detrimental to health and that the practice should be terminated until more concrete evidence established the effects. In September Mr. Justice Nunn of the Nova Scotia Supreme Court handed down a lengthy decision, the essence of which was:

> I am unable to accept that the plaintiffs have proved any strong probability or a sufficient degree of probability of risk to health to warrant the granting of the remedy sought, a *quia timet* [based on fear of harm] injunction.[59]

Environmentalists were especially disappointed and discouraged because the plaintiffs were also required to meet court costs.[60]

Former employees of the New Brunswick Electric Power Commission who sprayed defoliants under power lines in the 1950s and 1960s have joined in court action against the company. They claim that supervisors did not inform them of the hazards of herbicides. Of some two hundred men who did this spraying, it is reported that sixty-six have died and many are suffering from health problems. Their case is pending.[61]

These facts and circumstances show how different organizations interact with government in the political process. A somewhat simplified but, we hope, not wholly unrealistic version of liberal democratic theory suggests that the state should stand as an autonomous force in society. It should be an independent arbiter, responsible for reconciling disputes between conflicting interests within a plural society. Governments, which exercise the power of the state, should ensure that all individuals and groups have an opportunity to voice their position in the political process. After all the arguments are heard, governments should make public decisions in response to public desires, recognizing that in a plural society, citizens are unlikely to be unanimous in what they want. Thus the freedom to argue a case and marshal support for a cause is one of the cornerstones of liberal democratic politics.

In the Maritimes provincial governments were required to make a decision. Natural resources, forests in New Brunswick and Nova Scotia, were threatened by an insect. Superficially, this might seem to be a simple issue. The administrative departments in each province, the Department of National Resources in New Brunswick and the Department of Lands and Forests in Nova Scotia, would license spraying in order to protect the trees that were vital to their economies. Provincial government responsibility, however, also includes protecting the environment. Thus individuals and groups who felt threatened by spraying could oppose it with arguments based on environmental protection. They claimed sprays posed a hazard to the health of anyone caught in the fallout and that sprays destroyed wildlife. Their arguments included evidence gathered in other provinces, the United States, and some European nations. They tried to convince the government of each province to delay spraying until definitive information was available on the safety of spraying.

Thus, as so often is the case, the Cabinets in both provinces were caught between two forces on a controversial issue. On the one side, environmentalists mobilized citizen groups on their behalf, using the media when possible to rally support. Some of the electronic and print media responded, often focussing their coverage on the potential health problems. The claim in New Brunswick, however, has been that the environmentalists' lack of access to the media gave the industry and government bureaucracies an unfair advantage in making their decision. Groups that took an environmental position felt they were unable to combat the powerful resources available to the industry and the state bureaucracy. Thus they were stifled in taking their case to the people of New Brunswick.

On the other hand, the administrative departments concerned, the industry, and some labour unions pressed for spraying to save the resource. Their arguments were essentially economic: that wood products were the largest component of the industrial base in the provinces and that if the budworm was allowed to run its course, continued defoliation would have an adverse effect. Jobs were at stake in a region of Canada that could ill afford increased unemployment. Moreover, government health departments countered environmentalists' arguments, suggesting that the effects of spraying on health were exaggerated.

With regard to pesticide spraying, the two Cabinets initially took different positions. In 1952 New Brunswick began to spray and has maintained a continuous program using a variety of sprays to combat the budworm. Nova Scotia chose to refrain from spraying until 1981, when it finally did undertake a limited program. In both cases, economic arguments ultimately prevailed.

Two additional features of the process in this case should be noted. Political parties, or at least the grass-roots membership of the political parties, did not play a key role. Interest groups, at times using the media, were the prime force pressing the governments from the environmental side. Thus political parties, as institutions representing citizens' interests, were circumvented by the interest groups. This pattern of political activity is not uncommon in the parliamentary process. Under such a system, the powerful parliamentary leadership of a party can dominate the party's position in the legislative process and influence the role any constituency organizations may try to play. Thus while the grass-roots party organizations may be effective at elections, between elections they are largely inactive as conveyors of popular opinion. In this case also, opposition parties were not always eager to take up a cause that had such economic implications.

A second interesting feature was the role of the courts. As groups or the government seek a legal clarification of the issue, courts can be drawn into the process. This is precisely what one citizens' group attempted to do. It sought an injunction against the granting of licences by administrative departments to spray Crown or private land, arguing that governments should disallow spraying until specific consequences could be established. The Nova Scotia Supreme Court took the position that the groups should prove damages. But the evidence on the effects of spraying was inconclusive, and the judge did not order to halt the spraying.

Accurate factual information did indeed seem to be lacking, especially early in the confrontation. Governments were initially inclined to go ahead and spray without any attempt to allay the fears of the public. Also, in some cases, they were almost secretive about granting permits for spraying and were hesitant to release information on the content of the sprays. This air of secrecy only heightened the fears of those who opposed spraying.

At the same time, environmentalists emphasized health over economic issues when they demanded that spraying be halted. This stance was not well received by individuals who earned their living from the forests, nor did it win many friends in the departments of Natural Resources or Lands and Forests. Thus the tactics employed by forces on both sides of the issue tended to intensify feelings rather than reduce emotion.

Although the details of this controversy are unique, the issue is typical of the political process in modern liberal democracies. A public decision sets up pressures on opposing sides, both motivated by their own interests. The two sides use whatever resources they possess in order to affect the outcome. In this case, the forest industry used its strategic economic position to influence government departments and the political executive. Government officials used their control of information to influence public opinion. Environmentalists, initially the weaker side, had to resort to more difficult tactics of grass-roots organization and media campaigns. When they were unsuccessful in the legislative, executive, and bureaucratic arenas, they turned to the courts. In the end, neither side won or ever can win a clear-cut victory. Balancing environmental concern against economic necessity is not a "problem" with a "solution." Like almost all issues in the political process, it is an enduring dilemma that calls for the art of persuasion and conciliation to produce a "settlement" with which various interests can live. That settlement is itself bound to be only temporary and to become the starting point for a new cycle of conflict. This case study has shown the political process in action—as an endless process of adjustment and decision making in response to changing social interests.

Notes

1. See Ludwig von Bertalanffy, *General System Theory* (New York: George Braziller, 1968).

2. David Easton, *A Systems Analysis of Political Life* (New York: John Wiley & Sons, 1965), p. 32.

3. Gabriel A. Almond and G. Bingham Powell, Jr., *Comparative Politics: A Developmental Approach* (Boston: Little, Brown, 1966), pp. 16–41.

4. Thomas Sowell, *The Economics and Politics of Race* (New York: William Morrow, 1983), pp. 47, 49.

5. For a discussion of political culture and politics, see Gabriel A. Almond and Sidney Verba, *The Civil Culture: Political Attitudes and Democracy in Five Nations* (Boston: Little, Brown, 1963), ch. 1.

6. Almond and Verba, *The Civil Culture*, ch. 1.

7. Almond and Powell, *Comparative Politics*, p. 23.

8. Howard J. Wiarda, "Toward A Framework For the Study of Political Change in the Iberic-Latin Tradition: The Comparative Model," *World Politics* 25, No. 2 (January 1973), pp. 206–235.

9. Gabriel A. Almond, "A Comparative Study of Interest Groups and the Political Process," *The American Political Science Review* 52, No. 1 (March 1958), pp. 270–282.

10. James A. Bill and Robert L. Hardgrave, *Comparative Politics: The Quest for Theory* (Columbus, Oh.: Charles E. Merrill, 1973), ch. 4.

11. Ibid., ch. 3.

12. The *Financial Times of Canada*, January 30–February 5, 1978, p. 1.

13. Joseph LaPalombara, *Politics Within Nations* (Englewood Cliffs, N.J.: Prentice-Hall, 1974), p. 323.

14. Gabriel A. Almond and James S. Coleman, eds., *The Politics of Developing Nations* (Princeton: N.J.: Princeton University Press, 1960), pp. 33–34.

15. Mancur Olson, *The Logic of Collective Action* (Cambridge, Mass.: Harvard University Press, 1965).

16. David B. Truman, *The Governmental Process* (New York: Alfred A. Knopf, 1951).

17. Mancur Olson, *The Rise and Decline of Nations: Economic Growth, Stagflation, and Social Rigidities* (New Haven, Conn.: Yale University Press, 1982).

18. Jean-Jacques Rousseau, *The Social Contract* (New York: Hafner, 1947), pp. 26–27.

19. Alexander Hamilton, John Jay, and James Madison, *The Federalist* (New York: Modern Library, n.d.), p. 54.

20. E. E. Schattschneider, *The Struggle for Party Government* (College Park: University of Maryland, 1948).

21. Joseph LaPalombara, *Politics Within Nations*, p. 509.

22. *Webster's New Collegiate Dictionary*, 8th ed., s.v. *pragmatism*.

23. Keith Archer, "The Failure of the New Democratic Party—Unions, Unionists, and Politics in Canada," *Canadian Journal of Political Science* 18 (1985), pp. 362–363.

24. One might even call Canada a "one-party-plus" system. The Conservatives have been in power for only twenty-eight of the ninety years between 1896 and 1986.

25. Herbert J. Gans, *Deciding What's News* (New York: Pantheon Books, 1979), p. 88.

26. Victor Lasky, *It Didn't Start with Watergate* (New York: Dell, 1977).

27. Rosemary Righter, *Whose News? Politics, the Press and the Third World* (London: Burnett Books, 1978), p. 190.

28. John Plamenatz, "Electoral Studies and Democratic Theory," *Political Studies* 6 (February 1958), p. 9.

29. The term gerrymander, meaning to draw constituency lines so as to achieve a deliberate result, comes from the name of Elbridge Gerry, governor of Massachusetts in 1812, who tried to favour his party at the time of redistricting.

30. John Stuart Mill, *Considerations on Representative Government* (Chicago: Henry Regnery, 1962), p. 141.

31. Much of this material on electoral systems is taken from J. S. Corry and Henry J. Abraham, *Elements of Democratic Government*, 4th ed. (New York: Oxford University Press, 1964), ch. 11; and John C. Wahlke and Alex N. Dragnich, eds., *Government and Politics*, 2nd ed. (New York: Random House, 1971), pp. 540–573.

32. For the debate see William P. Irvine, *Does Canada Need a New Electoral System?* (Kingston: Queen's University Institute of Intergovernmental Relations, 1979); and John C. Courtney, "Reflections on Reforming the Canadian Electoral System," *Canadian Public Administration* 23 (1980), pp. 427–457.

33. Seminal works in the Canadian debate are Alan C. Cairns, "The Electoral System and the Party System in Canada, 1921–65," *Canadian Journal of Political Science* 1 (March 1968), pp. 55–80; and J. A. A. Lovink, "On Analysing the Impact of the Electoral System on the Party System in Canada," ibid. 3 (December 1970), pp. 497–516.

34. See in general Hanna Pitkin, *The Concept of Representation* (Berkeley: University of California Press, 1967); and A. H. Birch, *Representation* (London: Macmillan, 1971).

35. *Burke's Speeches and Letters on American Affairs* (London: E. P. Dutton, 1980), p. 73.

36. John Adams, "Thoughts on Government," in *The Political Writings of John Adams* (Indianapolis: Bobbs-Merrill, 1954), p. 86.

37. R. MacGregor Dawson, *The Government of Canada*, 4th ed. (Toronto: University of Toronto Press, 1963), p. 185.

38. Government of Canada, Minister of Supply and Services, Ottawa.

39. W. L. White, R. H. Wagenberg, and R. C. Nelson, *Introduction to Canadian Politics and Government*, 3rd ed. (Toronto: Holt, Rinehart and Winston, 1981), pp. 143–144.

40. Colin Leys, *Politics in Britain* (Toronto: University of Toronto Press, 1983), p. 269.

41. William A. Niskanen, Jr., *Bureaucracy and Representative Government* (Chicago: Aldine-Atherton, 1971), pp. 36–42.

42. *Edwards et al. v. Attorney General of Canada et al.,* [1930] A. C. 124.

43. [1979] 2 S.C.R. 1032.

44. M. Elizabeth Atcheson, Mary Eberts, and Beth Symes, *Women and Legal Action: Precedents, Resources and Strategies for the Future* (Ottawa: Canadian Advisory Council on the Status of Women, 1984), p. 168.

45. Ibid., pp. 166–167.

46. Originally, the Bill of Rights applied only to the federal Congress, but the Supreme Court has held that it was extended by the Fourteenth Amendment to the state legislatures.

47. See, for example, Theodore J. Lowi, *The End of Liberalism*, 2nd ed. (New York: W. W. Norton, 1979), ch. 11.

48. *Queen v. Paul Mathew Therens*, May 23, 1985, [1985] S.C.C.D. 5568-01.

49. F. L. Morton, "Charting the Charter—Year One: A Statistical Analysis," *Canadian Human Rights Yearbook* 1984–1985, pp. 237–261.

50. Statistics Canada, Catalogue 61-202, pp. 25, 27, 28.

51. The *Halifax Chronicle-Herald*, March 13, 1985, p. 7.

52. Government of New Brunswick, Department of Natural Resources, "Forest Management: Prevention-Protection," n.d., p. 2.

53. Province of New Brunswick, *Journal of Debates* (*Hansard*), Second Session, Forty-Ninth Legislative Assembly, 1980, p. 159.

54. A good account of the activities of citizen groups is found in Elizabeth May, *Budworm Battles: The Fight to Stop the Aerial Insecticide Spraying of the Forests of Eastern Canada* (Tantallon, N.S.: Four East Publications, 1982).

55. The *Globe and Mail*, June 3, 1978, p. 10.

56. Most major news outlets have reported extensively on the spraying issue. A few examples are the *Globe and Mail*, June 3, 1978, p. 10; *Science Forum* 11, No. 4, Nov.-Dec. 1978, pp. 20–23; the *Calgary Herald*, January 30, 1982, p. D27; the *Financial Post*, May 8, 1983, p. 7; and *Maclean's*, June 25, 1984, p. 48.

57. The two governments' positions are made very clear in the annual department reports: Government of New Brunswick, Department of Natural Resources, *Annual Report*, 1981–1982; and Government of Nova Scotia, Department of Lands and Forests, *Annual Report*, 1982.

58. Government of Nova Scotia, Department of Lands and Forests, *Annual Report*, pp. 33–34.

59. *Palmer et al. v. Stora Kopparbergs Bergslags Aktiebolag, carrying on business as Nova Scotia Forest Industries*, [1983] 12 C.E.L.R 157 [N.S. S.C. (T.D.)], pp. 236–237.

60. The decision was ironic because within a month of the judgment, the United States Environmental Protection Agency withdrew Dow Chemical's licence to manufacture the herbicide. Dow, the Canadian supplier, said it would no longer produce the compound. Thus the product became unavailable for Canadian users.

61. *Maclean's*, June 25, 1984, p. 48.

Vocabulary

political process
political system
structure
function
informal
formal-legal
political culture
political socialization
interest (pressure) group
anomic group
associational group
institutional group
non-associational (latent) group
lobbying
faction
political party
aggregation of demands
pragmatic party
ideological party
interest party
personal party
movement party
single-party system
one-party-dominant system
two-party system
two-party-plus system

representation
trustee
delegate
party member
microcosm
political executive
prime minister
ministry
Cabinet
Priorities and Planning Committee
Prime Minister's Office
Privy Council Office
Treasury Board
Privy Council
central agency
responsible government
portfolio
ministerial responsibility
bureaucracy (administration)
tenure
merit recruitment
patronage
Crown corporation
deputy minister
auditor general
ombudsman

multi-party system
Cabinet instability
communications (mass) media
first-past-the-post system
gerrymander
run-off system
preferential (alternative) ballot
proportional representation
list system
quota system
legislature

appellate
provincial courts
superior courts
Judicial Committee of the
    Privy Council
judicial review
ultra vires
judicial activism

Appendix

Constitution Act, 1982

Schedule B to Canada Act 1982 (U.K.)

PART I

CANADIAN CHARTER OF RIGHTS AND FREEDOMS

Whereas Canada is founded upon principles that recognize the supremacy of God and the rule of law:

Guarantee of Rights and Freedoms

Rights and freedoms in Canada

1. The *Canadian Charter of Rights and Freedoms* guarantees the rights and freedoms set out in it subject only to such reasonable limits prescribed by law as can be demonstrably justified in a free and democratic society.

Fundamental Freedoms

Fundamental freedoms

2. Everyone has the following fundamental freedoms:
(*a*) freedom of conscience and religion;
(*b*) freedom of thought, belief, opinion and expression, including freedom of the press and other media of communication;
(*c*) freedom of peaceful assembly; and
(*d*) freedom of association.

Democratic Rights

Democratic rights of citizens

3. Every citizen of Canada has the right to vote in an election of members of the House of Commons or of a legislative assembly and to be qualified for membership therein.

Maximum duration of legislative bodies

4. (1) No House of Commons and no legislative assembly shall continue for longer than five years from the date fixed for the return of the writs at a general election of its members.

Continuation in special circumstances

(2) In time of real or apprehended war, invasion or insurrection, a House of Commons may be continued by Parliament and a legislative assembly may be continued by the legislature beyond five years if such continuation is not opposed by the votes of more than one-third of the members of the House of Commons or the legislative assembly, as the case may be.

Annual sitting of legislative bodies

5. There shall be a sitting of Parliament and of each legislature at least once every twelve months.

Mobility Rights

Mobility of citizens

6. (1) Every citizen of Canada has the right to enter, remain in and leave Canada.

Rights to move and gain livelihood

(2) Every citizen of Canada and every person who has the status of a permanent resident of Canada has the right
(*a*) to move to and take up residence in any province; and
(*b*) to pursue the gaining of a livelihood in any province.

Limitation

(3) The rights specified in subsection (2) are subject to
(*a*) any laws or practices of general application in force in a province other than those that discriminate among persons primarily on the basis of province of present or previous residence; and
(*b*) any laws providing for reasonable residency requirements as a qualification for the receipt of publicly provided social services.

Affirmative action programs

(4) Subsections (2) and (3) do not preclude any law, program or activity that has as its object the amelioration in a province of conditions of individuals in that province who are socially or economically disadvantaged if the rate of employment in that province is below the rate of employment in Canada.

Legal Rights

Life, liberty and security of person

7. Everyone has the right to life, liberty and security of the person and the right not to be deprived thereof except in accordance with the principles of fundamental justice.

Search or seizure

8. Everyone has the right to be secure against unreasonable search or seizure.

Detention or imprisonment

9. Everyone has the right not to be arbitrarily detained or imprisoned.

Arrest or detention

10. Everyone has the right on arrest or detention
(*a*) to be informed promptly of the reasons therefor;
(*b*) to retain and instruct counsel without delay and to be informed of that right; and
(*c*) to have the validity of the detention determined by way of *habeas corpus* and to be released if the detention is not lawful.

Proceedings in criminal and penal matters

11. Any person charged with an offence has the right
(*a*) to be informed without unreasonable delay of the specific offence;
(*b*) to be tried within a reasonable time;
(*c*) not to be compelled to be a witness in proceedings against that person in respect of the offence;
(*d*) to be presumed innocent until proven guilty according to law in a fair and public hearing by an independent and impartial tribunal;

(*e*) not to be denied reasonable bail without just cause;

(*f*) except in the case of an offence under military law tried before a military tribunal, to the benefit of trial by jury where the maximum punishment for the offence is imprisonment for five years or a more severe punishment;

(*g*) not to be found guilty on account of any act or omission unless, at the time of the act or omission, it constituted an offence under Canadian or international law or was criminal according to the general principles of law recognized by the community of nations;

(*h*) if finally acquitted of the offence, not to be tried for it again and, if finally found guilty and punished for the offence, not to be tried or punished for it again; and

(*i*) if found guilty of the offence and if the punishment for the offence has been varied between the time of commission and the time of sentencing, to the benefit of the lesser punishment.

Treatment or punishment

12. Everyone has the right not to be subjected to any cruel and unusual treatment or punishment.

Self-crimination

13. A witness who testifies in any proceedings has the right not to have any incriminating evidence so given used to incriminate that witness in any other proceedings, except in a prosecution for perjury or for the giving of contradictory evidence.

Interpreter

14. A party or witness in any proceedings who does not understand or speak the language in which the proceedings are conducted or who is deaf has the right to the assistance of an interpreter.

Equality Rights

Equality before and under law and equal protection and benefit of law

15. (1) Every individual is equal before and under the law and has the right to the equal protection and equal benefit of the law without discrimination and, in particular, without discrimination based on race, national or ethnic origin, colour, religion, sex, age or mental or physical disability.

Affirmative action programs

(2) Subsection (1) does not preclude any law, program or activity that has as its object the amelioration of conditions of disadvantaged individuals or groups including those that are disadvantaged because of race, national or ethnic origin, colour, religion, sex, age or mental or physical disability.

Official Languages of Canada

Official languages of Canada

16. (1) English and French are the official languages of Canada and have equality of status and equal rights and privileges as to their use in all institutions of the Parliament and government of Canada.

Official languages of New Brunswick

(2) English and French are the official languages of New Brunswick and have equality of status and equal rights and privileges as to their use in all institutions of the legislature and government of New Brunswick.

Advancement of
status and use

(3) Nothing in this Charter limits the authority of Parliament or a legislature to advance the equality of status or use of English and French.

Proceedings of
Parliament

17. (1) Everyone has the right to use English or French in any debates and other proceedings of Parliament.

Proceedings of New
Brunswick legislature

(2) Everyone has the right to use English or French in any debates and other proceedings of the legislature of New Brunswick.

Parliamentary statutes
and records

18. (1) The statutes, records and journals of Parliament shall be printed and published in English and French and both language versions are equally authoritative.

New Brunswick
statutes and records

(2) The statutes, records and journals of the legislature of New Brunswick shall be printed and published in English and French and both language versions are equally authoritative.

Proceedings in courts
established by
Parliament

19. (1) Either English or French may be used by any person in, or in any pleading in or process issuing from, any court established by Parliament.

Proceedings in New
Brunswick courts

(2) Either English or French may be used by any person in, or in any pleading in or process issuing from, any court of New Brunswick.

Communications by
public with federal
institutions

20. (1) Any member of the public in Canada has the right to communicate with, and to receive available services from, any head or central office of an institution of the Parliament or government of Canada in English or French, and has the same right with respect to any other office of any such institution where

(*a*) there is a significant demand for communications with and services from that office in such language; or

(*b*) due to the nature of the office, it is reasonable that communications with and services from that office be available in both English and French.

Communications by
public with New
Brunswick institutions

(2) Any member of the public in New Brunswick has the right to communicate with, and to receive available services from, any office of an institution of the legislature or government of New Brunswick in English or French.

Continuation of
existing constitutional
provisions

21. Nothing in sections 16 to 20 abrogates or derogates from any right, privilege or obligation with respect to the English and French languages, or either of them, that exists or is continued by virtue of any other provision of the Constitution of Canada.

Rights and privileges
preserved

22. Nothing in sections 16 to 20 abrogates or derogates from any legal or customary right or privilege acquired or enjoyed either before or after the coming into force of this Charter with respect to any language that is not English or French.

Minority Language Educational Rights

Language of instruction

23. (1) Citizens of Canada

(*a*) whose first language learned and still understood is that of the English or French linguistic minority population of the province in which they reside, or

(*b*) who have received their primary school instruction in Canada in English or French and reside in a province where the language in which they received that instruction is the language of the English or French linguistic minority population of the province,

have the right to have their children receive primary and secondary school instruction in that language in that province.

Continuity of language instruction

(2) Citizens of Canada of whom any child has received or is receiving primary or secondary school instruction in English or French in Canada, have the right to have all their children receive primary and secondary school instruction in the same language.

Application where numbers warrant

(3) The right of citizens of Canada under subsections (1) and (2) to have their children receive primary and secondary school instruction in the language of the English or French linguistic minority population of a province

(*a*) applies wherever in the province the number of children of citizens who have such a right is sufficient to warrant the provision to them out of public funds of minority language instruction; and

(*b*) includes, where the number of those children so warrants, the right to have them receive that instruction in minority language educational facilities provided out of public funds.

Enforcement

Enforcement of guaranteed rights and freedoms

24. (1) Anyone whose rights or freedoms, as guaranteed by this Charter, have been infringed or denied may apply to a court of competent jurisdiction to obtain such remedy as the court considers appropriate and just in the circumstances.

Exclusion of evidence bringing administration of justice into disrepute

(2) Where, in proceedings under subsection (1), a court concludes that evidence was obtained in a manner that infringed or denied any rights or freedoms guaranteed by this Charter, the evidence shall be excluded if it is established that, having regard to all the circumstances, the admission of it in the proceedings would bring the administration of justice into disrepute.

General

Aboriginal rights and freedoms not affected by Charter

25. The guarantee in this Charter of certain rights and freedoms shall not be construed so as to abrogate or derogate from any aboriginal, treaty or other rights or freedoms that pertain to the aboriginal peoples of Canada including (*a*) any rights or freedoms that have been recognized by the Royal Proclamation of October 7, 1763; and

(*b*) any rights or freedoms that now exist by way of land claims agreements or may be so acquired.[1]

Other rights and freedoms not affected by Charter

26. The guarantee in this Charter of certain rights and freedoms shall not be construed as denying the existence of any other rights or freedoms that exist in Canada.

Multicultural heritage

27. This Charter shall be interpreted in a manner consistent with the preservation and enhancement of the multicultural heritage of Canadians.

Rights guaranteed equally to both sexes

28. Notwithstanding anything in this Charter, the rights and freedoms referred to in it are guaranteed equally to male and female persons.

Rights respecting certain schools preserved

29. Nothing in this Charter abrogates or derogates from any rights or privileges guaranteed by or under the Constitution of Canada in respect of denominational, separate or dissentient schools.

Application to territories and territorial authorities

30. A reference in this Charter to a province or to the legislative assembly or legislature of a province shall be deemed to include a reference to the Yukon Territory and the Northwest Territories, or to the appropriate legislative authority thereof, as the case may be.

Legislative powers not extended

31. Nothing in this Charter extends the legislative powers of any body or authority.

Application of Charter

Application of Charter

32. (1) This Charter applies

(*a*) to the Parliament and government of Canada in respect of all matters within the authority of Parliament including all matters relating to the Yukon Territory and Northwest Territories; and

(*b*) to the legislature and government of each province in respect of all matters within the authority of the legislature of each province.

Exception

(2) Notwithstanding subsection (1), section 15 shall not have effect until three years after this section comes into force.

Exception where express declaration

33. (1) Parliament or the legislature of a province may expressly declare in an Act of Parliament or of the legislature, as the case may be, that the Act or a provision thereof shall operate notwithstanding a provision included in section 2 or sections 7 to 15 of this Charter.

Operation of exception

(2) An Act or a provision of an Act in respect of which a declaration made under this section is in effect shall have such operation as it would have but for the provision of this Charter referred to in the declaration.

---

[1]Paragraph 25(b) was repealed and the present paragraph 25(b) was substituted by the Constitution Amendment Proclamation, 1983.

Five year limitation

(3) A declaration made under subsection (1) shall cease to have effect five years after it comes into force or on such earlier date as may be specified in the declaration.

Re-enactment

(4) Parliament or the legislature of a province may re-enact a declaration made under subsection (1).

Five year limitation

(5) Subsection (3) applies in respect of a re-enactment made under subsection (4).

Citation

Citation

34. This Part may be cited as the *Canadian Charter of Rights and Freedoms*.

PART II

RIGHTS OF THE ABORIGINAL PEOPLES OF CANADA

Recognition of existing aboriginal and treaty rights

35. (1) The existing aboriginal and treaty rights of the aboriginal peoples of Canada are hereby recognized and affirmed.

Definition of "aboriginal peoples of Canada"

(2) In this Act, "aboriginal peoples of Canada" includes the Indian, Inuit and Métis peoples of Canada.

Land claims agreements

(3) For greater certainty, in subsection (1) "treaty rights" includes rights that now exist by way of land claims agreements or may be so acquired.

Aboriginal and treaty rights are guaranteed equally to both sexes

(4) Notwithstanding any other provision of this Act, the aboriginal and treaty rights referred to in subsection (1) are guaranteed equally to male and female persons.[2]

Commitment to participation in constitutional conference

35.1 The government of Canada and the provincial governments are committed to the principle that, before any amendment is made to Class 24 of section 91 of the *"Constitution Act, 1867"*, to section 25 of this Act or to this Part,

(*a*) a constitutional conference that includes in its agenda an item relating to the proposed amendment, composed of the Prime Minister of Canada and the first ministers of the provinces, will be convened by the Prime Minister of Canada; and

---

[2]Subsections (3) and (4) of s. 35 were added by the Constitution Amendment Proclamation, 1983.

(*b*) the Prime Minister of Canada will invite representatives of the aboriginal peoples of Canada to participate in the discussions on that item.[3]

PART III

EQUALIZATION AND REGIONAL DISPARITIES

Commitment to promote equal opportunities

36. (1) Without altering the legislative authority of Parliament or of the provincial legislatures, or the rights of any of them with respect to the exercise of their legislative authority, Parliament and the legislatures, together with the government of Canada and the provincial governments, are committed to

(*a*) promoting equal opportunities for the well-being of Canadians;

(*b*) furthering economic development to reduce disparity in opportunities; and

(*c*) providing essential public services of reasonable quality to all Canadians.

Commitment respecting public services

(2) Parliament and the government of Canada are committed to the principle of making equalization payments to ensure that provincial governments have sufficient revenues to provide reasonably comparable levels of public services at reasonably comparable levels of taxation.

PART IV

CONSTITUTIONAL CONFERENCE

Constitutional conference

37. (1) A constitutional conference composed of the Prime Minister of Canada and the first ministers of the provinces shall be convened by the Prime Minister of Canada within one year after this Part comes into force.

Participation of aboriginal peoples

(2) The conference convened under subsection (1) shall have included in its agenda an item respecting constitutional matters that directly affect the aboriginal peoples of Canada, including the identification and definition of the rights of those peoples to be included in the Constitution of Canada, and the Prime Minister of Canada shall invite representatives of those peoples to participate in the discussions on that item.

Participation of territories

(3) The Prime Minister of Canada shall invite elected representatives of the governments of the Yukon Territory and the Northwest Territories to participate in the discussions on any item on the agenda of the conference convened under subsection (1) that, in the opinion of the Prime Minister, directly affects the Yukon Territory and the Northwest Territories.

---

[3]Section 35.1 was added by the Constitution Amendment Proclamation, 1983.

PART IV.1

CONSTITUTIONAL CONFERENCES

Constitutional conferences

37.1 (1) In addition to the conference convened in March 1983, at least two constitutional conferences composed of the Prime Minister of Canada and the first ministers of the provinces shall be convened by the Prime Minister of Canada, the first within three years after April 17, 1982 and the second within five years after that date.

Participation of aboriginal peoples

(2) Each conference convened under subsection (1) shall have included in its agenda constitutional matters that directly affect the aboriginal peoples of Canada, and the Prime Minister of Canada shall invite representatives of those peoples to participate in the discussions on those matters.

Participation of territories

(3) The Prime Minister of Canada shall invite elected representatives of the governments of the Yukon Territory and the Northwest Territories to participate in the discussions on any item on the agenda of a conference convened under subsection (1) that, in the opinion of the Prime Minister, directly affects the Yukon Territory and the Northwest Territories.

Subsection 35(1) not affected

(4) Nothing in this section shall be construed so as to derogate from subsection 35(1).[4]

PART V

PROCEDURE FOR AMENDING CONSTITUTION OF CANADA

General procedure for amending Constitution of Canada

38. (1) An amendment to the Constitution of Canada may be made by proclamation issued by the Governor General under the Great Seal of Canada where so authorized by
(*a*) resolutions of the Senate and House of Commons; and
(*b*) resolutions of the legislative assemblies of at least two-thirds of the provinces that have, in the aggregate, according to the then latest general census, at least fifty per cent of the population of all the provinces.

Majority of members

(2) An amendment made under subsection (1) that derogates from the legislative powers, the proprietary rights or any other rights or privileges of the legislature or government of a province shall require a resolution supported by a majority of the members of each of the Senate, the House of Commons and the legislative assemblies required under subsection (1).

Expression of dissent

(3) An amendment referred to in subsection (2) shall not have effect in a province the legislative assembly of which has expressed its dissent

---

[4]Part IV.1, consisting of s. 37.1, was added by the Constitution Amendment Proclamation, 1983.

thereto by resolution supported by a majority of its members prior to the issue of the proclamation to which the amendment relates unless that legislative assembly, subsequently, by resolution supported by a majority of its members, revokes its dissent and authorizes the amendment.

Revocation of dissent   (4) A resolution of dissent made for the purposes of subsection (3) may be revoked at any time before or after the issue of the proclamation to which it relates.

Restriction on proclamation   **39.** (1) A proclamation shall not be issued under subsection 38(1) before the expiration of one year from the adoption of the resolution initiating the amendment procedure thereunder, unless the legislative assembly of each province has previously adopted a resolution of assent or dissent.

Idem   (2) A proclamation shall not be issued under subsection 38(1) after the expiration of three years from the adoption of the resolution initiating the amendment procedure thereunder.

Compensation   **40.** Where an amendment is made under subsection 38(1) that transfers provincial legislative powers relating to education or other cultural matters from provincial legislatures to Parliament, Canada shall provide reasonable compensation to any province to which the amendment does not apply.

Amendment by unanimous consent   **41.** An amendment to the Constitution of Canada in relation to the following matters may be made by proclamation issued by the Governor General under the Great Seal of Canada only where authorized by resolutions of the Senate and House of Commons and of the legislative assembly of each province:

(*a*) the office of the Queen, the Governor General and the Lieutenant Governor of a province;

(*b*) the right of a province to a number of members in the House of Commons not less than the number of Senators by which the province is entitled to be represented at the time this Part comes into force;

(*c*) subject to section 43, the use of the English or the French language;

(*d*) the composition of the Supreme Court of Canada; and

(*e*) an amendment to this Part.

Amendment by general procedure   **42.** (1) An amendment to the Constitution of Canada in relation to the following matters may be made only in accordance with subsection 38(1):

(*a*) the principle of proportionate representation of the provinces in the House of Commons prescribed by the Constitution of Canada;

(*b*) the powers of the Senate and the method of selecting Senators;

(*c*) the number of members by which a province is entitled to be represented in the Senate and the residence qualifications of Senators;

(*d*) subject to paragraph 41(*d*), the Supreme Court of Canada;

(*e*) the extension of existing provinces into the territories; and

(f) notwithstanding any other law or practice, the establishment of new provinces.

Exception

(2) Subsections 38(2) to (4) do not apply in respect of amendments in relation to matters referred to in subsection (1).

Amendment of provisions relating to some but not all provinces

43. An amendment to the Constitution of Canada in relation to any provision that applies to one or more, but not all, provinces, including

(a) any alteration to boundaries between provinces, and

(b) any amendment to any provision that relates to the use of the English or the French language within a province, may be made by proclamation issued by the Governor General under the Great Seal of Canada only where so authorized by resolutions of the Senate and House of Commons and of the legislative assembly of each province to which the amendment applies.

Amendments by Parliament

44. Subject to sections 41 and 42, Parliament may exclusively make laws amending the Constitution of Canada in relation to the executive government of Canada or the Senate and House of Commons.

Amendments by provincial legislatures

45. Subject to section 41, the legislature of each province may exclusively make laws amending the constitution of the province.

Initiation of amendment procedures

46. (1) The procedures for amendment under sections 38, 41, 42 and 43 may be initiated either by the Senate or the House of Commons or by the legislative assembly of a province.

Revocation of authorization

(2) A resolution of assent made for the purposes of this Part may be revoked at any time before the issue of a proclamation authorized by it.

Amendments without Senate resolution

47. (1) An amendment to the Constitution of Canada made by proclamation under section 38, 41, 42 or 43 may be made without a resolution of the Senate authorizing the issue of the proclamation if, within one hundred and eighty days after the adoption by the House of Commons of a resolution authorizing its issue, the Senate has not adopted such a resolution and if, at any time after the expiration of that period, the House of Commons again adopts the resolution.

Computation of period

(2) Any period when Parliament is prorogued or dissolved shall not be counted in computing the one hundred and eighty day period referred to in subsection (1).

Advice to issue proclamation

48. The Queen's Privy Council for Canada shall advise the Governor General to issue a proclamation under this Part forthwith on the adoption of the resolutions required for an amendment made by proclamation under this Part.

Constitutional conference

49. A constitutional conference composed of the Prime Minister of Canada and the first ministers of the provinces shall be convened by the Prime Minister of Canada within fifteen years after this Part comes into force to review the provisions of this Part.

PART VI

AMENDMENT TO THE CONSTITUTION ACT, 1867

Amendment to
Constitution Act,
1867

50. *The Constitution Act, 1867* (formerly named the *British North America Act, 1867)* is amended by adding thereto, immediately after section 92 thereof, the following heading and section:

"Non-Renewable Natural Resources, Forestry Resources and Electrical Energy

Laws respecting non-renewable natural resources, forestry resources and electrical energy

92A. (1) In each province, the legislature may exclusively make laws in relation to

(a) exploration for non-renewable natural resources in the province;

(b) development, conservation and management of non-renewable natural resources and forestry resources in the province, including laws in relation to the rate of primary production therefrom; and

(c) development, conservation and management of sites and facilities in the province for the generation and production of electrical energy.

Export from provinces of resources

(2) In each province, the legislature may make laws in relation to the export from the province to another part of Canada of the primary production from non-renewable natural resources and forestry resources in the province and the production from facilities in the province for the generation of electrical energy, but such laws may not authorize or provide for discrimination in prices or in supplies exported to another part of Canada.

Authority of Parliament

(3) Nothing in subsection (2) derogates from the authority of Parliament to enact laws in relation to the matters referred to in that subsection and, where such a law of Parliament and a law of a province conflict, the law of Parliament prevails to the extent of the conflict.

Taxation of resources

(4) In each province, the legislature may make laws in relation to the raising of money by any mode or system of taxation in respect of

(a) non-renewable natural resources and forestry resources in the province and the primary production therefrom, and

(b) sites and facilities in the province for the generation of electrical energy and the production therefrom,

whether or not production is exported in whole or in part from the province, but such laws may not authorize or provide for taxation that differentiates between production exported to another part of Canada and production not exported from the province.

"Primary production"

(5) The expression "primary production" has the meaning assigned by the Sixth Schedule.

Existing powers or rights

(6) Nothing in subsections (1) to (5) derogates from any powers or rights that a legislature or government of a province had immediately before the coming into force of this section."

Idem

51. The said Act is further amended by adding thereto the following Schedule:

"THE SIXTH SCHEDULE
Primary Production from Non-Renewable
Natural Resources and Forestry Resources

1. For the purposes of section 92A of this Act,

(a) production from a non-renewable natural resource is primary production therefrom if

(i) it is in the form in which it exists upon its recovery or severance from its natural state, or

(ii) it is a product resulting from processing or refining the resource, and is not a manufactured product or a product resulting from refining crude oil, refining upgraded heavy crude oil, refining gases or liquids derived from coal or refining a synthetic equivalent of crude oil; and

(b) production from a forestry resource is primary production therefrom if it consists of sawlogs, poles, lumber, wood chips, sawdust or any other primary wood product, or wood pulp, and is not a product manufactured from wood."

PART VII
GENERAL

Primacy of
Constitution of
Canada

52. (1) The Constitution of Canada is the supreme law of Canada, and any law that is inconsistent with the provisions of the Constitution is, to the extent of the inconsistency, of no force or effect.

Constitution of
Canada

(2) The Constitution of Canada includes

(*a*) The *Canada Act 1982*, including this Act;

(*b*) the Acts and orders referred to in the schedule; and

(*c*) any amendment to any Act or order referred to in paragraph (*a*) or (*b*).

Amendments to
Constitution of
Canada

(3) Amendments to the Constitution of Canada shall be made only in accordance with the authority contained in the Constitution of Canada.

Repeals and new
names

53. (1) The enactments referred to in Column I of the schedule are hereby repealed or amended to the extent indicated in Column II thereof and, unless repealed, shall continue as law in Canada under the names set out in Column III thereof.

Consequential
amendments

(2) Every enactment, except the *Canada Act 1982*, that refers to an enactment referred to in the schedule by the name in Column I thereof is hereby amended by substituting for that name the corresponding name in Column III thereof, and any British North America Act not referred to in the schedule may be cited as the *Constitution Act* followed by the year and number, if any, of its enactment.

Repeal and
consequential
amendments

54. Part IV is repealed on the day that is one year after this Part comes into force and this section may be repealed and this Act renumbered, consequentially upon the repeal of Part IV and this section, by proclamation issued by the Governor General under the Great Seal of Canada.

Repeal of Part IV.1
and this section

54.1 Part IV.1 and this section are repealed on April 18, 1987.[5]

French version of
Constitution of
Canada

55. A French version of the portions of the Constitution of Canada referred to in the schedule shall be prepared by the Minister of Justice of Canada as expeditiously as possible and, when any portion thereof sufficient to warrant action being taken has been so prepared, it shall be put forward for enactment by proclamation issued by the Governor General under the Great Seal of Canada pursuant to the procedure then applicable to an amendment of the same provisions of the Constitution of Canada.

English and French
versions of certain
constitutional texts

56. Where any portion of the Constitution of Canada has been or is enacted in English and French or where a French version of any portion of the Constitution is enacted pursuant to section 55, the English and French versions of that portion of the Constitution are equally authoritative.

English and
French versions of
this Act

57. The English and French versions of this Act are equally authoritative.

Commencement

58. Subject to section 59, this Act shall come into force on a day to be fixed by proclamation issued by the Queen or the Governor General under the Great Seal of Canada.

Commencement
of paragraph 23(1)(*a*)
in respect of Quebec

59. (1) Paragraph 23(1)(*a*) shall come into force in respect of Quebec on a day to be fixed by proclamation issued by the Queen or the Governor General under the Great Seal of Canada.

Authorization of
Quebec

(2) A proclamation under subsection (1) shall be issued only where authorized by the legislative assembly or government of Quebec.

Repeal of this section

(3) This section may be repealed on the day paragraph 23(1)(*a*) comes into force in respect of Quebec and this Act amended and renumbered, consequentially upon the repeal of this section, by proclamation issued by the Queen or the Governor General under the Great Seal of Canada.

Short title and
citations

60. This Act may be cited as the *Constitution Act, 1982,* and the Constitution Acts 1867 to 1975 (No. 2) and this Act may be cited together as the *Constitution Acts, 1867 to 1982.*

References

61. A reference to the "*Constitution Acts, 1867 to 1982*" shall be deemed to include a reference to the "*Constitution Amendment Proclamation, 1983*".[6]

---

[5]Section 54.1 was added by the Constitution Amendment Proclamation, 1983.

[6]Section 61 was added by the Constitution Amendment Proclamation, 1983.

SCHEDULE

to the

Constitution Act, 1982

Modernization of the Constitution

Item	Column I Act Affected	Column II Amendment	Column III New Name
1.	British North America Act, 1867, 30–31 Vict., c. 3 (U.K.)	(1) Section 1 is repealed and the following substituted therefor: "1. This Act may be cited as the *Constitution Act, 1867*." (2) Section 20 is repealed. (3) Class 1 of section 91 is repealed. (4) Class 1 of section 92 is repealed.	Constitution Act, 1867
2.	An Act to amend and continue the Act 32-33 Victoria chapter 3; and to establish and provide for the Government of the Province of Manitoba, 1870, 33 Vict., c.3 (Can.)	(1) The long title is repealed and the following substituted therefor: "*Manitoba Act, 1870*." (2) Section 20 is repealed.	Manitoba Act, 1870
3.	Order of Her Majesty in Council admitting Rupert's Land and the North-Western Territory into the union, dated the 23rd day of June, 1870		Rupert's Land and North-Western Territory Order
4.	Order of Her Majesty in Council admitting British Columbia into the Union, dated the 16th day of May, 1871		British Columbia Terms of Union
5.	British North America Act, 1871, 34-35 Vict., c. 28 (U.K.)	Section 1 is repealed and the following substituted therefor: "1. This Act may be cited as the *Constitution Act, 1871*."	Constitution Act, 1871

SCHEDULE

to the

Constitution Act, 1982—continued

6. Order of Her Majesty in Council admitting Prince Edward Island into the Union, dated the 26th day of June, 1873		Prince Edward Island Terms of Union
7. Parliament of Canada Act, 1875, 38-39 Vict., c. 38 (U.K.)		Parliament of Canada Act, 1875
8. Order of Her Majesty in Council admitting all British possessions and Territories in North America and islands adjacent thereto into the Union, dated the 31st day of July, 1880		Adjacent Territories Order
9. British North America Act, 1886, 49-50 Vict., c. 35 (U.K.)	Section 3 is repealed and the following substituted therefor: "3. This Act may be cited as the *Constitution Act, 1886.*"	Constitution Act, 1886
10. Canada (Ontario Boundary) Act, 1889, 52-53 Vict., c. 28 (U.K.)		Canada (Ontario Boundary) Act, 1889
11. Canadian Speaker (Appointment of Deputy) Act, 1895, 2nd Sess., 59 Vict., c. 3 (U.K.)	The Act is repealed.	
12. The Alberta Act, 1905, 4-5 Edw. VII, c. 3 (Can.)		Alberta Act

SCHEDULE

to the

Constitution Act, 1982—continued

13. The Saskatchewan Act, 1905, 4-5 Edw. VII, c. 42 (Can.)		Saskatchewan Act
14. British North America Act, 1907, 7 Edw. VII, c. 11(U.K.)	Section 2 is repealed and the following substituted therefor: "2. This Act may be cited as the *Constitution Act, 1907.*"	Constitution Act, 1907
15. British North America Act, 1915, 5-6 Geo. V, c. 45 (U.K.)	Section 3 is repealed and the following substituted therefor: "3. This Act may be cited as the *Constitution Act, 1915.*"	Constitution Act, 1915
16. British North America Act, 1930, 20-21 Geo. V, c. 26 (U.K.)	Section 3 is repealed and the following substituted therefor: "3. This Act may be cited as the *Constitution Act, 1930.*"	Constitution Act, 1930
17. Statute of Westminster, 1931, 22 Geo. V, c. 4 (U.K.)	In so far as they apply to Canada, (*a*) section 4 is repealed; and (*b*) subsection 7(1) is repealed.	Statute of Westminster, 1931
18. British North America Act, 1940, 3-4 Geo. VI, c. 36 (U.K.)	Section 2 is repealed and the following substituted therefor: "2. This Act may be cited as the *Constitution Act, 1940.*"	Constitution Act, 1940

SCHEDULE

to the

Constitution Act, 1982—continued

19. British North America Act, 1943, 6-7 Geo. VI, c. 30 (U.K.)	The Act is repealed.	
20. British North America Act, 1946, 9-10 Geo. VI, c. 63 (U.K.)	The Act is repealed.	
21. British North America Act, 1949, 12-13 Geo. VI, c. 22 (U.K.)	Section 3 is repealed and the following substituted therefor: "3. This Act may be cited as the *Newfoundland Act*."	Newfoundland Act
22. British North America (No. 2) Act, 1949, 13 Geo. VI, c. 81 (U.K.)	The Act is repealed.	
23. British North America Act, 1951, 14-15 Geo. VI, c. 32 (U.K.)	The Act is repealed.	
24. British North America Act, 1952, 1 Eliz. II, c. 15 (Can.)	The Act is repealed.	
25. British North America Act, 1960, 9 Eliz. II, c. 2 (U.K.)	Section 2 is repealed and the following substituted therefor: "2. This Act may be cited as the *Constitution Act, 1960*."	Constitution Act, 1960
26. British North America Act, 1964, 12-13 Eliz. II, c. 73 (U.K.)	Section 2 is repealed and the following substituted therefor: "2. This Act may be cited as the *Constitution Act, 1964*."	Constitution Act, 1964

SCHEDULE

to the

Constitution Act, 1982—continued

27. British North America Act, 1965, 14 Eliz. II, c. 4, Part I (Can.)

Section 2 is repealed and the following substituted therefor:
"2. This Part may be cited as the *Constitution Act, 1965*."

Constitution Act, 1965

28. British North America Act, 1974, 23 Eliz. II, c. 13, Part I (Can.)

Section 3, as amended by 25-26 Eliz. II, c. 28, s. 38(1) (Can.), is repealed and the following substituted therefor:
"3. This Part may be cited as the *Constitution Act, 1974*."

Constitution Act, 1974

29. British North America Act, 1975, 23-24 Eliz. II, c. 28, Part I (Can.)

Section 3, as amended by 25-26 Eliz. II, c. 28, s. 31 (Can.), is repealed and the following substituted therefor:
"3. This Part may be cited as the *Constitution Act (No. 1), 1975*."

Constitution Act (No. 1), 1975

30. British North America Act (No. 2), 1975, 23-24 Eliz. II, c. 53 (Can.)

Section 3 is repealed and the following sustituted therefor:
"3. This Act may be cited as the *Constitution Act (No. 2), 1975*."

Constitution Act (No. 2), 1975

Bibliography

PART ONE BASIC CONCEPTS

Society, Government, and Politics

Amstutz, Mark R. *An Introduction to Political Science: The Management of Conflict.* Glenview, Ill.: Scott, Foresman, 1982.

Ball, Alan R. *Modern Politics and Government.* 2nd ed. London: Macmillan, 1977.

Bowie, Norman E., and Robert L. Simon. *The Individual and the Political Order.* Englewood Cliffs, N.J.: Prentice-Hall, 1977.

Conn, Paul H. *Conflict and Decision Making: An Introduction to Political Science.* New York: Harper & Row, 1971.

Connolly, William E. *The Terms of Political Discourse.* 2nd ed. Princeton, N.J.: Princeton University Press, 1983.

Crick, Bernard. *In Defence of Politics.* rev. ed. London: Pelican, 1964.

Dahl, Robert A. *Modern Political Analysis.* 3rd ed. Englewood Cliffs, N.J.: Prentice-Hall, 1976.

de Grazia, Alfred. *Politics for Better or Worse.* Glenview, Ill.: Scott, Foresman, 1973.

Deutsch, Karl W. *Politics and Government: How People Decide Their Fate.* 3rd ed. Boston: Houghton Mifflin, 1980.

Duverger, Maurice. *The Idea of Politics.* London: Methuen, 1966.

Friedrich, Carl J. *Man and His Government.* New York: McGraw-Hill, 1963.

Hood, Chrisopher C. *The Tools of Government.* London: Macmillan, 1983.

Kariel, Henry S. *The Promise of Politics.* Englewood Cliffs, N.J.: Prentice-Hall, 1966.

Khan, Rais A., Janes D. McNiven, and Stuart A. MacKnown. *An Introduction to Political Science.* rev. ed. Georgetown, Ont.: Irwin-Dorsey, 1977.

Kolb, Eugene J. *A Framework for Political Analysis.* Englewood Cliffs, N.J.: Prentice-Hall, 1978.

Laski, Harold J. *An Introduction to Politics.* rev. ed. London: George Allen & Unwin, 1951.

Lasswell, Harold D. *Politics: Who Gets What, When, How.* New York: Meridian Books, 1958.

MacIver, R. M. *The Web of Government.* rev. ed. New York: The Free Press, 1965.

MacKenzie, W. J. M. *The Study of Political Science.* London: Macmillan, 1971.

Mair, Lucy. *Primitive Government.* 2nd ed. Harmondsworth: Penguin, 1964.

McDonald, Neil A. *Politics: A Case Study of Controlled Behaviour.* New Brunswick, N.J.: Rutgers University Press, 1965.

Merkl, Peter H. *Political Continuity and Change*. New York: Harper & Row, 1967.

Miller, J. D. B. *The Nature of Politics*. Harmondsworth: Penguin, 1960.

Pickles, Dorothy M. *Introduction to Politics*. rev. ed. London: Methuen, 1964.

Pocklington, T. C. *Liberal Democracy in Canada and the United States: An Introduction to Politics and Government*. Toronto: Holt, Rinehart and Winston, 1985.

Pouton, Geoffrey, and Peter Gill, in collaboration with John Vogler. *Introduction to Politics*. Oxford: Martin Robertson, 1982.

Renwick, Alan, and Ian Swinburn. *Basic Political Concepts*. Essex: The Anchor Press, 1980.

Reynolds, H. T. *Politics and the Common Man: An Introduction to Political Behaviour*. Homewood, Ill.: The Dorsey Press, 1974.

Spiro, Herbert J. *Politics as the Master Science*. New York: Harper & Row, 1970.

Taylor, Charles. *The Pattern of Politics*. Toronto: McClelland and Stewart, 1970.

Weldon, T. D. *The Vocabulary of Politics*. London: Penguin, 1953.

Welsh, William A. *Studying Politics*. New York: Praeger, 1973.

Power; Legitimacy and Authority

Champlin, John R. *Power*. New York: Atherton Press, 1971.

Connolly, William, ed. *Legitimacy and the State*. Oxford: Basil Blackwell, 1984.

de Jouvenel, Bertrand. *On Power*. Boston: Beacon Press, 1945.

Friedrich, Carl J., ed. *Authority*. Cambridge, Mass.: Harvard University Press, 1958.

Lukes, Steven. *Power: A Radical View*. London: Macmillan, 1974.

Open University. *Power*. Milton Keynes: Open University Press, 1975.

Pirages, Dennis. *Managing Political Conflict*. New York: Praeger, 1976.

Russell, Bertrand. *Authority and the Individual*. Boston: Beacon Press, 1960.

Sennet, Richard. *Authority*. New York: Alfred A. Knopf, 1980.

Vidrich, Arthur J., and Ronald M. Glassman, eds. *Conflict and Control: Challenge to Legitimacy of Modern Governments*. Beverly Hills: Sage Publications, 1979.

Wrong, Dennis H. *Power: Its Forms, Bases and Uses*. Oxford: Basil Blackwell, 1979.

Sovereignty and the State; The Nation

de Jouvenel, Bertrand. *Sovereignty*. Chicago: University of Chicago Press, 1963.

Dyson, Kenneth. *The State Tradition in Western Europe*. Oxford: Martin Robertson, 1980.

Gellner, Ernest. *Nations and Nationalism*. Oxford: Basil Blackwell, 1983.

Harrison, Frank. *The Modern State*. Montreal: Black Rose Books, 1983.

Klein, Robert A. *Sovereign Equality Among States: The History of an Idea.* Toronto: University of Toronto Press, 1974.

Krader, Lawrence. *Formation of the State.* Englewood Cliffs, N.J.: Prentice-Hall, 1968.

Laski, Harold J. *Studies on the Problem of Sovereignty.* New Haven, Conn.: Yale University Press, 1917.

Lubasz, Heinz. *The Development of the Modern State.* New York: Macmillan, 1964.

McLennan, Gregor. *The Idea of the Modern State/The State and Society.* Milton Keynes: Open University Press, 1984.

Merriam, Charles E. *History of the Theory of Sovereignty since Rousseau.* New York: Columbia University Press, 1900.

Oppenheimer, Franz. *The State.* Montreal: Black Rose Books, 1975. First published 1914.

Stankiewicz, Wladyslaw Josef. *In Defense of Sovereignty.* New York: Oxford University Press, 1969.

Tivey, Leonard, ed. *The Nation State: The Formation of Modern Politics.* Oxford: Martin Robertson, 1981.

Law; Constitutionalism

Allott, Antony. *The Limits of Law.* London: Butterworths, 1980.

Dicey, A. V. *Introduction to the Study of the Law of the Constitution.* 10th ed. London: Macmillan, 1959.

Fuller, Lon L. *The Morality of Law.* 2nd ed. New Haven, Conn.: Yale University Press, 1975.

Hart, H. L. A. *The Concept of Law.* London: Oxford University Press, 1961.

Jennings, W. Ivor. *The British Constitution.* 4th ed. London: Cambridge University Press, 1961.

Langford, J. Stuart. *The Law of Your Land.* Toronto: CBC Enterprises, 1982.

Lederman, W. R. *Continuing Canadian Constitutional Dilemmas.* Toronto: Butterworths, 1981.

Lloyd, Dennis. *The Idea of Law.* rev. ed. London: Penguin, 1976.

McWhinney, Edward. *Canada and the Constitution.* Toronto: University of Toronto Press, 1982.

———. *Constitution-Making: Principles, Process, Practice.* Toronto: University of Toronto Press, 1981.

Pennock, James Roland, and John William Chapman. *Constitutionalism.* New York: New York University Press, 1979.

Summers, Robert S., and Charles G. Howard. *Law: Its Nature, Functions and Limits.* 2nd ed. Englewood Cliffs, N.J.: Prentice-Hall, 1972.

Waddams, S. M. *Introduction to the Study of Law.* 2nd ed. Toronto: Carswell, 1983.

International Politics and International Law

Akehurst, Michael. *A Modern Introduction to International Law*. 5th ed. London: George Allen & Unwin, 1984.

Archer, Clive. *International Organizations*. London: George Allen & Unwin, 1983.

Art, Robert J., and Robert Jervis, eds. *International Politics*. 2nd ed. Boston: Little, Brown, 1985.

Fox, William T. R. *A Continent Apart: The United States and Canada in World Politics*. Toronto: University of Toronto Press, 1985.

Holsti, K. J. *International Politics: A Framework for Analysis*. 3rd ed. Englewood Cliffs, N.J.: Prentice-Hall, 1977.

Maris, Gary L. *International Law, An Introduction*. Lanham, Md.: University Press of America, 1984.

Miller, Lynn H. *Global Order: Values and Power in International Politics*. Boulder, Colo.: Westview Press, 1985.

Morgenthau, Hans J. *Politics Among Nations*. 5th ed. New York: Alfred A. Knopf, 1973.

Robertson, Charles L. *International Politics Since World War II*. 2nd ed. New York: John Wiley & Sons, 1975.

Spanier, John. *Games Nations Play: Analyzing International Politics*. New York: Praeger, 1972.

Vincent, Jack Ernest. *International Relations*. Lantham, Md.: University Press of America, 1983.

PART TWO IDEOLOGY

General Works

Baradat, Leon P. *Political Ideologies: Their Origins and Impact*. Englewood Cliffs, N.J.: Prentice-Hall, 1979.

Christenson, Reo M., et al. *Ideologies and Modern Politics*. New York: Dodd, Mead, 1971.

Christian, William, and Colin Campbell. *Political Parties and Ideologies in Canada*. 2nd ed. Toronto: McGraw-Hill Ryerson, 1983.

Ebenstein, William, and Edwin Fogelman. *Today's Isms*. 8th ed. Englewood Cliffs, N.J.: Prentice-Hall, 1980.

Eccleshall, R., V. Geoghegan, R. Jay, and R. Wilford. *Political Ideologies*. Toronto: Copp Clark Pitman, 1984.

Feuer, Lewis S. *Ideology and the Ideologists*. New York: Harper & Row, 1975.

Larrain, Jorge. *The Concept of Ideology*. London: Hutchinson, 1979.

Manning, D. J. *The Form of Ideology*. London: George Allen & Unwin, 1980.

Minogue, Kenneth R. *Alien Powers: The Pure Theory of Ideology*. London: Weidenfeld & Nicolson, 1985.

Parekh, Bhikhu. *Contemporary Political Thinkers*. Oxford: Martin Robertson, 1982.
Plamenatz, John. *Ideology*. London: Pall Mall Press, 1970.
Sargent, Lyman T. *Contemporary Political Ideologies*, 4th ed. Homewood, Ill.: The Dorsey Press, 1978.
Seliger, Martin. *Ideology and Politics*. London: George Allen & Unwin, 1976.
————. *The Marxist Conception of Ideology*. Cambridge: Cambridge University Press, 1977.
Watkins, Frederick M. *The Age of Ideology: Political Thought, 1750 to the Present*. Englewood Cliffs, N.J.: Prentice-Hall, 1964.

Liberalism

Berlin, Isaiah. *Four Essays on Liberty*. London: Oxford University Press, 1969.
Bolkestein, F., ed. *Modern Liberalism*. Amsterdam: Elsevier Publishers, 1982.
Bramsted, E. K., and K. J. Melhuish. *Western Liberalism: A History in Documents from Locke to Croce*. London: Longman, 1978.
de Ruggiero, Guido. *The History of European Liberalism*. Boston: Beacon Press, 1959. First English edition 1927.
Girvetz, Harry K. *The Evolution of Liberalism*. New York: Collier, 1963.
Hartz, Louis. *The Liberal Tradition in America*. New York: Harcourt, Brace, 1955.
Hobhouse, L. T. *Liberalism*. New York: Oxford University Press, 1964. First published 1911.
Laski, Harold J. *The Rise of European Liberalism*. London: George Allen & Unwin, 1936.
Lowi, Theodore J. *The End of Liberalism*. New York: W. W. Norton, 1969.
MacLean, Douglas, and Claudia Mills. *Liberalism Reconsidered*. Totowa, N.J.: Rownam and Allanheld, 1983.
Minogue, Kenneth. *The Liberal Mind*. London: Methuen, 1963.
Schapiro, J. Salwyn. *Liberalism: Its Meaning and History*. New York: Van Nostrand Reinhold, 1958.
Spitz, David. *The Real World of Liberalism*. Chicago: University of Chicago Press, 1982.
Underhill, Frank H. *In Search of Canadian Liberalism*. Toronto: Macmillan, 1961.

Conservatism

Allison, Lincoln. *Right Principles*. Oxford: Basil Blackwell, 1984.
Coser, Lewis A., and Irving Howe. *The New Conservatives: A Critique from the Left*. New York: Quadrangle, 1974.
Harbour, William R. *The Foundations of Conservative Thought*. Notre Dame, Ind.: University of Notre Dame Press, 1982.
Hogg, Quintin M. (Lord Hailsham). *The Case for Conservatism*. Harmondsworth: Penguin, 1947.

Kendall, Willmoore. *The Conservative Affirmation*. Chicago: Henry Regnery, 1963.

Kirk, Russell. *The Conservative Mind*. 3rd ed. Chicago: Henry Regnery, 1960.

Kristol, Irving. *Reflections of a Neoconservative*. New York: Basic Books, 1983.

Lora, Ronald. *Conservative Minds in America*. Westport, Conn.: Greenwood Press, 1979. First published 1971.

O'Sullivan, Noel. *Conservatism*. London: Dent, 1976.

Rossiter, Clinton. *Conservatism in America: The Thankless Persuasion*. rev. ed. New York: Alfred A. Knopf, 1962.

Scruton, Roger. *The Meaning of Conservatism*. Harmondsworth: Penguin, 1980.

Viereck, Peter. *Conservatism from John Adams to Churchill*. Princeton, N.J.: Van Nostrand Reinhold, 1956.

_____. *Conservatism Revisited: Revolt against Revolt*. New York: Scribners, 1949.

Socialism and Anarchism

Avakumovic, Ivan. *Socialism in Canada*. Toronto: McClelland and Stewart, 1978.

Cohen, Arthur A. *The Communism of Mao Tse-tung*. Chicago: University of Chicago Press, 1964.

Cole, G. D. H. *A History of Socialist Thought*. 5 vols. London: Macmillan, 1953–1960.

Gray, Alexander. *The Socialist Tradition, Moses to Lenin*. London: Longmans Green, 1946.

Gregor, A. James. *A Survey of Marxism*. New York: Random House, 1965.

Hunt, R. N. Carew. *The Theory and Practice of Communism*. Harmondsworth: Penguin, 1963. First published 1950.

Joll, James. *The Anarchists*. London: Eyre & Spottiswoode, 1964.

_____. *The Second International, 1889–1914*. London: Weidenfeld & Nicolson, 1955.

Levine, Andrew. *Arguing for Socialism*. Boston: Routledge and Kegan Paul, 1984.

Lichtheim, George. *A Short History of Socialism*. New York: Praeger, 1970.

McLellan, David. *Karl Marx: His Life and Thought*. London: Macmillan, 1973.

Meyer, Alfred G. *Leninism*. New York: Praeger, 1962. First published 1957.

_____. *Marxism: The Unity of Theory and Practice*. Ann Arbor: University of Michigan Press, 1963. First published 1954.

Patsouras, Louis, and Jack Ray Thomas. *Varieties and Problems of Twentieth-Century Socialism*. Chicago: Nelson-Hall, 1981.

Tucker, Robert. *The Marxian Revolutionary Idea*. New York: W. W. Norton, 1970.

White, Stephen, John Gardner, and George Schopflin. *Communist Political Systems: An Introduction*. London: Macmillan, 1982.

Woodcock, George. *Anarchism*. New York: World Publishing Co., 1962.

Nationalism and Fascism

Breuilly, John. *Nationalism and the State*. Manchester: Manchester University Press, 1982.

Cameron, David. *Nationalism, Self Determination, and the Quebec Question*. Toronto: Macmillan, 1974.

Carsten, F. L. *The Rise of Fascism*. London: Methuen, 1967.

Cassels, Alan. *Fascism*. New York: Crowell, 1975.

Cook, Ramsay. *French Canadian Nationalism*. Toronto: Macmillan, 1969.

Emerson, Rupert. *From Empire to Nation*. Cambridge, Mass.: Harvard University Press, 1960.

Hayes, Carlton J. H. *Nationalism: A Religion*. New York: Macmillan, 1960.

Kedourie, Elie. *Nationalism*. New York: Praeger, 1960.

Kitchen, Martin. *Fascism*. London: Macmillan, 1976.

Kohn, Hans. *The Idea of Nationalism*. New York: Macmillan, 1944.

_____, ed. *Nationalism: Its Meaning and History*, 2nd ed. Princeton, N.J.: D. Van Nostrand, 1965.

Nolte, Ernst. *Three Faces of Fascism*. New York: Holt, Rinehart and Winston, 1966.

O'Sullivan, Noel. *Fascism*. London: J. M. Dent, 1983.

Russell, Peter. *Nationalism in Canada*. Toronto: McGraw-Hill Ryerson, 1966.

Sathyamurthy, T. V. *Nationalism in the Contemporary World*. London: F. Pinter, 1983.

Shafer, Boyd C. *Nationalism: Myth and Reality*. New York: Harcourt, Brace, 1955.

Smith, Anthony D. *Theories of Nationalism*. London: Duckworth, 1983.

Weber, Eugen. *Varieties of Fascism*. New York: D. Van Nostrand, 1964.

PART THREE FORMS OF GOVERNMENT

General Works

Bishop, Vaughn F., and J. William Meszaros. *Comparing Nations: The Developed and Developing Worlds*. Lexington, Mass.: D. C. Heath, 1980.

Blondel, Jean. *Comparative Government*. London: Weidenfeld & Nicolson, 1969.

_____. *The Organization of Government*. London: Sage Publications, 1982.

Brogan, D. W., and Douglas V. Verney. *Political Patterns in Today's World*. 2nd ed. New York: Harcourt, Brace and World, 1968.

Crick, Bernard. *Basic Forms of Government: A Sketch and a Model*. London: Macmillan, 1973.

Davies, Morton R., and Vaughan A. Lewis. *Models of Political Systems*. London: Macmillan, 1971.

Finer, S. E. *Comparative Government*. London: Penguin, 1970.

Loewenberg, Gerhard, and Samuel C. Patterson. *Comparing Legislatures*. Boston: Little, Brown, 1979.

Macridis, Roy C., and Bernard E. Brown. *Comparative Politics: Notes and Readings*. 5th ed. Homewood, Ill.: The Dorsey Press, 1977.

Merkl, Peter H. *Modern Comparative Politics*. 2nd ed. Hinsdale, Ill.: Dryden, 1977.

Merritt, Richard L. *Systematic Approaches to Comparative Politics*. Chicago: Rand McNally, 1970.

Price, J. H. *Comparative Government*. 2nd ed. London: Hutchinson, 1975.

Wesson, Robert G. *Modern Governments: Three Worlds of Politics*. 2nd ed. Englewood Cliffs, N.J.: Prentice-Hall, 1985.

Liberal Democracy

Bachrach, Peter. *The Theory of Democratic Elitism*. Boston: Little, Brown, 1967.

Brooks, Stephen, ed. *Political Thought in Canada*. Toronto: Irwin, 1984.

Cassinelli, C. W. *The Politics of Freedom: An Analysis of the Modern Democratic State*. Seattle: University of Washington Press, 1961.

Clement, Wallace. *The Canadian Corporate Elite*. Toronto: McClelland and Stewart, 1975.

Cook, Terrence E., and Patrick M. Morgan. *Participatory Democracy*. San Francisco: Camfield, 1971.

Dahl, Robert A. *Polyarchy: Participation and Opposition*. New Haven, Conn.: Yale University Press, 1971.

Downs, Anthony. *An Economic Theory of Democracy*. New York: Harper & Row, 1957.

Levine, Andrew. *Liberal Democracy*. New York: Columbia University Press, 1981.

Lijphart, Arend. *Democracies: Patterns of Majoritarian and Consensus Government in Twenty-One Countries*. New Haven, Conn.: Yale University Press, 1984.

_____. *Democracy in Plural Societies*. New Haven, Conn.: Yale University Press, 1977.

Lindsay, A. D. *The Modern Democratic State*. New York: Oxford University Press, 1962.

Macpherson, C. B. *The Life and Times of Liberal Democracy*. New York: Oxford University Press, 1977.

Mayo, Henry B. *An Introduction to Democratic Theory*. New York: Oxford University Press, 1960.

Parry, Gerraint. *Political Elites*. London: George Allen & Unwin, 1969.

Pateman, Carole. *Participation and Democratic Theory*. Cambridge: Cambridge University Press, 1970.

Pennock, J. Roland. *Liberal Democracy: Its Merits and Prospects*. New York: Rinehart, 1950.

Powell, G. Bingham. *Contemporary Democracies*. Cambridge, Mass.: Harvard University Press, 1982.

Sartori, Giovanni. *Democratic Theory*. New York: Praeger, 1965.

Totalitarianism

Arendt, Hannah. *The Origins of Totalitarianism*. rev. ed. Cleveland: World Publishing Co., 1958.

Aron, Raymond. *Democracy and Totalitarianism*. New York: Praeger, 1969.

Birch, Betty, ed. *Dictatorship and Totalitarianism*. New York: D. Van Nostrand, 1964.

Curtis, Michael. *Totalitarianism*. New Brunswick, N.J.: Transaction Books, 1980.

Friedrich, Carl J., and Zbigniew K. Brzezinski. *Totalitarian Dictatorship and Autocracy*. 2nd ed. New York: Praeger, 1965.

Friedrich, Carl J., Zbigniew K. Brzezinski, Benjamin Barber, and Michael Curtis. *Totalitarianism: Its Changing Theory and Practice*. New York: Praeger, 1969.

Howe, Irving, ed. *1984 Revisited*. New York: Harper & Row, 1983.

Menze, Ernest A. *Totalitarianism Reconsidered*. Port Washington, N.Y.: Kennikat Press, 1980.

Talmon, J. L. *The Origins of Totalitarian Democracy*. New York: W. W. Norton, 1970.

Authoritarianism

Altemeyer, Bob. *Right-Wing Authoritarianism*. Winnipeg: University of Manitoba Press, 1981.

Collier, David, ed. *The New Authoritarianism in Latin America*. Princeton, N.J.: Princeton University Press, 1979.

Germani, Gino. *Authoritarianism, Facism and National Populism*. New Brunswick, N. J.: Transaction Books, 1978.

Herz, John H. *From Dictatorship to Democracy: Coping with the Legacies of Authoritarianism and Totalitarianism*. Westport, Conn.: Greenwood Press, 1982.

Huntington, Samuel P., and Clement H. Moore, eds. *Authoritarian Politics in Modern Society: The Dynamics of Establishing One Party Systems*. New York: Basic Books, 1970.

Moore, Barrington, Jr. *Social Origins of Dictatorship and Democracy*. Boston: Beacon Press, 1967.

Neumann, Frantz. *The Democratic and Authoritarian State*. New York: The Free Press, 1964.

Perlmutter, Amos. *Modern Authoritarianism*. New Haven, Conn.: Yale University Press, 1981.

Wittfogel, Karl A. *Oriental Despotism*. New Haven, Conn.: Yale University Press, 1967.

Parliamentary Systems

Ameller, Michel. *Parliaments*. London: Cassell, 1966.

Aydelotte, William O., ed. *The History of Parliamentary Behavior*. Princeton, N.J.: Princeton University Press, 1977.

Coombes, D., ed. *The Power of the Purse: A Symposium on the Role of European Parliaments in Budgetary Decisions*. New York: Praeger, 1976.

D'Aquino, Thomas, G. Bruce Doern, and Cassandra Blair. *Parliamentary Democracy in Canada*. Toronto: Methuen, 1983.

Dodd, L. C. *Coalitions in Parliamentary Government*. Princeton, N.J.: Princeton University Press, 1976.

Herman, V. *Parliaments of the World*. London: Macmillan, 1976.

Jennings, W. Ivor. *Parliament*. 2nd ed. Cambridge University Press, 1957.

Loewenberg, Gerhard, ed. *Modern Parliaments: Change or Decline*. Chicago: Atherton, 1971.

MacKinnon, Frank. *The Crown in Canada*. Toronto: McClelland and Stewart, 1976.

Mackintosh, John P. *The Government and Politics of Great Britain*. 4th ed. London: Hutchinson, 1977.

March, Roman R. *The Myth of Parliament*. Scarborough, Ont.: Prentice-Hall, 1974.

Marshall, Edmund. *Parliament and the Public*. London: Macmillan, 1982.

Rose, Richard, and Ezra N. Suleiman, eds. *Presidents and Prime Ministers*. Washington, D.C.: American Institute for Public Policy Research, 1980.

Rush, Michael. *Parliamentary Government in Britain*. London: Pitman, 1981.

Verney, Douglas V. *British Government and Politics*. 3rd ed. New York: Harper & Row, 1976.

Presidential Systems

Bessette, Joseph M., and Jeffrey Tulis, eds. *The Presidency in the Constitutional Order*. Baton Rouge, La.: Louisiana State University Press, 1981.

Binkley, Wilfred F. *President and Congress*. 3rd ed. New York: Vintage Books, 1962.

Burns, James MacGregor. *Presidential Government*. Boston: Houghton Mifflin, 1966.

Califano, Joseph A., Jr. *A Presidential Nation*. New York: W. W. Norton, 1975.

DiBacco, T. V. *Presidential Power in Latin American Politics*. New York: Praeger, 1977.

Fisher, Louis. *President and Congress*. New York: The Free Press, 1972.

Griffith, Ernest S. *The American Presidency*. New York: New York University Press, 1976.

Gwyn, W. B. *The Meaning of Separation of Powers*. The Hague: Martinus Nijhoff, 1965.

Heclo, Hugh, and Lester M. Salamon, eds. *The Illusion of Presidential Government*. Boulder, Colo.: Westview Press, 1981.

McConnell, Grant. *The Modern Presidency*. 2nd ed. New York: St. Martin's, 1976.

Nelson, Michael. *The Presidency and the Political System*. Washington, D.C.: Congressional Quarterly Inc., 1984.

Nwabueze, B. O. *Presidentialism in Commonwealth Africa*. New York: St. Martin's, 1974.

Sickels, Robert J. *The Presidency*. Englewood Cliffs, N.J.: Prentice-Hall, 1980.

Federalism

Bakvis, Herman. *Federalism and the Organization of Political Life*. Kingston, Ont.: Institute of Intergovernmental Relations, Queen's University, 1981.

Bird, Richard M., ed. *Fiscal Dimensions of Canadian Federalism*. Toronto: Canadian Tax Foundation, 1980.

Boogman, J. C., and G. N. Van der Plaat. *Federalism: History and Current Significance of a Form of Government*. The Hague: Martinus Nijhoff, 1980.

Duchacek, Ivo D. *Comparative Federalism: The Territorial Dimension of Politics*. New York: Holt, Rinehart and Winston, 1970.

Elazar, David J. *The Politics of American Federalism*. Lexington, Mass.: D. C. Heath, 1969.

Friedrich, Carl J. *Trends of Federalism in Theory and Practice*. New York: Praeger, 1968.

Gibbins, Roger. *Regionalism: Territorial Politics in Canada and the United States*. Scarborough, Ont.: Butterworths, 1982.

King, Preston. *Federalism and Federation*. London: Croom Helm, 1982.

MacMahon, Arthur W. *Administering Federalism in a Democracy*. New York: Oxford University Press, 1972.

Meekison, J. Peter, ed. *Canadian Federalism: Myth or Reality*. 3rd ed. Toronto: Methuen, 1977.

Reagan, Michael D. *The New Federalism*. New York: Oxford University Press, 1972.

Riker, William H. *Federalism: Origin, Operation, Significance*. Boston: Little, Brown, 1964.

Simeon, Richard. *Federal-Provincial Diplomacy: The Making of Recent Policy in Canada*. Toronto: University of Toronto Press, 1972.

Smiley, D. V. *Canada in Question: Federalism in the Eighties*. 3rd ed. Toronto: McGraw-Hill Ryerson, 1980.

Stevenson, Garth. *Unfulfilled Union: Canadian Federalism and National Unity*. Toronto: Macmillan, 1979.

Wheare, K. C. *Federal Government*. New York: Oxford University Press, 1964.

White, W. L., et al. *Canadian Confederation: A Decision-Making Analysis*. Toronto: Macmillan, 1979.

PART FOUR THE POLITICAL PROCESS

Systems Theory

Almond, Gabriel A., and G. Bingham Powell, Jr. *Comparative Politics: System, Process and Policy*. 2nd ed. Boston: Little, Brown, 1978.

Chapman, Henry, and Denis Deneau. *Citizen Development in Public Policy-Making: Access and the Policy-Making Process*. Ottawa: Canadian Council on Social Development, 1978.

Curtis, Richard Kenneth. *Evolution or Extinction*. New York: Pergamon Press, 1982.

Deutsch, Karl W. *The Nerves of Government: Models of Political Communication and Control*. 2nd ed. New York: The Free Press, 1966.

Easton, David. *A Systems Analysis of Political Life*. New York: John Wiley & Sons, 1965.

Gordon, Morton. *Comparative Political Systems*. New York: Macmillan, 1972.

McLennan, Barbara N. *Comparative Political Systems: Political Processes in Developed and Developing States*. North Scituate, Mass.: Duxbury Press, 1977.

von Bertalanffy, Ludwig. *General System Theory*. New York: George Braziller, 1968.

Waddington, Conrad Hal. *The Man Made Future*. London: Croom Helm, 1978.

Wiseman, H. V. *Political Systems*. New York: Praeger, 1966.

Political Culture and Political Socialization

Almond, Gabriel A., and Sidney Verba. *The Civic Culture*. Princeton, N.J.: Princeton University Press, 1963.

Borman, Kathryn M., ed. *The Social Life of Children in a Changing Society*. Hillsdale, N.J.: Lawrence Erlbaum Associates, 1982.

Dawson, Richard E., and Kenneth Prewitt. *Political Socialization*. Boston: Little, Brown, 1969.

Hartz, Louis. *The Founding of New Societies*. New York: Harcourt, Brace and World, 1964.

Hyman, Herbert H. *Political Socialization*. rev. ed. New York: The Free Press, 1969.

Jaros, Dean. *Socialization to Politics*. New York: Praeger, 1973.

Lane, Robert. *Political Man*. New York: The Free Press, 1972.

Langton, Kenneth P. *Political Socialization*. New York: Oxford University Press, 1969.

Mead, George Herbert. *The Individual and the Social Self*. Chicago: University of Chicago Press, 1982.

Pye, Lucian, and Sidney Verba. *Political Culture and Political Development*. Princeton, N.J.: Princeton University Press, 1965.

Rosenbaum, Walter A. *Political Culture*. New York: Praeger, 1975.

Rushton, J. Phillippe. *Altruism, Socialization and Society*. Englewood Cliffs, N.J.: Prentice-Hall, 1980.

Wentworth, William M. *Context and Understanding*. New York: Elsevier Publishers, 1980.

Canadian Political System

Bon, Daniel L., and Kenneth D. Hart. *Linking Canada's New Solitudes*. Ottawa: Conference Board of Canada, 1983.

Dawson, R. MacGregor. *The Government of Canada*. 5th ed. Revised by Norman Ward. Toronto: University of Toronto Press, 1970.

Doern, G. Bruce, and Peter Aucoin, eds. *Public Policy in Canada: Organization, Process and Management*. Toronto: Macmillan, 1979.

Fox, Paul W. *Politics: Canada*. 5th ed. Toronto: McGraw-Hill Ryerson, 1982.

Gibbins, Roger. *Conflict and Unity: An Introduction to Canadian Political Life*. Toronto: Methuen, 1985.

Hockin, Thomas A. *Government in Canada*. Toronto: McGraw-Hill Ryerson, 1975.

Mallory, J. R. *The Structure of Canadian Government*. rev. ed. Toronto: Macmillan, 1984.

Merritt, Allan S., and George W. Brown. *Canadians and Their Government*. rev. ed. Toronto: Fitzhenry & Whiteside, 1983.

Rea, K. J., and Nelson Wiseman, eds. *Government and Enterprise in Canada*. Toronto: Methuen, 1985.

Redekop, John H., ed. *Approaches to Canadian Politics*. Scarborough, Ont.: Prentice-Hall, 1978.

Schultz, Richard, Orest M. Krulak, and John C. Terry, eds. *The Canadian Political Process*. 3rd ed. Toronto: Holt, Rinehart and Winston, 1979.

Van Loon, Richard J., and Michael S. Whittington. *The Canadian Political System: Environment, Structure and Process*. 3rd ed. Toronto: McGraw-Hill Ryerson, 1981.

White, W. L., R. H. Wagenberg, and R. C. Nelson. *Introduction to Canadian Politics and Government*. 3rd ed. Toronto: Holt, Rinehart and Winston, 1981.

Whittington, Michael S., and Glen Williams, eds. *Canadian Politics in the 1980s*. Toronto: Methuen, 1981.

Zureik, Elias, and Robert M. Pike, eds. *Political Socialization*. Vol. I of *Socialization and Values in Canadian Society*. Toronto: McClelland and Stewart, 1975.

Interest Groups

Duverger, Maurice. *Party Politics and Pressure Groups: A Comparative Introduction*. New York: Thomas Y. Crowell, 1972.

Ehrmann, Henry W. *Interest Groups on Four Continents*. Pittsburgh, Pa.: University of Pittsburgh Press, 1958.

Hayes, Michael T. *Lobbyists and Legislators: A Theory of Political Markets*. New Brunswick, N.J.: Rutgers University Press, 1981.

Key, V. O., Jr. *Politics, Parties, and Pressure Groups*. 5th ed. New York: Thomas Y. Crowell, 1964.

Kwavnick, David. *Organized Labour and Pressure Politics: The Canadian Labour Congress 1956–1968*. Montreal/Kingston: McGill-Queen's University Press, 1972.

Malecki, Edward S., and H. R. Mahood, eds. *Group Politics*. New York: Scribners, 1972.

Moe, Terry M. *The Organization of Interests*. Chicago: University of Chicago Press, 1980.

Olson, Mancur. *The Logic of Collective Action*. Cambridge, Mass.: Harvard University Press, 1965.

Ornstein, Norman J., and Shirley Elder. *Interest Groups, Lobbying and Policy-making*. Washington, D.C.: Congressional Quarterly Press, 1978.

Pross, A. Paul. *Governing Under Pressure*. Toronto: Institute of Public Administration of Canada, 1982.

Pross, A. Paul, ed. *Pressure Group Behaviour in Canadian Politics*. Toronto: McGraw-Hill Ryerson, 1975.

Richardson, J. J., and A. G. Jordan. *Governing Under Pressure: The Policy Process in Post-Parliamentary Democracy*. Oxford: Martin Robertson, 1979.

Thompson, Fred, and W. T. Stanbury. *The Political Economy of Interest Groups in the Legislative Process in Canada*. Ottawa: Institute for Research on Public Policy, 1979.

Truman, David B. *The Governmental Process*. New York: Alfred A. Knopf, 1958.

Willetts, Peter, ed. *Pressure Groups in the Global System*. London: Francis Pinter, 1982.

Wootton, Graham. *Interest Groups: Policy and Politics in America*. Englewood Cliffs, N.J.: Prentice-Hall, 1985.

———. *Pressure Politics in Contemporary Britain*. Lexington, Mass.: D. C. Heath, 1978.

Political Parties

Alexander, Robert J. *Latin American Political Parties*. New York: Praeger, 1973.

Brodie, M. Janie, and Jane Jenson. *Crisis, Challenge and Change: Party and Class in Canada*. Toronto: Methuen, 1980.

Castles, Francis G., ed. *The Impact of Parties*. Beverly Hills, Calif.: Sage Publications, 1982.

Christian, William, and Colin Campbell. *Political Parties and Ideologies in Canada*. 2nd ed. Toronto: McGraw-Hill Ryerson, 1983.

Duverger, Maurice. *Political Parties*. rev. ed. New York: John Wiley & Sons, 1959.

Engelmann, F. C., and M. A. Schwartz, eds. *Political Parties and the Canadian Social Structure*. Scarborough, Ont.: Prentice-Hall, 1967.

Epstein, Leon D. *Political Parties in Western Democracies*. New York: Praeger, 1967.

Frears, J. R. *Political Parties and Elections in the French Fifth Republic*. London: C. Hurst, 1977.

Goodman, William. *The Party System in America*. Englewood Cliffs, N.J.: Prentice-Hall, 1980.

Katz, Richard S. *A Theory of Parties and Electoral Systems*. Baltimore: Johns Hopkins University Press, 1980.

Kornberg, Allan, Joel Smith, and Harold D. Clarke. *Citizen Politicians—Canada: Party Officials in a Democratic Society*. Durham, N.C.: Carolina Academic Press, 1979.

Lawson, Kay. *The Comparative Study of Political Parties*. New York: St. Martin's, 1976.

Macridis, Roy C., ed. *Political Parties: Contemporary Trends and Ideas*. New York: Harper & Row, 1967.

Michels, Robert. *Political Parties*. New York: The Free Press, 1962. First published 1911.

Milnor, Andrew J., ed. *Comparative Political Parties: Selected Readings*. New York: Thomas Y. Crowell, 1969.

Paletz, David L., and Robert M. Entman. *Media Power Politics*. New York: The Free Press, 1981.

Paterson, William E., and Alastair H. Thomas, eds. *Social Democratic Parties in Western Europe*. London: Croom Helm, 1977.

Rose, Richard. *Do Parties Make a Difference?* 2nd ed. London: Macmillan, 1984.

Schapiro, Leonard B. *The Communist Party of the Soviet Union*. 2nd ed. New York: Random House, 1971.

Sorauf, Frank J. *Party Politics in America*. 4th ed. Boston: Little, Brown, 1980.

Thorburn, Hugh G., ed. *Party Politics in Canada*. 4th ed. Scarborough, Ont.: Prentice-Hall, 1979.

Winn, Conrad, and John McMenemy, eds. *Political Parties in Canada*. Toronto: McGraw-Hill Ryerson, 1976.

Young, Walter D. *Democracy and Discontent: Progressivism, Socialism and Social Credit in the Canadian West*. 2nd ed. Toronto: McGraw-Hill Ryerson, 1978.

Communications Media

Arora, Satish K., and Harold D. Lasswell. *Political Communication: The Public Language of Political Elites in India and the United States*. New York: Holt, Rinehart and Winston, 1969.

Canada, Government of. *Report of the Royal Commission on Newspapers* (Kent Report). Hull: Canadian Government Publishing Centre, 1981.

Crotty, William J., ed. *Public Opinion and Politics: A Reader*. New York: Holt, Rinehart and Winston, 1970.

Deutsch, Karl W. *The Nerves of Government: Models of Political Communication and Control*. 2nd ed. New York: The Free Press, 1966.

Fagen, Richard. *Politics and Communication*. Boston: Little, Brown, 1966.

Fletcher, Frederick J. *The Newspaper and Public Affairs*. Vol. 7 of the Royal Commission on Newspapers. Research Publications. Ottawa: Supply and Services Canada, 1981.

Gans, Herbert J. *Deciding What's News*. New York: Pantheon Books, 1979.

Joslyn, Richard. *Mass Media and Elections*. Reading, Mass.: Addison-Wesley, 1984.

Kesterton, Wilfred H. *The Law and the Press in Canada*. Toronto: McClelland and Stewart, 1976.

Paletz, David L. *Media Power Politics*. New York: The Free Press, 1981.

Patterson, Thomas E. *The Mass Media Election*. New York: Praeger, 1980.

Righter, Rosemary. *Whose News? Politics, the Press and the Third World*. London: Burnett Books, 1978.

Wells, Alan. *Mass Media and Society*. 3rd ed. Palo Alto, Calif.: Mayfield, 1979.

Elections and Electoral Systems

Clarke, Harold. *Political Choice in Canada*. Toronto: McGraw-Hill Ryerson, 1979.

Clarke, Harold, et al. *Absent Mandate*. Toronto: Gage, 1984.

Elton, David K. *Electoral Reform*. Calgary: Canada West Foundation, 1981.

Holler, Manfred J. *Power, Voting and Voting Power*. Vienna: Physica-Verlag, 1982.

Irvine, William P. *Does Canada Need a New Electoral System?* Kingston, Ont.: Institute of Intergovernmental Relations, Queen's University, 1979.

Kornberg, Allan, and Harold Clarke, eds. *Political Support in Canada*. Durham, N.C.: Duke University Press, 1983.

Lipset, Seymour M., and Stein Rokkan, eds. *Party Systems and Voter Alignments: Cross-National Perspectives*. New York: The Free Press, 1967.

Lyons, W. E. *One Man—One Vote*. Toronto: McGraw-Hill Ryerson, 1970.

Milnor, A. J. *Elections and Political Stability*. Boston: Little, Brown, 1969.

Mishler, William T. E. *Political Participation in Canada*. Toronto: Macmillan, 1979.

Penniman, Howard Rae. *Canada at the Polls, 1979 and 1980*. Washington: American Enterprise Institute for Public Policy Research, 1981.

Pierce, John C., and John L. Sullivan. *The Electorate Reconsidered*. Beverly Hills, Calif.: Sage Publications, 1980.

Rae, Douglas W. *The Political Consequences of Electoral Laws*. rev. ed. New Haven, Conn.: Yale University Press, 1971.

Rose, Richard, ed. *Electoral Participation*. Beverly Hills, Calif.: Sage Publications, 1980.

Verba, Sidney, Norman H. Nie, and Jae-On Kimo. *Participation and Political Equality*. Cambridge: Cambridge University Press, 1978.

Legislative Assemblies and Representation

Birch, A. H. *Representation*. London: Pall Mall Press, 1971.

Campbell, Colin. *The Canadian Senate: A Lobby from Within*. Toronto: Macmillan, 1978.

Fisher, Louis. *The Politics of Shared Power: Congress and the Executive*. Washington, D.C.: Congressional Quarterly Press, 1981.

Jackson, Robert J., and Michael M. Atkinson. *The Canadian Legislative System*. Toronto: Macmillan, 1974.

Kornberg, Allan. *Canadian Legislative Behavior: A Study of the 25th Parliament*. Toronto: Macmillan, 1974.

Kornberg, Allan, William Mishler, and Harold D. Clarke. *Representative Democracy in the Canadian Provinces*. Scarborough, Ont.: Prentice-Hall, 1982.

Kunz, F. A. *The Modern Senate of Canada, 1925–1963*. Toronto: University of Toronto Press, 1965.

Loewenberg, Gerhard, and Samuel C. Patterson. *Comparing Legislatures*. Boston: Little, Brown, 1979.

Mezey, M. L. *Comparative Legislatures*. Durham, N.C.: Duke University Press, 1979.

Neilson, W. A. W., and J. C. MacPherson, eds. *The Legislative Process in Canada: The Need for Reform*. Toronto: Butterworths, 1978.

Ornstein, Norman J., ed. *The Role of the Legislature in Western Democracies*. Washington, D.C.: American Enterprise Institute for Public Policy Research, 1981.

Pitkin, Hanna F. *The Concept of Representation*. Berkeley: University of California Press, 1967.

Ripley, Randall B. *Congress: Process and Policy*. 2nd ed. New York: W. W. Norton, 1978.

Sandquist, James L. *The Decline and Resurgence of Congress*. Washington, D.C.: Brookings Institute, 1981.

The Executive

Burns, James MacGregor. *Leadership*. New York: Harper & Row, 1978.

Campbell, Colin. *Governments Under Stress: Political Executives in Washington, London and Ottawa*. Toronto: University of Toronto Press, 1983.

Carter, Byrum E. *The Office of the Prime Minister*. Princeton, N.J.: Princeton University Press, 1956.

French, Richard D. *How Ottawa Decides: Planning and Industrial Policy Making, 1968–1980*. Ottawa: Canadian Institute for Economic Policy, 1980.

Griffith, Ernest S. *The American Presidency: The Dilemmas of Shared Power and Divided Government*. New York: New York University Press, 1976.

Hirschfield, Robert S. *The Power of the Presidency*. New York: Aldine, 1982.

Hockin, Thomas A. *Apex of Power: The Prime Minister and Political Leadership in Canada*. 2nd ed. Scarborough, Ont.: Prentice-Hall, 1977.

Lynn, Laurence E., Jr. *Managing the Public's Business: The Job of the Government Executive*. New York: Basic Books, 1981.

Mackintosh, John P. *The British Cabinet*. 3rd ed. London: Stevens & Sons, 1977.

Matheson, W. A. *The Prime Minister and the Cabinet*. Toronto: Methuen, 1976.

Monet, Jacques. *The Canadian Crown*. Toronto: Clarke Irwin, 1979.

Perlmutter, A. *The Military and Politics in Modern Times*. New Haven, Conn.: Yale University Press, 1977.

Punnett, R. M. *Front Bench Opposition: The Role of the Leader of the Opposition, the Shadow Cabinet and Shadow Government in British Politics*. London: Heinemann, 1973.

————. *The Prime Minister in Canadian Government and Politics*. Toronto: Macmillan, 1977.

Selassie, Bereket H. *The Executive in African Governments*. London: Heinemann, 1974.

The Administration

Bird, Richard M. in collaboration with Meyer W. Bucovetsky and David K. Foot. *The Growth of Public Employment in Canada*. Ottawa: Institute for Research on Public Policy, 1979.

Brown, R. G. S., and D. R. Steel. *The Administrative Process in Britain*. 2nd ed. London: Methuen, 1979.

Campbell, Colin, and George J. Szablowski. *The Superbureaucrats: Structure and Behavior in Central Agencies*. Toronto: Macmillan, 1979.

Downs, Anthony. *Inside Bureaucracy*. Boston: Little, Brown, 1967.

Etzioni-Halevy, Eva. *Bureaucracy and Democracy*. London: Routledge and Kegan Paul, 1983.

Gawthrop, Louis C. *Bureaucratic Behavior in the Executive Branch*. New York: The Free Press, 1969.

Granatstein, J. L. *The Ottawa Men*. Toronto: Oxford University Press, 1982.

Hodgetts, J. E. *The Canadian Public Service: A Physiology of Government, 1867–1970*. Toronto: University of Toronto Press, 1973.

Hodgetts, J. E., and O. P. Dwidedi. *Provincial Governments as Employers*. Montreal: McGill-Queen's University Press, 1974.

Kernaghan, W. D. K., ed. *Public Administration in Canada: Selected Readings*. 5th ed. Toronto: Methuen, 1985.

Schultz, Richard J. *Federalism, Bureaucracy and Public Policy*. Montreal: McGill-Queen's University Press, 1980.

Self, Peter. *Administrative Theories and Politics*. Toronto: University of Toronto Press, 1973.

Stevens, T. J. *The Business of Government: An Introduction to Canadian Public Administration*. Toronto: McGraw-Hill Ryerson, 1978.

von Mises, Ludwig. *Bureaucracy*. New Haven, Conn.: Yale University Press, 1944.

Weiss, Carol H., and Allen H. Barton, eds. *Making Bureaucracies Work*. Beverly Hills, Calif.: Sage Publications, 1979.

Wilson, Vincent Seymour. *Canadian Public Policy and Administration*. Toronto: McGraw-Hill Ryerson, 1981.

The Judiciary

Abraham, Henry J. *The Judicial Process: An Introductory Analysis of the Courts of the United States, England, and France*. 4th ed. New York: Oxford University Press, 1980.

American Assembly, The. *The Courts, the Public, and the Law Explosion*. Englewood Cliffs, N.J.: Prentice-Hall, 1965.

Gall, Gerald L. *The Canadian Legal System*. 2nd ed. Toronto: Carswell, 1983.

Horowitz, Donald. *The Courts and Social Policy*. Washington, D.C.: The Brookings Institution, 1977.

Lederman, W. R., ed. *The Courts and the Canadian Constitution*. Toronto: McClelland and Stewart, 1964.

McWhinney, Edward. *Judicial Review in the English-Speaking World*. 3rd ed. Toronto: University of Toronto Press, 1965.

Morton, F. L. *Law, Politics and the Judicial System*. Calgary: University of Calgary Press, 1984.

Murphy, Walter, and C. Herman Pritchett. *Courts, Judges, and Politics*. 3rd ed. New York: Random House, 1979.

Nagel, Stuart S. *The Legal Process from a Behavioral Perspective*. Homewood, Ill.: The Dorsey Press, 1969.

Schmidhauser, John R., ed. *Constitutional Law in the Political Process*. Chicago: Rand McNally, 1963.

Schubert, Glendon. *Judicial Policy Making*. rev. ed. Chicago: Scott, Foresman, 1974.

Shapiro, Martin M. *Courts, a Comparative and Political Analysis*. Chicago: University of Chicago Press, 1981.

Strayer, Barry Lee. *The Canadian Constitution and the Courts*. Toronto: Butterworths, 1983.

Theberg, Leonard J., ed. *The Judiciary in a Democratic Society*. Lexington, Mass.: D. C. Heath, 1979.

Index